Methods in Clinical Psychology

Volume 1
Projective Assessment

METHODS IN CLINICAL PSYCHOLOGY

Methods in Clinical Psychology

Volume 1
Projective Assessment

Robert R. Holt

Research Center for Mental Health
New York University

Plenum Press · New York and London

Library of Congress Cataloging in Publication Data

Holt, Robert R
  Methods in clinical psychology.

  Bibliography: p.
  Includes index.
  1. Clinical psychology. 2. Personality assessment. 3. Prediction (Psychology) 4.
Psychological research. I. Title. [DNLM: 1. Projective techniques — Collected
works. 2. Psychology, Clinical — Methods — Collected works. 3. Research —
Methods — Collected works. WM145 H758m]
RC467.H65   157   77-10429
ISBN 0-306-31053-8 (v. 1)

© 1978 Plenum Press, New York
A Division of Plenum Publishing Corporation
227 West 17th Street, New York, N.Y. 10011

Printed in the United States of America

157
H742 m
v. 1

Acknowledgments

The author and the publisher would like to thank the following for permission to reprint, with revisions and additions, the author's previously published articles in this volume.

American Psychological Association

The accuracy of self-evaluations: Its measurement and some of its personological correlates [pp. 298–317], originally published in *Journal of Consulting Psychology*, 1951, *15*, 95–101.

Creativity and primary process: A study of adaptive regression by F. Pine and R. R. Holt [pp. 235–248], originally published in *Journal of Abnormal and Social Psychology*, 1960, *61*, 370–379.

Duke University Press

Individuality and generalization in the psychology of personality [pp. 7–29], originally published in *Journal of Personality*, 1962, *30*, 377–404.

Grune & Stratton, Inc.

A blind interpretation of Doe's TAT [pp. 164–183], originally published in Edwin S. Shneidman et al., Eds. *Thematic Test Analysis*. New York: Grune & Stratton, Inc., 1951, pp. 101–112; also, 237–240, 268–272.

Journal of Psychological Researches

Cognitive controls and primary processes [pp. 225–233], originally published in *Journal of Psychological Researches*, 1960, *4*, 105–112.

Menninger Foundation

An inductive method of analyzing defense of self-esteem [pp. 309–317], originally published in *Bulletin of the Menninger Clinic*, 1951, *15*, 6–15.

Prentice-Hall, Inc.

The Thematic Apperception Test [pp. 33–76], originally published in H. H. and G. L. Anderson, Eds. *An Introduction to Projective Techniques*. Englewood Cliffs: Prentice-Hall, Inc., 1951, pp. 181–229.

Society for Personality Assessment, Inc.

An approach to the validation of the Szondi test through a systematic study of unreliability [pp. 288–297], originally published in *Journal of Projective Techniques*, 1950, *14*, 435–444.

A blind interpretation of Jay's TAT [pp. 184–208], originally published in *Journal of Projective Techniques*, 1952, *16*, 457–461.

Formal aspects of the TAT—A neglected resource [pp. 150–162], originally published in *Journal of Projective Techniques*, 1958, *22*, 163–172.

Gauging primary and secondary processes in Rorschach responses [pp. 211–224], originally published in *Journal of Projective Techniques*, 1956, *20*, 14-25.

Charles C Thomas

The nature of TAT stories as cognitive products: A psychoanalytic approach [pp. 123–149], originally published in J. Kagan and G. Lesser, Eds. *Contemporary Issues in Thematic Apperceptive Methods*. Springfield: Charles C Thomas, 1961, pp. 3–43.

University of Nebraska

Measuring libidinal and aggressive motives and their controls by means of the Rorschach test [pp. 249–283], originally published in D. Levine, Ed. *Nebraska Symposium on Motivation, 1966*. Lincoln: University of Nebraska Press, 1966, pp. 1–47.

To the memory of my sister
DOROTHY WATSON WHITELAW
whose courage, serenity, and concern for others
live in the minds of all who knew her

Preface

I do not think of myself as primarily interested in method, but in the substance of psychology. Nevertheless, our discipline has such difficulties in coming to grips with its substance that I have found myself getting involved in *how* to do it persistently and since the beginning of my career. That career has been divided between diagnosis and research, the balance between them swinging gradually from the former to the latter. To the astonishment of many of my students and colleagues, I have never become a psychotherapist nor a psychoanalyst, though I have looked closely over the shoulders of many friends at their work, have attended continuous case seminars, and have participated in research on psychotherapy and psychoanalysis enough to feel that I have a pretty good grasp of what that kind of endeavor is like.

So I have been writing about method, diagnostic and investigative, for over 25 years, and was happy to accept the suggestion of Seymour Weingarten, of Plenum Press, that I publish a collection of these papers. What has ended up as two volumes was originally conceived as one, for I feel that there is more similarity of method in assessment, prediction, and research than appears on the surface. The General Introduction and Chapter 1 of Volume 1 state the point of view of the entire work. Nevertheless, it became apparent that the papers on projective assessment were enough to constitute one volume, while those on the closely related methodological topics of the clinical-statistical prediction controversy and investigative techniques made up a well-balanced companion. Realizing that not every reader would want to buy both volumes, I have tried to make each self-contained while repeating a minimum of material from the other.

Taken together, the two volumes do not include everything I have written on either diagnostic testing or research methods. Some of my earliest publications were simplistic or naive enough not to be worth reprinting; others simply did not fit in for one reason or another. Neither volume pretends to be comprehensive in a second sense, either, for I have not tried to discuss all aspects of clinical methods other than therapeutic. I have, however, made some effort to increase the usefulness of this collection by

ix

adding to it four chapters not previously published, and by rewriting and updating some of the other chapters rather extensively. I have also included (at the end of Volume 2) a complete personal bibliography for the curious or those who would like to see what kinds of investigative and theoretical substance has engaged me in between the writing of the papers here collected. In addition, I have prepared brief introductions to all of the chapters intended to give the context of each and help knit them together into something more than a set of reprints.

A good many of these papers have grown out of my teaching, as is doubtless true for most academics. That applies to three of the chapters (Vol. 1, No. 3; Vol. 2, Nos. 9 and 10) that are now published for the first time here. I do not expect that many readers will find either the first or the second of these three very rewarding simply to read through. They are intended as resources or reference works, and I do not apologize for their low level of readability. The second volume's Chapter 9, in particular, is a progress report, which threatens to sprout a new shoot every time I review another complex or innovative report of research; no doubt I shall continue to add to and revise it, and welcome the suggestions of readers. Critical and constructive feedback about anything in this book is welcome, and I pledge myself to respond to anyone who wants to engage in conversation or correspondence about any matter of diagnostic or research method discussed here.

In general, aside from Chapters 1 and 2 of Volume 1, I have tried to resist the temptation to rewrite; but I have made a few terminological changes to bring the theoretical stance of the papers more or less up to date. That has meant deleting most metapsychological concepts, changing terms like "need" and "drive" to "motive" or "wish," and the like. It is another small indication of the superfluousness of the metapsychological level of theorizing that it could usually be merely excised without leaving a gap. Where alterations of the text have gone beyond the just-indicated changes and minor corrections of phrase in the service of clearer communication, I have set square brackets around contemporary interpolations, including footnotes added now.

The papers in this volume are about personality assessment in general, with a particular focus on psychodiagnosis by means of projective techniques. Ever since my Topeka training in diagnostic testing, I have firmly advocated that psychodiagnosticians should use well-rounded batteries including tests of intelligence and concept formation, and a variety of more expressive techniques by no means limited to the most popular, the Rorschach and TAT. Yet on looking back I find that most of my scattered writings on assessment *methods* (as distinct from findings) concentrate on these two tests. This collection therefore is not presented as a comprehensive work on projective techniques but as a focused and supplementary one; in no way does it compete with either *Diagnostic Psychological Testing* (Rapaport, Schafer, & Gill, 1968) or *Assessing Personality* (Holt, 1971c). It expands, exemplifies, and in some respects updates the general point of view expressed in those books. I hope that graduate students and working professionals in personality assessment alike will find it useful for its sustained effort to supply a theoretically grounded basis for understanding the significance of assessment data.

The book starts off with a paper on individuality and generalization in personology, because I feel that that piece provides a theoretical rationale for personality assessment. Then follow six chapters on the TAT (Thematic Apperception Test), a substitute for the book on that test's interpretation I once planned to write. I have fleshed out Chapters 2 and 3 from my teaching notes so that they and the two following chapters contain most of the generalizations I can make about administering the TAT and making sense out of the stories. The rest has to be transmitted case by case, in a way I have tried to exemplify in Chapters 6 and 7.

Chapters 8 through 11 deal with my way of looking at the Rorschach test, using a person's responses as a way of assessing his access to primary-process thinking and the ways he controls it or defends himself against it. The reader can trace several important stages in the development of this method and get an overview of the approach and of the information about people it yields. Unfortunately, full directions for scoring occupy so much space that another entire book will have to be devoted to them, which I hope to publish in the next few years.

This volume ends with three miscellaneous empirical studies in personality assessment. Chapter 12 is included partly for the relevance of its general message about reliability for other methods of assessment, and partly to remind psychologists that despite all attempts to dismiss it, the Szondi test remains a challenge to our understanding—less an easily applicable test than a reminder that there is much we do not fully understand about what goes on in the process of perceiving another person's face. The final two chapters deal with methods of evaluating aspects of the self. Neither technique is projective in the usual sense, though both exemplify the general point of view toward measuring and understanding qualities of fellow human beings that I have tried to detail in the earlier chapters. They are among my earliest papers, yet the kind of multiform personality assessment they deal with still seems to be news to some colleagues who did not share my good fortune of having worked intensively at the Harvard Psychological Clinic and the Menninger Foundation.

Readers of this volume may be particularly interested in the first five chapters of Volume 2, on the controversy over clinical and statistical prediction and measurement. They constitute a complete collection of all that I have written on this topic. I realize that many graduate courses on personality assessment spend some time on the controversy, but it actually has very little to do with learning how to understand people (which is the focus of this volume) and a lot to do with attaining clarity on methodological issues (which occupy the rest of Volume 2. Hence I put them in the other volume.

Since 1962, all of my work (including the composition of Chapters 3 and

11 of Volume 1, 1, 4, 5, and 7–10 of Volume 2) has been supported by a Public Health Service Research Career Program Award (K06 MH 12455), which I am happy to acknowledge. I express my gratitude to NIMH for the many ways this award has facilitated my work, including the semester of leave (fall, 1976) during which I put the finishing touches on this collection. I am grateful, as well, to my colleagues at the Research Center for Mental Health for the stimulating setting they have provided for me to do most of the work recorded here, and to the many students in my courses on the interpretation of the TAT and various seminars and courses on research methods, for their helpful criticism and stimulation. Sponsoring or serving on the dissertation committees of many graduate students of clinical psychology has taught me a great deal of what I have tried to set down here concerning research. I would not have been able to learn from that experience, however, if it had not been for the didactic and practicum training in psychodiagnosis I received from such great teachers as Henry A. Murray, Robert W. White, and David Rapaport, and the tacit knowledge they enabled me to absorb by working alongside them. In that way I gained a great deal from close association in Topeka with Martin Mayman and Roy Schafer for periods of time that seem in retrospect all too brief. From these same men, and from colleagues in the Research Department of the Menninger Foundation—Paul Bergman, Margaret Brenman, Sibylle Escalona, Merton Gill, Louisa Howe, George Klein, and Lester Luborsky—I had most of my training in methods of research in clinical psychology. But I have gained a good deal from working with my statistician friends Daniel Horn, Jacob Cohen, Mark Fulcomer, and Noel Dunivant, as well.

Fred Pine and Edwin S. Shneidman have earned my special thanks for allowing me to include parts of their work in Volume 1. Mrs. Bettie Brewer, paragon among secretaries, has my lasting gratitude for the many ways in which her serene competence and cheerful unflappability have made all of my work easier as well as for special efforts to bring this book into reality.

I am grateful also to Mary Ann Dishman for the retyping of several chapters, and to Robyn Dawes, Irene Kaus, and David Wolitzky for a critical reading of individual chapters.

It is not possible to specify the many ways in which a family support, encourage, and motivate the writing of a book, particularly one that collects the labors of several decades. Concretely, Joan and Danny helped with the index, but I want them and Michael to know my appreciation of many more important though less tangible ways in which they help get all my jobs done.

Robert R. Holt

New York

Contents

Other Methods

Contents of Volume 2

General Introduction

To look backward on 25 years of one's own work seems at times an exercise in narcissistic self-indulgence, but it can also yield new perspectives that seem to transcend the purely personal. I am struck by a number of recurring themes in my own work, which the distance of some years helps me to see as a slightly idiosyncratic expression of problems endemic to all of psychology. Perhaps the most persuasive is my struggle to come to terms with a peculiarly psychological antinomy, which may be expressed in the often-encountered, skeptical question: is a science of psychology possible at all? For science is an attempt to be impersonal and objective in the pursuit of public knowledge, of invariances, laws, and precise measurements and formulations; whereas the most distinctive subject matter of psychology is personal, subjective, privately known thoughts, feelings, fantasies, dreams, yearnings, dreads, free choices, and states of consciousness—evanescent and constantly changing impalpables that seem to defy codification, exact description, or measurement.

Two contrasting strategies of dealing with this dilemma have found favor with most psychologists. One is the procrustean solution of behaviorism: whatever is not objective, public, and measurable is simply declared off limits—in the most extreme formulations, nonexistent or only illusion; in softer formulations, it is called epiphenomenal, or trivial, or literally negligible—and the subject matter of psychology is limited to *behavior*. The other pseudo solution says, in effect, if there is a clash between objective scientific method and the nature of our subjective subject matter, so much the worse for the method. The most extreme position is that of contemporary mystics who reject the proposition that psychology should be a science at all, while softer forms of this position are declarations that the method must be changed in fundamental ways to adapt it to its ambiguous and obscure materials.

From the beginning, I have felt intuitively that neither of these strategies was right; not for me, anyway. Only now have I been able to formulate the issue this clearly, and I have been much helped by a book on seemingly quite a different topic—Gerald Holton's *Thematic Origins of Scientific Thought*

1

(1973). The following passage is particularly helpful in providing historical perspective. After noting that "there have coexisted in science, in almost every period since Thales and Pythagoras, sets of two or more antithetical systems or attitudes, for example, one reductionist and the other holistic," Holton proposes:

> In addition, there has always existed another set of antitheses or polarities, even though, to be sure, one or the other was at a given time more prominent—namely, between the Galilean (or, more properly Archimedean) attempt at precision and measurement that purged public, "objective" science of those qualitative elements that interfere with reaching reasonable "objective" agreement among fellow investigators, and, on the other hand, the intuitions, glimpses, daydreams, and a priori commitments that make up half the world of science in the form of a personal, private, "subjective" activity. Science has always been propelled and buffeted by such contrary or antithetical forces (p. 375).

Earlier, he put the fundamental dichotomy this way:

> First, one must delineate more clearly science in the sense of the personal struggle, by distinguishing it from a different activity, also called "science," which is its public, institutional aspect. The two activities may be labelled S_1 and S_2 respectively.

It was in the work of Polanyi (1958) that I first saw vividly portrayed the world of S_1 in the hard sciences, for he gives many striking examples of the passion, the stubborn and seemingly irrational clinging to convictions, the exhilaration and despair, the intuitive, tacit, and unverbalizable component of creative thought, all of which have been so evident in the lives and work of many great scientists. That strengthened my conviction that such intangible and mysterious processes as empathy, intuition, and inspiration, such value-laden processes as esthetic preference and clinical judgment (all aspects of S_1), have as honorable a place in science as the public and generally revered procedures of the context of justification (S_2), such as experimental design and statistical testing of hypotheses.

The dichotomy we are dealing with goes beyond the boundaries of science itself, however. At least for me personally, I feel that my interest in the holistic and subjective approach to psychology has two principal roots: my personal psychoanalysis (and the neurosis that occasioned it), and my esthetic interests, which go back as far as I can remember. Some of my most vivid early memories preserve experiences of wonder and ecstasy occasioned by a dewy spring morning, by the sight and scent of wild flowers, even by a painting in a magazine advertisement. My first publications were poems (in literary magazines at prep school and at college), before I discovered the endless fascination of psychological research. Some years before, the first reflection I can remember about a possible career was a wavering between being an artist and an astronomer. The former seems odd today since I am almost devoid of any graphic talent; but the latter became real enough for a period in my adolescence when I helped form an astronomy club and worked for months grinding a mirror for a telescope.[1]

Clinical psychology has made it possible for me to retain and integrate all these interests and values. Along the way I have been gratified by finding teachers and role models who embodied much of the artist as well as the scientist: Gordon W. Allport, Henry A. Murray, Robert W. White, David Rapaport, and Gardner Murphy. These men seemed easily able, in their own lives, to transcend the split between what C. P. Snow called the "two cultures" of art and the humanities, and of science. All of which is not to deny that I have experienced the conflict, and have found myself pulled in opposite directions by the effort to ride two such different-looking horses simultaneously. The insight into the underlying unities has come slowly, though helped by identification.

My continuing effort to find a way of combining objective and subjective, of remaining faithful to the essence of scientific method while refusing to give up any of the human relevance of clinical psychology's central subject matter, lends these two volumes whatever unity they possess. I have long felt that there was a structural homology between good diagnostic work and scientific research, and argue the point specifically in Volume 1, Chapter 2. All of the papers in Volume 1 on diagnostic testing attempt in various ways to retain, explicate, and clarify the intuitive procedures of the best clinicians I have known while showing how to verify and objectify them as much as possible. In Chapter 3 of Volume 2, I sought to find unity in diversity through another means, that of examining the actual methods used by hard scientists, by diagnostic and therapeutic clinicians, and by literary critics; and was heartened by the homologies that emerged. In the other papers on the clinical-statistical prediction controversy, I tried in various ways to redefine and defuse a conflict that has always seemed to me an unnecessary distraction from the main task, which is how to find ways of retaining the best of both approaches. Finally, the other chapters of the second volume return repeatedly to this same (to me, surprisingly conservative) task, in the context of research.

In the long run, I have more faith in the quest than in whatever findings (of substance or of method) I have come up with. If these pages help others to see the need to confront the paradoxes of a truly psychological science and of disciplined professional practice, and to keep up the struggle toward the high ground that may eventually provide perspective for synthesis, I will feel greatly rewarded.

---

[1] One by one, all the club members dropped out except for Bradshaw Wood, who finished building the instrument and went on to become a professor of astronomy at Princeton.

1

The paper with which I have chosen to begin this book (here reprinted with a new subtitle) was written during the year 1960–1961, though I had been brooding about many of the issues it considers for two decades. In a real sense as a kind of starting point for all my work in clinical and personality psychology, it seems an appropriate first chapter.

Appropriately enough, it appeared cheek by jowl in the Journal of Personality *with a paper by Allport (1962) on the same general topic. It was to study with him that Hadley Cantril sent me to do my graduate studies at Harvard, and though Allport fended off my hero-worshipping efforts to become his close disciple by a kind of pained and embarrassed withdrawal, he was one of my main teachers. Sitting in his seminar on personality theory I became increasingly skeptical about his basic approach, and by the time I had completed my dissertation—with his considerable help—I had on my drawing board the sketch of an attack on his methodological position. Fortunately, the pressure of making a living forced me to put off writing it, for I did not yet have the historical perspective on the issues that only the teaching of personality theory would help me gain. During the respite of a delightful year in the congenial setting of the Center for Advanced Study in the Behavioral Sciences (where I also wrote Chapters 3 and 6 of Volume 2), I was able to take a fresh look at the problems and write the following pages.*

In his accompanying paper, Allport restated a vision he followed with admirable tenacity all his professional life, of a psychology of personality that should devote itself to understanding how the structure of the unique person comes about. In his latter years, after becoming acquainted with general systems theory, he took over some of its terminology and tried to adopt its outlook (Allport, 1960; 1961, Chapter 23). Here (Allport, 1962) he called for a morphogenetic approach to the system that a personality constitutes, as opposed to the traditional dimensional tack of analytic reductionism or positivism. Yet he failed to see that the systems outlook amounted to a Kuhnian revolution, a fundamental transformation of formative principles in terms of which many of psychology's traditional antinomies became reconciled. It vindicated his faith in the molar and structural approach to personalities, his stubborn insistence that there could and should be a science of individuals, but not his ambivalent polemical rejection of atomism. Part of the beauty and power of the systems approach is that it finds an appropriate place for both molar and molecular observations and laws, for both analytic and synoptic methods, as Weiss (1969) argues so cogently with respect to the life sciences.

As a graduate student, I turned away from Allport partly because his methodology led to so little by way of useful method. Twenty years later, he still had come up with few techniques by which to carry out his program of morphogenetic study of individual persons. He persistently favored matching, despite the fact that research using this method had led nowhere (or at least, to very little), concluding lamely: "Although the method gives us no insight into causal relationships it is, so far as it goes, a good example of a 100 per cent morphogenic procedure" (1962, p. 416). In the same paper, he goes on to recommend several more useful procedures which actually boil down to two: Baldwin's (1942) personal structure analysis, a simple statistical method of identifying reliably recurring coöccurrences of content themes in a person's productions; and interviewing in order to discover important themes, problems, structural foci, stylistic features, values, or other traits in a person, sometimes followed up by the use of generalized rating scales like those of Kilpatrick and Cantril (1960).

Partly, I believe, Allport's difficulty was his personal lack of clinical training and experience, a circumstance that kept him always at a distance from the personalities he wished to study. In his entire career, he never made an intensive study of a single personality at first hand! The apparent exception (Allport, 1965) was a study of a collection of Letters from Jenny, *carried out after its subject's death; Allport had never met her.*

Because he could never see the usefulness of dimensions as more than weak compromises with true individuality, Allport only fitfully addressed himself to the task of trying to find useful dimensions. One obvious difficulty in the realm of personality is the abstractness or nonmateriality of our subjectmatter, as compared to that of a biologist. The latter has no difficulty with using a concept like mitochondrion or chromosome, because the things in question are visually recognizable, having a recurrent distinctiveness of form despite their manifestly unique and fluctuating configurations in the individual cell. What is a corresponding element, individually variable, that goes to make up the unique personality? To answer, the trait (as Allport generally did) is simply to substitute another generalized term for "element." By and large, the traditional approach has been to fall back on the resources of nonscientific language, as Allport did himself (in collaboration with Odbert, 1936), accepting such a descriptive adjective as punctual *or* dominant *as the functional equivalent of an organelle. Yet such terms are inevitably interactive: they are impressions made on an observer by a person, judgments rather than perceptions, in which the orientation of the judge demonstrably plays a very large role. Sometimes it is more important than what is in the person under scrutiny, especially when we get into the very extensive areas of personal behavior that are socially* valued *either positively or negatively—the halo problem.*

Somehow, we need to find a way of taking a fresh look at people, without the blinders of standard trait vocabulary. I believe that a case can be made that concepts like self *(a person's reflexive experience and conception of his own personality),* wish, fear, value, ability, *and* temperament *are the analogues of the cell's fine structure. The psychology of personality, then, should seek for general laws or generalizations about regular structural relations among these elements, which may hold regardless of the unique content of such terms when applied to individuals. (It seems much less fruitful to look for generalizations on the level of these actual contents—e.g., the targets of people's values, which are given in such large part by culture, the appropriate level on which to seek regularities in the value realm.) Likewise, I am doubtful that it will be necessary to proceed just by making case studies, even though that may be an indispensable ground on which to work. We can pursue general goals even while ostensibly bending our efforts to the understanding of unique lives. That at least is the spirit in which I have tried to work, both as a diagnostic tester and as a researcher.*

Individuality and Generalization in the Psychology of Personality: A Theoretical Rationale for Personality Assessment and Research

One of the hardiest perennial weeds in psychology's conceptual garden is the notion that there are nomothetic (generalizing) and idiographic (individualizing) branches, types, or emphases of science. Many respected and important contributors to psychology—especially to personology, the psychology of personality—have quoted these terms with respect and have used them as if they contributed something useful to methodology (e.g., Allport, 1937a; Beck, 1953; Bellak, 1956; Bertalanffy, 1951; Colby, 1958; Dymond, 1953; Falk, 1956; Hoffman, 1960; Sarbin, 1944; Stephenson, 1953; the list could be considerably extended). It is the purpose of this essay to examine the historical origins of this cumbersome pair of concepts, their logical implications, the reasons psychologists espouse them, and alternative solutions to the underlying problems. In so doing, I hope—no doubt fondly, but none the less ardently—to lay this Teutonic ghost which haunts and confounds much of modern psychology.

The principal exponent of the nomothetic-idiographic dichotomy in this country has been Gordon W. Allport (1937a, 1940, 1942, 1946, 1955), a pioneer in academic personology and a man who has brilliantly clarified many important issues in the field. On this particular point, I shall try to show, the artist in him has probably dimmed the vision of the scientist. The underlying problem with which Allport wrestles is vexing enough: the unusual nature of personality as a scientific subject matter. Allport readily concedes that everything in nature is unique, but maintains that natural sciences are not interested in the unique leaf, stone, or river. Only personology, the argument continues, takes as its very subject matter the unique personality as opposed to the generalized human mind or the behavior of organisms at large. The rest of psychology takes care of the general laws of behavior and experience and is thus nomothetic (literally, setting down laws);[1] what is left over is the impressive fact that every personality is different and must be studied in such ways as respect and try to capture this uniqueness—in short, by an idiographic science (literally, portraying what is private or peculiar, i.e., individual). With these two curious words adopted from Windelband, then, Allport describes what he sees as two complementary branches of psychology, both of which are necessary for complete coverage.

---

[1]This is the generally accepted meaning. Brunswik (1943), however, used it in a different sense, which occasionally causes confusion: as pertaining to a science of exact laws expressible as functions or equations, and opposed to statistical generalizations. Both are within the scope of the nomothetic, as understood here. Rickert used a slightly different term, nomological.

On the other hand, many distinguished contributors to personology, from Freud to Murphy (1947), have found no need for such an approach to the scientific study of individuality, and the sharp voice of Eysenck (1954) has been heard rebutting Beck (1953) and proclaiming that psychology should be nomothetic throughout. Clearly, the issue is controversial.

HISTORICAL BACKGROUND: THE ROMANTIC MOVEMENT IN SCIENCE[2]

Kant, writing in the middle and late 1700s and reacting against reductionism, is one of the intellectual ancestors of this issue (which can, of course, be traced back to Plato and Aristotle—like any other problem in psychology; see Popper, 1957). Though he did not himself fall into the dualistic belief that mind and matter were so different that different methods had to be applied to their study, he wrote about these issues on too sophisticated a level for his followers. Thus, the analytic and generalizing methods of natural science were fine for the study of matter, but the mind, according to the post-Kantians, had to be studied also by an additional method, intuition of the whole. Being impressed with the concrete uniqueness and individuality of personality, they did not want to analyze it but to grasp it by a direct empathic act.[3]

Yet for the next century, no one developed such an intuitive approach to personality into anything; meanwhile, physics and chemistry, and even some branches of biology, grew rapidly and used the developing scientific methods with great success in the realm of matter. Mechanics developed early, and Newton's laws of motion were misunderstood as being foundation stones of mechanism and materialism. As C. Singer (1959) points out, Newton's laws were quite abstract and did not deal with physical bodies at all; but in their early great successes they were applied to the motions of the planets, and thus were thought of as the laws of material masses. It could hardly have been otherwise, because of the prevailing tenor of philosophical and scientific thought. The world was simply not ready for the field-theoretical implications of Newton's theories. Even so great a physicist as Lord Kelvin found "meagre and unsatisfactory" any physical knowledge that could not be expressed in a mechanical model.

Though the facts of their own disciplines did not require it, then, natural scientists—helped along by the overgeneralizations of contemporary

---

[2]In preparing this historical summary, I have relied principally on Roback (1927), Allport (1937a, 1937b), Boring (1929), Parsons (1937), L. Stein (1924), Tapper (1925), Friess (1929), Klüver (1929), and the *Encyclopedia of the Social Sciences*, I am aware of some oversimplification in speaking about *the* romantic movement in science; a variety of figures and currents of thought that could be characterized as romantic may be distinguished in the history of nineteenth-century science, some of them only loosely related to the movement described here.

[3]For clarification of Kant's role in these matters, I am indebted to my friend Abraham Kaplan.

philosophers—adopted a hard-headed, materialistic, and mechanistic positivism. It was assumed that all reality was orderly, classifiable, and susceptible of mechanistic explanation; to the extent that it seemed not to be, the province of science ended. It was expected that the secrets of life itself would shortly be reduced to physico-chemical formulas. The resulting clash with religion and humanism seemed an inevitable consequence of being a good scientist. "What was not realized was that the success of science was due to the faithfulness of its practice, while its destructiveness [of humanistic, cultural values] arose from the error of its philosophy which saw that practice as though it were the outcome of a world-view with which it was in fact fundamentally incompatible" (C. Singer, 1959, p. 420).

This was a classic atmosphere, ripe for the romantic revolt that started in poetry at the turn of the nineteenth century and swept through the arts. The humanities are accustomed to see the pendulum swing from classicism to romanticism and back again; from a time of reason, order, control, and clarity to one of passion, ambiguity, free expression, and revolt. To a degree, such movements are felt in the sciences as well, though usually less clearly. In science, we have a temperamental difference between the tough-minded and the tender-minded, as James put it, or in Boring's phrase, the advocates of *nothing but* against those of *something more*; in the nineteenth century, it was objectivism and positivism versus subjectivism and intuitionism. The hardheaded positivists had had their way for a long time; near the end of the century, however, there was something of a romantic revolt in science, tipping the balance toward the subjectivists. Independently, in two different parts of Germany, Wilhelm Dilthey in Berlin and the "southwesterners" Windelband and Rickert proclaimed the primacy of understanding *(Verstehen)* in certain kinds of science over quantification of elements, in the part of the general intellectual current with which we shall be concerned here.

They elaborated the distinction between two kinds of science: the *Naturwissenschaften,* natural sciences, and *Geisteswissenschaften,* the German translation of J. S. Mill's "moral sciences." The latter term, often retranslated as "social sciences," meant actually a good deal more, for it included philosophy and the humanities as well as history, jurisprudence, and much else that is often excluded from social science today. In an attempt to develop separate methodologies for the *Naturwissenschaften* and *Geisteswissenschaften,* Windelband and Rickert took up, developed, and popularized a distinction between two types of science that had been proposed by Cournot, the French founder of mathematical economics.[4] Cournot, who was also something of a philosopher of science, had a sophisticated concept of chance and examined the role

[4]See the article on *Geisteswissenschaften* in the *Encyclopedia of the Social Sciences* and Cournot (1851). The reader who is interested in a richly detailed picture of the issues and their background will do well to read Popper (1957) and Chapters 13 and 17 in Parsons (1937). An excellent briefer account is given by Klüver (1929), in which references to the principal relevant works of Windelband and Rickert may be found.

it played in various fields of knowledge in the process of classifying them. In the exact sciences, precise laws were possible, he said, but in history, chance played such a large role that only a probabilistic discipline was possible. As a later philosopher of history, Meyer, put it: any particular event "depends on chance and on *the free will of which science knows nothing but with which history deals.*" (Quoted by Weber, 1949, p. 115, from Meyer's *Zur Theorie und Methodik der Geschichte,* Halle, 1900.)

It should be clear by now that we are dealing with not just a pair of isolated terms but a complex set of methodological concepts and viewpoints. The nomothetic-idiographic distinction can no more be understood out of the context of the *geisteswissenschaftliche* movement than can any isolated culture trait torn from its cultural embeddedness. For the sake of convenience, I shall refer to this complex of ideas as the romantic movement in science. There have been so many major and subtle shifts in our outlook that it is difficult for us to see the issues with the eyes of *ca.* 1900; recall, however, that vitalism was a live doctrine then, and the ideas of chance and free will[5] were closely connected, respectable concepts. Many scholars conceived of history as having been shaped primarily by the acts of great men; as we shall see, the theme of the relation between personality and achievement is a recurrent preoccupation of the romantics.

It is factually true that history, biography, and literary criticism are primarily interested in increasing our understanding of particular events, persons, or works, rather than in treating these as incidental to the discovery of general laws. But men like Windelband and Rickert took the jump from this proposition to the sweeping declaration that all of the disciplines concerned with man and his works should not and by their very nature cannot generalize, but must devote themselves to the understanding of each particular, and its integration "as a real causal factor into a real, hence concrete *context*" (Weber, 1949, p. 135). The repetition of the word "real" in this passage underscores the conception that only the concrete was real, hence abstractions could not be conceived of as causes of particular events. Moreover, abstract analysis of specific events or persons was thought to be fallacious, since it destroyed the unique unity that was the essence of any such particular. This essence was qualitative, not quantitative, and often consisted of verbal meanings (as opposed to objective facts, the subject matter of natural science), which cannot be measured but only interpreted. By identifying Cournot's methodological distinction with their own between the knowedge of Being *(Sein),* obtained in physical science, and the consciousness of and relatedness to norms *(Sollen)* in the cultural sciences,

---

[5][At the time I wrote this, I shared the prevailing and largely thoughtless rejection of free will, accepting as self-evident the proposition that it was opposed to the scientifically necessary assumption of determinism. I have since mended my ways; see my papers of 1967a and 1972a. Similar arguments may be found in Chein (1972), M. B. Smith (1974), and Weiss (1969).]

Windelband and Rickert started the great debate on the role of values in science [see Volume 2, Chapter 10].

For psychology, Dilthey was the most important figure in this movement. He was a philosopher, an admirer of Goethe and Schopenhauer, rebelling against Christianity and Hegel, though influenced by the Biblical hermeneutics of Schleiermacher. He wanted to respect the heart's reasons the head will never know, to understand life in its own terms, not to explain it. The anti-intellectual element in such a goal is perceptible, and indeed, he is part of the current in German thought that provided the philosophical background for Nazism. He wanted, not a reduction of data either to physical-material or to idealistic terms, but a direct insight into the vital nature of things as articulated wholes. His approach was empirical, but in a different sense from the atomistic English tradition, stressing the importance and primacy of the unbroken whole, the *Strukturzusammenhang*. Obviously, he helped prepare the seedbed for Gestalt psychology. He was optimistic, unlike some of his successors (e.g., Spengler), and very influential in Germany.

Basic to the development of the social and culural sciences, he thought, was the development of a new psychology, which he called *verstehende* psychology—a descriptive discipline concerned with the systematic knowledge of the nature of consciousness and of the inner unity of the individual life, and with the understanding of its development. It did not analyze or start with elements, but with experienced relationships. The most important unifying forces in a man were purpose and moral character. He saw the intimate relation of the person to his social setting and insisted that individual human character was an outgrowth of institutions, not vice versa.

These are only fragments from Dilthey's large output of ideas, which lacked system and order; his work was brought together only after his death, by friends. Nevertheless, it stimulated many workers in diverse fields: jurisprudence, economics, sociology, philosophy, genetics, history, and psychology.

Dilthey's most important psychological follower was Spranger, who is known chiefly for his book *Lebensformen* (Spranger, 1922; translated as *Types of Men*). He too distinguished sharply between explanatory and descriptive psychology, favoring the latter, *verstehende*, type. *Verstehen*, he says, is the mental activity "that grasps events as fraught with meaning in relation to a totality." He was opposed to the analysis of personality into elements, but wanted to stay on the level of "intelligible wholes." As a focus for the study of individuality, he followed Dilthey again in proposing that the person's values, which determined the direction of his strivings, be considered of primary interest.

Dilthey had propounded three forms of *Weltanschauung* which underlie and pervade the personalities as well as the doctrines of the philosophers whom he studied. Spranger proposed his famous six ideal types of values, to which actual individual values more or less correspond: the theoretical, economic, aesthetic, social, political, and religious. He did not recognize the possible cultural determination of his choosing just these six, but traced them back to instincts. Each value type has its own ethics (economic: utilitarianism; aesthetic: harmony), and its own style of life in many other ways. The entire scheme was rather ingeniously worked out.

This theory followed the new ideas in stressing the unity of personality, the way in which many details of behavior become comprehensible when we know such key facts about the total structure as the principal values toward which a man is oriented; to underline the contrast between the prevailing atomistic psychology and his own, Spranger called it *Structur* psychology. As a general theory of personality, it suffers from incompleteness, and its main influence today comes from its having stimulated the production of a widely used paper and pencil test, the Allport-Vernon-Lindzey Study of Values, which is still in active use as a research instrument.

The history of the psychology of *Struktur* and *Verstehen* since Spranger is not yet finished; its influence is still felt in personology, and as a school it still has adherents in Germany. Allport has done the most to bring it to this country; there were a number of lesser figures, but they have not made significant contributions.

William Stern, a man of some influence in psychology, must be at least briefly mentioned even though he began in intelligence testing and his work converged only rather late with the main line of development traced above. The nomothetic-idiographic distinction played no part in his writings, though he was influenced by *verstehende* psychology. He had been a pioneer and an established figure in child psychology and the psychology of individual differences, when he became convinced that conventional psychology was wrongly conceived. As differential psychologists, he said, we are studying isolated mental functions, the ranges and correlates of their variations, but overlooking the important fact that all such functions are embedded in personal lives. As child psychologists, we talk about the growth of intelligence or the like, forgetting that only *persons* grow. Reasoning thus, and basing his psychology on his personalistic philosophy, he decided that a radical rebeginning was imperative; psychology had to be rebuilt with the indivisible, individual person as the focus of every psychological investigation. Even Gestalt psychology with its emphasis on totalities and its similar antielementarism was insufficient, for: *"Keine Gestalt ohne Gestalter."* Stern went into most of psychology's classical problems, such as perception, making the point that there are not separate problems of spatial perception in hearing, vision, touch, etc.—there is only one space, *personal* space, and it is perceived by whatever means is appropriate. Most of the facts that had been established in traditional general psychology were brought in, with this new twist.

Stern's theory of motivation was a complex one, including drives (directional tendencies), instincts (instrumental dispositions), needs, urges, will, pheno-motives and geno-motives, etc., in too subtle and highly elaborated a structure to be recounted here. He did not have a theory of personality as such; rather, the personalistic viewpoint pervaded all of his general psychology. There was a specific theory of character, however, conceived of as the person's total make-up considered from the standpoint of his acts of will, his conscious, purposive striving. Though stratified, character is a unified structure and may be described by a list of traits, but this is only the beginning; much stress was laid on the particular, concrete structure. Particular traits, said Stern, no matter how precisely described, have meaning only when you see what function they play in the structure of the whole personality.

These are the principal psychological figures in the stream of ideas that produced the distinction between nomothetic and idiographic *Wissenschaften* and then applied the latter approach to the problems of psychology. Perhaps the name of Jaspers, in psychopathology, should be added. He helps to establish the continuity between the romantic movement at the turn of the century and the contemporary existentialist-phenomenological movement in psychiatry. The *geisteswissenschaftliche* point of view made even more headway in the social sciences, from which some influence still comes to bear on psychology. Popper (1957) has applied the term *historicism* to one of the main streams in sociology, history, and economics that developed as part of the romantic reaction against positivist, natural-scientific methodology. Such potent names as Marx, Engels, Spencer, Bergson, Mannheim, and Toynbee are among the historicists, and the movement is by no means dead today, despite the vigor of attacks by logical positivists which have refuted the underlying logic of this position. I will not further consider this important group of theorists, who have been adequately routed (Popper, 1957; cf. also Popper, 1950).

How useful were the new ideas to the group of psychologists discussed above? What they took from the romantic revolt was its emphasis on the permission to study as legitimate objects of inquiry, personality, values, motivation, and the interrelation of such factors with cognition (e.g., ideology, perception). Starting with Dilthey's first disciples and going on through the solid contributions of Spranger and Stern, these men did not adhere to a strict distinction between idiographic and nomothetic approaches, and were disinclined to make any substantial change in their accustomed ways of scientific work. Any follower who wholly gave up general concepts and stuck closely to intuitive contemplation of indivisible Gestalten simply dropped out of the picture; the men who are remembered used the new battle cries to help shift their fields of activity slightly, and to develop new types of concepts—which as concepts were on no different level of abstractness from the ones Dilthey and the southwesterners attacked so vehemently.

Note, for example in the above summaries, the generalizing, abstract nature of the motivational concepts used by Spranger and Stern: both retained values and instincts, which were assumed to be found in all persons.

As soon as they stopped their polemics and got down to work, the men of this romantic revolt strayed off the intuitive reservation and came up with conceptual tools methodologically indistinguishable from those of so-called nomothetic science. In a way, Stern was the most consistent in the attempt of his *General Psychology from a Personalistic Standpoint* (1938) to reshape all of psychology from bottom to top; but on closer examination, the changes turn out to be largely verbal. It is all very well to talk about personal space, for example, but no idiographically personalistic research methods were developed. One could hardly say that there has been any further development of a personalistic psychology of perception, except in the sense that Stern has helped focus attention on new types of generalized variables derived from a study of individual differences in perceptual behavior (see Klein & Schlesinger, 1949).

Nevertheless, all of this work did represent an important ground swell in the history of ideas, and it had some useful influence on the behavioral sciences. It did not make them idiographic, but it directed their attention to new or neglected problems and novel kinds of variables, as well as to the issue of structure: the ways the variables are organized. Like many rebellions, it revolted against a tradition that was stultifying, only to produce an opposite extreme, which if taken literally would have been equally useless or more so. Fortunately, scientists only occasionally take their concepts quite that literally and with such logical consistency; especially at a time that old ideas are overthrown, the important content of the new movement is often emotional. Through the drama of overstatement, a prevailing but opposite overemphasis may be overthrown, and in calmer times other men may find a sensible position from which to move forward.[6]

Certainly the psychology and social science that held the stage in Germany during the 1880s and 1890s were in many ways inadequate as scientific approaches to important human problems. It was a day when not only value judgments but even an interest in the psychology of values was banned from scientific concern. Fechner and Wundt had started with problems it is easy to dismiss as trivial, minute, or far removed from what the man on the street thinks of as psychology. Experimental psychology had to start that way, and it can now look back on an illustrious, slow development of methods and concepts, which today permit laboratory studies of personality and some of life's more pressing issues. But 70 years ago, is it any wonder that a person who was interested in man the striver, the sufferer, the spinner of ideologies---as Dilthey was—thought that the classical scientific approach itself might be at fault? Surely the world· of inner knowledge, of passions and ideals, had been left out, and the *verstehende* movement was a revolt against this one-sidedness.

[6][As stated here, the text seems to imply that the solution is a compromise, whereas I am now convinced that nothing less than a change of ethos or age, in Ackoff's phrase, is involved. See footnote 18, below.]

THE HISTORICAL ROLE OF DIFFERENTIAL PSYCHOLOGY

In psychology, the romantic movement has been felt particularly in personology, the psychology of personality. And one reason that its impact was particularly great there is the fact that personology grew out of differential psychology, the psychology of individual differences.

The first efforts of the "new psychology" of the 1890s were devoted to finding empirical generalizations and abstract laws about such functions as sensation and perception (concepts which themselves were the heritage of faculty psychology). It was what Boring has called the science of the average, healthy, adult (and, one might add, male) mind, a subtly Aristotelian conception that relegated the study of women and children, and of abnormal and exceptional behavior, generally to a subordinate status. Even so, there remained embarrassing observations of exceptions to the general laws even when the subjects were "average, healthy adults"; and so the field of differential psychology was invented as a kind of wastebasket to take care of these annoying anomalies. From the standpoint of the highest type of psychology, which was concerned with laws in a way not expected of differential psychology, the unexplained residual variance continued to be considered error and to be treated as if it were random and unlawful.

The psychologists who were content to work with the miscellany of leavings from all the high-caste tables in psychology were further handicapped by the taint of practical application, for they were principally involved in applying psychology to mundane problems like educating children, treating the disturbed, and selecting employees. Such work called for the prediction of behavior, and it quickly became apparent that the general laws provided by "scientific psychology" left a great deal unpredicted; it was practically imperative to supplement them by some kind of lore that dealt with all the other important determinants.

As time went on, differential psychologists made a radical shift in approach. In the era when individual differences were thought of as error— as not lawful, really—they were catalogued and measured, and a few attempts were made to parcel out the variance in terms of sex, age, ethnic group, and other gross demographic categories. During the past couple of decades, however, personologists have increasingly begun to recognize that all the error-terms of standard psychological equations are their own happy hunting grounds. Individual differences in such hallowed perceptual phenomena as time-error, size-estimation, and shape-constancy proved to be not random at all but reliably related to other dimensions of individual differences in cognitive phenomena and in noncognitive realms, too (see Gardner, Holzman, Klein, Linton, & Spence, 1959).

The fallacy involved in treating individual differences as if they were random and unlawful resembles that of the eighteenth-century scientists who concretized Newton's laws as propositions concerning mechanical bodies. In both cases, the grasp of certain principles lagged behind what could have been expected. Objectively viewed, the laws that govern individual variation in the perception of apparent movement are just as abstract as the laws that cover the general case, and seem to have a different methodological status only because of the accident of history that brought about the discovery of the latter first. And, despite the implied promise in Klein and Schlesinger's title (1949), the study of such general principles does not bring the perceiver, the person in Stern's sense, back into perceptual psychology; it is merely a change in the axis of generalization, so to speak, not a way of becoming less abstract about perception.

THE LOGIC OF THE ROMANTIC POINT OF VIEW IN PERSONOLOGY

Let us now consider each of the main propositions that make up the romantic point of view, and state the logical objections to them systematically. In brief, they are an indictment of natural sciences as having no room for a meaningful approach to personality; the argument is thus plausible only to the extent that science has approximated the nomothetic caricature.

1. *The Goal of Personology Is Understanding, While That of Nomothetic Science Is Prediction and Control.*[7] Here is a particularly subtle and mischievous dichotomy, which has been accepted by all too many, even within psychology. Actually, all of the highly developed sciences aim at prediction and control *through* understanding; the goal is compound and indivisible. Most scientists, as contrasted with technologists, are themselves more motivated by the need to figure things out, to develop good theories and workable models that make nature intelligible, and less concerned with the ultimate payoff, the applied benefits of prediction and control that understanding makes possible. But it is only in recent years that the dual nature of the scientific enterprise has been made clear by philosophers of science, the fact that it has hypothesis-forming and hypothesis-testing phases; moreover, methodolo-

---

[7][This section on understanding was rewritten (in 1966) to take into account some of the ideas of Polanyi (1958), to whom I am indebted for clarifying these subtle matters, of which I did not have an adequate grasp at the time this paper was first written. The would-be tough-minded misconception of science, which denigrates intuition, empathy, and understanding, is endemic in psychology: most of us have been trained to a kind of automatic obeisance to the ideal of objectivity to the point where we lose sight of its proper sphere of relevance. Therefore, I have little hope that this brief section will convince many who were trained in the tradition of behaviorism and logical positivism; I urge them to study Polanyi (1958), who writes from an inside and expert knowledge of several of the "hard sciences." Kaplan (1964, especially Chapter IX) is another good source on the limitations of prediction as an ultimate criterion in science. His summary is worth quoting: "explanations provide understanding, but we can predict without being able to understand, and we can understand without necessarily being able to predict. It remains true that if we can predict successfully on the basis of a certain explanation we have good reason, and perhaps the best sort of reason, for accepting the explanation" (p. 350). See also Volume 2, Chapter 10.]

gists have concentrated almost entirely on explicating a reconstructed logic of proof and have neglected to describe the very part of scientific work that is most exciting and personally rewarding. Therefore, it was easy enough to portray "hard science" as uninterested in understanding, and solely guided by the aim of verifying or refuting predictions that were rigorously deduced from theory.

This misconception of what actually goes on in such sciences as chemistry and physics was enthusiastically taken up by many psychologists; indeed, it is central to behaviorism. One should not underestimate the emotional appeal of such an ideal of a completely rigorous, objective, machine-like science, especially for such an intrinsically difficult and ambiguity-ridden field as psychology. It is a close analogue of the obsessive-compulsive ideal of completely rational thought and action; the behaviorist and the obsessional alike hoped to escape from the frightening entanglements of emotional subjectivity by banishing it entirely. Affects can indeed be a source of error. But Freud saw clearly as long ago as 1900 that effective, adaptive thought must reduce the scope of affect not to zero but to that minimum necessary for the signal functions involved in judgment. When emotions are completely ruled out, the neurotic has no sense of what course of possible action is promising and what is not. His defenses protect him from hunches and intuitions, leave him without a sense of what data are to be trusted and which ones are probably artifacts, and allow him no way of knowing what is an important problem rather than a trivial one. Clearly, this kind of "freedom from subjectivity" is crippling for a scientist.

Smaller numbers of psychologists, concentrated largely among clinical practitioners, resisted the successive vogues of behaviorism and logical positivism and embraced the notion of an idiographic discipline. They were happy to have philosophical auspices under which to reject scientific method and control, so they could be free to indulge in irresponsible speculation and undisciplined intuition. To distinguish their ideal from the understanding of natural scientists, let us call it *Verstehen*. The true scientist's goal is an explanation—a cognitive grasp of the significant inner structure and functioning of a phenomenon, an intelligible model arrived at by disciplined analytic and synthetic processes. In *Verstehen*, however, the emphasis was not on figuring out how something really worked but on gaining an empathic feeling of it as directly as possible, a sense of knowing it from the inside by nonintellective means. As its exponents described it, *Verstehen* was not so much Kekulé's insight into the structure of organic molecules in his famous fantasy of the carbon atoms joining hands in a ring, as it was the feeling of understanding a person more deeply after seeing a portrait of him painted by a master. This latter type of nonexplanatory understanding, therefore, is a subjective effect properly aimed at by artists, not scientists. A vivid, compelling portrait, whether in paint, stone, or words, achieves its communicative effect by judicious selection and artful distortion, not by complete fidelity to reality. Indeed, a scrupulous realism that tries to copy nature exactly is the death of an artistic endeavor, though it is necessary to science.

If personology were to be devoted to word portraits that seek to evoke in the reader the thrill of recognition, the gratifying (if perhaps illusory) feeling of understanding unique individuals, it would become not an idiographic science but an art. There is such an art of personality, of course: literary biography. We can enjoy and profit from it, while recognizing that an artist's quest for "truth" differs from a scientist's in being a striving not for strict verisimilitude but for allusive illumination. The criterion of this kind of understanding is the effect on some audience; the ultimate criterion of scientific understanding may be verified prediction, or—depending on the particular science—an elegant and comprehensive accounting of facts already available, like the Darwinian theory of evolution.

In all of these matters, it is difficult to tread a middle path, and the dichotomous thinking engendered by the contrast of idiographic and nomothetic makes it even more so. To the neobehaviorist, the avowed search for understanding, the interest in major (which means messy and uncontrollable) human problems, the respect for introspective data and subjective phenomena, the use of empathy as a method—all of that makes personology look indistinguishable from armchair speculation and self-deluded mysticism. To the idiographer, the determination to use as much scientific method as possible (including statistics and experimental design), to control unwanted sources of variance, to test hyptheses rigorously instead of simply proclaiming them—all that makes personology look indistinguishable from the alleged sterilities of psychophysics and the irrelevancy of rat learning. Yet the heritage of the older, more developed sciences themselves is exactly this middle way.

The difference between the scientist and the artist is at bottom not so great as dichotomous thinking would make us believe. Gardner Murphy points out (in a personal communication) that there are many cases, "all the way from Leonardo da Vinci to John J. Audubon and John Muir, of scientist-artists, in whom it is not conceptually very feasible to make the roles distinct." Some personologists too (notably Freud, Murphy, Allport, and Murray) have had much of the artist in them as well as the scientist and have been masters of prose writing; small wonder, therefore, that at times the artistic side of their identities has come uppermost. If Allport had been less aesthetically sensitive, he might not have failed to distinguish between artistic and scientific goals. Often, too, poor scientists are at the same time poor writers, and an inferior case study may be poor either because its facts are wrong and its interpretations undiscerning, or because it is poorly put together and lacks the literary touch that can put the breath of life into even a routine case report. The more art a scientist possesses—so long as he does not let it run away with him—the more effective a scientist he can be, because he must use his aesthetic sense in constructing theory as well as in communicating his findings and ideas to others.

2. *The Proper Methods of Personology Are Intuition and Empathy, Which Have No Place in Natural Science.* As has been indicated above, intuition and empathy were used by the romantics as ways of gaining direct and definitive understanding, and were considered to be complete scientific methods. The contemporary personologist has no quarrel with their use in the practical arts of clinical psychology and psychoanalysis, nor as ways of making discoveries and formulating hypotheses. Indeed, the more secure scientists are in their methodological position, the more respect they usually have for intuition (and in psychology for the closely related methods of empathy and recipathy[8]). Thus, the claim that these operations have no place in natural science is false; they are used by all scientists in the most exciting and creative phase of scientific work: when they decide what to study, what variables to control, what empirical strategies to use, and when they make discoveries within the structure of empirical data. As to their sufficiency, I need only remind the reader that the methodology of verification, the hypothesis-testing phase of scientific work, involves well-developed rules and consensually established procedures, and that intuition and empathy have no place in it.

3. *Personology Is a Subjective Discipline As Contrasted to Objective Branches of Psychology, Being Concerned with Values and Meanings, Which Cannot Be Subjected to Quantification.* Elsewhere (Holt, 1961 [Volume 2, Chapter 3]), I have dealt with the contention that there is a fundamental methodological difference between disciplines that deal with verbal meanings and values, and those that deal with objective facts. Briefly, the argument is the familiar one that objectivity is only intersubjectivity, and that meanings (including values) may be perceived and dealt with in essentially the same ways as the data of natural science, which must be discriminated and recognized also. Moreover, a logical analysis of the operations carried out in disciplines such as literature, concerned with the understanding of individual works and little (if at all) with generalization, shows that these workers outside of science use many of the *same* methods of analyzing texts as the quantitative content-analysts of social psychology, with their exclusive concern with generalization. Their work has shown that meanings may be quantified and in other ways treated as objectively as any other facts of nature. Other objections to quantification grow out of antipathy to abstract variables of analysis and will be considered in the following section.

4. *The Concepts of Personology Must Be Individualized, Not Generalized As Are the Concepts of Natural Science.* The belief that the concern of personology with unique individuals (see below) contrasts fundamentally with the exclusive concern of nomothetic science with generalities logically implies that the two types of discipline must have different types of concepts. As the chief

---

[8]Recipathy is the method of "becoming as open and sensitive as possible" not only to "the subject's movements and words" but to one's own feelings of "how the subject's attitude is affecting him [the observer] . . . if he feels that he is being swayed to do something he imagines Dominance; if he feels anxious or irritated he infers Aggression, and so forth" (Murray, 1938, p. 248).

spokesman for the romantic point of view in psychology, Allport calls for the use of individual traits, which are specific to the person being studied, not common traits, which are assumed to be present to some degree in all persons. But to describe an individual trait, we have to take one of two courses: either we create a unique word (a neologism) for each unique trait, or we use a unique configuration of existing words. The first approach is clearly impossible for communication, let alone science; personology would be a complete Babel. The second solution, however, turns out to be a concealed form of nomothesis, for what is a unique configuration of existing words but a "fallacious attempt to capture something ineffably individual by a complex net of general concepts"? Allport himself has explicitly ruled out this possibility:

> ... each psychologist tends to think of individuals as combinations of whatever abstractions he favors for psychological analysis. This proce-dure, common as it is, is wholly unsuitable for the psychology of person-ality. For one thing, such abstract units are not distinctively personal[9] (1937a, p. 239).

An idiographic discipline thus must be a dumb or an incomprehensible one, for intelligible words—even some of Allport's favorite, literary ones, like *Falstaffian,* which he does consider "personal"—abstract and generalize, proclaiming a general pattern of resemblance between at least two unique individuals, Falstaff and the case being described. Any such trait thus becomes common, not individual.

One of the great methodologists of social science, Max Weber (1949) developed an apposite analysis of scientific concepts and their development in reaction against the romantic movement in his country at the turn of the century (see Parsons, 1937). He had the insight to see that the exponents of *Geisteswissenschaft* were trying to do the impossible: to capture the full rich-ness of reality. There are three identifiable stages in the scientific study of anything, Weber said. To begin with, one selects from nature the historical individual (or class thereof) one wishes to focus on; for example, the Boston Massacre, the personality of Einstein, the cathedral at Chartres. Even though limited, each of these is infinitely rich in potentially specifiable aspects and configurations. One could study one of these, or even a tiny "flower in a crannied wall," until doomsday and not exhaust everything that could be known about it. Without doing any more abstracting than focusing on a particular topic, one can only contemplate it; and this is where the idio-graphic approach logically must stop. The method of intuition or *Verstehen* is essentially a wordless act of identification with the object, or some other attempt to "live in it" without analyzing its Gestalt.

[9]Allport wrote these words in the context of rejecting Murray's system of needs (1937a); yet elsewhere (Allport, 1937b) he praises as "strikingly personal" such concepts (or dimensions) of W. Stern (1938) as depth-surface, embeddedness-salience, nearness-remoteness, and expec-tancy-retrospect!

The second stage, that of the ideal type, is a rudimentary attempt to see similarities between historical individuals, while staying as close as possible to their concrete particularity. Ideal types are much used in psychology, especially in diagnosis, for any syndrome such as schizophrenia is a complex of identifiably separate but loosely covarying elements, never encountered in exact textbook form. The lure of ideal types is that they give the brief illusion of getting you close to the individual while still allowing a degree of generality. But this advantage is illusory, the apparent advantage of a compromise that denies satisfaction to either party. Concrete reality (fidelity to the unique individual) *is* forsworn, and the advantages of truly general concepts are not attained. An ideal type does not fit any particular case exactly, and the failure of fit is different in kind as well as degree from one case to another. For an ideal type "is a conceptual construct which is neither historical reality nor even the 'true' reality. It is even less fitted to serve as a schema under which a real situation or action is to be subsumed as one *instance*. It has the significance of a purely ideal *limiting* concept with which the real situation or action is compared and surveyed for the explication of certain of its significant components" (Weber, 1949, p. 93).

Weber's final stage of scientific development, therefore, is the fractionation of ideal types into their constituent dimensions and elements, which he called abstract analytical variables.[10] Paradoxically, only a truly abstract concept can give an exact fit to any particular individual! I cannot say exactly how Falstaffian or how schizophrenic or how big any particular subject may be, but I can name a particular value of an abstract analytical variable, height, that fits him as closely as his skin. The example would be less convincing if chosen from psychology because we do not have as well-established, unitary dimensions as the physical ones, and not as simple and unarguable operations for measuring them as the use of the meter stick; the principle, however, is the same.

The fit is exact, of course, only because an abstract analytical concept does not purport to do more than one thing. If I try to measure the breadth of a person's interests, I make no pretensions to have "captured the essence of his personality." Not having tried, I cannot properly be accused of failing. But I have chosen a variable that can be measured, and thus potentially its relations to other aspects of personality can be discovered and precisely stated. Curiously, Allport attacks general variables on the ground that they "merely *approximate* the unique cleavages which close scrutiny shows are characteristic of each separate personality" (Allport, 1946; his emphasis). His preferred *ad hoc* approach may seem less approximate because many of the general variables used in personology are ideal types, lacking true abstract generality. The solution, however, lies in a direction diametrically opposed to the one toward which Allport beckons. And it does not consist in escaping

---

[10] [In his analytical emphasis and his neglect of total system properties—which most personality traits seem to be—Weber showed his rootedness in nineteenth-century thinking.]

from approximation. Scientific models of reality can *never* fit perfectly; the attempt to force such identity between concept and referent sacrifices the flexibility and power of abstract concepts in a chimerical quest for the direct grasp of noumena.[11]

Parenthetically, the recent vogue of existentialism and Zen Buddhism in psychology may be partly attributed to the promise they extend of providing a way of grasping the total richness of reality. Part of the lure of *satori* or any other mystical ecstasy of a direct contact with the world, unmediated by concepts, may stem from the necessary distance imposed by the scientific necessity to abstract. But despite their confusing jargons, which make them seem superficially quite different from the late nineteenth-century romantic movement we have been considering, both of these fashionable doctrines suffer from the same fallacies. Mystical experience offers nothing to the scientist qua scientist except an interesting phenomenon that may be subjected to scientific study.

5. *The Only Kind of Analysis Allowable in Personology Is Structural, Not Abstract, While Natural Science Is Not Concerned with Structure.* It is true that the scientific psychology of Dilthey's heyday had no place for structural analysis in the sense introduced by the romantics. Psychology dealt with a number of functions, which were treated implicitly or explicitly as quite independent of one another. It had no methods parallel to those of exegetic Biblical scholarship (hermeneutics) or literary criticism, which seek out the internal organization of ideas in a specific text. And the reductionistic enthusiasts for analyzing things were not interested in putting the pieces back together again, nor very clear themselves that analysis need not mean dismemberment. This state of affairs made it easy to think that analysis could be destructive, and that structural relations between the parts of the personality could be studied only in concrete, unique individuals, so that structure[12] seemed to be an exclusive concern of idiographic disciplines.

There are really two points here: the distrust of analysis, and the emphasis on structure. The first of these has been partly dealt with in the preceding section; it was based on a misunderstanding of the nature of abstract concepts.[13]

---

[11][Fifteen years later, I feel less inclined to reject typological concepts or to consider them only way stations to attaining the analytical goal of a set of abstractions. Following Weiss (1969), I would say now that some types are attempts to delineate recurrent patterns of system-organization, which are not wholly reducible to their components. At the least, the issues seem much more complicated today than they did when I wrote this paper.]

[12]Ironically, in psychology the early adherents of structuralism were among those who carried atomistic, reductionistic analysis to its most absurd extreme: the Titchenerian introspectionists. The Gestalt psychologists, though appalled by the equally atomistic behaviorism and structuralism alike, concentrated their efforts on perceptual patterning, leaving untouched most of the structural problems that concern personology, particularly the enduring invariances of molar behavior.

[13][But also on a valid recognition that analysis, even supplemented by a synthetic effort to put the pieces back together, is not enough: analysis need not kill, but it does fail to say all that needs to

On the second point, structural concepts and structural analyses are commonplace in science at large today. Such structural disciplines as stereochemistry and circuit design were (at best) in their infancy at the time of the idiographic manifestoes. Today, natural science uses abstract, structural, and dispositional concepts simultaneously with a minimum of confusion. Presumably, the same may be true of personology someday, too.

One merit of the romantic tradition in personology is that it has consistently highlighted the problem of structure. At the time Allport was taking his position on these matters (in the late 1920s and early 1930s), the predominant American conceptions of personality were "and-summative" (it was defined as the sum total of a person's habits, traits, etc.), and the problem of structure was ignored. The early academic personologists who concentrated their efforts on personality inventories, single variables, or factor analyses, all tended to disregard entirely the structuring of these elements or to assume simple, universal answers (e.g., orthogonal factor-structure).

At the same time, however, Freud (1923b) was developing the structural point of view in psychoanalysis, and today psychoanalytic psychology is increasingly concerned with the problem and has developed a variety of variables to deal with it (Rapaport & Gill, 1959; Holt, 1960b; and see the work of G. S. Klein and his associates on cognitive controls as structural variables: Gardner *et al.*, 1959 [but see also Holt, 1975b]). Drawing on this tradition and that of psychopathology generally, psychodiagnosis concerns itself with structural variables and their constellation into a limited number of ideal types (e.g., the obsessive-compulsive type of ego-structure) which, in the best practice, are used not as pigeonholes but as reference-points in terms of which the clinician creates individualized analyses of personality structure.

6. *There Can Be No General Laws of Personality Because of the Role of Chance and Free Will in Human Affairs.* There are hardly any contemporary personologists who openly espouse this argument. It played an important part in the development of the romantic point of view, as we have seen, and persists in Catholic psychology. It is generally admitted, however, that scientific work requires the basic assumption of strict determinism throughout.[14] Closely examined, chance becomes ignorance; when we discover systematic effects where "error" existed before, the chance (at least in part) disappears. It may well be that the exact events of an individual life could never be predicted,

---

be said. Systems must be described on their own level, not just that of their constituent elements. The point has been beautifully developed by Weiss (1969). For another clear exposition of general system theory's resolution of the false antithesis between holistic and analytic approaches, see Koestler (1967).]

[14][Until the past decade, I did not see that free will and determinism are not antithetical; indeed, personal freedom would be impossible in a nondeterministic world. See footnote 5, above; I am considering these issues at greater length in another book (in preparation). See also Weiss (1969) for a refutation of the position I took in the first version of this paper; his hierarchical conception of determinism is an important contribution to the systems outlook on an ancient philosophical problem.]

any more than the exact path of a falling raindrop; but that does not in any way rule out the possibility of general laws that determine these two kinds of "behavior."

7. *General Laws Are Not Possible in Personology Because Its Subject Matter Is Unique Individuals, Which Have No Place in Natural Science.* It is not difficult to dispose of this last, supposedly critical point of difference between *Naturwissenschaft* and *Geisteswissenschaft*.

The mechanistic, reductionistic science of Windelband's day contained a curious dictum that has been one of the principal sources of confusion on this whole issue: *Scientia non est individuorum*—science does not deal with individual cases. This hoary slogan dates back to the days when Aristotle was the last word on matters scientific, and the whole point of view it expresses is outdated in the physical sciences. According to this philosophy, the individual case was not lawful, since laws were conceived of as empirical regularities. This is the point of view (Plato's idealism or what Popper [1957] calls *essentialism*) that considers an average to be the only fact, and all deviation from it mere error.

Freud and Lewin have taught us that psychic determinism is thoroughgoing (see above), and the individual case is completely lawful. It is just difficult to know what the laws *are* from a study of one case, no matter how thorough. We can surmise (or, if you will, intuit) general laws from a single case in the hypothesis-forming phase of scientific endeavor, but we can verify them only by resorting to experimental or statistical inquiry or both.

There is truth in the old adage only in one sense, then: we cannot carry out the complete scientific process by the study of an individual.[15] It is true that in certain of the disciplines concerned with man, from anatomy to sensory psychology, it has usually been assumed that the phenomena being studied are so universal that they can be located for study in any single person, and so autonomous from entanglement in idiosyncratically variable aspects of individuals that the findings of intensive investigation will have general applicability to people at large. Every so often, however, these assumptions turn out not to be tenable. For example, when Boring repeated Head's study (in one case, himself) of the return of sensation after the experimental section of a sensory nerve in his arm, he did not find the protopathic-epicritic sequential recovery, which had been so uncritically accepted as to be firmly embedded in the literature. No matter how intensively prolonged, objective, and well-controlled the study of a single case, one can never be sure to what extent the lawful regularities found can be generalized to other persons, or in what ways the findings will turn out to be contingent on some fortuitously present characteristic of the subject—until

---

[15][And also in Weiss's (1969) sense that many aspects of individuals are indeterminable, hence we might as well view them as "chance," even though the individual is thereby playing his part in producing an intelligible and predictable (or lawful) regularity on a higher level of analysis.]

the investigation is repeated on an adequate sample of persons. As excellent a way as it is to make discoveries, the study of an individual cannot be used to establish laws; bills of attainder (that is, laws concerned with single individuals) are as unconstitutional in science as in jurisprudence. Note, however, that law of either kind, when promulgated, is still conceived as holding quite rigorously for the single individual. [See also Volume 2, Chapter 8.]

Science is defined by its methods, not its subject matter; to maintain the opposite, as Skaggs (1945) did in an attack on Allport, is to perpetuate the confusion, not resolve it, and Allport (1946) was an easy victor in the exchange. There can be and is scientific study of all sorts of individuals. Particular hurricanes are individualized to the extent of being given personal names and are studied by all the scientific means at the meteorologist's command. A great deal of the science of astronomy is given over to the study of a number of unique individuals: the sun, moon, and planets, and even individual stars and nebulae. There may not be another Saturn, with its strange set of rings, in all of creation,[16] yet it is studied by the most exact, quantitative, and—if you must—nomothetic methods, and it would be ridiculous to suggest that astronomy is for these reasons not a science or that there should be two entirely different astronomical sciences, one to study individual heavenly bodies and the other to seek general laws. Further examples are easily available from geology, physics, and biology. Once we realize that individuals are easily within the realm of orthodox scientific study and that science does not strive for artistic illusions of complete understanding, the issue is easily seen as a pseudoproblem. Psychology as a science remains methodologically the same, whether its focus be on individual cases or on general laws.

Granted, then, that individual personalities may and must be studied by the scientific method in personology, with the use of general concepts, what is the role of general laws in such a science? Where does it get us to make scientific studies of personalities, if each is unique, and if that uniqueness is the heart of the matter?

Personalities *are* in many ways unique, but as Kluckhohn and Murray (1953) point out, every man is also like all men in some ways and like a limited number of others in still other ways, making generalization possible. If every personality structure were as much a law unto itself as Allport implies, it would be impossible to gain useful information in this field; there would be no transfer from one case study to another. As anyone knows who has tried it, there is a great deal.

It is a mistake to focus personology on just those aspects of a person that

---

[16]After these words had been written, I was amused to find that Cournot used this same example, and even similar wording, in supporting his position that "it is no longer necessary to accept to the letter the aphorism of the ancients to the effect that the individual and particular have no place in science" (1851, p. 443).

are unique, as Weber (1949) saw clearly half a century ago. "The attempt to understand 'Bismarck,'" he said for example, "by leaving out of account everything which he has in common with other men and keeping what is 'particular' to him would be an instructive and amusing exercise for beginners. One would in that case . . . preserve, for example, as one of those 'finest flowers' [of such an analysis of uniqueness] his 'thumbprint,' that most specific indication of 'individuality.'" And some of the most critical points about him for predicting his behavior would have to be excluded because he shared them with other persons. Indeed, in contemporary psychodiagnosis, it is considered most useful to treat as a quantitative variable the degree to which a person's responses resemble those of the group as a whole.

The only kind of law that Allport could conceive for personology was one (like his principle of functional autonomy) that describes how uniqueness comes about. Personology has not been much restrained from seeking general relationships among its variables by this narrow view, however; the journals are full of investigations in which aspects of personality are studied genetically (that is, are related to the abstract variable of age) or are correlated, one with another. Once one treats uniqueness not with awe but with the casual familiarity due any other truistic fact of life, it ceases to pose any difficulty for personology.

Writing intensive case studies (on the genesis and structure of individual personalities) turns out not to be a particularly fruitful method, except for the generation of hypotheses. This is a very important exception, but the point is that personology does not proceed mainly by adding one exhaustive scientific biography to another, looking for generalizations afterwards. The Gestaltist taboo on studying any variable out of its context in the individual life is an overstatement. There is, of course, such a phenomenon as the interaction of variables, but it is not so far-reachingly prevalent as to make impossible any study of two variables at a time. As Falk (1956) has shown, this condition of interactive nonsummativeness is found in many other kinds of subject matter besides personality and creates no major difficulties of method or procedure.[17]

In summary, in this section we have looked at the major propositions of the romantic point of view as applied to personology and have found that the "basic differences" between this field and natural science are completely illusory. No basis for a separate methodology exists, and the objections to applying the general methodology of science to personalities turn out to be based on misunderstandings or on a narrow conception of natural science that is an anachronism today.

It by no means follows, as Eysenck (1954) puts it, that the science of

---

[17][At the same time, we have to accept a low ceiling on the possible size of relationships discoverable in this way, and a lower one the further our level of analysis is from that appropriate to the kind of system under study. At the time I wrote this paragraph, I did not grasp the fact that obtainable information about a system is not exhausted by studying its elements and their interactions.]

personality should therefore be considered nomothetic. The nomothetic conception of science must be rejected as a caricature of what any contemporary scientist does. The only way to justify the application of the term nomothetic to the natural science of the present is to change the definition of the term so much that it no longer resembles its original meaning and becomes an unnecessary redundancy. It can only lead to confusion to introduce such (unacknowledged) changes of definition; the nomothetic is as dead a duck today as the idiographic, and neither term adds anything to contemporary philosophy of science.[18]

Many psychologists have followed Allport in taking the apparently sensible "middle position" of trying to deal with the objections that have been raised to his extreme idiographic pronouncements by saying, let's have a personology that is *both* nomothetic and idiographic (e.g., McClelland, 1951; MacKinnon, 1951). Thus, whenever he approaches the realization that the idiographic discipline of which he dreams is unworkable, Allport says, in effect, "I am not an extremist; common traits have their uses, even though they are only approximations, and personology can use both nomothetic and idiographic contributions." In practice, what this amounts to is that whenever attention is focused on individual cases, the inquiry is called idiographic, and otherwise it is considered nomothetic.

My objection to this "solution," this apparently reasonable compromise between antithetical positions, is that it is achieved only by a perversion of the original definitions and that it accomplishes nothing except the preservation of a pair of pedantic words for our jargon. If one really accepts the arguments for an idiographic *Geisteswissenschaft* he can logically have no truck with nomothetic methods. They exist no longer, anyway, except in the history books; scientific method, as understood and practiced today in natural science and personology alike, is not a combination nor blend of nomothetic and idiographic approaches, but something bigger and better than both of them.[19] The original dichotomies were badly formulated and based on misconceptions. The accompanying terminology might best be forgotten along with them.

[18][Specifically, the nomothetic conception of science is basically the nineteenth-century tradition of mechanistic reductionism (Holt, 1971a), or what Whitehead (1925, p. 18) called scientific materialism (see also Yankelovich and Barrett, 1970; and Ackoff, 1974, Chapter 1). Since nomothetic and idiographic are antithetical, the conflict cannot be solved by compromise, either that of the moderate middle way or of the "sometimes one, sometimes the other" variety. What is needed is a true synthesis, a decentering shift in point of view or theory to a new level of observation and conceptualization. The systems outlook gives just such a synthesis in terms of which we can see the truth and the error in both prior positions (Bertalanffy, 1968; Laszlo, 1972).]

[19][Alas, I was too optimistic when I wrote these words, underestimating the extent to which mechanistic reductionism flourishes in contemporary psychology. The fact is that Eysenck, Skinner, and other proponents of what Koestler (1967) tellingly calls "flat-earth psychology" continue to dominate our discipline, with many of their zealous followers occupying prominent roles in personology and clinical psychology.]

IS THERE AN IDIOGRAPHIC METHOD?

The last stand of the proponents of the romantic dichotomy is the contention that there are distinct generalizing (nomothetic) and individualizing (idiographic) *methods* in personology. This is the point of departure for Stephenson (1953) and some others who are enchanted by the mystique of *Q*. Inflating his ingenious rating technique into a whole so-called methodology, Stephenson has argued that his device of rating on an "ipsative" instead of a "normative" scale creates a specifically idiographic method for personology. When one *Q*-sorts a group of items for a subject, he makes a set of ratings which are forced into a normal distribution and scaled according to each item's applicability to this particular person (which is ipsative scaling, as opposed to the usual normative ratings where the standard is the distribution in a population of comparable persons). The device is clever and often useful; it enables a judge to give quantitative ratings to a great number of variables for one person without any reference to any sort of standard population; the population is intrapersonal (Block, 1961).

Here is a technique suited to individual cases. Is it therefore idiographic, something fundamentally different from conventional scientific methods of rating personality? Hardly. *Q*-sorts are typically used in large studies in which the individual case is an anonymous statistic. Moreover, it is a kind of Procrustean bed, imposing a standard pattern of ratings on every personality: all must have the same mean, standard deviation, and distribution (normal, flat, or other). What is even further from the spirit of Allport's crusade for individual traits, the "items" are common traits, applied to everyone with no allowance for their failure to fit certain cases. In summary, then, the *Q*-sort is quite unacceptable in the traditional meaning of the term idiographic, and the use of that term to signify the fact that it is applied to individuals is simply a grandiloquent pose.

Following Allport (1942), others (e.g., Dymond, 1953; Hoffman, 1960) have revived the tired old terms either in an attempt to bolster, or in an attack on, the contention that clinical predictions must be superior to statistical predictions, because the clinician uses idiographic methods which alone are appropriate to predictions about individual cases. Here is another badly formulated pseudo-issue [see section on Prediction in Volume 2]. Whether a clinician or a formula does better in making a particular kind of prediction is an empirical question and one of little general interest. Clinicians and statisticians have their own proper spheres of activity, which overlap but little, and the difference between their activities has nothing to do with methodological issues. The method of clinical judgment has a great deal in common with the hypothesis-forming and theory-building phases of work in all the sciences [see Volume 2, Chapter 3].

In the end, we see that there is no need for a special type of science to be applied to individual personalities and that the attempt to promulgate such a science fell into hopeless contradictions and absurdities. Today, Windelband's terms continue to appear in psychological writing but largely as pretentious jargon, mouth-filling polysyllables to awe the uninitiated, but never as essential concepts to make any scientifically vital point. Let us simply drop them from our vocabularies and let them die quietly.[20]

SUMMARY

The conception of two kinds of disciplines, a nomothetic science to study general principles and find abstract laws, and an idiographic science to study individuality, arose as a protest against a narrow conception of science in the nineteenth century. But the romantic movement of which it was a part started from fallacious premises, such as the conception that science is defined by its subject matter rather than its method, and its radical principles were never actually applied in pure form by any of its adherents. The idiographic point of view is an artistic one that strives for a nonscientific goal; the nomothetic, a caricature that bears little resemblance to the best contemporary work in the "hard" sciences. Since no useful purpose is served by retaining these mischievous and difficult terms, they had best disappear from our scientific vocabularies.

[20]Surely a trivial but none the less annoying characteristic of the word *idiographic* furnishes a further argument for its consignment to oblivion: the strong tendency of printers to assimilate it to the more familiar but wholly different word *ideographic* (pertaining to ideographs or picture-writing). For example, Skaggs's paper (1945) contains *only* the misspelled version. [After this paper's publication, a friend pointed out to me the ironic fact that the last statement is (almost) true also of Holt and Luborsky, 1958!]

The TAT

2

At the Harvard Psychological Clinic, graduate students like myself had plenty of opportunities to learn the methods of multiform personality assessment pioneered in Explorations in Personality *(Murray, 1938)—informally, not as part of a curriculum. From R. W. White and later from Murray and Morgan I learned the fundamenents of interpreting the Clinic's favorite instrument, the TAT. Then, during my first clinical job in Topeka, David Rapaport taught me his own, quite different and more theoretically grounded approach (Rapaport, Gill, & Schafer, 1968). An invitation to contribute a chapter to a book on projective techniques (Anderson & Anderson, 1951) gave me the opportunity to synthesize these two interpretive schemes. This volume's second chapter is basically a reprint of my old paper, with some minor adjustments of terminology and some supplementation. As usual, the recent interpolations of any considerable length are indicated by being set inside square brackets, though it was not feasible to use the latter with Tables 2.1 and 2.2, here published for the first time.*

The Thematic Apperception Test: Rationale, Administration, and Interpretation

Le style c'est l'homme. Writers, from the creators of classics to comic strip hacks, put their own values, their own personalities into their works. Who would doubt that Dickens was a moralistic, sentimental person, or that Swift was bitter and lonely? It is a commonplace of literary criticism to point out, as was widely done, for example, of Thomas Wolfe's *Look Homeward, Angel,* that the story has much of autobiography in it; the somewhat subtler psychological exegesis of a man's less obviously autobiographic works is also frequently found in contemporary letters. When we go beyond the step of reading simply to be distracted or to lose ourselves in the excitement of a yarn, we turn to a new novelist or poet to see what aspect of experience he has found most vivid and has passed on to us; we try to get a fresh perspective on the world—and we seldom hesitate to assume that this perspective is the author's own. The more we read of his work, the more we can see what remains

33

constant while individual stories change; through the nature of these con-
stancies we get a feeling for the author as a man.

From an extensive and expert acquaintance of this kind with literature
and literary criticism, Murray and Morgan asked themselves why the same
kinds of deductions could not be drawn from study of a series of stories
written or told by anyone. They hit upon the happy idea of developing a set
of 20 pictures around which tales could be constructed. The pictures stimulate the imagination; they give definite grist for the less imaginative person's
mill, so that he does not soon run out of ideas. They permit more or less
systematic exploration of specific areas of potential conflict or motivational
importance. And the subject's perceptual reactions to the pictures yield an
added source of valuable data about the ways he looks at his world. The
result, then, was the *Thematic* (in reference to the themes that are elicited)
Apperception (in reference to the perceptual-interpretive use of the pictures)
Test, or TAT, for short. Experimental use revealed that Murray and Morgan
had created a multidimensional instrument that elicits from a subject a rich
source of data about himself. In spite of the difficulties in recording, scoring,
and interpreting the TAT, the test today ranks second only to the Rorschach
in widespread clinical use.

The difficulties mentioned and the lack of a generally accepted scoring
scheme have given the test, in some quarters, a reputation for slipperiness or
even mystery that it hardly deserves. One of the purposes of this chapter is to
show that the TAT story is no more inscrutable than any other product of
human thinking. The plan of the chapter is, first, a discussion of rationale, an
attempt to outline ten important classes of psychological determinants that
are operative in the creation of a TAT story; second, a section on some
problems of administering the test; and finally, an introduction to some
methods of interpreting the responses to it.

RATIONALE

The late Kurt Lewin was fond of remarking that nothing is as practical
as a good theory. In the field of clinical psychology, intuitive ingenuity and
accumulated practical experience have considerably outstripped theoretical
development. One can go a long way with purely empirical rules for interpreting specific constellations in psychological tests, but rules of thumb
always tie one to concrete patterns and give no help at all when the particulars of known significance fail to appear. There are very few such "signs"
with anything like invariant meaning in TAT stories; furthermore, the
flexibility that a good theoretical grasp can give is particularly necessary for
the successful use of the test.

A good way to approach a rationale for the TAT is to try to understand
what takes place, psychologically, as a story comes into being. To unravel a

knot, it is helpful to know how it was tied; to decipher hieroglyphic traces of the unique person in his stories, it helps if one can first get some clarity about the ways in which stories come about. Unfortunately, we do not have much empirical knowledge about this kind of problem. We have a number of insightful hypotheses, however, and it is worth while to review them, remembering always that what follows is not as well established as one should like for proper scientific rigor.

Some Propositions from Freud's Theory of Dream-Formation

Perhaps nothing will be so useful in this connection as some speculations about the mental processes involved in a somewhat different kind of phenomenon, written at the turn of the century. In the monumental seventh chapter of his *Interpretation of Dreams,* Freud (1900a) gives a hypothetical reconstruction of the mental alchemy of dreams, from which the following points may be abstracted.

1. Some event of the preceding day (the day's residue) starts a train of unconscious reactions going.

2. *This train of thought usually leads to a repressed wish or conflict.* As long as it is unsatisfied, it tends to keep propelling derivatives—ideas or memories— into consciousness. But it may be opposed by incompatible wishes or fears. Direct expression may be intolerable to the conscious mature personality, whose standards would require guilt, shame, or mortification (loss of self-esteem) if the person were to have the thoughts or commit the acts he secretly wants to. Or, he might become anxious, fearful of being overwhelmed by his own dangerous impulses. Therefore, direct expression is closed off by repression and other *mechanisms of defense.* The motivating wish, still unfulfilled, continues to generate derivatives.

3. The events represented by the day's residue, having been present in ordinary consciousness, need not be repressed. Thus, *the day's residue offers to the beleaguered unconscious wish an opportunity for partial satisfaction.* But how can the idea of an ordinary event play such a role for an unacceptable impulse? It is one of Freud's important discoveries that a wish can obtain some partial gratification through the agency of an act or thought that is related in some way to it. Thus, checkmating an opponent's king may offer some fulfillment to the necessarily unconscious wish to murder one's father; taking part in a revolution, dreaming about it, or telling a TAT story on the subject may all likewise give some gratification to this same motive (though, of course, to different degrees).

4. The wish and associated ideas still cannot usually find any direct route to the semiconsciousness of the dream state and are long-circuited through a variety of devious by-ways, undergoing certain kinds of distortions and transformations.

5. Under the influence of directing ideas, the nascent dream undergoes

secondary elaboration—is fashioned into a more or less coherent, usually dramatic form.

This is not intended to be an exhaustive summary of Freud's formulations; to mention only the most obvious omission, for example, I have dropped all references to forces and energies. Only the generalizable aspects of the Freudian account have been outlined. A dream is not a TAT story, and it cannot be maintained that all aspects of Freud's theory are relevant.

If we consider an actual story, it will be easy to see the extent to which these formulations help in understanding how it came into being. In card 8BM, an adolescent boy looks straight out of the picture. The barrel of a rifle is visible at one side, and in the background is the dim scene of a surgical operation, like a reverie-image. Here is a story told by a young college man, called Nailson, to card 8BM.

> Gee, it looks like a young fellow. (Pause.) Oh, fellow is about fifteen, I guess. It's (pause). He's either seen or read about some operation in which the patient had gone through all kinds of tortures, and he decided he's going to become a doctor. He's going to fix things, they're not going to happen like that any more. These are old doctors, very old, long time ago, I guess. They're going to town, probably no ether or anything else. The kid was probably just a young baby at the time, maybe. Looks like he had a nightmare or two. And (pause) that determined his life for him. He's going to spend his whole time trying to be a doctor and not have any more operations like this. He's going to (pause). Well, it could be that he's something like Bliss or some one of the great doctors that invented anaesthetics, something to bring ease to the patient during the operation. Probably spend his whole life trying to develop something like that. Anyway, he's going to be a doctor, he's not going to have anything like this happen again.

If we take the story as analogous to the finished dream, what corresponds to the day's residue, the original stimulus that set going a process resulting in the story?

1. Surely the picture, or part of the picture, must stand in the same relation to the story as the day's residue does to the dream. Neither is wholly responsible for the finished product, yet the influence of the originating content can be seen in the final product in both cases. The story is less personal than the dream in that the picture is not a personal experience in the same sense as the day's residue, but there is the compensating advantage of greater interindividual comparability.

2. Now, it is true that the perceptual impact of a TAT picture may or may not touch off very important underlying motives or problems. Some stories (like the one quoted here) go right to the heart of the subject's important formative experiences; others remain superficial and reveal little of the deep themes for which the psychologist usually searches. But the contrast to dreams is not such an exaggerated one, after all: not all experi-

ences in daily life result in dreams, either; only the ones that have some kind of relatedness to important motives. Just so, only pictures the contents of which give tongue to the silent forces of the unconscious result in psychodynamically significant stories. Fortunately, the range of vital human problems is not so wide that one cannot find a few important gaps in almost any subject's defenses with a set of 20 pictures. It obviously becomes important just what the content of the pictures is; they have been chosen to touch on the basic human situations and sources of conflict that are important to most people in our culture.

Let us return to Nailson and the operation scene. The great and strikingly repeated emphasis on preventing the recurrence of scenes of torture like this primitive attempt at surgery, the event's decisiveness in the life of the story's central figure, or hero, the use of language, which (for this subject) is vivid—all point to the conclusion that *the perceptual process has made contact with important configurations in his emotional and conative life, which are using it to come to indirect conscious expression.*

3. If we are to adhere to a dynamic point of view, we must assume always that *some motives are at work determining the particular content chosen.* In the case of the TAT story, one cannot dogmatically say that the wishes that find some partial outlet are necessarily unconscious. When the subject matter of the picture is relatively indifferent, *and* when the inner pressure of unsatisfied, repressed, or conflicted wishes is *not* great, relatively peripheral conscious motives may be chiefly involved. Of course, if an emotionally disturbed person is under great pressure of a psychic conflict, he may foist the latter upon any picture, express it somehow in any story—for that matter, in the content of Rorschach responses or almost any other test given to the patient.

In any event, since the subject is not personally responsible for the content of the picture, he can usually allow himself at least to describe it, or to tell a story in which there is little apparent deviation from what is objectively given. Thus any repressed wish that becomes implicated can escape censorship to some degree. In the present instance, the repressed traumatic incident was determined with fair certainty to be the shock at an early age ("a long time ago . . . just a baby at the time") of seeing his mother brutally mistreated by his father (or so he thought). It may even have taken the form of the *primal scene* (observation of parental intercourse). It is by no means to be assumed that any such deep interpretation could confidently be made on the basis of this story alone. It is a conclusion reached by Nailson's biographer after careful analysis of many other sources of data, including interviews as well as tests.[1] A great deal of the subject's life actually has been

[1] A sketch of Nailson containing most of the relevant data may be found in Bellak and Jaques (1942). Under another pseudonym, Nack, he is also discussed at length in Murray and Morgan (1945). In the latter monograph, there is a report of an interview in which the subject himself confirmed the hypothesis of exposure to the primal scene.

organized around this very slogan: "he's not going to have anything like this happen again."

4. It is clear, however, that *the basic complex remains unconscious,* in spite of its being stirred by the picture. Instead of its being a sexual scene that "determines his life for him," it is an operation in the story. One may well argue that no distortion is involved here, that, in fact, there would be gross distortion if the pictured scene were called a rape. Of course there would be *perceptual* distortion in such a case; one would be justified in hypothesizing that someone who disregarded reality to such an extent was psychotic. But it is characteristic of psychotics that material related to childhood traumas does sometimes break through directly, with little distortion, into consciousness, warping perceptual contact with reality in doing so. In this case, then, the picture both arouses the traumatic material and furnishes it with a respectable disguise, so that the distorting effect of defenses on the latent content is hard to see.

5. The similarity between dream and TAT story in the final steps has already been referred to. The perceptual data, the cognitive associations, and the feelings and wishes that are activated are all organized by the set to satisfy the instructions of the test and are synthesized into a relatively orderly story. The result in this case is a great deal more coherent than most dreams, being mainly the product of the *secondary process* (rational thinking) rather than the *primary process* of dreams (unconscious, nonrational thinking). This is not the best place to go into an examination of differences between TAT stories and dreams; suffice it to say that the two mental products have very important differences as well as similarities, and that it is far from my intention to to give the impression that TAT stories are to be analyzed just as if they were dreams. [See also Chapter 4.]

Categories of Determinants

Do the above five stages exhaust all that we know or can reasonably hypothesize about how a story comes into being? Not at all. There follows a set of ten different categories of determinants that shape TAT stories. They are presented in approximately the order in which they seem to come into operation as the mental process corresponding to a story develops. In tracing the operation of these determinants, I will use Nailson's story further as an example.

1. **The Situational Context.** One must go back beyond the point when the first picture is presented if he is to understand the important determinants of a story. Any dynamic psychology must work with some equivalent of Lewin's formula, $B = f(P,E)$: all behavior is a function of the nature of the person and of his environment. In psychological testing, we sometimes overlook the effect of the E in this equation, because of our concern with the nature of P. A person will make up different stories for a friend who is doing

some research, for a prospective employer, for a psychiatrist who is treating his neurosis, or for a prison psychologist who is investigating his motives for a crime he has committed. A different side will be turned to each, in all likelihood; somewhat different attitudes, sets, defenses, and motivations will be called up by each situation.

To understand Nailson's story, it should be realized that he was a healthy college man who was serving as a subject in a research program in order to earn some extra money.[2] Furthermore, he was being tested by a friendly, informal examiner who liked him and put him at his ease. There were therefore no pressing personal reasons for Nailson to reveal himself, and no strong pressure from the outside either, though there was plenty of encouragement. It is reasonable to suppose that he might have been much more cautious or guarded in another situation. As it was, he felt free to speak quite informally, and his use of slang (as in the phrase, "going to town," with its perhaps important sexual implication [in contemporary usage, it could mean "having sexual intercourse"]) is not as inappropriate as it would be coming from a patient.

2. The Directing Sets. Another determinant closely related to the situational context and in large part growing out of it is the group of anticipations, guiding ideas, or directing sets that the subject forms. They are made up of his preconceptions of what the test and tester are like, his subjective interpretation of the instructions, and his conception of what it means to be tested. His motivation for participating may be considered a part of this group of determinants, which make the difference between such extremes as his passively giving minimal compliance to a red-tape routine, and his being challenged to maintain his self-esteem and the examiner's approbation by telling as interesting, dramatic, and finely wrought stories as possible. [Another principal group of sets, cultural and subcultural in origin, constitutes the teller's conception of what a *story* is—a precipitate of his experiences of being told tales, being read to, reading everything from comic strips to novels, and absorbing narrative materials from radio, television, and other mass media.] This understanding of "what it's all about" has a pervasive influence throughout the formation of a story and is naturally something the examiner must do his best to understand and influence. Since it is a function of the nature of the subject as well as of the setting and the examiner's efforts, it is often difficult to modify. [Skillful administration consists mostly of fostering appropriate sets.]

A reading of Nailson's stories gives the impression that he felt he ought to do the best he could; that he saw the task primarily as finding the best interpretation of the picture rather than telling a plotted narrative; that he did not find it much of a threat to his self-esteem or to his revealing anxiety-laden unconscious material.

[2]A cooperative research program, in which I was involved, at the Harvard Psychological Clinic under the direction of Dr. Henry A. Murray, during 1941–1943.

3. The Perceptual Impact. With these more or less conscious anticipations in mind, Nailson was handed the card. The consensus of most healthy, intelligent persons is that this picture contains four figures: a youth looking straight out of the picture, and behind him, the dimly seen figures of a man lying on his back, a bearded man leaning over him cutting into his abdomen with some kind of knife, and another man holding a lantern. A window is visible in the background, and a rifle is sharply delineated on the other side of the picture from the boy. The instructions do not specify that all of this be brought into the story, but most subjects get the definite implication that they are to take some note of everything important in the picture. Unconscious violations of this implied requirement are, however, fairly common; Nailson commits one. He does not mention the gun.

From his first remark, it is plain that the normally most salient figure, the boy, first caught his eye. Then he probably saw the operation and was so taken up by the associations it aroused that he did not turn his attention to the gun. We cannot assume, however, that he did not see it. On the contrary, *we must almost always assume that the subject does see and, on some level of awareness, recognize everything in the picture,* unless we have good evidence to the contrary. What he omits or interprets idiosyncratically becomes very important, for it is a clue to the kinds of dangers against which he has erected important defenses. If one prefers a less elaborate explanation, it is possible that Nailson saw the gun well enough but could not see how to fit it into the story. Since he had recognized the gun in another picture at once (3BM) when it was presented, and since the gun in 8BM does not fit well into this particular story that he practically *had* to tell, this explanation is plausible. It is unfortunate that there was no inquiry. It would have been simple enough for the examiner to have asked afterwards, casually, "Did you notice anything else in the picture that you didn't bring into your story?" The answer would have told at once whether repression or a conscious decision was responsible for the omission. Actually, this is not a very important deviation. The various elements of the picture are so difficult to integrate that the rifle is often left out. [See Chapter 3.]

In one other way, we learn about Nailson from our speculations about the perceptual impact. In their very useful table of apperceptive norms, Rosenzweig and Fleming (1949) note that 66 percent of normal men see the patient being operated on as a man; it is usual for the sex to be specified if there is any reference to the patient. Nailson leaves the sex indefinite. Here, as before, it is only because acquaintance with a long series of other cases tells us what to expect that we notice anything amiss. The Rosenzweig-Fleming norms are very helpful as far as they go, but they do not deal with all of the pictures, nor with all aspects of the 16 cards that were included in their study. Until satisfactory norms have been published on all such matters as these, the TAT worker has to accept the fact that his facility in using the test must, and will, grow as he tests more and more persons and builds up his own, largely unconscious, norms.

But what if he does say just, "the patient." What then? Ordinarily, we might not assign it much significance; in Nailson's case, it is congruent with the hypothesis that in his unconscious memory or fantasy, the victim of an attack such as this is seen to be is more likely to be a woman than a man. Possibly, he would even have said that the patient looked like a woman if during the inquiry, after the card had been taken away, he had been matter-of-factly asked whether or not he noticed the sex of the patient. From other evidence, it seems a little doubtful that he would have called the patient a woman, but ordinarily the possibility would be worth looking into. (Of course, not in such a way as to make the subject overalert to all features of subsequent pictures.) More emphasis has been given to this point, for illustrative reasons, than it deserves from a practical standpoint. As in the case of the omitted rifle, this is a rather slight clue that requires the support of more evidence before it can carry interpretative weight.

4. The Arousing of Motives and Affects. It is only conceptually possible to separate the perceptual impact of the picture from the logically subsequent phase, the touching off of motives [including emotions] and their derivatives.[3] When we examine a series of stories told by different subjects to the same picture, they can be seen to differ in a number of ways, but often outstandingly in the kinds of motives that actuate the characters in the stories. We assume that such differences must be due to the differential importance of the motives for the subjects themselves.

In discussing the parallel to dreams, above, I touched on this fourth phase, but only so far as it involves the deeper, unconscious wishes and complexes. The story we are using as a reference point may be misleading because it clearly involves motivation of this basic sort so much more clearly than do most TAT stories. Indeed, interpretation of the test would be vastly simpler if one could always assume that the strivings of the heroes represented unconscious urges of the subject.

The truth, however, is complex. I once tried, with a small group of very thoroughly studied subjects, to test the hypotheses that (1) when a motive was actually stronger in a subject's overt behavior than he admitted, and when it involved a form of behavior that was relatively unacceptable to him, it would then be prominently present in his TAT stories; and (2) when a motive was weaker in a subject's overt behavior than he judged it to be, and was considered by him to be relatively desirable, it would then likewise be found in unusual strength in his stories. The data tended to support both hypotheses (which were derived from the concepts of *projection* and of *wish-fulfillment*, respectively), but the important point is that there were many exceptions, many whose frequency and intensity in the stories were not explained. Take, for example, the motive Murray called *n Sex*. It was found most prominently in the stories of subjects who had the strongest interest in sex in overt behavior, who felt that sexual expression was quite acceptable,

[3][For my present views on motivation, see Holt (1976a).]

and who might therefore be supposed to be in little need of any fantasy outlet or projection. In the college population being studied, it seemed that when superego controls were strong enough to restrain the sexual motive in the everyday lives of the more inhibited subjects, they also kept it out of their TAT stories to a large extent, while in the case of the "emancipated" subject, the letting down of the barriers so far that he could engage in considerable sexual activity also made it easier for him to talk about it for whatever reasons.

It is necessary to assume, therefore, that any motive present in a person may be aroused sufficiently in the course of the test to enter into a story, provided that stronger *restraints* are not present. Beyond that statement, it does not seem to be possible to lay down any very helpful principles about the kinds of motives that will be expressed most strongly.

Depending on the nature of a person's defenses, as soon as he looks at a picture he may be flooded with emotional feeling that spills over into exclamations, weeping, or other direct display; or he may completely isolate and repress all affective experience, never varying his delivery or tone of voice a whit; or his affective experiences and expressions (for example, silly giggling) may be inappropriate to the situation—or a number of other possibilities might obtain. Whatever a person's mode of dealing with affects, they may show up in two ways: either directly, as just described, or indirectly, through attribution to the characters in the stories.

How did Nailson react to the perceptual impact of the picture? First, it stirred up aggressive motives (which we knew from other sources were strong but well-controlled); but they did not obtain direct outlet in the story, nor was there any overt affective display. The unconscious presence of strong destructive wishes can be inferred from his dwelling on the patient's tortures and the doctors' apparent zest in inflicting them. But he could not allow himself to identify directly with the sadists (who were, incidentally, put at a great remoteness in time, so that Nailson could all the more dissociate himself from their deeds); he did, however, have his hero take over an approved version of their role, in which the aggression was subordinated to nurturance (tender care).

In terms of Murray's (1938) motivational classification, the *needs* that are directly expressed in the story are *Dominance:* nonpersonal (strong efforts to master the situation), and *Achievement* (hard and persistent work). Less prominent are the related pair, *Cognizance* (the need to see, find out, know) and *Construction* (to invent, create). The former two make an interesting comparison: Nailson considered himself to be very dominant, but actually made few efforts to lead or influence others, so that this wish was not actually manifested much in overt behavior; but the need for *Achievement* was quite strong. Nailson was an effective, hard worker, who liked to solve difficult mathematical problems for fun (*Cognizance* and *Construction*) and who put successful effort into mastering the nonhuman aspects of his environment—

breaking horses, shooting rapids, and so on. Thus, his behavior reflected a kind of dominance directed toward the mastery of difficult situations, rather than people, and this is the very kind of dominance expressed in his story. The example shows how difficult it is to generalize about a motive from one form of its expression in a story. Assuming that dominance in general was strong would have been incorrect; so would the assumption that dominance was expressed only in the effort to solve this one personal problem.

The nature of the situation as Nailson perceived it caused the motives above mentioned to be aroused and to shape the courses of action attributed not only to the hero but to the other characters in the story. As usually happens, Nailson did not endow the central figure—fictitious shadow though he was—with the kinds of wishes he himself found unacceptable and kept unconscious. Such motives appeared instead as actuating other characters. We have not been able to talk about these motives, it seems, without discussing what logically belongs in the next stage.

5. Identification and Identity. An important principle regulating the incitement of wishes, and many other aspects of the stories as well, is *identification.* One of the differences between the perceptual process set going by a TAT card and by a day's residue is that the subject is not directly involved in the former, as he is in the latter. Fortunately for man's social existence, most persons do have a natural tendency to identify with others when there is no important barrier in the way. So when they are confronted by card 1, showing a boy and a violin, the great majority of subjects unconsciously and unhesitatingly think about a story from the point of view of the boy, identifying themselves with him. This patch of grays and blacks on a piece of paper becomes implicitly a projection of oneself and is thereby naturally endowed with attributes of the self-concept, on some level: what one is, what he wishes he were, or what he fears he may become.

Many of the cards present more than one person, however, and some of them present persons of different ages and sexes. It is easiest for anyone to identify with someone else who has important attributes of his own identity (Erikson, 1946), so the subject usually adopts the point of view of the figure who is most like him in some crucial way, and makes this person the central character, or *hero* of his story. In fact, if there is no apparent identification with any of the pictured figures, we have good reason to suspect that the subject is unusually narcissistic or has strong characterological defenses against forming interpersonal relationships of any emotional depth.

[One of the unexpected by-products of the early program of research on subliminal influences on perceptual and cognitive processes at the Research Center for Mental Health (e.g., Klein, Spence, Holt, & Gourevitch, 1958; G. J. Smith, Spence, & Klein, 1959) was a conviction of the importance, in perception, of the identification that people form with a pictured human being. In a number of our experiments, when the subliminal presentation was a picture of a person or part of a person, the findings could be understood only on the hypothesis that the registration in some way made contact with the subject's own self-concept or identity. The perceptual report and judgments about what the subject could see were clearly affected by an interaction of these two sets of influences (the subliminal presentation and the self-concept), though the inferred interaction was sometimes one of fusion, sometimes one of contrast-formation. Clinical experiences suggest an even wider relevance of a tendency to compare perceptual inputs with an image of the self. Very often, for example, persons who show in many ways that they have deep-seated convictions of being physically inadequate or mutilated produce many Rorschach responses of twisted, deformed, injured, or otherwise defective animals, trees, and even objects as well as human beings (see also Schafer, 1967). Coming back to the TAT, I was struck by the same phenomenon in a story given by an applicant to the Menninger School of Psychiatry to card 11: he described a huge castle with thick walls and a threatening appearance, within which lived a small, frightened person. He himself was unusually large and strong, a formidable physical specimen, who put up a front of being a "strong, silent man," but whose actual behavior was often so timid as to indicate an inner sense of being insecure and weak.

Just what these identification-like processes are and how they work I cannot say;[4] it is a deplorably neglected problem in cognitive psychology. But by making use of the hypothesis that such processes go on, one can often form valuable hypotheses about a storyteller's conception of himself. It follows from the conception presented here that a storyteller's interpretation of *all* figures in a picture (and all other characters in the story) will be affected in some way by his/her self-concept. As indicated in the previous section, the hero is likely to be given motives and other characteristics from the teller's identity about which (s)he feels least conflict, or even features of her/his ideal self-conception (ego ideal). The more a character in a story differs from the teller and the more he is presented as a villain or otherwise as someone who is held up to scorn or obloquy, the more likely he is to be used to express consciously rejected ("ego alien") aspects of identity, even negative identity (Erikson, 1958, 1968).

In one further respect the theory of identification and identity helps us understand TAT stories. Erikson (1950) and L. P. Howe (1948, 1955) have postulated that when a child learns what a parent is like, (s)he learns relationships in which the parent is involved—especially, but not exclusively, relationships involving the child. Thus, if a parent reacts with nurturance to the child's succorant (dependent) needs, the latter learns a reciprocal role relationship—that the appropriate response to press Succorance is need Nurturance (in Murray's terms)—and not only practices the dependent role but in fantasy rehearses its inverse, the role of kindly parent. That much is

---

[4][Schafer's (1976) conception appeals to me, that the central process in identification is forming a recurrent, enduring fantasy of being one with another person.]

obvious in the play of young children ("You be the baby and I'll be the mommy"), an enactment of fantasies that later typically become unconscious (see Chapter 4, below).

One of the most important reciprocal role-relationships learned in childhood in our culture is dominance-submission and its pathological extreme, sadism-masochism. If a set of stories contains several with a dominant man and a submissive woman, you can infer that the teller—whether male or female—(1) is likely to have fairly conventional conceptions of sex roles, (2) has the potentiality of assuming either the dominant or the submissive posture, and (3) if forced or encouraged by circumstances to enact the unconventional role, will probably feel a threat to his/her sense of sexual identity. In Nailson's case, we can expect that his sense of identity would combine masculinity, dominance, nurturance, and a kind of professionally sublimated, unconscious sadism. This discussion does hardly more than hint at the many ways Erikson's rich conception of identity affects the storytelling process; but see Chapter 7, below.]

6. Defensive Circuiting. As has been indicated, the developing story-process enters into some devious byways as soon as motives have been set going by the perceptual material. Important persisting wishes left from childhood can rarely be expressed directly even in dreams, much less in stories of the kind the TAT elicits. The transformations and long-circuits the socialized human being must force upon his wishes are called strategies of defense. They are defensive because, as above indicated, they serve the purpose of warding off the anxiety, shame, guilt, or loss of self-esteem that would result from unmodified exercise of one's primitive potentialities.

Historically, Nailson went through a period of overt sadism, torturing animals in his early childhood; thus, his first defense against the anxiety caused by his early trauma was *identification* with an aggressive father. Then he began to take over some of his mother's softer ideals and made a dramatic about-face: in a *reaction formation,* he became determined to defend the weak against the strong, to care for his ailing mother and all animals. He then became a great lover and defender of animals, and decided on medicine as a career. At the same time, he could still indirectly gratify his aggressive wishes, because one of his measures in instituting a new era of kindliness on his father's farm was to take over the butchering of the calves himself—"so that it would be done in the most humane manner." [This admixture of a return of the repressed with what is consciously intended is one of the best signs that nurturance is reaction formative, as opposed to the loving kind based on an identification with unambivalently tender parents.]

In his story, we can see him doing the same kind of things with an aggressive wish. First, he gave it a remote (in Tomkins' [1947] sense of the term) expression through the description of the brutal doctors. That it was a source of unconscious anxiety is hinted at in the statement, "he had a nightmare or two." Then the hero identified himself with the aggressors, but he did so in order to bring about a denial of aggression at the same time, in the *prevention* of pain (reaction formation). Thus we may assume that the story-process was shunted about, developing according to the defense mechanisms characteristic of the subject's life history. Likewise, the desire to look (which must have taken on great importance if Nailson was exposed to the primal scene) could not be expressed in its most direct form. Instead, it led to a preliminary, remote, and passing reference to seeing or reading about an operation; then it reappeared in the *sublimated* form that the need had actually taken in Nailson's life, an intense interest in scientific knowledge and discovery.

7. The Cognitive Elaboration. The next (only conceptually separate) stage is the accretion to the story-process of a variety of cognitive ("associative") material. So far, logically, we have only the content given by the picture as the subject interprets it, the motivational meanings that it stirs up, and the defensive routes these themes must take in order to achieve expression. But as has been indicated, it is characteristic of the emotions and wishes that motivate us that we tend to bring their derivatives into consciousness, including the goals toward which we strive and the associated means (objects, situations) of getting to them. Of course, the specific nature of these derivatives is determined by the individual's past history; so that here already we have one important kind of cognitive material, personal-historical content, being made ready to be included in the stories under the organizing influence of the existing sets.

A. Personal-Historical Content. One of the most common errors of beginners in TAT interpretation is the assumption that all stories are autobiographical and that interpretation consists merely of changing names and tenses here and there, leaving the content essentially as the subject gives it. There is a perfectly good reason for such an error: frequently the content of the stories *is* derived almost entirely from personal history. The story we are using for an example is considerably more autobiographical than most; it happens that Nailson gave us a barely disguised account of what is perhaps his life's most central theme. Yet for every story of this kind, there are several others in which the manifest content has little to do with the teller's past. For the content is usually determined primarily in salient features by the picture and certain socially shared meanings that each picture tends to have. Only if events and sentiments from one's own personal past are particularly fraught with emotional meaning are they likely to be worked into stories when the picture does not have some direct associative link to them.

Here we must reconsider the importance of the anticipations, or sets, under the influence of which the constructive aspects of thinking take place. The raw materials for this constructive work are the ones we have considered so far (the perceptual givens, the needs and affects), plus all the storehouse of memories available to the teller. While the arousal of the aggressive ideas in Nailson might conceivably have led him to think of hunting, an activity he had frequently enjoyed, he had the set to tell a coherent story consistent with the picture; so the set operated to activate only *relevant* memories.[5] That is true, at least, in intact, healthy persons. Various kinds of breakdown in this function [which Rapaport called anticipation] can be seen in stories that wander, proceed by sudden jumps, or become bogged down in a mire of many possible associations; and corresponding kinds of pathology can be inferred therefrom.

However effective the set, a person has only his own experiences, direct or indirect, to call on to put flesh on the skeletal story-process we have so far conceived. And unless he is unusually suspicious, creative, or evasive, it is far easier for the subject to think of his own direct experiences. They are not only more interesting and more vivid to him, but they may be involved in dynamic complexes like the traumatic early experience of Nailson. In such a case, the person has a positive need to bring the repressed memory back to consciousness in some form, so that it can gradually be "decontaminated" and mastered. For reasons like these, the contents most likely to be brought into the story in addition to what the picture suggests directly are autobiographical.

But it may also happen that nothing in the picture moves the subject, either because of the neutrality of its contents or because his defenses are so strong that they prevent communication between the perceptual process and latent emotional trends. In such a case, the story will be relatively stereotyped, containing no evidences of personal involvement, little by way of motives for the action, and that little all drawn from external experience—stories he has read or observation of others. Stereotyped stories of this kind usually differ very little from the bare "popular" interpretation, are not long, and have little life in them. They exist in pure form only rarely; actually, most records contain a few more or less stereotyped stories in which there is little involvement, but very few protocols are devoid of any involvement of the subject's own wishes and strivings. Learning to distinguish between what is stereotyped, indicating merely that a person participates in a certain subculture, and what is indicative of more personal material, is essential to skilled use of the TAT. Unfortunately, it is not quickly learned. Like any other projective technique, the TAT must be worked with patiently and with a sustained interest in learning, if one is to exploit its real usefulness.

B. *Sentimentive Content.* Another important part of the associative storehouse that a person has to call on derives from personal experience, yet is

[5]Actually, one of the popular stories told to this picture does integrate all of the perceptual givens into a story of a man injured (often accidentally shot by the boy) while hunting. Why did Nailson fail to give this better interpretation? Very probably because he could not fantasy killing his father and because of his tendency to see the person in pain as equivalent to his mother. He solved his Oedipal conflict by identifying himself with his strong, brutal father, not by a fantasy of killing him. For these reasons, the popular hunting-accident story was probably not available to him.

not exactly autobiographical. That is his fund of values and attitudes. As Nailson rounded out his story, he expressed very clearly his sentiment (value attitude) about suffering and medical ignorance: they would not recur if he could help it. There was a surgeon in the picture, so he talked about doctors; but having such strong positive sentiments toward skilled medical men, particularly the discoverers of "something to bring ease to the patient," he could not talk about doctors without expressing these attitudes. Of course, if he had been suspicious and evasive, or had thought that he stood to lose something by betraying his true feelings, he could fairly easily have disguised them and put in the stories expressions of attitudes that were not his own. In practice, however, deliberate attempts to mislead are so infrequent that the possibility of their occurrence may be ignored most of the time. Such defensiveness usually makes itself known obviously enough and is typically expressed by a refusal to give anything beyond the bare essentials.

The most important kind of sentimentive content in the TAT, for most purposes, is the attitudes toward other persons. Here the subject's characteristic *interpersonal relationships* make their nature known, since they too are a function of basic sentiments toward classes of people: older males, older females, competitors, love-objects, the weak and helpless, and so forth. Something about the warmth and importance to the subject of his relationships with others is likely to get into his stories as sentimentive content of this sort. Nailson's interpersonal ties did not seem, on the basis of this story, to be particularly intense, though his ambivalent respect for authority figures and his tender feeling for those who are suffering were obviously determining elements of the story's content.

C. General Informational Content. As long as a story sticks very closely to the picture, with little real invention, it may contain a minimum of any kind of content. Since it is always possible for a subject to take the test in such a meager, constricted way, the TAT cannot be thought of as a test of information. Yet it is obvious that a person must use his fund of general information even in recognizing the contents of the pictures, as well as in introducing further ideas to make complete stories. If a subject calls the monster in card 11 a diplodocus, then we clearly know that he either has a general store of information indicative of a high educational level or that he probably has special interests and attainments in geology or paleontology. (There are implications of a different sort in the fact that he chooses to use such a word; they will be considered below.) Nailson's reference to Bliss is rather obscure. Since there is actually no such "great doctor" in the history of medicine, he hit upon a little-known figure by dint of very specialized reading, or was confused and inexact in his memory, or else was merely being pretentious and arbitrary, counting on the examiner's not looking up his apparently erudite reference. Inquiry would have helped here; without it, the second possibility seems the most likely, from internal evidence.

It has been implied in the above three subsections that a person's possible associations are patterned in personally revealing ways. But they are also more subtly patterned, as are his needs, defenses, and other aspects of personality, by the culture in which he takes part. Only what is known to his culture will be known to the individual, and the values and goals he expresses will be determined in large part by the culture, either directly or through his protest against them. (See Henry, 1951, and Lindzey, 1961.)

8. The Enabling and Limiting Effects of Abilities. We have by now accounted for the appearance of most of the elements of a story and have a number of ideas about influences that shape the content into particular forms. One rather silent influence not so far spoken about is that of abilities. To a large extent, what goes into a story is fixed by the range of a person's experience and by the nature of his defenses; and, indeed, we have to think about most of these influences in terms of their interactions. But the marks of one ability—general intelligence—are sometimes plain to see. No matter how favorable the defensive structure, no matter how great the exposure to a variety of experiences, if native wit is at a low enough level, TAT stories will be primitive in their structure. They may be very useful, may contain a great deal that is of value; but that is not the question. In explaining any one story, one must take into account the author's level of intelligence—and of other abilities. Nailson's story, for all its simplicity, could hardly have been told by a very dull person. Likewise, his somewhat limited *verbal facility* set an upper limit on the literary quality of the stories he turned out. Without *creative imagination*, ingenious and original stories cannot be written, though of course one may have imagination and not exercise it.

One may infer that Nailson had an average degree of *observational ability* from this story, since his interpretation was largely in line with popular trends. On another picture, card 15, Nailson took note of small gray blemishes near the left corner of the top margin, interpreted them as running men, and brought them into the story, an interpretation requiring an observational ability apprehensively sharpened to pathological acuity. On the same picture, a paranoid schizophrenic actually saw the gray blemishes as two figures pursuing the hero.

It was mentioned that card 8BM puts some strain on the organizing ability of most subjects; a number of other cards likewise picture disparate elements or a variety of them, so that something of what constitutes a "good *W*" in the Rorschach test is required to integrate what is given in the picture into a consistent story. Even such features of the stories as the interpersonal relationships between characters can be looked at from the standpoint of abilities, too. Without *empathy,* the ability to feel with others, one cannot describe in detail in a story about card 2, for example, the point of view of more than one of the persons pictured.

The effect of abilities, then, in producing a TAT story, is first, to set upper limits for a number of the production's dimensions. Second, a modicum of certain abilities is necessary for the development of real stories sufficiently rich and extensive to allow other influences on a story to make their weight felt.

9. The Internal Milieu. The TAT story is the end product of the operation of a complex mental process that takes place, not in an indifferent medium, but in the mind of a person. In the subjective life of a human being, there are characteristic and pervasive states that subtly and indirectly affect whatever is transacted. They may be spoken of as the prevalent emotional tone, the emotional climate, or the *internal milieu* of the subject.

Nailson's story gives a distinct impression of forcefulness, or determination, perhaps even zest for activity and effort. They are, in fact, qualities that are ubiquitous in his behavior. So is optimism, a generally hopeful outlook. These prevailing winds in the inner climate of his mind have their effects quite without his awareness; they are hard to measure, but they are highly reliable. In other subjects, anxiety, depression, euphoria, or fatigue may be present in consciousness or just below its surface, as the by-products of a variety of dynamic configurations of more genotypical variables. Whatever their origin, there they are; they help to set the tone of the stories. One of the marks of the experienced interpreter of the TAT is his sensitivity to this atmospheric quality. It helps to give a basic orientation to the understanding of a person.

10. The Personal Style. With all of the above categories, we still need to invoke another group of determinants, referred to as personal style [in Klein's (1970) phrase, cognitive style] in order to explain how Nailson told just this story in just this way. Take his choice of words, for example; how unpretentious, simple, even naive it was at times. Even though we might ultimately be able to derive it from a complete understanding of defenses and abilities, it is simpler at the present stage to consider what Allport (1961) calls *stylistic traits* as determinants on their own emergent level. Whenever we can see that a hasty *tempo*, for example, is a result of anxiety, or that a slow one is a means of expressing passive hostility, then there is no reason not to interpret it as such. But it is safe, and legitimate enough, to refer things to the level of personal style as a useful first approximation.

One feature of Nailson's personal style that emerged quite clearly in the operation story is an uneven rhythm. Note that he made two somewhat abortive starts before he finally got into his story. One hypothesis would be that he had trouble starting because of the intense emotional nature of his associations to the picture. He did about the same thing, however, with every story. Also, examples from his everyday life could be cited to show that he was a slow and uncertain starter, who nevertheless usually made a strong finish.

The matter of verbalization deserves more emphasis than it has received above. The appropriateness, felicity, prolixity, primitivity, conventionality, and many other qualitites of the way a person uses words reveal much about him. Sanford (1942) has shown how faithfully the characteristics of a person's verbal style may reflect basic aspects of his personality. More of this later, however, when we consider the implications of each determinant for interpretation.

Summary

In trying to understand how a particular TAT story came to be just the way it is, we have distinguished ten classes of determinants: the situational context, the directing sets, the perceptual impact, the arousal of motives and affects, identification and identity, defensive circuiting, associative elaboration, the limiting and facilitating effect of abilities, the internal milieu, and personal style. Some of these headings are more inclusive than others, but all of them are to some degree operative in every story. The relative importance of these determinants may vary greatly in the responses of different subjects to the situation. Complete blocking and rejection—for example, the statement "I can't make up a story this time"—can be explained without necessarily invoking associative elaboration any further than to say that there is none.

A complex phenomenon such as the TAT story is produced differently in different persons. Therefore, we must not expect to get the same things out of one person's TAT that may be inferred from another's. The stories of an intelligent, cooperative, inwardly free person will often contain an inexhaustible wealth of materials for various kinds of insights about him, permitting an extensive description and analysis of personality to be written, covering diagnostic considerations, personality traits and structure, developmental trends, relations with important persons in his life, motives and defenses, sentiments, qualities of intellect, vocational adjustment, and other areas. Just because this is often possible, it is not fair to claim that the TAT is a test of all these regions of personality, any more than such a claim can be made for any other projective technique. We must recognize the fact that inhibited, constricted personality structures often lead to results with projective tests that tell us that the subject is organized in such a way, and little more.

It may be said further that frequently a great deal more can be interpreted from a set of "cliché stories," or from a protocol obtained question-by-question, almost by a process of extraction, than is frequently claimed. It is more difficult; it requires more experience and more sensitivity to subtle ways in which a stereotyped story differs from dead average; but, as Freud (1900, p. 525) said about the interpretation of difficult dreams, "It is always possible to go *some* distance."

ADMINISTRATION

The third revision of the TAT (Murray, 1943), which is the one in current use, consists of 30 pictures and a blank card. The pictures have been selected and marked in such a way that there are four sets of 20 cards each: one for boys, one for girls, one for males over 14, and one for females over 14. A card marked "BM" is used for both boys and men; one marked "GF" is used for both girls and women, etc. A card number not followed by a letter designates a picture used for both sexes and all ages. The serial number and letter designations are printed on the backs of the cards. [For descriptions of the cards and discussion of their utility and significance, see Chapter 3, below.]

In the administration of the TAT, the examiner should strive to create a situation that will be as therapeutic to the subject, or at least as nontraumatic, as possible. Some of the pictures carry strong implications of aggression (especially 8BM and 18GF and to some extent, 4), others of sexuality (13MF; less strongly 10), or suicide (3BM and 17GF). Sometimes 12M and 18BM are an unconscious homosexual threat to the subject.

The examiner should neither shrink back overcautiously from exposing disturbed persons to such sights, nor press too hard for a story if the patient is obviously upset by one of them. Emotionally vulnerable patients sometimes experience a kind of "black shock" on cards 14 and 15, comparable to that seen in the Rorschach test. The examiner must guard against the possibility of doing the patient more harm than good by being too insistent on a story, or by forcing a patient to recognize something that for very good reasons he has distorted or omitted.

What can the examiner do to create a situation in which the subject will respond in the most useful ways? The most general answer is that the methods of administration must vary according to the examiner's purpose. For research in personality, especially when healthy college students are the subjects, Murray's suggestions, given in the manual that accompanies the printed pictures, are appropriate. With the reclining position, the challenge to the university student's claim to intelligence and imagination, and other devices, Murray succeeded in obtaining unusually long, detailed, rich, and revealing stories. For diagnostic use, such elaborated stories are neither needed nor wanted. The number of cards used and the particular ones chosen, as well as the nature of inquiry, also vary according to the purpose for which the test is being given. Most of the differences in styles of administration can be reconciled by reference to this one principle.

Some Specific Suggestions

The procedure of administration may best be considered in relation to the determinants of TAT stories already listed.

1. The Situational Context. The situational context is affected by the way the test is administered. Of course, certain aspects of the situational context cannot be changed by the examiner; the subject may be anxious because the test he is taking will help to determine whether or not he gets a job or an educational opportunity, and not because of anything the examiner himself says or does. Nevertheless, the examiner should always be aware of the situation from the subject's viewpoint. With such awareness, he can offer appropriate mollifying explanations, or assume a role of warm friendliness, distinterested impersonality, or whatever will be most supportive and conducive to a letting-down of defenses. In general, he should try to arrange for a minimum of distractions and a maximum of relaxation.

One fortunate thing about the standard arrangement of the pictures is that card 1, the boy and violin, usually brings out the subject's reaction to an imposed task. Sometimes the examiner can advantageously avoid in the test situation the kind of behavior attributed to the "bad parents" who are making the boy do something he hates, or can emulate the attitudes of the "good parents" who foster the boy's talent. In any event, he must usually maintain a neutral, accepting attitude, no matter what the subject says. The most important aspect of the situational context is the interpersonal relation between examiner and patient, and the emotional attitudes of the examiner are far more important than the exact words he uses. If one dislikes a difficult patient and is not skilled in self-control, he can use the most neutral and nondirective wording in everything that he says, and yet, because of inflection and emphasis, make the patient feel dominated and hounded. Conversely, if rapport is good, if the subject feels basically not threatened by the examiner's approach to him but recognizes that the examiner is trying to help him or is genuinely interested in him as a person, the examiner can often make extensive demands on the subject.

2. **Directing Sets.** The purpose of the instructions is to produce the particular kind of *directing sets* that the examiner wants. Broadly speaking, one wants to motivate the subject to do his best; one wants stories with a plot having a beginning, a middle, and an end, and with characters whose thoughts and feelings as well as external actions are described. Again, the particular words that are used in the instructions are not as important as getting these objectives across to the subject in his own terms, and in such a way as to motivate him to cooperate—or, for some patients, in such a way as to arouse only a minimum of resistance. The TAT requires a rather complex set for many subjects to maintain over a period of an hour, and they forget part of it. It is necessary both to take note of any difficulty in maintaining a set and to remind the subject as tactfully as possible of the parts of his task that have been forgotten. Efforts to challenge the subject's self-esteem by intimating that one is going to test important abilities are out of place for most patients in clinical settings; the test is better introduced simply as something else one wants him to do in order to get information necessary to help him.

[I find it useful, after the subject comes to a stop in his response to the first card, to inquire specifically for each of the specified parts of the story that he has omitted. Then I "restructure"; that is, I say: "OK, that's good. I'm going to show you several other pictures, and you are to make up a story each time, which the picture might illustrate. Be sure each time to include the events leading up to the scene pictured, what's going on in the picture, what the characters are thinking and feeling, and then give it an ending—tell how it all turns out. Got it? All right, try this one." If necessary, inquire for omitted specifications after the second story too; occasionally it will be desirable to restructure this second time. It is safe to assume for adults of normal intelligence that, by the end of two tries with this kind of (as it were) editorial assistance, they have had ample instruction. A failure to establish and maintain the relevant sets is probably attributable to psychopathology, and careful attention to the patient's test behavior in comparison to similar handling of other tests can often give valuable leads about the nature of that pathology.]

As to the other kind of sets—those that guide the development of particular stories—they must be determined by the subject himself, his own needs, defenses, and abilities. It follows that directive inquiry, when used, should be employed very deliberately, under special circumstances, and with full understanding of what one is doing. If a subject cannot be led into an important area of potential conflict in any other way, structured questions may be asked after the spontaneous story is over; in the final test protocol, they should always be written out in full, in parentheses, so that it is clear where and how the examiner departed from the nondirective approach. Suppose, for example, a subject tells a story to picture 6BM, in which the son tells his mother that he is going to another city to take a job, and she disowns him. The examiner has reason to know that it is important to find out what the subject's reaction to maternal rejection is; so he asks a nondirective question: "What are his thoughts and feelings?" If the answer is, "He is wondering how his new job is going to turn out," the examiner has only indirect evidence on the crucial point. It is then permissible to ask, "How does he feel about his mother's saying that she has disowned him?" Of course, one should never ask, "Does he feel bad?" or in any other way put words in a subject's mouth. Generally, one should avoid questions that can be answered by a simple yes or no.

With some subjects, the examiner need say nothing after the initial instructions except to praise the stories, though not too lavishly. The occasions that call for him to intervene actively, as Rapaport (1946) says, are lack of clarity (verbal, perceptual, and meaningful); failure to include one of the specified aspects of the story; and running far over or far under the average time allotted per story. The principal disagreement among writers about TAT administration concerns this matter of inquiry. In my judgment, inquiry is frequently useful and works best if done immediately after the picture is taken away. It is not necessary to get *all* aspects of every story. For example, if the thoughts of the characters in the stories are persistently omitted and are not very revealing when inquired into for the first few pictures, it is better to abandon this line of inquiry. Done with the proper attitude and in the manner referred to above, the inquiry can be fairly extensive without upsetting or inhibiting the patient and his later productions. It is better for the examiner to underinquire than to overinquire, and in case of doubt, to save his question until after the test is completed.

3. The Perceptual Impact. Since the perceptual impact of specific pictures is important in determining the stories, it is a matter of concern which pictures are used. There is much to be said for each of the pictures in the published set, and for those in the most widely used earlier revision, but this is not the place to discuss the special merits of particular pictures. Whenever possible, all 20 pictures should be administered, in two or more sessions. Often the pressure of work in a busy clinic does not allow the time required for the complete test, but it is generally inadvisable to use fewer than 10 cards. The 11 most frequently used (for adult males) seem to be the following: 1, 2, 3BM, 4, 6BM, 7BM, 8BM, 12M, 13MF, 16, 18GF. For adult females, 1, 2, 4, 7GF, 9GF, 10, 13MF, 16, 18GF, and often 12M and 3BM. In clinical use, one usually adds (or substitutes) pictures with demand characteristics ("pull") relevant to the patient's problems. There is nothing final about the selection of pictures devised by Murray and Morgan; other workers have used other pictures with very good results. The blank card, 16, particularly deserves wider use, as does 11, but both with special instruction. [See Chapter 3, below, for further information on these and other cards, their indications and contraindications.] For practical reasons, however, it is best to build up experience with cards that are widely used, so that one can make use of the recorded experience of others.

4. The Arousal of Motives and Affects. The arousal of affects by the pictures and their associations may be quite apparent in the patient's behavior and tone of voice as well as in what he says. A very important part of a complete protocol therefore is a description of the patient's behavior, changes or breaks in the tone of voice, and somatic signs of anxiety such as sweating and heavy breathing, particularly as these things change in relation to story content.

[Since it is often desirable to assess a person's handling of hostility, 18GF is useful with many male subjects. It is the only card that contains a scene of violence, yet is rather often given a nonviolent interpretation. See also Chapter 3, below.]

[**5. The Role of Identification.** If a picture presents no one at all similar to the subject with whom to identify himself, he is likely to have more difficulty in telling stories. It is therefore advisable to present, at the beginning of the testing session, pictures containing persons with whom identification is easy. Cards 11 and 16, for example, are usually best presented late. Bearing in mind the widely observed phenomenon of an age-lag in the sense of identity, expect that most people will find it easier to tell stories when the picture presents someone younger, harder when the only choices are older than the subject.

Well-educated persons from the middle class (as TAT testers tend to be) usually have a considerable investment in being—and in being considered by others to be—productive, imaginative, and responsive to legitimate authorities. To such a person it will often come as a surprise to find subjects who produce little when the TAT is presented as a challenge or as a directive from a person in an authoritative role. Many people seem to accept without shame an identity that lacks creative, literary abilities or even general achievement motivation. Presented with Murray's instructions, they feel content to explain, "I don't have much imagination," and then sit back as if they are thereby excused from further effort. If the authoritative approach does not work either ("This is something your doctor needs for you to do so that he can help you better"), the tester has to use whatever clues he has obtained up to that point concerning the subject's values and motives, and shape his instructions accordingly to motivate the subject to produce usable story material.]

6. Defensive Circuiting. We have seen above how defenses play a dual role in TAT stories: they may disguise or prevent the emergence of hidden content; and yet from the defenses one learns about what Rapaport, Gill, and Schafer (1968) called the ego structure of the subject. Like the early psychoanalysts, some examiners are impatient with the subject's defenses as resistances that merely impede the work; such a one may want to find technical means in administration to avoid them. If so, he may reflect on the later experiences of psychoanalysts, which showed that often these defenses and resistances were most worthy of the analyst's attention because they were the most crippling aspects of a personality. For this and similar reasons, psychoanalysis turned from preoccupation with the id to increasing interest in the ego via analysis of resistances. When allowance is made for this consideration, it still remains true in some cases that defenses are so rigid and ubiquitous that they prevent the production of anything more than barren descriptions of pictures. When this happens, one can try to see the subject at another time when there is reason to think he will be less threatened. Or, after exhausting one's wiles in efforts to induce the subject to relax and to respond to the first two or three cards, a strategic retreat may be made: the test may be turned into a perceptual one by showing each card briefly and asking what the situation was, or what was pictured. Then, at least, one gets the perceptual impact of the whole set of cards in a brief time.

7. Associative Elaboration. Sophisticated subjects sometimes start giving *personal-historical content* directly, without more than a gesture or two at putting it into story form. If you believe that the subject has interpreted his task as merely to produce short segments of his remembered past, it is appropriate to stop him (usually only if there are slips into the use of the first personal pronoun or other unmistakable evidence) and ask if that is not what he is doing. You may explain that the test calls for *stories,* that the subject is to use his imagination rather than his memory, and make them up. The reason is that the TAT is not—except in unusual cases—an efficient way of taking a personal history. The TAT's special usefulness comes in eliciting attitudes, motives, and aspects of personal experience that are *not* readily accessible to conscious efforts at remembering. It is much more feasible to gain access to these levels when the subject has the set to make up an imaginative story, not to tell a chapter of his autobiography.

8. Abilities. It is similarly necessary, with an occasional patient, to remind him that a coherent story is wanted, not free associations. Again, this step is taken not because free association is not a valuable method; it is just a different method, yielding different kinds of results. Only when the subject tries to tell a regular story with a plot are you able to find out about certain *abilities* that are relevant to this kind of task. Of course, the principal way in which abilities concern the examiner in administration is that he must tailor his instructions and questions to the subject's intellectual level.

9. Internal Milieu;   10. Personal Style. The last two categories, the internal milieu and personal style, carry no particular implications for administration that have not already been covered. It might only be mentioned that the subject's style is likely to be visible in his stories more clearly, the less interference there is with his natural tempo, phrasing, and architectonic sense. The exigencies of the examiner's writing stories by hand, when no recording equipment or other special aids are available, will sometimes cramp the subject's style (as well as the examiner's hand), but the advantages of this simple method outweigh the loss, for practical use in the clinic. If the patient is told ahead of time that the examiner is going to try to write down everything that he says and is occasionally reminded not to go too fast, he will usually match the tempo of the writing. It should go without saying that for the TAT, as in almost all psychological testing, *verbatim recording is an absolute essential.*

This section on administration has been intentionally selective in its coverage of the problem. The intent here has been, primarily, to delineate the principal attitudes and points of view from which the individual examiner may derive specific procedures that are most congenial to his own personal style of testing; and secondarily, to present certain points about administration that are not already covered in other easily available sources. [Further hints about administration are given in negative form, in Table 2.1]

Table 2.1.   Common Errors in Administration of the TAT*

1. Failure to maintain professional atmosphere in testing.
2. Failure to observe and record test behavior—*S*'s overall approach and demeanor, tone of voice, expression, gestures, attitude to *E*, and changes in any of these from time to time as testing goes on, in relation to specific pictures or themes.
3. Failure to record verbatim, which should include side-remarks, and *E*'s questions as well as his answers to *S*'s questions.
4. Not making it clear that a slip, mistake, etc., is *S*'s, not *E*'s, by putting *(sic)* after it.
5. Failure to use optimal wording for instructions.
6. Failure to use special instructions for cards 11 and 16.
7. Failure to restructure carefully after first couple of stories, when necessary, and to get across clearly to *S* what's wanted.
8. Failure to get reaction time and total time for each story.
9. Not setting time limits for overproductive *S*s.
10. Failure to praise and encourage.
11. Pursuing and trying to develop stories that clearly won't amount to anything much. Don't hurry the *S* or make him feel greatly pressured; you're not a D.A.
12. Faulty order: don't give the more difficult cards (e.g., 11, 16, 19, 20) or the more personal and traumatic ones (e.g., 13MF, 18GF, 6BM, 15) *early* in the series. Start with a few relatively easy and innocuous ones to warm *S* up—e.g., 1, 2, 4.
13. Continuing testing session past *S*'s tolerance.
14. Overpermissive replies to questions about content of pictures ("Whatever you want it to be" instead of "What does it look like to *you*?").
15. Failure to wait until *S* has finished spontaneous story to do the inquiry. Be patient!
16. Over-inquiry; and inquiry about nonessential points (e.g., age of hero).
17. Failure to inquire about nonmentioned aspects of 3BM, 4, 8BM, 11. [See Chapter 3.]
18. Subtly encouraging idea that there is a right answer or that the story is a *deduction* from picture rather than *S*'s own imaginative product. "What do you think *will* happen?" or "Which possibility is more *likely*?" or "What leads you to think that?"—These are examples of questions you should *not* ask.
19. Failure to inquire into possible peculiarities and possible misperceptions.
20. Failure to ask the right kind of questions. *Don't* ask questions that can be answered with a single word if you want to encourage *S* to give more than a single bit of information; don't ask complicated or double-barrelled questions.

*In this table, *E* means the examiner or tester, *S* the subject.

INTERPRETATION

Books have already been written on the interpretation of the TAT, and enough has been left unsaid for many a volume more. A part of one chapter in one book cannot pretend to do more than open up the topic and attempt a general orientation. [See also Holt, 1971c, Chapter 6.]

There is a great deal to be said for a set of fixed variables to be scored for each story, after the model of the insightful formulae of Rorschach, but there are many difficulties in applying such a plan to the TAT. A number of systems have been worked out; almost all of them are useful for some purposes, chiefly for research and for training in sensitivity to easily overlooked aspects of stories. The better known scoring systems have been developed by Murray (1943), M. I. Stein (1948), Tomkins (1947), Wyatt (1947), Henry (1947), Bellak (1947a, b), and Eron (1950) [with the help of Eagle (1964), I have perpetrated one myself (Holt, 1969d)]. None of these, however, is more than an aid to systematic observation, and none can be recommended for routine clinical use, though they are very helpful in research.

Strictly speaking, there are scarcely any generally applicable rules for analysis and interpretation of the TAT. One general statement can be made, however: one's skill in interpreting the TAT is greatly enhanced by, and can proceed no further than, his *thorough understanding of personology*. Specifically, many TAT workers have found that their insightfulness in interpretation has been enriched most by a knowledge of psychoanalysis.

Different specific approaches are appropriate to different purposes for which the test is being used. The vocational counselor will seldom find it helpful to indulge in speculative reconstruction of his subject's early history; the psychodiagnostician may be quite uninterested in exploring the patient's sentiments; the researcher on the emotional springs of prejudice will care little to trace indications of the abilities for which the psychologist looks when consulted about the selection of highly trained professional personnel.

The first step in interpretation is to get straight just what your aims are. If you are working for an institution, or as part of a clinical team, that will usually involve finding out *exactly* what service you are expected to supply, and perhaps, working out a realistic compromise on the basis of what you are able to deliver. All too often, dissatisfaction with the clinical psychologist's contributions arises out of unrealistic expectations and the lack of a common understanding of the purpose of the testing.

More specifically, decide, on the basis of the detailed purposes of testing, what kinds of data [i.e., information about the subject to be derived from the TAT] are needed to satisfy those purposes. Suppose the setting is a psychiatric one, the job is diagnostic testing, and the specific problem is the differential diagnosis of paranoid schizophrenia versus psychotic depression. You have given the Rorschach test, which is meager, suggestively peculiar in spots, but not decisive. What other kinds of data will be needed? An answer to this last question requires a knowledge of psychopathology. To name a few things, you will want to try to distinguish between depressive blocking and paranoid caution; perhaps between delusions of unworthiness and delusions of persecution; between constriction of the perceptual field and projective distortion. These then are some specifications of the kinds of information you will want to get from a test, or from a whole battery of tests. Depressive blocking and paranoid cautiousness may both produce meager stories with long reaction times, but the latter may make itself known through an inferential, descriptive approach that *derives*, often by explicit steps, everything in the story from details of the picture itself (Rapaport, Gill,

& Schafer, 1968). As far as the different types of delusions are concerned, neither will necessarily be reflected in the test, but the plots of the stories may give direct hints about one or the other kinds of delusion. And by paying attention to the perceptual impact of the pictures, you can see paranoid influences at work in distortions, particularly misidentifications of sex, while the effects of depression are more likely to be seen in inert omissions of the less obvious aspects of the pictures.

[Second, orient yourself generally in terms of the facts you will have about the storyteller or subject, and about the situational context. In other words, you take into consideration what you know about the nature of the test situation, about the tester (if it was not yourself), the purpose of testing, and what kind of person your subject is. Obviously, you need to know whether the subject is a male or female, his/her approximate age, marital status, educational level, and ethnicity. There is no point in trying to find out from the TAT these things that are so easily ascertainable directly; and they make a great deal of difference to the interpretations of some kinds of test findings.

Remember, your job is to find out what produced the stories, and to the extent that any relatively external and trivial determinants had an effect on them, you ought to know about it. For example, if the patient was ravenously hungry and you were having to defer his lunch while you finished up, and this seems to show up in a story, you need to know about that and make a note of it, and not make the goof of assuming that there are unusually strong oral needs in this person at all times.

The third step is to become thoroughly familiar with the stories. Read them over several times—quickly for an orientation, slowly examining every detail, preferably coming back to them again after some time spent in doing other things (for a fresh perspective), but taking notes each time on what you notice. The implication is that you will not try to interpret everything, only what is particularly revealing about your subject (the teller). In this process of search, your intentions, your interests, and other task sets operate as *open schemes* (in Piaget's sense), implicitly readied to assimilate whatever they can that fits their particular niches. The more such schemes or (in Duncker's phrase) search models you have, the more you can get out of a set of stories—or any other clinical data.

Some of the most useful open schemes are not specific to the TAT but are applicable to almost any clinical data. They are not to be despised for this nonspecificity; I have seen experienced and well-trained psychiatrists with no specific knowledge about the TAT do a very respectable and insightful job of interpreting TAT stories just on the basis of such nonspecific principles of interpretation. For example, obsessional stewing, hysterical lability of affect, sexual preoccupation, schizophrenic peculiarity of language, depressive slowness and heaviness, or the prim propriety of an inhibited and conventional person—these and similar categories of clinical case description are applicable to what patients say and do in relation to an examiner, whether the situation is an intelligence test, a physical or neurological examination, or any projective technique. For the most part, your interpretation of test behavior and the general qualities of verbalization will make use of these nonspecific conceptions or schemes and will depend heavily on the extent and concrete basis of your grasp of descriptive psychopathology (symptomatology) if you are using the TAT diagnostically. If not, it will depend on a comparable kind of experience with the ways live human beings exemplify the general categories of behavior with which you are working.

The specific principles of interpreting the TAT are based on the particular nature of the test materials and task, including the technique of administration used in interaction with the pictures themselves. It is therefore most important to get to know the pictures about which the stories were told, and their "pull"—what kinds of stories (and other reactions) they usually evoke from people of the kinds you are testing. Extensive but exclusive experience with white middle-class American adults will be of limited value to anyone confronted by stories told by a poor Haitian preadolescent, for example.

Ideally, the TAT interpreter would have on his desk a set of *norms* for every such population, members of which he works with. They would have to be subdivided by sex, age (or general developmental status), culture (including separate norms for American blacks and whites), intellectual level (at least such gross groupings as subnormal, normal, and superior), diagnostic type. . . . But why try to be complete? The task is already obviously far beyond reach and I have not even taken note of the hardest question: what is to be tallied in a normative study? Here the lack of a standard scoring scheme is particularly embarrassing. Little normative research has been done, and most of what is available is getting out of date as our culture changes. I have tried to assemble information of this kind, card by card, in the next chapter, but it can serve only as a rough guide. There is, unfortunately, no readily available alternative to building up your own familiarity with the kind of people you test and the ways they react to the cards you tend to use the most.

The function of norms (or their experiential equivalent) is to provide you with a set of average expectable assumptions from which to note divergences. Whether you think in terms of base rates (Meehl & Rosen, 1955), adaptation level (Helson, 1959), or assimilation and accommodation (Piaget, 1936), the logic is the same and rests on a well-established finding on the psychology of attention: we notice primarily what we do not expect—the surprising or unusual. *Un*usualness is plainly defined residually as what is not usual; hence, the need to be as explicit as possible about what we mean by usual. If you are trying to interpret the TAT stories of a 30-year-old, unemployed black father of three recently admitted to a state hospital in Boston after a suicide attempt, it would obviously be a waste of time to look for divergencies from general (i.e., white) expectations that would confirm the fact that your subject is black. Instead, you will want to look for whatever is "unusual" for a man with just these half-dozen characteristics, that is, for any new information this test can supply.

In a way, this emphasis on divergence seems to run counter to the advice to look for recurrences—repeated themes in the content, repeated "relationship paradigms" in test behavior, repeated stylistic features in formal aspects of the stories. But a moment's reflection will confirm the fact that this advice implicitly means repeated divergences from expectation. Recurrent turns of phrase that characterize "Black English," for example, will be of little interest in our hypothetical example and should attract less of your attention than repeated peculiarities in verbal usage that would not be expected from a normal (or even from a depressed) black American of whatever age, intellectual level, or subculture.

We are especially interested in recurrent features of the record, because of our assumption that if something keeps coming to the fore, it is likely to be strong, important for the person, and/or generally characteristic. The reverse does not hold, however: the person's central pathogenic complex may not show up at all in his stories, or may make only a fleeting and indirect appearance, because of defenses against it. Be on the lookout for qualitatively or quantitatively remarkable divergences, therefore, even when not repeated. By "quantitatively remarkable," I mean for example a theme that stands out by its intensity or by the vividness of affect accompanying it.

A contrasting kind of divergence has been called *negative content* by Henry (1956); it is the failure of the expected to appear. The type case is a story given to card 1 about a little boy who is learning to play the violin, loses interest in it, and turns to something else. This content seems quite ordinary and unexceptional until we notice something precisely because it is not there—the absence of any reference to the boy's parents. True, the picture portrays only a boy and a violin; but experience with almost all populations of American subjects shows that if more than the most meager story is produced, at least one parent plays some role in it. To be sure, such a discrepancy tells us mainly to be on the lookout for more positive evidence that will help solve the mystery; all divergences pose problems of accounting for them, but negative content does so in a particularly tantalizing way. Notice that the principle applies just as well for formal aspects and test behavior as to content. In the example above of the suicidal father, suppose that the emotional tone of the stories was consistently less gloomy than you would expect from the nature of the pictures you used and his presenting symptom—the divergence from expectation is, to begin with, the nonappearance of the expected somberness of internal milieu.

As we attempt to formulate the discrepancies we find, we are back to the role of open schemes, and into interpretation proper. To note recurrent, characteristic themes or ways of handling the task is hardly more than to begin the task. If the emotional tone of the stories is consistently less sad than expected, that is an important observation, but several tasks remain. You must characterize the tone *positively*, first—are the stories normally cheerful? frantically, relentlessly insistent on turning all darkness into light, all sadness into joy? jocular, facetious, and cynically satirical? blandly lacking in intense emotion of any kind? These four (out of many) possibilities all carry different implications, to which we get by processes of inference.

Inference is our principal tool of problem-solving in interpreting TAT stories. An attention-catching discrepancy from base-rate expectations poses a psychological problem: what kind of person would respond like *this*? It is therefore more than merely a generalization about the stories. The inferential process takes you from the stories to hypotheses about features of the story*teller* that may account for his having behaved this way—whether you are seeking an explanation for a single element (even the use of one word) or a pervasive general feature of the stories. It can be done on either a blind actuarial basis ("in my experience, or according to X's research, seeing the boy in the first picture as blind means . . .") or on the basis of theoretical understanding; ideally, both. Inference rooted in a theoretical rationale or understanding of how the various aspects of stories come about is more useful, because the empirical method leaves you with a collection of isolated bits and pieces, and what is inferred is usually rather general and external (e.g., diagnosis) because that is the easiest kind of criterion to use in research.

From another perspective, we work with two kinds of inference in interpreting the TAT: primary and secondary inferences. Whenever we develop a hypothesis about what determined any specific aspect of a person's test performance, that is a *primary inference*. Whenever we base one inference on another or on a group of primary inferences, I call it *secondary inference*. The latter come in at least three kinds. (1) If you find evidence of projective trends, and then infer that there must be a latent homosexual problem, you are showing your familiarity with classical psychoanalytical clinical theory, but you are not interpreting the TAT—unless you can also find direct evidence to back up a primary inference of this very kind. (2) If you find evidence of withdrawal and jump to a diagnosis of schizophrenia, you are taking a secondary inferential shortcut. Strictly speaking, a diagnosis is always a matter of secondary inference, for diagnostic categories are syndromes of the kinds of attributions about which we can make primary inferences. Since one symptom does not make an illness nor one trait a type, it takes a synthetic kind of secondary inference, putting together all that primary inference has suggested about pathological trends and personality structure, to reach a defensible diagnostic formulation. (3) If you see evidence in one story that your subject has strong wishes to achieve and in another that he has formed a clearcut identification with his father, you may be tempted to write that "*because of* his identification with his father, he has developed intense achievement motivation." If you do so without any direct test evidence that there is such a genetic connection between the two trends, you are making a secondary inference and usually an ill-advised one.

Each of these examples shows secondary inference in both its strength and its weakness. Secondary inferences of each type are excellent sources for hypotheses to be tested, open schemes in search of raw data to fill them. It is pretending—ultimately, intellectual dishonesty—to put forward an unsubstantiated hypothesis as if it were a fact, and that is the seductive danger about secondary inferences. Any good one ought to be true, and a good one is usually defined as the one that has just occurred to you.

The next step in interpreting the TAT is to develop and test a series of hypotheses. Every time you find evidence of a new trend, infer the working of some defense not previously noticed, note the workings of a value or see a stylistic trait being expressed, each such formulation becomes a primary inference and a hypothesis that the aspect of personality in question has enough generality to be important. (It is self-evident that a person who readily tells long stories as long as you keep bringing out pictures is productive—as a storyteller. It does *not* necessarily follow that he will be a productive research chemist, or life insurance salesman, or shoemaker; yet if he does work at one of these vocations, any consumer of your test report will be likely to translate a general statement, "a highly productive person," into such real-life terms.) Your task, then, is to test your hypotheses by looking for relevant data: is the subject productive in other tests? Particularly in nonverbal ones, if subject's occupation is not a wordy one. Are the characters in his stories—particularly the heroes, the ones whose behavior he most evidently admires or approves of—engaged in productive work, do they show signs of ambition, or conscientiousness, or the wish to be creative? Do the other aspects of personality about which you can make primary inferences fit with and support the idea of a man productive in his line of work, or clash with it, as evidences of glibness and avoidant defenses would or many stories about self-defeating central characters?

In this way, test interpretation is not really so very different from scientific work. Both have hypothesis-forming and hypothesis-testing phases. These require rather different orientations, different enough so that frequently one person is good at getting hunches and not very good at testing them, and another tester is fine at the more rigorous and hardheaded side of the work but has trouble thinking up any but a standard set of hypotheses. Ideally, then, you need to be two contrasting types of person. In the hypothesis-getting phase, you want to be as free, wild, loose, and intuitive as you can, opening yourself up to all kinds of possibilities. You can feed this process, of course, by a wide knowledge of personology and psychopathology, by a rich humanistic culture, by broad life experience and by the vicarious experience of literature, and by freeing access to all your inner resources of memory and fantasy (often by personal therapy). But then you need to doff your seer's robe and put on the lab coat of the hard-nosed experimenter, trying to scrutinize your own ideas as dispassionately as possible and seeing to what extent you can find evidence to back them up. It is all too easy to become so enchanted by the ingeniousness of your own hypotheses that the mere making of them seems an adequate substantiation. Guard yourself against that! Be as cold toward your own brain-children as you would be with someone else's, and look to *all* your data for evidence that will decide whether each one survives or is discarded. Exceptionally, a single unsupported bit of evidence will seem so impressive that a conclusion can be founded on it alone, but it should be stated tentatively. It is especially reassuring to be able to support an inference from content by a bit of relevant evidence from direct observation (test behavior) or from formal aspects, and best of all to see the same trait showing itself in all three ways as well as in non-TAT data.

So much for general principles. (Many of the above and a few others are summarized in Table 2.2.) Let us now take a quick look at some concrete data.]

Excerpts from the case of Harris, a 31-year-old, white, divorced veteran, will illustrate the use of the TAT in clinical practice, with the following objective: the patient's doctor referred him for a "full battery work-up" as an aid to long-term intensive psychotherapy that he was about to begin. The psychiatrist was interested in anything the tests might reveal—anything, that is, that would be relevant to a full understanding of the patient's personality and his illness, and that might help plan the course of therapy. The psychiatrist said that Harris had been diagnosed "schizophrenia, paranoid type." What, then, are the kinds of helpful information that the TAT can give?

Seven types of data relevant to this problem are often yielded by the TAT, namely, information about: (1) thought organization; (2) emotional organization (responsiveness and control); (3) motives, their strengths and ways in which they are manifested; (4) the subject's view of the world; (5) interpersonal relationships (object attachments); (6) the subject's conception of and attitudes toward himself; (7) dynamics of development and illness. Some information of all of these kinds was extracted from Harris' TAT stories. Limitations of space allow us to look at the protocols for only three pictures.

13MF (10"). They got some lulus here don't they? (sigh; 48") Well this is a boy and girl, they've been going together. They started going together, he was very . . . she was very pretty and he was attracted by her pulchritude. This boy was jumping around from one place to another, had no goal in mind seeking what pleasure he could find, and he carried on with her to the point of sexual intercourse. (sigh). . . . All this time he was beginning to become, well, he was becoming more nervous and uncertain. Because of that he continued to carry on relations more frequently, and the girl was unfortunately in love with him but he wasn't in love with her, in fact he wasn't in love with anybody. Finally he gets to the point where he stays all night

Table 2.2.   Common Errors in Interpreting the TAT

1. *Don't* present secondary inferences as if they were primary, and be sure you know which are which.

2. *Don't* confuse theoretical propositions with factual findings.

   The *test* does not suggest, for example, that the patient's present difficulties are attributable to an infantile neurosis or trauma, nor does it tell us that a latent homosexual fixation made indentification with his father impossible. It may at best provide evidence that is consistent with such interpretations, or supports them, but they are not findings. At best, they are secondary inferences.

3. *Don't* try to say what is *the most* active or central or important anything, *from this one test*, unless evidence is overwhelming and then only with caution. It is dangerous and unnecessary to try this kind of thing without a full battery, and even then one is often wrong.

4. *Don't* try to make specific inferences about personal history from content that is clearly derived from the picture. (More people have had some kind of music lessons than have studied the violin.)

5. *Don't* concentrate solely on history, defenses, and motives. Bring in values, attitudes, identity, personal style—try to capture some of the uniqueness of the subject.

6. *Don't* use historical or clinical material external to the test as if it is something you learned from the test data. Do, however, use such information to get more out of the data.

7. *Don't* make statements about the story hero as if they are about the subject or try to analyze the hero instead of the subject.

   For example, "In 3BM he rebels against his father several times, but in reality he is unable to rebel openly and forcefully. Only running away seems to be possible after which the father becomes more lenient for a short period"; etc., etc. One can write pages of this stuff without really coping with the interpretative problems set by the record. Absurd as the preceding may sound, beware—this is one of the easiest traps to fall into.

8. *Don't* engage in overgeneralization and hyperbole, trying to convince yourself of an inference you feel uncertain about by stating it in an extreme form. Not all expressions of doubt, uncertainty, or changing one's mind mean obsessiveness, not every expression of interest in education and learning means overintellectualization. It's a question not just of spotting a trend but seeing it in perspective, how well compensated it is, whether it takes adjustive or pathological forms, etc.

9. *Don't* fall into heavy reliance on technical jargon and extensive theorizing in test reports. Remember that a report is a communication about a patient, not a chance for you to show off or work out your pet theories. Also avoid vague, supposedly impressive use of big words ("patient displays a dysphoric reaction to the environment" instead of "patient is sad about his situation").

10. *Don't* rely on your own personal associations to something as a substitute for seeing what its context is and making inferences from that. Projection is a danger; but personal problems are also a resource: the better you know yourself, the better you can use them to pick up subtle cues and to understand these by (controlled) identification.

11. Be wary of carrying Henry's (1956) "negative content" approach very far. One can get ideas by noting what the subject did not say that he could be expected to have said, but you can't prove things that way, and surely it is dangerous to reason that a trend is not there from the *lack of any evidence* for it—even from a battery, but especially from a single test.

with her . . . and even though he, let's see (sighs) he—this particular night he stays all night with her for the first time. He wakes up in the morning, realizes the seriousness of the situation because she was a nice girl and it's his duty to go ahead and marry her whether he loves her or not. He feels very guilty, shameful about the situation as far as her and his family is concerned, but he goes ahead with the marriage, which is an unhappy one. (7 minutes)

18BM (76"). Could be the story of a fellow who was at one time a very happy man, satisfied with things in general. Then he started to stop in the local bar occasionally with a friend or two. It became more frequent as time went on till it got the best of him, that is he started drinking heavily, got the habit. He got to the point where he depended upon liquor to get along. It had a firm grip on him then. Because of his liquor why his family got broken up which aggravated his condition still more. Eventually wound up in an alcoholic institution. I believe that's all. (4½ minutes) (What is the scene shown in the picture?) Well that could be a scene when he was very drunk and the hands represent the hold liquor had on him.

10 (40"). A story of a middle-aged woman who never married. Very active in community affairs, sewing circles, etc. She had always avoided men up to—well up to quite ah—well quite a long time, because she was picking out, she was waiting to pick out the perfect husband. When she got to the point where she was rather elderly, middle-aged, she saw she was aging, saw that she had waited too long, so she sought outlet by entering into all these so-called activities. So during the course of the meeting they decided to have a noted lecturer give a talk on, oh something or other, and he was invited to, well, lecture before the club, a woman's club, and he was, it happened he came and gave a lecture. The fellow himself was very scheming, rather handsome sort, with an eye for a wealthy widow or someone he could finagle money from. So after the lecture he does his usual casing of the members to find the most eligible and he decides upon this woman because of her wealth, etc., and so he starts laying it on thick, and the spark in her returns. She thinks that this would be her last chance to ever marry and all the time she was believing all his words, etc., and all he was thinking about was ways of getting some of her money. The romance continues and by some means or other he—gets some money from her, the period before the marriage takes place. So as soon as he gets his money he skips out and she is left at the church. She realizes then that he was not good, that her only satisfaction in life was the community affairs that she had been pursuing, in helping others. I guess that's all, kinda corny. (9 minutes)

USING THE CATEGORIES OF DETERMINANTS IN INTERPRETATION

We have seen at the beginning of the chapter how nine different classes of determinants may be considered to play a part in shaping a story; let us see what we can figure out about Harris by studying the impress of each kind of determinant on these stories.

1. The Situational Context. Little that is directly relevant to interpretation ordinarily comes from the first class of determinants. You are, of course, trying to interpret the nature of the person from his stories, not the nature of his environment, so that the latter becomes important mainly in a negative way: you do not want to make the mistake of thinking that a certain reaction is generally characteristic of the subject if it is determined primarily by this particular situation. For example, some male patients have violent aversions to women, which seriously distorts the results of tests given them by feminine examiners. Female patients sometimes react similarly to male examiners.

2. The Directing Sets. There is one way in which the situational context may tell us much about the person himself; that is through the patient's own interpretation of the situation. We are considering this factor under the second class of determinants, however, since it comes into play almost entirely in terms of general sets and motivation for cooperating with the examiner. If a patient's interpretation of the examiner's efforts to help him is that the examiner is trying to prove him insane, for example, he must be called suspicious, perhaps even paranoid. To return to Harris—knowing that the author of the above stories is confined in a mental hospital with a diagnosis of paranoid schizophrenia, one might expect that he would be suspicious, evasive, or otherwise difficult to test. Yet from these stories one can see that he is not only compliant, telling unusually long and excellent stories, but even *self*-derogatory. ("Kinda corny," he said of his own story to picture 10; elsewhere in the test he had remarked, "I'm not very good at this.") When the situation of being sent from a locked ward to take some strange tests produces only this kind of set (the rest of the stories are similar in implied set), it is unlikely that the patient is a paranoid schizophrenic of the usual contentious, suspicious, rigid kind. If he *is* a paranoid schizophrenic at all, he is much more likely one of the very different, meek, intropunitive sort, who often seem very similar to depressives.

There is another important aspect of sets that must be noted by anyone who is testing for schizophrenia. One of the characteristic impairments associated with this disease is a breakdown in the ability to maintain appropriate sets long enough for any significant achievements. Of course, like almost any other specific deficit attributed to schizophrenia, this impairment does not necessarily appear in every case. But when a patient is as unusually well able to maintain continuity and smooth development of an idea as was Harris, one may begin to wonder just how psychotic he is. At least, the TAT suggests that there was no impairment of this function; the lack of any significant drop in the Picture Arrangement subtest score in his Wechsler-Bellevue profile supports this interpretation.

3. The Perceptual Impact. In this area, too, Harris' stories were almost more remarkable for what they were *not* than for what they were. There were no serious perceptual distortions; he was not even overimpressed by details of the pictures, but usually seemed to have good average percepts (cf., in the Rorschach test, F + percent, 70; no small or rare areas chosen; average proportion of popular responses). There was, however, one important deviation. In his story to 18BM there was something about the way he said, "It had a firm grip on him," that made the examiner suspect that there might be some symbolic, overliteral apperception of the three hands in the picture. Note that the inquiry used was completely nonleading and gave no hint of this suspicion, yet it did bring him to verbalize the autistic idea that was woven into his perception of the card. (At this point, the Wechsler-Bellevue scatter pattern offers some support for the assumption that his perceptual interpretations were more generally affected, since the lowest subtest score of all—four points below Vocabulary—was for Picture Completion, a perceptual test.)

Of course, the significance of what Harris did here is not wholly in the realm of perception; the fact that he gave an explanation of the kind he did suggests the encroachment of symbolic modes of thinking on his otherwise good thought organization. It is mentioned here largely because it was the concern of the examiner to establish just what Harris' perception of the scene was that led to the psychotic-like idea. It is perhaps worth digressing here for a moment to point out that there is very little inquiry in these stories; little was needed. Yet in this one instance, waiting until the end of the test would very likely have meant losing the opportunity to test the hypothesis—that is, the hypothesis on which the inquiry is based, for questioning must always have a definite purpose.

4. The Arousal of Motives and Affects. The three stories quoted above, and Harris' others, are unusually rich in hints about his motivational life. Many interesting subtleties of interpretation could be illustrated by reference to them, but a full analysis would take a number of pages. Only a few interrelated themes can be considered. One that pervades all of the stories is passivity. When one reads these stories looking to see how adequate the heroes are in achieving satisfaction of their needs, one is struck by the fact that not one of the heroes made an effort to struggle against the fate that was imposed upon him; all were caught in the grip of circumstance or inner compulsion (of guilt, or of dependence on drink). Consider also the self-defeating (and in other stories, self-destructive) effect of the actions Harris was able to think of for his characters. For picture 13, the young man got himself more and more embroiled so that he finally felt compelled to enter into a marriage that was foredoomed to failure; in 18, the hero's responsibility for his eventual failure in life was carefully not seen. In 10, the woman did not seem to bring defeat on her own head, though she certainly was the victim of what was almost a persecuting villain. The consistency of these themes, and their deviation from the usually given stories for the several pictures, must lead to the conclusion that there was in fact a strong passive masochistic wish in Harris that forced such themes into his consciousness.

As far as affects are concerned, Harris said little about the feelings and emotions of the characters. The anxiety and guilt of the man in picture 13MF, however, and the disappointed yearning of the woman in picture 10 were expressed so clearly that we may justifiably set up the hypotheses that these were his own feelings. The only affect that broke through his defenses into overt manifestation during testing was *depression,* in the many sighs that punctuated his story to card 13MF. Another important negative statement deserves to be made: there was little that could be called disharmonious or inappropriate affect. In the affective realm, as well as in the intellectual, there was little evidence of a schizophrenic process.

[**5. Identification and Identity.** When we look at the stories from this standpoint, we are led (by secondary inference) to an additional important motivational theme. He seems to have a high degree of feminine identification (or unconscious fantasy of being a woman) and probably the usually accompanying homosexual wishes.] Card 10 offers an excellent opportunity for a subject to identify himself with either of the two, equally prominent figures. There can be no doubt that Harris identified himself with the victim in this case, and his ability to create a picture of her yearnings and feelings is additional evidence of his having experienced many things in a "feminine" way himself. This hypothesis is partly confirmed by the slip at the beginning of the story for picture 13MF, when he nearly said that *he* was very pretty. (Actually, the patient himself was unusually handsome.) Although in the story Harris identified himself with the man, the heterosexuality was clearly unsatisfactory and compulsive in quality; that is, the motivation for more frequent sexual relations was directly stated to be because of the man's nervousness and uncertainty; "he wasn't in love with her, in fact he wasn't in love with anybody." In none of Harris' productions was there a happy marriage or any other satisfactory heterosexual relationship; in 10, the underlying conviction that there is no real love between man and woman must be particularly clear. This picture is very frequently seen as a loving couple. In my experience, only patients—usually paranoid—with strong homosexual wishes, and neurotic characters who cannot conceive of a genuine tender relationship between any two persons, think that the scene is a sham, that there is really no reciprocal affection. There is nothing to indicate that the homosexual fantasies were conscious; in fact, the compulsive heterosexual acting out, strongly suggesting a denial of homosexuality, in 13MF was striking.

The motives that have been discerned in these stories are quite consistent with paranoid developments of some kind, and so contribute to confirming the diagnosis. In addition, we have learned much about the patient's personality and have established the severity of his underlying disorder, even though his formal thought functioning may be good in most respects.

We have as yet learned relatively little about Harris' identity from these three stories. The last one provides data for an inference of this kind, however, in the qualities attributed to the male figure. Since Harris clearly made the woman the central character and portrayed the man in unflattering terms, the latter's psychopathic-like traits (exploitativeness toward women, caring only for money, trickery, using his sexual attractiveness as a weapon) may make up part of a negative identity—an evil self-image in sharp contrast to the "slave of duty" who is hero of the 13MF story and who seems to be acting in a way the subject feels is right. To some extent, the weak drunkard hero of 18BM may be another embodiment of such a hedonistic, egocentric, bad self. The "good self" implied by 13BM showed up in other stories, also, not given here.]

6. **Defensive Circuiting.** In discussing a case, it is almost impossible to discuss motives without saying something about the defenses against them, or about the strategies through which their expressions are controlled. The fact that certain wishes seemed to be unconscious implies the operation of repression in keeping any direct recognition of them out of the stories. The self-defeating, masochistic trend implies that Harris turned aggression against himself, as does also the stress on guilt. Projection, which is certainly expected in a paranoid case, was less apparent than usual, though the symbolic idea of the hands as representing "the hold liquor had on him" is interpretable as an instance of the related defense of externalization.

One of the most significant contributions to the understanding of Harris that came from looking for evidences of his defenses was the uncovering of the character disorder that antedated his schizophrenia. With respect to this important feature of the case, the diagnosis was as blind as one could wish; if anything, my attention should have been called *away from* characterological difficulties by the diagnostic impression given. Yet the efforts Harris made to avoid coming to grips with his true feelings and to avoid responsibility were quite striking. When he looked at the scene in card 13MF, his story revealed that strong feelings of guilt, shame, and anxiety were aroused, yet he tried at once to laugh off these feelings with a feebly facetious comment which was in vivid contrast to his later gloom. When he voiced some rather poignant feelings indirectly in the last of these three stories, he had to devaluate them by calling his story "corny." His heroes likewise were conspicuously avoidant in their behavior—"jumping around from one place to another, had no goals in mind"; "she had always avoided men"; "he skips out." In story 18BM, the denial of the hero's personal responsibility for his alcoholism is striking. The other typical defense of character disorder, acting out, has already been indicated in the discussion of story 13MF. When the specific content of alcoholism was present so blatantly, one is justified in a strong hunch, at least, that the premorbid personality structure had many of the features of character disorder. In this case, it was particularly important to establish the nature of the prepsychotic adjustment, because the therapist was prepared for what happened when Harris became almost entirely free from schizophrenic symptoms: he showed a tendency to turn to alcohol, which the therapist was able to forestall fairly well.

7. **Cognitive Elaboration.** A number of determinants, including the associative elaboration, can be considered from the standpoint of *form* as well as content: that is, not just *what* are the needs, but *how* appropriately, impulsively, and so on, are they expressed; not just *what* are the memories that are awakened and brought into the story, but *how* the associative process

works. Is it rambling, chain-like, going off the point (as in many manics)? Is it brought almost to a standstill by depression? Does it proceed by jumps and by obscure idiosyncratic associations, so that the listener cannot easily follow the trend of thought (an indication of a schizophrenic process)? Harris' sequential thinking passed this kind of inspection fairly well; it seemed to be intact. By now we have found so many aspects of his personality that were untouched by schizophrenia, so far as we can see, that we must consider the possibility that he was not psychotic in spite of story 18BM and one confabulation (in Rapaport's sense) in the Rorschach. The final conclusion reached was, in fact, that there was very substantial remission from a schizophrenic episode.

A. Personal-Historical Content. To what extent did Harris draw on his own life and his present problems in making up his stories? To a very large extent, undoubtedly, varying considerably from one story to another. It would seem very unlikely that anything in story 10, for example, was directly autobiographical, though the story to 13MF turned out to be almost entirely a condensed account of circumstances leading to his marriage. How does one decide? Certainly, plausibility and internal consistency must play a considerable role. It would not make sense for so passive and helpless a fellow as Harris obviously was to have swindled any wealthy maiden ladies. Yet we can take something from that very secondary character, put it together with the other "lover" in 13MF, and piece together a generalization that does hold true of his past: that he was psychosexually immature, incapable of a real love relationship, and that there was a parasitic, exploitative undercurrent in his affairs with women. It is rarely safe (and rarely does it contribute anything to the study of a case) to try to be much more specific than this. Interpretation of personal-historical material, then, is best confined to a rather general level, concerned principally with the nature of the emotional relationships between the subject and important kinds of figures in his life.

B. Sentimentive Content. One of the easiest ways to approach the analysis of a TAT is to look for indications of the subject's sentiments, his basic emotional attitudes toward certain classes of persons and objects. From these, one can often set up hypotheses that can be tested out on other levels. Or certain sentiments themselves may have diagnostic significance. For example, in the story Harris told to picture 18BM, he clearly expressed a utilitarian attitude toward liquor—that it was something to depend on, in order to get along—which is conducive to the development of alcoholism.

C. General-Informational Content. Nothing particularly significant on this level emerged in the three stories under consideration. As an indirect indicator of intelligence, the kind of information a person is able to call on is sometimes helpful in questioning an impression of mental deficiency, just as may be a patient's spontaneous use of unusual words ("pulchritude").

8. Abilities. Taken as a group, these three stories are better than average in construction and in interest. It is reasonable to infer that Harris' intelligence and imaginative ability were considerably better than average, though of course no one would attempt to use the TAT to get an IQ. Certain kinds of abilities, however, are indicated more directly by the TAT than by any other test. One thing the psychiatrist obviously wanted to know about Harris was, would he respond well to psychotherapy? A case of schizophrenia with character disorder also involved would seem, on the face of it, to be particularly unpromising. But in his stories, Harris showed a noteworthy ability to empathize, to take the point of view of more than one character in a story and to create a convincing picture of feelings (Dymond, 1948; see also Feffer & Jahelka, 1968). Furthermore, his recognition that nervousness and uncertainty may be causally related to sexual activity represented an insight considerably above the average level. These slight indications point to a capacity for psychological mindedness, an ability to examine his own behavior in psychological terms and to accept psychological explanations. This ability was not invariably present (there were no indications of it in some of his other stories) but it existed as a potentiality that made expressive psychotherapy a suitable technique for him.

9. The Internal Milieu. These stories are enough, in Harris' case, to give the "tune" of the whole test. An atmosphere of hopelessness, of fatalism, of being caught in a vicious circle of some kind, pervades his stories. It bespeaks an inner pessimism that was quite deep-rooted and was cause for some qualification of the hopeful prognosis suggested by his abilities. I inferred that Harris' spirit had been broken, that his feelings of validity and worth as a man had been so severely damaged that he might have great difficulty in ever making a successful adjustment. The fact that there is danger in letting oneself go too far in speculations about a person on the basis of the atmosphere of the stories, which could have been a function of temporary mood, was brought home clearly by a retest of Harris after one and one-half years of therapy. Once he had achieved a better control over his passive wishes, he was able to take a more positive and optimistic outlook on life.

10. Personal Style. Harris' way of talking, judged from this sample, seemed to be rather easy, informal without being disrespectful, generally fluent, and free of schizophrenic peculiarities. A stilted word crept in once in a while, and he blocked to some extent when he came up against emotional difficulties. Perhaps the most noticeable feature of his style was his tendency to become vague at points during a narrative when more mental effort would have enabled him to produce a definite idea that in turn would have made a better story. In picture 10, this trait was particularly outstanding: the lecturer is to talk on "oh, something or other"; "by some means or other he gets some money from her"; note also the liberal use of et cetera. Here is a clue to the intellectual indolence that is very clearly seen in contrast between a Wechsler-Bellevue IQ of 126 and the meager Rorschach: 26 responses, half of them animals, with only one good whole response other than popular and near-popular responses.

The style of verbalization is very often one of the best sources of evidence for important defenses and types of pathology. From the lack of pedantry, rumination, and intellectually ambitious references, one can see that Harris was not a very obsessive person. If he had used more slang, particularly of the flippant and rather callous sort into which he slipped in describing the schemer of story 10, if he had joked with the tester, or, in general, had tried to make it plain that he was not going to get personally involved, the character disorder would have been considered much more severe and ingrained. As it was, the negative evidence of the lack of schizophrenic autism in speech was used to buttress the conclusion that schizophrenia had not seriously undermined the patient's intellectual and emotional functioning.

The abundance of test data from Harris has been very thinly sampled here; but some of the ways it can be used in interpretation are evident. Occasional references to other tests have been included as an example of cross-checking between tests.

A few final words about Harris: he had been kept in a state of exaggerated passive dependency by an overpowering mother and strict father. After some rather nomadic years following high school, he impregnated a girl and then entered into a rather brief and unsatisfactory marriage. While overseas in military service, he became involved in a heterosexual affair, which occasioned guilt that went to delusional extremes. He was an airplane pilot, and completed a number of missions while actively deluded about the harmful effect of his glance upon other persons, which he attributed to his own sinfulness. He finally turned himself in to a hospital, was cooperative and seemingly in good contact with reality in spite of his delusions, though he was easily embarrassed. After a year and a half of intensive psychotherapy, his delusions had left. Though he still had some difficulty in looking directly at anyone he talked to, he made an excellent social adjustment, and was able to obtain and hold a job.

RELIABILITY AND VALIDITY

The TAT is not a test in the same sense that an intelligence scale is, and consequently the usual canons of reliability and validity cannot be applied without considerable qualification. The TAT provides a segment of human behavior, which may be analyzed in a tremendous variety of ways, and which may serve as the basis for inferences about a myriad of personal characteristics. Almost as well ask: what is the reliability or validity of everyday behavior? These questions begin to make sense only when we consider a particular method of abstracting from the data that are provided.

The problem of reliability may be restated for the TAT: to what extent do the stories reflect transient and fugitive states of the person, such as moods or the traces of recent experience, and to what extent are they determined by more slowly changing dynamic and structural features? The reliability of the TAT has never been investigated in quite these terms, so an answer is not available. Relevant data are furnished by W. Coleman (1947): the TAT stories told by 41 children soon after they had seen a movie showed insignificant evidence of influence by its content.

Some data are available on the stability of need-press scorings (according to Murray's scheme) of repeated TATs. In an excellent, extended discussion of these problems, Tomkins (1947) reports that the repeat reliability of the test, as scored in this way, may be as high as .80 or .90, depending upon the lapse of time between administrations and upon the fluidity-rigidity of the particular subjects concerned.

A second important aspect of reliability is the agreement of different scorers or interpreters working with the same protocols. The simpler and grosser the scoring scheme, the easier it is to obtain good reliability. As a result, the observer reliabilities of complex and highly differentiated sets of categories like Aron's (1949) are usually not high, while those obtained by investigators who have worked with a few simple categories have been as good as anyone would wish (Garfield & Eron, 1948; Mayman & Kutner, 1947). In some unpublished work at the Harvard Psychological Clinic, Murray demonstrated that a highly differentiated analytic scheme (his need-press categories) could be used with high interobserver reliability. By intensively training two Radcliffe undergraduates, he was able to bring them to the point where their ratings correlated consistently around .90 with his.

The validity of any particular set of statements based upon the TAT must be a function of at least the following factors: (a) the ability and experience of the interpreter; (b) the system of scoring and interpretation he uses; (c) the particular kind of statements, predictions, or ratings the interpreter is called upon to make. The interpreter is inseparable from the test when the validity of a technique like the TAT is in question. It is unfortunately true that the ability of Harrison (1940) to make blind diagnoses of psychiatric patients with 82.5% accuracy using his own method of analysis says virtually nothing about the likelihood that anyone else's diagnosis of a case, prediction of a subject's success in a vocation, or interpretation of a personality will be accurate.

Reported studies indicate that in the hands of competent interpreters using a variety of analytic techniques, the TAT may form the basis for valid inferences about a wide variety of personality traits and abilities (Harrison, 1940; Henry, 1947) and facts of personal history (Combs, 1946; Markmann, 1943). It may lead to valid predictions of leadership ability in officer candidates (Murray, 1943) or of psychotherapeutic ability in psychiatric candidates (Holt & Luborsky, 1958), predictive ratings in both studies correlating above .60 with criterion ratings. TAT results have been found to agree well with the results of psychoanalytic investigation, other tests, and a variety of sources for case data (Harrison, 1940; Henry, 1947; Morgan & Murray,

1935; Murray, 1938). Meaningfully and statistically differentiating characteristics have been found in the TATs of known groups ranging from prejudiced and nonprejudiced normal persons (Frenkel-Brunswik, 1948) to various nosological groupings (Balken & Masserman, 1940; Renaud, 1946). The limits of the possible kinds of valid inferences from the TAT are yet to be explored, but by the same token, its validity for any particular task, as applied by any particular clinician, remains unknown until it has been tested, and may be poor.

It should be stated in all frankness that neither the reliability nor the validity of the method of interpretation advocated in this chapter has been rigorously tested, though clinical experience supports the contention that it is teachable and that it yields a variety of statements about personality that agree with independent sources of data. It can also be used with such related instruments as the Four-Picture Test (van Lennep, 1948, 1951), the MAPS test (Shneidman, 1948, 1949), the Children's Apperception Test (Bellak & Bellak, 1949), the Michigan Picture Test (Hartwell, Hutt, Andrew, & Walton, 1951), and story-completion methods like the Insight Test (Sargent, 1944).

3

When I began teaching the interpretation of the TAT about 30 years ago, I felt keenly the lack of any useful norms. The most helpful thing I could find was Rapaport's brief comments about some of the cards in his monograph, which had just appeared (Rapaport, Gill, & Schafer, 1946). As the years went on, books about the TAT began to appear with their authors' more or less normative notations about the kind of material usually pulled by each picture, notably M. I. Stein (1948), Bellak (1954b), and Henry (1956). During this period were published three reports of formal normative research by Rosenzweig and Fleming (1949), and Eron (1948, 1950). In 1949, I came across an unpublished compilation of such material by Dr. Robert L. McFarland, which he was kind enough to let me reproduce in 1956 for my students along with some supplementation from the above-mentioned books that had appeared by that time and from two unpublished masters theses (Fleming, 1946; Kiefer, 1950), plus commentary based on my own clinical experience.

Many successive classes of graduate students reported to me that they found my enlargement of McFarland's compilation highly useful, and I have distributed countless copies in the two decades since I first produced it, without any revisions. When I decided to put together the present book, my first thought was simply to include it here with the most minor retouching. When I read it over, however, I became aware that it contained a good deal of redundancy, with extended quotations from generally available books, and that opinion has since been established—and in some instances, refuted—by normative research, some of it my own unpublished work.

All in all, it seemed best to boil the old document down, introducing as much hard information from quantitative normative studies as possible. I have made an effort to locate and use as much of the published normative material as possible, but it is a frustrating task. To begin with, since there is no generally used scoring system, each normative study uses its own variables, tabulating data in different and nonequivalent ways, so that is is extremely difficult to cumulate a series of them. Most of the work dates back to the decade immediately following the publication of the cards; it is impossible to say how differently contemporary American samples would respond to the pictures, though I believe that the gross outlines—which is what we mainly want from norms—have not changed much. Most of the samples used leave a great deal to be desired: numbers of cases were generally small, sampling methods not specified and never truly satisfied, and supportive data on subjects usually skimpy. The work generally used available groups of college undergraduates of both sexes, or of patients, predominantly fairly young male veterans in VA hospitals and clinics. All studies have sampled whites, relatively few outside the middle class. The only time I know of when a national probability sample of U.S. adults was given a thematic test, ironically no TAT cards

77

were used. Veroff (1961) and his colleagues used two sets of six pictures each, specially drawn to be suitable for general samples of men and women, respectively, and he provides no norms for these unpublished pictures.

In everything that I have seen, nothing yet seems to me comparable to the job that Edith E. Fleming did in her MA thesis, only the cream of which was skimmed off and published in her joint paper with Saul Rosenzweig. Her breakdown of the material was detailed enough to be exhaustive but clear enough to be reliably used by others. Her sample (50 men, 50 women) was gathered mostly by ten examiners, all students in Rosenzweig's fall 1944 course, each of whom had the assignment to test five males and five females, who were not to be in a professional field, although some students were undergraduate majors in psychology. The average age of both sex subgroups was 27.5 years (S.D. 6 and 6.3); all subjects were American-born urban whites, 80% of whom had had at least two years of college. Consequently, I had my research assistant (now Dr. Lolafaye Coyne, of the Menninger Foundation) apply it to several other bodies of data I managed to lay my hands on, all of them from rather educated males and each using a slightly different set of TAT cards. Anne Roe kindly lent me TATs from the eminent biologists, physicists, and artists whom she tested (Roe, 1946, 1952); William E. Henry generously made available stories told by successful and unsuccessful business executives he had studied (Henry & Gardner, 1949); and the local files produced TAT data from the control group of Rapaport's Diagnostic Psychological Testing *study (Rapaport, Gill, & Schafer, 1945–1946) and from psychiatric residents who were subjects in the selection research project (Holt & Luborsky, 1958).*

In writing this chapter, therefore, I have tried to digest all the foregoing, plus published normative research by Eron (1948, 1950, 1953), Wittenborn (1949), Murstein (1963, 1972), Ullmann (1957), and Gurel and Ullman (1958). I have made relatively little use of the recent trend of TAT research to have judges (mostly college students) rate or scale the pictures themselves for such variables as ambiguity (Bijou & Kenny, 1951), pleasantness (Murstein, 1958), hostility (Murstein, David, Fisher, & Furth, 1961), or achievement (Murstein, 1965), because such work tells us nothing directly about the kinds of stories we get using each picture, which is what we need. It is unfortunate that most of the recent normative research has used the scaling approach, even employing multidimensional scaling techniques, semantic differentials, etc., instead of dealing with the clinically useful features of the stories. I have tried to concentrate on the latter in this chapter.

A Normative Guide to the Use of the TAT Cards

In preparing this small handbook for the clinical use of the TAT, which I hope will be useful to personality researchers as well, I have assembled all of the normative data I could find, published or unpublished. In the course of doing so, I have been over the entire cumulative bibliography of the TAT— my own (which I allowed Henry to publish in his 1956 book and which is quite exhaustive through the early 1950s) and those published in Buros's indispensable handbooks (1965, 1970, 1972). Only a few dozen titles out of approximately 2000 even suggest the presence of norms, and many of those proved of little value. Except for Eron's valuable work (1950, 1953), I have found the unpublished material more complete, detailed, and extensive than what has made its way into print. There are many deficiencies of the normative literature besides its paucity—many studies give data for sets of cards, not for the individual pictures; or they comprise information on only a few cards, or they use nonstandard administration (e.g., stories written in response to projected images of the cards), aside from the sampling difficulties mentioned in the introduction. Further, the slight differences in definition of categories (for example, some authors lump "murder" with "suicide" while others distinguish them as I would prefer) or failure to define categories precisely make it frustrating to try to combine categories. For these reasons, I have leaned especially heavily on Fleming's data on 100 adult males and females, supplemented by an application of her detailed, precise, and perceptually focused categories to data from up to 20 biologists, 19 physicists, and 18 artists (kindly given me by Roe; not all subjects were given the same cards), 53 Kansas highway patrolmen, 30 businessmen (Henry), and 31 to 50 psychiatric residents. Unfortunately, that makes a male, mostly middle-class, highly educated and sophisticated sample; where possible, I have compared frequencies with those given by the female half of Fleming's sample, Eron's (1953) norms for women, and Kiefer's unpublished norms on 75 women and girls.

If we keep it in mind that the purpose is not to make a study of sex differences or of differences between occupational or age groups, then the inadequacies of sampling become less important. For the most part, we need a set of normal benchmarks against which to measure psychopathological subjects. Where possible, I have examined data on neurotic and psychotic men and have cited figures when there were large and probably reliable differences. Remember, however, that you can get a very significant difference between, say, a group of hospitalized VA schizophrenics and a "normal control" group without its being of any value. The two groups may and usually do differ in age, education, intelligence, socioeconomic status and other demographic characteristics all of which are hopelessly confounded with diagnosis. But even if groups are well-matched, a reliable mean difference usually tells us nothing useful about base rates and the gain in discrimination efficiency from using the cue in question, a gain that is almost always disappointingly slight when there is any substantial degree of overlap in the two distributions (Meehl & Rosen, 1955; Meehl, 1973).

The purpose of norms, therefore, is not to give you a set of "pathognomonic signs," which can be mechanically used to classify people into pigeonholes. It is to correct certain clinical traditions and to give some guidance about what to expect so that you do not treat as an interesting and interpretable discrepancy something that is given fairly often by people who are making a go of their lives and who do not define themselves as patients.

Before turning to the specific pictures, let me make a few comments about the set as a whole. Eron (1950, 1953) has shown that most persons tested gave stories with negative emotional tone in response to most pictures. That is, a set of stories containing little cheeriness, joy, contentment, tranquility, or optimism is no cause for alarm, but merely an appropriate reaction to pictures that—by design—concentrate on conflictful, problematic, and uncertain or threatening aspects of life. Furthermore, Fleming's finding that approximately one-fourth of the stories told to most pictures had indefinite or inconclusive endings indicates that the lack of a crisp, definitive conclusion cannot be taken as evidence for much of anything except possibly a somewhat lax style of administration. It speaks for the fact that storytelling is not a universally cultivated art and reminds us that in giving the TAT we are asking people to undertake a task at which they typically have had little practice and cannot be expected to perform at a very high level of competence. Do not relax your standards of test administration for that reason, however, only your notions about the importance of what Rapaport called compliance with the instructions. Fortunately, a story can be a limp literary product and still be valuable grist for the psychologist's mill.

CARD 1

Murray's description: A young boy is contemplating a violin which rests on a table in front of him. (Drawing by Christiana D. Morgan, after a photograph of Yehudi Menuhin as a child.)

The first thing the norms tell us is that the main figure in the picture is unambiguously a boy. No one—not even in Eron's group of patients—misrecognized his sex or age. It is not uncommon for normal adults to describe the boy's eyes (or face) as defective: 12% of Fleming's 100 subjects and 10% of Roe's 37 biologists and physicists did so, as well as 6% of the latter's 18 artists. Among educated people who are fully familiar with the appearance of violins, virtually everyone recognizes the violin, but I have found surprising numbers of nonpsychotic but culturally limited people who had difficulty figuring out what it was. Eron (1950) reports that 6% of the stories about No. 1 given by his mixed male psychopathological group included perceptual distortions, defined as "any departures from the standard description of the picture" as given by Murray, giving as an example "identifying the violin in Card 1 as a typewriter." Such misrecognitions were somewhat more common among neurotic than among psychotic veterans surprisingly enough; because of the way the data are reported, however, there is no way to tell whether the neurotics' distortions included anything so extreme as the example cited. More likely, they are of the following kinds. No member of our very superior professional samples saw violin or bow as broken, but from 4% to 7% of Fleming's men, Henry's businessmen, and Rapaport's highway patrolmen did so, and 8% of Fleming's women said one or the other was broken. From two-thirds to virtually all members of each sample said nothing about the sheet music; seeing it as simply paper or a piece of cloth is rare but hardly pathological, whereas calling it a book is so unusual as to indicate a psychotic distortion of realistic perception.

It is not unusual for people to launch into autobiography with this picture (7% of Eron's male and 2% of his female sample did so), a misunderstanding of instructions that should be corrected at once.

A boy is confronted by a violin, in our culture, for either of two main reasons—because his parents think he should study it or because he has some more self-generated interest. Among Eron's males, both the themes of parental pressure and of aspiration were equally common, given by 37%. Thus, for at least half of the normal population it provides information about reactions to an imposed task or duty—hence, it often gives clues to the subject's reaction to the (imposed) task at hand, telling stories. It is relatively uncommon for the hero to develop a positive interest or to succeed when the story begins with parental pressure. Among 88 male Harvard students in the early 1940s (Markmann, 1943), 60% of the themes given in response to this picture dealt with positive, self-generated achievement interests, and only a little over 20% of the themes dealt with rebellion, escape, or passive resistance; while in the stories told by the Kansas highway patrolmen, 42% focused on the boy's dislike of the violin and/or his desire instead to play ball with friends. A subordinate but fairly common theme (given by 16% of Eron's men) is curiosity about the violin.

In published discussions of this card (e.g., Bellak, 1954b; Henry, 1956), I think somewhat too much emphasis has been put on sexual symbolism. In the books on TAT interpretation, there are cautions and warnings about symbolic interpretations of this type, mostly by way of admonishing the psychodynamically naive student to stay away from such things, or that other evidence is necessary, etc. The main point to be made about this type of interpretation, in my view, is that it is generally not very useful. It is quite rare in my experience that a story has very directly suggested conflict about masturbation or the like, though I don't deny that the material is easily adaptable to carrying this symbolic freight. Masturbation guilt is extremely common, though it varies a great deal in intensity and in importance for a patient's illness, but it is just these latter issues that are not illuminated by symbolic interpretations of this picture, except in very rare instances. The latter do occur, but they are not frequent enough to warrant much space.

Other points to look for are indications of the hero's motivation for taking up and following through the study of the violin—whether it is his own motivation or induced, and if the latter, whether it "takes" or not: does he succeed in internalizing induced motivation? Note the role of parents (helping, overprotecting, forcing, demanding, giving) and the degree of achievement and gratification the hero gets in relation to the particular way that the parental role has been depicted. In achievement-oriented stories, it is important to note how much actual work is described as taking place, how realistically the effort is portrayed, particularly if there is an outcome stressing great success and fame, and how adequate or inadequate the hero is and feels. Other important themes: parental ego idealism (the attempt of the parents to achieve their own frustrated ambitions vicariously), achievement-orientation versus recognition-orientation (does the hero enjoy music and playing the violin for its intrinsic satisfaction, or is he only thirsting after glory?); curiosity about the violin (which of course may and probably does have roots in sexual curiosity, but is more likely to appear in neutralized and sublimated forms); and the broken violin (which may have the significance of various kinds of castration-equivalents). On the matter of curiosity, genetic interpretations concerning sexual voyeurism are generally more speculative and less useful than attempts to assess its contemporary manifestations. It is much more important to know whether someone with strong voyeuristic wishes is sublimating them in photography, scientific research, the practice of psychotherapy, or the like, as against being preoccupied with direct voyeuristic fantasies and experiencing conflictful breakthroughs of such a kind that disrupt his work, than it is to know that a particular patient was once exposed to the primal scene or some other infantile event that strengthened his sexual curiosity.

In the *Achievement Motive* by McClelland, Atkinson, Clark, and Lowell (1953), findings are reported from a study of n Achievement (as scored by McClelland) using eight pictures, including four from Murray's set. Picture 1 alone was uncorrelated with the others in the n Ach. that it pulled. The meaning of this finding is equivocated by the fact that we do not understand wholly what McClelland's scoring technique measures. If there is a difference, then, in the achievement-relevant material from No. 1 and No. 7BM or 8BM, consider the hypothesis that the story with the younger hero represents wishes, attitudes, etc., from an earlier era in the subject's life and that the material from the stories with more mature heroes is representative of more contemporary strivings. Consider also findings from research by Murstein (1963, 1965), in which pictures such as this one, which were judged by college students as having only a moderate achievement-relevance, were most effective in predicting actual performance. Pictures 7BM, 12M, 10, and 17BM were all rated as increasingly "higher in achievement," while top ratings were given to cards 2 and 8BM.

—All sources agree that this is a highly useful card for all ages and sexes.

CARD 2

Murray's description: Country scene: in the foreground is a young woman with books in her hand; in the background a man is working in the fields and an older woman is looking on. (Mural, "Fertility," by Leon Kroll.)

This is a highly detailed and structured picture, and normal persons have no difficulty recognizing the sexes and relative ages of the three main figures, so that failure to do so carries considerable pathological weight. The implied relationship among the figures is not so obvious. Some authors seem much too confident that the girl in the foreground should be seen as daughter of the other two; majorities of all normative samples concur, but she may also be seen as the man's wife or sweetheart, or as a sister. Approximately 10% of several samples portray her as not a member of the family, but stories in which none of the three are related are rare, being given by 7% of Eron's hospitalized and 3% of unhospitalized men. In my experience such stories have been given mainly by schizophrenics with strong feelings of estrangement from the family. From 20% to 50% of all samples specified that the woman on the right is pregnant, so it is fairly safe to assume that her condition is generally recognized even though not mentioned (and sometimes defended against). It is even safer to assume that everyone sees the books, even though only about half of normal subjects (2% of Eron's male sample) mention them specifically. Not one of the eight artists to whom Roe gave this picture mentioned the tree, but one or two of every six persons does allude to it. Except for the horse (which 40% of the biologists mentioned), no other item in the picture is mentioned by any substantial segment of any sample; in general, it is safe to assume that description of such minute details as the pond, forest, and buildings indicates obsessiveness. Some authors seem to imply that there is something of a choice open to male subjects to identify themselves with the girl or the man; actually, stories with the man as hero are quite unusual, and the prominence of the girl in the foreground creates such a strong pull to have her as the hero that I don't think any information on sexual identification can be obtained merely from the choice of her as hero.

In considering the family relationships, notice how close, warm, supportive as against distant, restrictive, tradition-bound the family is pictured as being. The closeness and specificity of kinship attributed to the figures can tell a good deal, as is nicely demonstrated in the research by Goldstein, Gould, Alkire, Rodnick, and Judd (1970) on the families of disturbed adolescents. This paper is, incidentally, an excellent example of the way the TAT can be used to develop a picture of a family as a system of conscious and unconscious emotional relationships. Goldstein and his collaborators rated each of the three main figures on a 6-point scale (from clear statements of nuclear family relationship—e.g., husband, daughter; through extended family member—e.g., aunt, cousin, friend, business associate, etc.; to total avoidance of character) and compared the average kinship ratings for each figure by fathers, mothers, and children within each of four types of families based on the child's presenting symptom. For example, aggressive-antisocial adolescents had the highest kinship scores, portraying a tight nuclear family, but their fathers rarely saw the man as father or husband though attributing close relationships to the female figures, and their mothers did not see the man and woman as related at all and the girl to them was typically a member only of the extended family.

Stories about this picture often give a good general picture of the subject's view of the environment, especially the family, in somewhat symbolic terms: people with generally favorable and strength-giving childhood relations with the family often remark on the fruitfulness of the field, while the more stress there is on the rocky, barren nature of the farm and the struggle to wrest a living from it, the more a person feels he has been deprived and that the world is a tough place to live in. (The "poor" interpretation is more common among males, the "rich" among females.)

The picture also tends to pull stories dealing with conflicts between personal ambition and family ties, between the old and the new, country life and city life, or between the generations. I agree with Henry's remark that this story may provide evidence about how far the subject sees the traditional as valuable or as inhibiting. Because of these implied conflicts and the large number of persons, it is a particular challenge to the teller's integrative capacity. And because it may be recognized as a painting, or the background interpreted as a painting in front of which the bookish girl is standing, this picture lends itself to easily recognizable defense against these conflicts by evasive and avoidant tactics.

In women subjects, look for the prominence of the theme of role-conflict and how it is resolved: career (via education) versus old-fashioned conception of subservient, child-bearing feminine role.

This picture offers the greatest variety of persons, thus giving a particularly good opportunity to observe range and depth of spontaneous identification (empathy?). Also it is a good one for the theme of work and achievement generally, with many of the same overtones to be looked for in analysis as in stories to picture 1, though the strong pull for achievement themes mentioned above indicates that no particular weight can be given the mere fact of a story to No. 2 dealing with career, work, etc. This is an instance of a more generally applicable point: the weaker the card pull for a given theme, the more diagnostic weight can be given that theme when it emerges. That is, of course, only an application of the general logic of interpreting divergences from expectation, given in Chapter 2, above.

—Another highly useful card, recommended for general use.

CARD 3GF

Murray's description: A young woman is standing with downcast head, her face covered with her right hand. Her left is stretched forward against a wooden door. (Drawing by Samuel Thal; F-15 in the old series redrawn.)

Relatively little by way of normative data is available for this picture, and like most other workers, I have not had much experience with it. In Hartman's (1970) study, it was ranked 22 among 31 cards by 90 experienced clinicians asked to choose a basic set of 10 cards for adults, and was tied for 17th place in a child series by 80 judges. All of the rating studies agree on finding this card among those with the most negative emotional tone, which is of course what was intended.

Again, the sex and general age status of the single person pictured are clear to virtually everyone; though 28% of Murstein's 67 college women referred to her as a "girl," the term is ambiguous. Most subjects in Fleming's normative group of 50 women mentioned nothing else, but reference to the door is common (40%) and to one or the other room fairly common. Remarkably enough, every one of them described the woman as experiencing distress, grief, or unhappiness of some kind. It would require a noteworthy degree of denial or other defense to perceive her as happy, tranquil, or the like. On the other hand, a story involving a despairing woman who eventually finds her way to happiness, if realistically presented, could indicate resiliency and a hopeful strength of character (or, if you like, "ego strength").

The commonest story involves the woman's emotional reaction to the death of a loved person (half or more of the subjects in Fleming's study and Eron's 1953 study). Many of the remaining subjects in both studies told stories about less severe losses or threatened loss—illness, disappointment in love, a quarrel with or rejection by her man; much less often, parental pressure of some kind.

It is important not to make the mistake of assuming that 3BM and 3GF are equivalent, simply because they were intended by Murray to be so. The picture pull for both, of course, stresses unhappy mood, but otherwise it is rather different. Suicidal themes are far more frequent for 3 BM than for 3GF; in the Fleming norms, suicide was mentioned by only 2% of a normal group of women for card 3GF whereas it was mentioned by 12% of her males for card 3BM; similarly, 2% of her women mentioned "committed murder," and an additional 2% "found murdered person," as compared to 10% of the males giving the theme "committed murder" to 3BM. Obviously, the lack of anything suggesting a weapon in this picture must play an important role in this difference. Therefore, a suicidal story to this picture has far more significance than a suicidal story to 3BM. The pictures also differ greatly in sexual ambiguity.

CARD 3BM

Murray's description: On the floor against a couch is the huddled form of a boy with his head bowed on his right arm. Beside him on the floor is a revolver. (Drawing by Christiana D. Morgan; M-13 in the old series.)

Despite the matter-of-fact, declarative tone of Murray's description, the picture was deliberately drawn to be ambiguous in two respects—the sex of the figure and the nature of the object on the floor. Here is one place where having norms is of considerable value, for they show how successful Murray and Morgan were. In Fleming's group of 50 men, 44% saw this figure as male, 50% saw it as female, the other 6% not committing themselves as to sex. Even stronger majorities of male artists, psychiatric residents, and businessmen and 84% of Murstein's (1972) mixed college group called it female; only the Kansas highway cops reversed the trend (76% said it was male). A majority of Eron's (1950) 150 male subjects either identified the figure as female or expressed uncertainty, and there was no difference in the proportion among normal and psychopathological subjects. Among a group of 100 troubled Yale students, 59% called it a girl, 40% a boy (Wittenborn, 1949). Moreover, among applicants for psychiatric residency in Topeka, quite a number of people spent a good deal of time worrying about this problem; and we made a number of bad predictive errors in assuming that concern over the figure's sex was necessarily an indication of strong latent homosexuality or the like. Rather, it seems to be—at least in this group—an indication of tolerance for ambiguity. The figure *is* ambiguous; it is appropriate enough to discuss the problems of whether it is supposed to represent a man or a woman, as long as the discussion is not accompanied by anxiety and is not too prolonged. Be very cautious about diagnosing homosexuality, overt or latent trends, from stories about this picture, despite the experts' statements!

The age of the figure is ambiguous enough so that nothing much can be inferred from it. A plurality—40%—of Fleming's men treated him/her (at least implicitly) as an adult but 20% thought the age to be preadolescent and 26% adolescent.

As to the "revolver," only 18% of Fleming's group identified it as "gun or weapon" (unfortunately, she does not break down this somewhat inclusive category), 20% called it something else specific (toy, keys, pipe, comb, tool, etc.—even a pool of blood), and 12% were undecided; a full 40% (from 19%

to 51% of other groups) did not refer to it. Similarly, 41% of Eron's total male sample were concerned with the object; 12% of them questioned the examiner whether it was a gun, 9% identified it as scissors, comb, knife, etc., 4% asked if it isn't such an object, and 5% could not decide what it is, only about 11% positively identifying it as a gun. My miscellaneous normative groups average out about the same. Therefore, failure to recognize the object as a gun has no serious implications about reality contact. Nevertheless, it is generally safe to assume that the aggressive implications of the object do get through to most subjects on some level and that in most cases the story is a reaction to them, at least in part. One does not have to assume that a failure to mention the object is an evasion, denial, or perceptual defense. I still find it striking that 62% of our highly rated psychiatric residents and only 13% of residents who performed poorly correctly recognized it, and the percentage of perceptual distortions among the latter was 47%, even though this single cue lost a great deal of its discriminative power on cross-validation. —Most subjects (about three out of four) do not mention anything else in the picture.

Not for nothing do some clinicians call this "the suicide card." Stories in which the hero contemplates or commits suicide were given by 26% of Eron's hospitalized veterans, by 16% of his nonhospitalized group, 12% of Fleming's, 23% of artists and businessmen, and from 38% to 50% of patrolmen and psychiatric residents. Even 21% of a sample of (British) 10-year-old boys told stories classified as "central figure has been killed or has committed suicide" (J. C. Coleman, 1969). That means that the mere fact of a suicidal story should not cause alarm. It is much more important to consider what the *resources* of the hero are for coping with the situation, as well as what kind of trauma has been seen as being important enough to warrant suicide. Consider how hopeful and realistic the conception of other people is, as supportive and helpful. Note also how disruptive is the impact of the picture, with its depressive tone and its ambiguity. Can the subject resist the gloom? Does he try to deny it, evade it, get callous or facetious? Whether the ending is happy or not, how *appropriate* is it? The other principal themes elicited by this picture are loss of a loved person (from 3% to 28% in various groups), aftermath of parental punishment or other pressure (highest, at 24%, in 10- and 13-year-old boys, given by 20% of Eron's men, down to 6% in several other adult samples), and failure in some striving (predictably highest among 202 working adults, 28%).

Since this figure is so easily seen as an adolescent or a child, it lends itself rather readily to the emergence of regressive tendencies, particularly as an escape from its depressive implications. For example, it may be portrayed as a little boy who is resting or sleeping, the "gun" being a toy water pistol or some other kind of toy. A word of caution, however: since 22% of Fleming's adult males saw the hero as "asleep or resting," that interpretation cannot be given much pathological weight, even though it is less common in other groups.

—In general, this is universally considered one of the most useful cards (ranked 7th and 2nd for adult and child use by Hartman's judges, for example), even though it is not one of my personal favorites.

CARD 4

Murray's description: A woman is clutching the shoulders of a man whose face and body are averted as if he were trying to pull away from her. (Illustration by C. C. Beall, from *Collier's*, 1940.)

A highly structured, clear picture, this one presents an unmistakable man and woman in their early adult years. Misrecognitions of sex did not occur in *any* normative group (including neurotics and psychotics). The main perceptual distortion (if it may be so described) that occurs is seeing the picture in the background as a real woman—only 6% of businessmen and psychiatric residents called it that or expressed doubt about whether it was real or a picture, 12 to 15% of artists, scientists, and Fleming's men, and 9% of Eron's men; while 10% of Fleming's women spoke of a real woman in the background and an additional 8% were uncertain. (From 4% to 16% of Fleming's subjects mentioned the window, curtains, and/or wall in background, none of them with any distortions.)

A couple of other perceptual points are noteworthy. The main woman in the picture is not infrequently seen as foreign or exotic looking, and 4% of Fleming's group (and slightly more of other samples) gave her a nonwhite ethnic identity; 5% of Eron's men saw her as black. She wears no ring on her ring finger, a minor detail noted by 4% and 8% of Fleming's men and women and by 7% of the businessmen, though by no one of Roe's subjects or of our 51 psychiatric residents. Thus, the mere fact that a subject mentions the lack cannot be taken as sufficient indication of a paranoid, overalert orientation; but when it is pounced on as "evidence" or used to prove something about the characters' intentions, you have something. Likewise, it is rare but possible for a normal person to see the picture in the background as representing his wishes or her fears—4% of Fleming's sample, both male and female, are joined by only a single physicist. Such a theme should be evaluated carefully, therefore, as a possible indicator of a thought disorder.

The man's face clearly expresses some negative affect (conflict, anxiety, anger, jealously are the most commonly mentioned), and the woman's face and posture show concern. From 12% to 50% of men see her as restraining the male figure (only 22% of women do), but pleading, arguing, urging, or making advances are all common interpretations. It ranks second among 20 in ability to pull stories with many emotional words (Ullman, 1957). Clearly, most people see some kind of male-female conflict as implied by this picture. Ask yourself, then, is it faced frankly, or pushed away through making this a stage or movie set or a scene from a story? (Notice that the picture lends itself to this by its obvious character as a magazine illustration.) It is also clearly implied that the woman wants the man to do or not to do something. Does she succeed in influencing him or not, and if so, how? For better or for worse? One common type of story is that the man is going to do something impulsive and often aggressive, such as fight someone because of an insult (to him or her); she represents reason and common sense, or timidity and caution. Another common theme is that the man is torn between sacred and profane love. How does he resolve it? How does she react to his conflict, infidelity, or rejection?

In any event, this is usually a good picture for getting at conceptions of male and female roles, as well as sexual attitudes and conflicts. Pseudomasculine protest often shows up in men (as in stories where the man stoutly resists any influence of the woman) as does competition between the sexes. With women, this picture easily brings out contemptuous and castrative attitudes toward men if present. Do not, however, jump to any conclusions about masculine identification if a woman tells a story in which the male figure is the central character. That occurred in 73% of Eron's female sample, and he cites an unpublished study by Cohen in which 80% of 50 women said, when directly asked, that the main character in their stories about this picture was the man.

If the picture in the background is not brought into the story, inquire after subject is through. ("Did you notice anything else in the picture that you didn't bring into the story?" with the picture turned face down, and then shown to the subject again if necessary.) My impression is that there is not any constant meaning and probably not any particularly important one, whether this is seen as a real woman or as a pinup or poster, though I believe that the latter is what is intended.

—Another highly popular, excellent picture, clearly among the ten best for use with men, women, or children (except, perhaps, the youngest).

CARD 5

Murray's description: A middle-aged woman is standing on the threshold of a half-opened door looking into a room. (Drawing by Samuel Thal; redrawn from 2 in the old series.)

Since its modification for formal distribution, this picture gives rise to many fewer sexual misrecognitions than it did in its original form, which was used by Rapaport. Only one of Eron's 150 men called the woman a man, though that one was a college student, not a patient! No other perceptual distortions were noted. No sexual misrecognition in Murstein's college sample, either.)

Introduced figures are quite common in stories told to this picture; in a group of 75 girls and women from ages 14 to 35 tested by Roberta Kiefer, only 23% did not introduce another person besides the pictured woman. Note what other figures are introduced into the story. If the subject has weak ties to other persons, this picture makes it easy for him to depict a solitary person.

Depending on age, largely, women may identify themselves with the woman and depict certain aspects of their own role-perception or conflict. For men, there is rarely much identification with the pictured woman; they are more likely than women to *introduce* a hero.

Among girls and women, a predominant theme is "curiosity" (Eron, 48%), what Kiefer calls "investigation, inquiry" (56%) or "discovery" (23%). Only 29% of her group give the theme, "investigates, disapproves, scolds for behavior or acts." On the other hand, Eron's (1953) female norms show that 35% of the themes offered were of "parental pressure," plus 7% "disappointment to parent."

For men, however, the main implication is often that this is some kind of mother figure watching (illicit sex, for 14% of Eron's men) with surprise or disapproval; curiosity (42%) is only slightly more frequent, in Eron's male norms, than "parent is prohibitive, compelling, censuring, punishing, quarreling with child" (37%). There seems to be some picture pull for the more negative aspects of mother, but the lack of a second figure may contribute to the fact that this picture rarely elicits stories of much emotional intensity; Eron and Kiefer agree that it is unusually high in the percentage of stories with neutral emotional tone or mood, and it was one of the seven lowest in emotional words produced in Ullmann's (1957) study of 175 male VA inpatients.

It should not be surprising, therefore, to find that this picture ranked 18th out of 20 on "transcendence" in Gurel and Ullmann's (1958) study. That means that stories tend to go little beyond picture description. It is accordingly not a particularly popular choice for a basic TAT set, and is best used for additional probing in the areas for which it is suited when other pictures (e.g., 6BM, 7GF) seem to need supplementation.

CARD 6GF

Murray's description: A young woman sitting on the edge of a sofa looks back over her shoulder at an older man with a pipe in his mouth who seems to be addressing her. (Part of an illustration from the *Saturday Evening Post*, 1941.)

In Kiefer's norms, the setting is usually unspecified and the heroine is typically not specifically characterized. But 32% of her girls and women saw the setting as being in a home, 4% in a hotel or a restaurant or at a dance. The heroine was a career woman in 16% of the cases, the wife of the man in 12%, his daughter in 4% (this interpretation was given by teen-agers only); 7% of Murstein's 81 college women called them father and daughter.

This last finding is interesting in light of the fact that Murray chose this picture specifically as a father-daughter picture. Instead, it gives the reaction of a woman to a somewhat older and dominant man, which undoubtedly has many implications about her relation to her father, particularly in its sexualized aspects, but it does not give the overt attitudes toward father in anything like the way that 6BM gives overt attitudes toward mother in men. 23% of Kiefer's subjects saw the man as some other kind of relative of the woman. Her feelings were described as surprise or shock by 43%, anger or annoyance by 27%, fear or anxiety by 16%, appreciation or interest by 7%, and other interpretations by 4%; only 3% gave no feelings. The main themes were as follows: girl surprised, startled, annoyed by suggestion or act of man, 33%; girl rejects, denies, suggestion or advice, 16%; girl discovers ulterior motive for act of man, 12%; wife and husband in conflict; [or?] girl runs away after disciplinary action (teen-agers primarily), 11%; girl forced to retract, accept suggestions or job, 4%. The following themes were given by teen-agers only: comforted, grateful for help, suggestion or actions, 4%; learns news of friend, meets old acquaintance, 4%.

Eron's women gave similar interpretations; he classified themes as "pressure from partner" (28%), "fear, worry" (17%), "ordinary activity" (15%), "pursuit of partner" (10%), "seduction" (10%), other sexual themes an additional 10%, "parental pressure" (7%), and "accusation" (7%). The mood elicited is more often on the negative than the positive side.

On the whole, I believe that Henry (1956, p. 247) underestimated the degree of pull for tense, unpleasantly toned reactions of the woman in the picture, and thus somewhat misleadingly gives us to believe that seeing "some difficulty or disruption in the relationship" between the pictured characters indicates that the teller "mistrusts interpersonal relations, especially in their sexual implications. . . . "

The failure of this picture to pull father-daughter stories may account for its relative neglect by clinicians. Judging by my own limited trials, Symonds' picture B8 seems better for the purpose.

CARD 6BM

Murray's description: A short elderly woman stands with her back turned to a tall young man. The latter is looking downward with a perplexed expression. (Drawing by Christiana D. Morgan; M11 in the old series.)

Murray and Morgan surely succeeded in producing a mother-son card: the sexes of the two figures are only very rarely misrecognized and then by psychotics, and better than nine out of ten tellers call them mother and son. Moreover, large majorities of all normative groups see both as anxious, upset, or otherwise stirred by negative emotions (not infrequently guilt on his part, anger on hers). His hat and her handkerchief are rarely mentioned, but lend themselves to obsessional or paranoid attempts to deduce the nature of the situation and the characters' future actions. Eron reports perceptual distortions only among his psychotic subjects, but in 10% of them (which is high, in my experience).

Story content tends to center on conflict between the generations, usually involving some rupture in their past relationship (through marriage, new job, being drafted, etc.). The importance of general life situation is dramatically shown by the fact that not one of Roe's eminent scientists or artists described a conflict over a new job, whereas 20% of our applicants for a psychiatric residency did so, and from a quarter to a half of the latter made the bone of contention the son's marriage (from 4 to 10% in other groups except artists—28%). The main alternative theme, given by approximately three out of ten men (but by 45% of male students seen for counseling by Wittenborn, 1949), is their reaction to bad news, which the son typically brings, often the death of a third person or the son's criminal actions. Altogether, 20% of the Yale men's, but only 4% of Eron's men's stories contained themes of the son's guilt.

Since the mother-son implications are so overwhelming, any story *not* on this theme is suspect as an evasion and points to some particularly painful conflict with respect to mother. The nature of the story must be taken in relation to characteristic conflicts of persons in the subject's age range. From college age through the twenties, the main thing is breaking away from the tie to mother; absence of this theme should attract your attention. The main question is how the conflict between the generations is handled. Does the man succeed? With how much guilt? Is he bitter about his mother's attempts to hold him? Does he have any ability to see the thing from his mother's viewpoint?

Note also that any mother-son situation implicitly involves the father somehow. How is he handled? Often enough, he is not introduced at all, but it is something to watch out for. Another theme that occurs not infrequently in the records of patients, particularly those who have great difficulty in expressing hostility directly toward their parents but who do so in passive and indirect ways, is that the son has got into some kind of trouble which is breaking his poor mother's heart, and he is very unhappy but there is nothing he can do about it. Remember that it is the subject's story, and the reaction of the mother, while obviously not a happy one from the picture pull, does not have to remain sad; the next moment after the picture, she can perfectly well turn around and embrace her son and wish him well, or the like. So, stories in which the action of the son cause the mother grief or pain can be interpreted as evidences of hostility toward her. In any event, this picture tends to evoke affect; it was top in the number of emotional words in the stories it stimulated in Ullmann's (1957) study.

In stories about the breaking of the silver cord, a mature and conflict-free resolution will often specify that the mother's grief is short-lived, that they do see each other afterwards and work out some new kind of relationship. Where the break has occasioned a good deal of pain, bitterness, or other difficulty, this story will often emphasize the finality of the son's departure, the unhappiness of both continuing in time, or other unhappy subsequent events.

—All sources agree that this is an excellent card, one of the most widely used and indispensable in any basic set with males; it was ranked third from the top by Hartman's judges for either adults or children.

CARD 7GF

Murray's description: An older woman is sitting on a sofa close beside a girl, speaking or reading to her. The girl, who holds a doll in her lap, is looking away. ("Fairy Tales" by Shulkin, The Metropolitan Museum of Art, New York.)

Fleming's norms show all of her adult female sample having no difficulty recognizing the sex and relative ages of the two figures, though only 78% of them called the relationship that of mother and daughter. The main alternative (given by 16% of both her sample and Murstein's) was a servant, governess, or nurse; in my experience, this is particularly characteristic of upperclass women whose own childhood experience was often with surrogates rather than with their mothers. Over a third interpreted the mother's attitude as consoling, loving, or concerned; 44% saw it as only reading, instructing, or amusing; and according to 14%, she is "not concerned, reluctant to respond to girl." The book was mentioned or implied by eight out of ten subjects, but 44% made no reference to the doll. The commonest perceptual distortion, interpreting the doll as a real baby, occurred in 4% of this normal sample and in 8% of Eron's subjects, but only uneducated, immature, or psychotic patients have ever told me that it is the girl's own baby. The girl is intended to be preadolescent, I believe; 6% of the Fleming sample called her "too old for dolls."

The typical story content is prosaic: the older woman is reading to the girl (58%) or telling her "the facts of life" (20%), or teaching her something (14%). Fleming's sample usually portrayed her as unresponsive, no doubt because she is looking away: 20% saw the girl's reaction as enjoyment; 20% as reluctance to accept a lesson; 20% said that she is daydreaming; 18% felt that she is rebellious, wanting to leave, and 22% said that she is moody, lonely, sad, or unhappy.

An important difference between this picture and either of the two pictures for males of relationships to parents is that the hero-figure is a child. Consequently the kind of postadolescent themes common to picture 6BM do not show up so much here, and stories with a strong undercurrent of desire to break away from the mother have somewhat more personal implications. When the particular characteristics of this picture are taken into account, however, it is an excellent one for bringing out attitudes toward the mother or maternal attitudes toward their own children in older women.

—This is a commonly used picture, ranked 7th by Hartman's clinicians for use in a child series but only 14th for an adult series (possibly because he did not ask for separate choices for use with men and with women). Because of good results with her transcendence measure, Weisskopf (1950) considered this one of the five potentially most productive cards.

CARD 7BM

Murray's description: A gray-haired man is looking at a younger man who is sullenly staring into space. (Redrawn by Samuel Thal from M-15 in the old series.)

Sexual misidentification on this card has not occurred in any normative sample, and other perceptual distortions were found by Eron in only 2% of his patient population. The relative ages of the men are much more unambiguous than the facial expressions; only 62% of Fleming's sample interpreted the younger man's affect in terms similar to Murray's (and as few as 37% of businessmen but over 80% of psychiatric residents—so this is a crude measure of psychological mindedness). In his college sample, Wittenborn found that 28% saw him as "compliant," 18% each "impetuous" and in conflict. From 5% (biologists) to 22% (artists, Fleming's males) interpreted the expression in such positive terms as "loving" or "capable." Such upbeat interpretations are more likely to indicate bland denial or sugary reaction-formations than deep-going self-trust and benignity of outlook. Roe's scientists were about equally likely to describe the older man's expression in positive as in negative terms, but in all other normative groups the benign interpretations predominate—again, more than half of the psychiatric residents called him kind, calm, glad, or the like, as against a little over 30% calling him grim, sly, sad, etc., while such terms were used by only 17% and 10% of the businessmen. Sixty percent of Wittenborn's college counsellees called him "objective and sympathetic," only 9% "evil." As compared to 6BM, there is less pull for the older figure to be seen specifically as parental; only about half of our normative males called him the father. Nevertheless, stories elicited by this picture are valuable sources of attitudes toward the father and paternal authority in general, and when the relationship is described as something other than father and son, the attitudes are more likely to be defended against (unconscious).

In both this and 6BM, a not infrequent theme is the young man who is in trouble of some kind, who comes to father willingly or not but provides his parent with unpleasant and distressing news. This very often stands for an underlying attitude of resentment and hostility that cannot be expressed openly, leading to self-defeating strategies of hitting back at parents (who have been partly internalized—an essentially depressive maneuver). Here is a sign of difficulty in the treatment situation; apparent compliance and cooperation followed by self-destructive acting out may be predicted from such a theme. Attitudes relevant to treatment may often be inferred from stories told to this picture.

In one form or another, the conflict between generations is likely to come up. Look for signs of basic respect of hero for older man, and of hero for self; if father-figure's attitude is kindly, can the young man make use of it in any but a parasitic way? If so, you have signs of ability to make a constructive identification and ultimately take over father's role, versus the hopeless feeling of inability ever to compete with the father in his own world.

See remarks on 6BM for significance of time of life at which subject tells the story, in relation to the theme he gives. The struggle to break away from the family often appears in postadolescents' 7BM stories, but in different and subtler forms.

Four main plots account for most of the stories told about this picture. (A) The older man helps, advises, consoles, or protects the younger. (B) The elder is critical of, rebukes, or is in conflict with the younger, pressuring, punishing, compelling him or the like. (C) The two are plotting or involved in a crime or "shady deal." (D) Other—mostly banal conversations, occasionally cooperative and positive activities:

	Type of story theme			
Normative group	(A)	(B)	(C)	(D)
English schoolboys: age 10	18%	21%	21%	39%
age 13	26%	21%	28%	25%
Eron's males	77%	25%	3%	?
Fleming's males	64%	26%	4%	6%
Psychiatric residents:				
Highest-rated	80%	6%	0%	14%
Unselected	60%	5%	15%	20%
Lowest-rated	53%	7%	20%	20%
Biologists and physicists	49%	8%	10%	33%
Artists	34%	28%	0%	38%
Businessmen	67%	0%	10%	23%

Type A themes generally connote a variety of favorable attitudes toward the father (especially in boys and young men who are not yet certain enough of their adult identity to have given up looking to their elders for support) and toward authorities in general. This type includes some unfavorable orientations as well, however, especially when the father figure is seen as smug, his advice well-meaning but useless or not wanted. These last interpretations often indicate reaction formations or protests covering love and dependence, and are not as deeply troublesome as the next two. Type B implies a struggle against a dominating, punitive, or authoritarian father, a rebellion that may not be inconsistent with basic respect. Type C suggests fantasies of victimization, even paranoid disgust, though its frequency in some of the normative groups should convey caution in any extreme interpretation; much depends on how it is given. At the least, it connotes distrust of conventional authority, a corruptible superego, or a tendency to externalize blame.

—Clearly a useful picture, third strongest puller of emotional words, and among almost everybody's basic set of ten for adults and children. It is occasionally used with women because of the lack of a good father-daughter picture.

CARD 8GF

Murray's description: A young woman sits with her chin in her hand looking off into space. ("Lili" by Taubes, The Metropolitan Museum of Art, New York.)

According to Eron (1953), the main themes are happy reminiscence, 33%; aspiration, 20%; occupational concern, 15%; economic pressure, 15%; reminiscence or rumination, 15%; ordinary activity, 15%; posing, 13% (always an indicator of some evasiveness, I think); and exhaustion, 10%. Despite his first category, above, his emotional tone ratings of the same stories include not positive ratings and mostly rather negative ones. Kiefer's norms indicate that positive affect is expressed about twice as often as negative. The object of the heroine's thoughts was, in Kiefer's words, "job, task, life-situation" for 31% of her subjects (but note that they were predominantly young, unmarried working women or girls going to school, while 40% of Eron's sample were pregnant women). Kiefer's sample gave the following stories: "poor working woman dreams of brighter future, travel, fame," 48%; "contemplates situation [or] activity, and is happy, content," 20%; "thinks carefully of career [or] change in plan," 12%.

On the whole, these bits of normative data confirm Bellak's characterization of most stories as having "shallow, contemplative themes" and his note that the card is rarely useful. I do not recall ever having used it, and see no reason to start doing so. In Hartman's survey, it was just about at the bottom in frequency of choice for either an adult or a child set.

CARD 8BM

Murray's description: An adolescent boy looks straight out of the picture. The barrel of a rifle is visible at one side, and in the background is the dim scene of a surgical operation, like a reverie-image. (Drawing by Samuel Thal, after an illustration by Carl Mueller from *Collier's*.)

This picture is the most difficult and challenging of the ones considered so far, containing a good deal of not very clearly depicted detail, which is hard to make out and perhaps even harder to integrate into a coherent whole. It is therefore a good one to test the kind of organizing ability tapped by W+ in the Rorschach. But it goes further, since there is not only perceptual organizing to be done but the need to account for conceptually disparate elements—the anachronistic contrast of a crude operation by lantern light and the foreground boy in more or less contemporaneous clothes, the implicit contrast between levels of reality of foreground and background, the contrast between the rifle and the scalpel, and the various degrees of tilt in the picture.

It is not surprising, then, that this picture gave rise to more perceptual distortions than any other in Eron's (1950) study, which used all 20 cards for males. The only distortion picked up by Fleming[1] was one subject's calling the figure being operated on a woman (2%); Eron tallied this one separately, finding a uniform 4% (again, a single subject) in each of his groups except 8% in one of his psychotic samples. Wittenborn also reports 4% among Yale men, Murstein 7% among his college men. Most subjects solve the perceptual problems posed by the various objects in the picture by not mentioning them. As to the persons, the boy was described as postadolescent or adult by 8% of Fleming's men, 10% of psychiatric residents, 6% of artists, and 17% of

[1]Unfortunately, the fact that Fleming found no distortions of most pictured objects meant that her scoring categories for this picture did not allow for them. I did not notice that fact until after my assistant had scored and refiled all the data, and her scoring leaves it somewhat unclear whether or not the "other" interpretations of the miscellaneous objects in the picture—gun, knife, lamp, table or bunk, and window—were distortions. Four percent of Fleming's men mentioned "books," presumably a distorted interpretation of the window in the upper right corner; if we include that and the "other" category, 5% to 10% of artists, psychiatric residents, and businessmen misperceived something in this picture. Eron's most common "distortion" was interpreting the background as an actual scene (hospitalized subsample, 35%; nonhospitalized, 20%). He also includes "background and foreground are two different events separated in time" (3%) and "reverses so that figure on table dreams of figure in foreground" (5%). Just over 1% of his subjects misidentified the sex of the boy in the foreground.

businessmen, so this deviation from Murray's description cannot be given pathological weight. Of the other three figures, only the man holding the light is more often omitted than mentioned.

Interpretations of the scene are divided between calling the background scene a fantasy or image (Fleming's men, 68%; about 90% of artists, psychiatrists, and businessmen) and seeing it as real. The former interpretation is typically that the boy dreams of his future as a doctor or visualizes operations of the past (given approximately equally often, by one- to two-fifths of each group). Less often, he is thinking about an operation currently going on (from 5% to 10% of all groups except artists, 24%) or imagining being a patient himself (from 4% to 10%, again artists being the exception: 18%; among Eron's men, 15%). His thoughts and feelings are usually ambitious longings to be a doctor (40% of Eron's sample, 50% of businessmen, 64% of Fleming's men, up to 75% of high-rated psychiatric residents, but only 24% of artists), or hopes that the injured man will live (no businessmen, very few psychiatrists, 12–20% of other groups); other attributed motives are scattered. Oddly enough, in 24% of Fleming's men, the boy has shot someone; 13% of businessmen say so, but this theme was not found in the stories of 51 psychiatric residents or 17 artists. In just over 1% of the total normative group, the boy has shot himself, clearly a pathological theme. Incidentally, the failure of the boy to become a doctor in the story should not be taken as a sign of inadequacy, lack of real achievement motivation, or the like; only a minority of any normative group, including highly successful and even eminent people, told stories in which the boy actually got his MD.

I have the impression that there is quite a marked class difference in interpretations of this picture. Boys and men who come from families in which professional aspirations are common are much more likely to give the dreaming-about-being-a-doctor story, whereas boys who come from economically underprivileged, unsophisticated backgrounds are more likely to take the whole thing literally and tell a story about a hunting accident. It is quite rare, actually, that a deliberate act of shooting occurs in stories to this picture, so that the accident theme should not be considered unusually defensive.

The basic motive touched on here is aggression, with implications of both direct and sublimated forms. So this gives us a chance to see how it is handled by the subject, on which level, where directed. Often, when direct, the boy pictured (hero) has shot someone "accidentally," and we can see who it was, what the outcome of the operation is, how the boy is punished, etc. Aggression may even be self-directed in the rather infrequent story in which hero fantasies self as being operated on.

—I have found this a useful picture, and others seem to agree: Ullmann found it 9th most frequently used by VA trainees, and Hartman reports it in similar rank but among the first ten for both adult and child use.

CARD 9GF

Murray's description: A young woman with a magazine and a purse in her hand looks from behind a tree at another young woman in a party dress running along a beach. (Illustration from *Collier's*, 1950.)

The figures are unambiguously young women, though the one behind the tree was seen as the older by 18% of Fleming's women, and was even called the other's mother by 4%. She (at right) has a rather ambiguous expression, however; 32% called her "calm, quiet, maternal" while an equal number saw her as "upset, afraid, [or] suspicious"; 10% called her "sad" and 6%, "triumphant" or "pleased." By contrast, the other was called anxious, angry, or upset by 78% of Fleming's women, only 10% saying anything like "happy, loving, [or] confident."

The other elements of the picture are more often not mentioned than specified; only 6% alluded to the purse, and the "magazine"—only slightly more often discussed—is easily seen as a book or papers. The water is the focus of most perceptual distortions. Among Eron's sample, 3% saw a reflection in it; 8% of Fleming's sample located the scene in the desert, hills, or country with no mention of water and probably misperception of it. Psychotics occasionally give even more bizarre interpretations of the mise-en-scene.

Typical stories are mostly concerned with conflict between the women (54%, Fleming), fairly often (32%, Fleming) rivalry for a man. Eron (1953) tallies an unusually large number of themes for this picture, led off by "escape from perilous environment," 33%, "curiosity," 28%, "jealousy," 22%, "fear, worry," 18%, "pressure from peer," 13%, "unfaithful male partner," 13%, and "sibling rivalry," 10%. He includes 16 other themes, ending with "suicide," 3%, which did not occur in Fleming's group. The latter did in 4% of the cases tell stories of crime or murder; compare Eron's "aggression from environment," 7%.

The fact that the picture presents one woman who is watching another in such a way that it is clear she does not want to be seen lends this picture very obviously to paranoid-like themes, which should be therefore interpreted somewhat cautiously. If there seems to be a problem of sibling rivalry in a woman, this is a good picture to bring it out, in its various ramifications. Since the girl running on the beach is wearing a long party dress and the woman behind the tree is dressed more plainly, often being seen in a servant's uniform, this picture lends itself also to expressions of concern with social differences, and envy.

—A good picture with adult or adolescent females, this one was ranked 20th by clinicians for use with children.

CARD 9BM

Murray's description: Four men in overalls are lying on the grass taking it easy.
(Drawing by Samuel Thal, after a photograph, "Siesta," by Ulric Maisel.)

Little by way of norms is available for this picture. From Eron we learn that this picture leads all the other 19 for males in "themes of equilibrium," and that 72% of his mixed group of college men and VA patients gave stories of "retirement"—i.e., "central character asleep, resting, etc." Other common themes were exhaustion (15%), lounging or wasting time (11%), tranquility (10%), and poverty (9%). There were no misrecognitions of sex, but from 6% to 12% of his groups saw one (or more) of the men as Negro, the only deviation I have encountered with any frequency.

In Wittenborn's (1949) study, the pictured men were "workers," 49% (Eron, 50%; Murstein, 40%), "idlers," 35% (Eron, "tramps," 31%; Murstein, 13%), "fugitives," 15%, and "pursuers," 1% (or "soldiers," Eron and Murstein, 11%). In only half of the students' stories was one figure singled out as hero.

Ullmann reports that stories told about this picture had the lowest average content of emotional words, and it ranked 14th out of 20 in transcendence (Gurel & Ullmann, 1958). It has very little apparent pull for hostility or achievement, but this last fact can occasionally make it useful. I have seen compulsively striving executives tell stories in which these resting figures are just having a lunch break from their hard work, and others in whom the "work ethic" was less fixed spinning out wishful tales of enjoyable bumming around. The bodily contact of the men may stir up longings for close companionship or sometimes homosexual anxieties. And their obviously lower-class appearance enables the picture to elicit prejudicial attitudes toward those who do not work, Blacks, hoboes, or the like. Of all the pictures in the set, this one is most likely to stimulate stories without a single hero.

—On the whole, most clinicians do not like this picture and it is seldom routinely used. Hartman lists it as tied with 8GF for last place for an adult set, tied for next-to-last place for a child set.

CARD 10

Murray's description: A young woman's head against a man's shoulder. (Drawing by Samuel Thal, after a photograph which was 5 in the old series.)

The sexes of the two characters are not nearly as clear as Murray's description implies; Eron (1950) reports that 5% of his males and 10% of his females misrecognizes the sex of one or both. There were no misrecognitions of the figure on the left among Fleming's 100 subjects, but 5% of physicists and 25% of artists saw "him" as female. The one on the right is even more ambiguous; 2% of Fleming's males and 4% of her females called "her" a male, while the percentages in our other groups were: physicists, 5%, artists, 6%, and biologists, 10%. Almost any adult age can be imputed to them. There is also something about the picture that tends to make many subjects (at least 10%) see these people as foreign in nationality. From 36% (artists) to 83% (Fleming's males and females) of subjects see them as a married couple or lovers. Correspondingly, love is the most frequently seen emotion; it was attributed to one or both of the characters by over 70% of Fleming's subjects (though the artists and scientists tended to attribute fewer feelings and a more even balance of loving and nonloving affect).

Stories tend to center about themes of consolation (e.g., for loss of a child), in about a third of the males and 18 to 38% of females; saying farewell or greeting one another after a separation, another third; the remainder being fairly evenly spread over reminiscing, dancing, or a love scene. (Frequencies of these themes differ slightly in the scientists, and artists a bit more so, but they seem to agree well with results from Eron's male and female samples). Not one member of either the Fleming or Eron male or female groups gave any story involving deception of one person by the other, pretended feelings with underlying hostility, or other defensive interpretation attempting to deny the obviously close and warm relationship. These latter types of interpretations are found in character disorders and paranoid patients not infrequently.

I have had a number of experiences of sexually preoccupied subjects' blocking and being embarrassed by this picture, which they see as one of sexual intimacy. The pull of the picture, however, is clearly for a more sublimated kind of love relationship. On the whole, it is the happiest of the adult pictures (in terms of Eron's emotional tone ratings, only his nonhospitalized males telling predominantly unhappy stories; and in rating studies by Goldfried and Zax, 1965, and by Newbigging, 1955).

—Generally considered a rather useful picture, it was rated 8th for an adult set, and tied for 11th place for a child set (Hartman, 1970).

CARD 11

Murray's description: A road skirting a deep chasm between high cliffs. On the road in the distance are obscure figures. Protruding from the rock wall on one side is the long head and neck of a dragon. ("Die Fels-Schlucht" by Boecklin, in the Schack Gallery, Munich; 6 in the old series.)

This picture is vague enough for perceptual distortions to be fairly common (though oddly enough Eron lists none for either males or females!).

The dragon, to begin with, was noted as such or described as a monster, dinosaur, etc., by only 58% of eminent and highly intelligent physicists, 68% of the Kansas highway patrol, 79% of biologists, but 98% of 51 applicants for psychiatric residency! The discrepancy in favor of the last group testifies not to the special affinity of psychiatrists for monsters but to the power of a set: only they were asked to "tell a fairy story, such as you might tell to a child." Even with this priming, one resident interpreted the dragon as a road with a fence further up the mountain, in which he was joined by one or two members each of the biologists, physicists, and policemen. Even those who spoke of a dragon occasionally saw the head as a tail—2% of patrolmen, 4% of residents, 11% of physicists, but of course no biologist. Another common "distortion" is to see what I believe is intended to be a group of persons and pack animals nearing the bridge as a single insect or other creature; from 5% to 21% of my four normative groups did so. (Those who gave this interpretation sometimes saw the whole scale as smaller, the dragon being a lizard— physicists, 5%, patrolmen, 6%.) The single human figure, who looks to me like a man running ahead across the bridge, was not noted by majorities of all groups except the psychiatrists, again, probably for the same reason. An even more striking effect of the fairy-story set is that only with it (and then in 30%–40%)[2] was there the introduced figure of a "fair maiden" or princess, or of a villain (7%–20%), even more remarkably, of the hero's father (12%– 20%) or nonhuman introduced figures (5%–14%).

Turning to the objects in the picture, the road was mentioned by majorities of all groups except the highway patrol, the pile of rocks by 15%– 28% of the four normative samples, the bridge by at least two-thirds of all groups except the patrolmen (24%), the chasm by 21%–50%, the luminous area by 5%–18%, and the cliffs by 11%–30%. The commonest perceptual distortion here was to see the rock walls or cliffs as the walls of a castle (4% of the patrolmen did so, 11% of the scientists, and 18% of the residents).

Typical stories may be grouped into two categories: those with human and those with animal heroes. I believe that the choice of one or the other gives a clue to the teller's maturity, an animal hero having much the same connotations as FM (animal movement) predominance over M in the Rorschach, though these two indicators do not always coincide. The available norms are of limited value, because the nature of the plot depends greatly on the instructions. I strongly recommend asking for a fairy story; otherwise, many patients and other subjects can do very little with it, and the picture is not infrequently thought poor on this account. The spontaneous incidence of fairy stories was only 2% in the patrolmen, 5% among scientists, 1% among Eron's hospitalized veterans but 12% in his unhospitalized group; with standard instructions, the results were plotless descriptions of the

---

[2]These percentages indicate ranges across three subgroups: an unselected class, a group of highest-rated residents, and a group of lowest-rated residents.

picture in 17% of Eron's hospitalized but 4% of his nonhospitalized men, in 5% of physicists, 11% of patrolmen, and 16% of biologists, while my special instructions obtained plots from *every* residency applicant. It is a little hard to know how many of the differences in plots between the psychiatric residents and other groups are attributable to the fact that we asked the former to tell fairy stories; but that seems to be responsible for the fact that *only* they told about the rescue of someone from captivity, or stories in which the hero must perform labors to win the heroine, or stories told with dragon as hero or from the dragon's viewpoint. If the last type are grouped together with all other plots with animal heroes, the proportions do not differ so greatly: 13% among both psychiatrists and cops, 10% of biologists and 20% of physicists, and 23% of Kiefer's female sample, while there is virtually no overlap in actual plots. About half of the psychiatrists' stories were of the above kind; in the other half a smaller animal overcomes the larger. Neither of those plots was given by the scientists or policemen, who tended to tell stories in which a large animal searches for food and attacks a smaller one. Across all male groups, however, the most popular single plot was one of travelers attacked or threatened by a monster (about 20%–30% or 41% if this is what is meant by Eron's "aggression from impersonal source").

Plots told by all but 13% of Kiefer's normative group of girls and women fall into four categories: "Monster attacks and gets man or smaller animals," 24%; "men or animals attacked by monster but escape," 17%; "civilization, people destroyed by slide; inhabited by animals," 16%; "man, boy, girl, animals discover and view scene," 13%. She notes that many adult women offered "fantastic and symbolic themes" based on the contrast of darkness and light; 7% of Eron's men's stories were symbolic.

The other available norms with women are Eron's, also based on standard instructions. He reports the following as the main themes: "aggression from environment," 38%; "escape from perilous environment," 18%; "fear, worry," 15%; "aggression to peer," 13%; and "curiosity," 10%; 17% merely described the picture.

By asking for a fairy story, you get a chance to see whether (and how far) the subject can allow himself to regress ("in the service of the ego") to a style of thinking a good deal closer to the primary process, or whether this idea is too threatening to him. With some patients it happens that the fairy story idea is not so threatening that they must avoid it, but it opens up the door to terrifying infantile fantasies; while for others, the threat is so great that only the most painfully stereotyped rescue-the-beautiful-princess stories come through. The dragon can be made the hero with real humor; if so, I think it has the implication of immaturity spoken of above plus a straining after effect. Particularly malign are stories in which the dragon is given explicitly sexual wishes or aims.

Whether—as is usually the case in fairy stories—the hero has to perform labors or to rescue a maiden from a horrible monster, you have an opportunity to get at basic fantasies of adequacy or inadequacy in the way that the hero copes with the threat posed by the dragon. An ingenious, appropriate, and successful method of killing the dragon or getting around him is a positive sign of "ego strength."

One type of story that occurs every so often with men, not only women, is the destruction of civilization. Sometimes this has all the earmarks of a schizophrenic world-destruction fantasy, with the damage being done by monsters who break through from subterranean caverns in a beautiful symbolism of "instinctual anxiety." But this may also be found in nonschizophrenic people! The way in which the theme is handled makes all the difference.

With the fairy-story instruction, one usually gets Oedipal themes, the infantile attitudes coming out much more clearly than in cards 6 or 7. I have also seen several striking parables of the primal scene in response to this picture. With special instructions, it is a valuable card; without it, not.

CARD 12F

Murray's description: The portrait of a young woman. A weird old woman with a shawl over her head is grimacing in the background. (Drawing by Christiana D. Morgan, after a painting by Augustus John; F-11 in the old series.)

Fleming's normative group as usual were unanimous in getting the sex correct in case of both women, and there was no reversal of the obvious age difference. Eron (1953) reports, however, that 3% of his group (2 out of 60) called the younger figure male, and Murstein reports that 4% of his college women misrecognized sex. Fleming's group split approximately in thirds over their basic interpretation. The 30% who saw them as related were equally split between mother-daughter and grandmother-granddaughter; Murstein reports 7% and 15%, however. Another third offered symbolic interpretations, most often (12% each) a woman with her real self, and the same woman in youth and old age. The remainder saw them in a scattering of miscellaneous ways.

Frequent themes, as classified by Eron, are few: "disappointment in parent," 22%; "parental pressure," 20%; "succorance [sic; he means nurturance, e.g., aid] from parent," 10%; and "reminiscence, sad," 10%. I find Fleming's classification of plots more helpful. She found that 30% of her women saw a woman with a vision or symbolic representation of her evil self (12%) or of old age, the future, etc. In 16% of the cases, the young woman is being tempted by an evil older one; in 8% the two are in some kind of conflict; to these might be added 2% each who saw them as witches and who were blocked, complaining that the picture was evil. In 12%, the younger woman cares for the older (compare Eron's 7%, nurturance to parent), and 8% told various stories of cooperation between them.

Sometimes, when paranoid or other psychotic trends are suspected, this picture will bring out material from a woman better than any other. Be careful, however, not to confuse malign interpretations proceeding from feelings of victimization with imaginative productions by nonpsychotic women who pick up and use the quality of weirdness that the picture was intended to have, and which serves as an invitation for and excuse for unrealistic stories. But that is just one more facet of the general problem of distinguishing between pathological and controlled, creative regression. Symbolic stories may have pathological implications, especially when given by relatively uneducated, unsophisticated people, but if there is as much card pull for them as with this picture, go slow in inferring thought disorder.

An interesting paper by Hunt and Smith (1966) reports a study of this card. Even at that time, the figure of the younger woman had taken on negative connotations not originally intended, at times being seen as lesbian, unattractive, too mannish, etc. When the picture was presented with this figure redrawn and brought up to date, there was a marked change in apperception of her and of the relationship between the two.

—All in all, considering the fact that 4% of Fleming's subjects were blocked and the percentage of indefinite endings was unusually high, plus low ratings in Hartman's study, this picture cannot be recommended for routine use in a basic set. It is useful for special problems of the kinds adumbrated above, however.

CARD 12M

Murray's description: A young man is lying on a couch with his eyes closed. Leaning over him is the gaunt form of an elderly man, his hands stretched out above the face of the reclining figure. (Drawing by Samuel Thal; M-14 in the old series, considerably modified.)

Normative data for this picture are skimpy, unfortunately. Eron reports that 13% of his mixed group misrecognized the sex of the reclining figure. This error was about as common among his college students as among neurotic and psychotic veterans; it occurred in 26% of college men and 16% of women (Murstein). An additional 10% of Eron's men said that the characters are same age (young). Seldom noted details of the picture, the hunched back of the older man and the halo-like light shading behind his head, are at times fastened on by obsessional or paranoid patients as the basis for reasoning about the picture. It is fair to say that the frequent misrecognition of sex points to an actual ambiguity, and that an interpretation that stresses effeminacy or bisexuality of the reclining figure may be a sensitive response to something that is there, even though a personal preoccupation may also be expressed.

Eron's (1950) norms contain a good many themes, the commonest of which are hypnosis, 40%; prayer, seeking consolation from God, religious conflict, or religious awakening, 21%; and death or illness of hero, 20%, or of the old man's son, 15%. Other fairly common themes, among psychiatric patients and college students, are: the young man is resting or sleeping, a physician is attending an invalid, or a therapist of some kind is attempting to treat a troubled person—in either event, often a psychiatric patient.

This picture often gives information about latent homosexual anxieties. Apparently the whole relationship between the extremely passive figure on the couch and the advancing, dominant figure of the older man, with his knee on the couch in what a number of subjects describe as an unprofessional manner, suggests the possibility of a homosexual attack. More generally, this picture lends itself to the projection of feelings of domination by father figures, who are not infrequently portrayed as evil, having a Svengali-like influence and forcing the young man into crime or destroying him. Thus, it is a good card to get at underlying emotional attitudes toward the father.

A good many years ago, White (1938) reported a striking relationship between hypnotizability and the telling of stories about the predecessor to this picture in which the hypnosis was successful. A good many other investigators have tried to replicate this finding with the present version but without success.

This picture was useful in testing psychiatric residents, because they frequently identified themselves with the older man and gave stories of hypnotherapy in which their attitudes toward the treatment situation, toward patients, and toward the whole problem of prognosis could be read. Very likely, the picture would have similar value in testing psychologists, psychotherapists, and psychoanalysts (especially applicants for training).

Likewise, patients who are contemplating psychotherapy or psychiatric treatment often give in their stories important clues to their subsequent orientations, conceptions of therapy, fears of intrusion, and other transferences, which can be helpful to treatment planning. It is not encouraging, for example, to have the potential patient tell a story about a quack who either fails to help an ill person or whose unscientific methods do actual harm, however well such stories can be justified by the older man's posture and appearance.

—On the whole, a good picture for general clinical use. It was ranked 9th as a candidate for a basic ten-card set for adults, and 11.5 for children (Hartman).

CARD 12BG

Murray's description: A rowboat is drawn up on the bank of a woodland stream. There are no human figures in the picture. (Photograph by H. G. Grainger.)

The lack of normative data indicates how seldom this picture is used, particularly with adults. Goldfried and Zax (1965), in their semantic differential rating study, found it to have strongly pleasant connotations for both male and female college students. It is probably the pleasantest, most relaxed picture in the set, and is special also in being the only structured, realistic picture without human beings. It poses the problem of accounting for the lack of people despite the presence of a boat, therefore, and also raises the question of how responsive the subject is to natural beauty, or images of peace, tranquility, and simple, passive, sensory gratifications. In general, it is a sign of health and adaptiveness if the subject can produce a story of fun, adventure, or a happy holiday trip. Social shyness or withdrawal can show itself in stories emphasizing the lack of people.

I have found this picture useful with patients who complain—either in so many words or through a monotonous succession of gloomy stories—that the pictures are sad, heavy, depressing, or the like. One can easily tell whether that is a superficial protest by giving this pleasant and cheerful picture; if then the subject produces another story with an unhappy ending, he is telling you clearly that the trouble is internal. Likewise, it is good as a way of showing up various kinds of preoccupation (e.g., sexual) since the lack of figures in the picture means that any introduced theme is solely the responsibility of the subject.

—Clinicians agree that this picture is not one for a standard set of ten, even with the children for whom it was intended; but do not overlook its potentialities in selected cases. Like a number of other special-purpose cards, it can be quite helpful if you approach the task of personality assessment in an individualized, not a routine, fashion, and make use of all the information you have about your subject.

CARD 13G

Murray's description: A little girl is climbing a winding flight of stairs. ("To Roof Garden," photograph by Hisao E. Kimura.)

No useful norms are available on this picture, which I have hardly ever used. Murstein (1972) administered it in group form to 53 male and 65 female college students, and reports that the figure was seen as everything from a child (17%) to an old person (6%), the modal description being classified as "young adult" (22%). The sex was seen as female by 83% of the women and 77% of the men. Rating studies find it quite bland, without any particular demand quality and notably low in any pull for hostility. Clearly, the child is exerting effort to go up steep-looking stairs, and according to Henry is often seen as exploring. It seems doubtful that the picture would often add much to what is pulled by other, more frequently used ones. Hartman reports that not a single clinician would make it part of a standard set for adults, so that it was in last place, and it was one of the three lowest-rated for a child set as well.

CARD 13B

Murray's description: A little boy is sitting on the doorstep of a log cabin. (Mr. Abe Lincoln, Jr., Farm Security Administration photograph by Nancy Post Wright.)

Though I have had little experience with it, I believe that this seldom-used picture has more potentiality than 13G. In the absence of norms other than Murstein's (1972) report that all of his mixed college sample saw the hero as a boy, or useful information from rating studies, which report that college students perceive it as rather bland, I see no reason not to accept Henry's treatment. He emphasizes the impression of the boy's smallness and loneliness, reporting that in the usual stories the hero is the child of share-croppers or other poor farmers whose parents are away. Though he is usually seen as just waiting for his family to return, sometimes he is day-dreaming of escaping from or working his way out of a deprived life.

—Rated 16th out of 31 for a child set, this picture cannot be strongly recommended for routine use. If there is a question of feelings of being underprivileged, however, in a child or even in the childhood of an adult, this may be a good picture to bring them out.

CARD 13MF

Murray's description: A young man is standing with downcast head buried in his arm. Behind him is the figure of a woman lying in bed. (Drawing by Samuel Thal; redrawn from F-19, in the old series.)

Confusions over the sexes of these figures are virtually unknown. "Other perceptual distortions" occurred in the stories of only 2% of Eron's college males and in 14% of his neurotic and psychotic veterans. He seems to mean, rather, deviant interpretations: father and daughter, mother and son, or sister and brother. The only "perceptual distortion" in his female sample was given as "father and daughter, 3%." I found nothing I would call a perceptual distortion in Fleming's male or female normative group. Relatively small minorities of normal groups mention the nonhuman aspects of the picture (except very incidentally, as "the woman in bed is . . ."), in decreasing order of frequency: bed, books, table, picture, chair.

The nudity of the woman and her relaxed posture most strongly imply the aftermath of a sexual encounter from which the man has arisen, and somewhat less plausibly suggest that she is unconscious—ill, dead, or asleep. It is safe to assume, therefore, that both the themes of sexual intercourse and of some harm to the woman are stirred up in most people by this picture, and the stories should be carefully examined for indications of conflict and defense concerning either or both when they do not appear in the manifest content.

Principal plots center around the interpretation of the scene in one of these basic ways. Among men, from 16% to 47% of my normative groups give stories centering on sex, the smaller proportions coming from scientists; 32% of Fleming's women gave sexual themes. Such stories usually involve considerable conflict or ambivalence; rape was mentioned by 7% or 8% of both males and females in Fleming's study and Eron's females; the sex was illicit—with a prostitute or extramarital—in 31% of Eron's men (though he also included premarital in the definition, which is probably why his figure is so large), in 12% of Fleming's men and from zero to 25% of my other male groups, averaging about the same, and in 16% or 17% of both female groups. By and large, however, most people see the woman as dead for one reason or another—from illness or childbirth (from 58% of biologists to 22% of psychiatrists, a quarter of both Fleming's males and females), murder (14% of Fleming's males down to 3% of scientists; 8% of females), or suicide (from zero to 6% in all groups, except 12% of Eron's women and 9% of his men—rare enough so that it is always to be taken seriously). Surprisingly enough, seeing the woman as merely ill is relatively uncommon in all groups; it did not occur to biologists, and ranged from 6% to 11% of other males, only 2% of Fleming's females. Unfortunately, Eron grouped together "death [or] illness of female partner" for both his (1948) male and female samples, with total incidence of 36% and 78% respectively. The emotion attributed to the man was guilt or remorse in 53% of Wittenborn's males, in 36% of Eron's (1948) males and about the same in scientists and psychiatrists but only 16% of Fleming's men; in 42% of Eron's women but none of Fleming's women, only 10% of whose characterizations she classified as "shame," plus 22% "regret." On the other hand, Eron reports only 7% "fear, worry" from his women and did not tabulate it for his male sample, but Fleming gives 30% "anxious, despairing" for males (from 5% to 35% of other male groups), and

24% "anxious, fearful, afraid" for women, plus 8%–10% "disgust" in both of her groups, the remainder being mainly shock or grief. Drunkenness cropped up in 12% of the stories of Eron's males.

Though some authorities say as much, I am not convinced that the theme of the woman's being sick and the man's being concerned about it, or even her death from illness, is necessarily indicative of a significant amount of hostility toward women or sex partners specifically. I think this somewhat more socially acceptable story is often used as a kind of second best to avoid telling a sex story. With women, it is of particular interest to notice the reaction of the woman to intercourse. Is she unconscious, peacefully relaxed, emotionally spent, frustrated and unfulfilled, etc.? Also particularly important to look for in stories told to this picture (as well as to 4 and 10) is the duration of the relationship. People with conflicts or maladjustment in the sexual area frequently tell stories of a brief contact, even emphasizing the fact that they will never see each other again. Much more hopeful for the subject's sexual adjustment are stories in which the eventual outcome is a continued close relationship between the partners, even if they start out unmarried, in conflict, etc. Incidentally, I have more often encountered stories of sadism and other perversion on this picture than elsewhere. I think in general it is somewhat more useful for the negative side of sexual relations than for the positive, which is to say that with male subjects, the position of the man tends to pull the less happy side of sexual relations. Compare carefully with stories to other pictures, particularly 10.

—An obviously valuable card, this one was the first choice of clinicians for a basic adult set and 5th for a child set, despite Murray's adults-only designation.

CARD 14

Murray's description: The silhouette of a man (or woman) against a bright window. The rest of the picture is totally black. (Drawing by Christiana D. Morgan; 4 in the old series.)

It seems odd that Murray should have mentioned the possibility of sexual ambiguity on only this picture, for not one person in any of Fleming's or Eron's normal male or female samples saw the figure as anything but a man; ditto for Henry's businessmen. A single Kansas highway patrolman called it a woman, as did 4% of Eron's psychotic veterans; 9% to 12% of the patrolmen and Roe's artists were puzzled or noncommittal ("this person . . ."), and Murstein (1972) classified 4% of the written responses of his 76 male students (but *none* of his 61 women's) as "other" than man or boy. I think it safe to say, therefore, that difficulty in recognizing the sex of this figure suggests confusion in the beholder's own sexual identity. Only Murstein reports substantial proportions of subjects as calling the figure a child or teen-ager (36% of men, 41% of women) rather than a man.[3]

Other perceptual distortions are rare. Eron reports them in 9% of his psychopathological samples; the only example he gives is "climbing in window," given by 8% of his hospitalized subsample only. Likewise, the examples he reports from his normal female sample are the man is "sitting on window ledge," 3%, "climbing in window," 2% (also given by 2% of Fleming's females). I would call these merely unusual interpretations.

In one respect, this picture is entirely ambiguous, for it could just as easily be that he is looking from a dark or a bright room, yet the former interpretation greatly predominates. That may be related to the fact that normal subjects so often project a theme of what Eron calls "aspiration: dreaming of future, hope for future, determination" and reports from 23% of his males and 32% of females. Fleming found that 34% of her men and 30% of her women described the young man as ambitious or determined; this was the only motive attributed specifically by Roe's artists (38%), and it was mentioned by 15% of the patrolmen and 13% of the businessmen. Curiosity was strong (26%) among Eron's men. Other emotions seen tended to be positive: "peaceful, satisfied"—20% of Fleming's men, 8% of patrolmen, 7% of businessmen; compare "tranquility," 17% of Eron's men and 8% of his women; "reminiscence, happy," 11%, men, and 7%, women—in Fleming's women, 28% "happy, satisfied." Negative affects, chiefly anxiety, conflict, and loneliness, were attributed to the man by 22% of Fleming's men, 31% of the highway patrol, and 16% of businessmen; 18% of her women gave such feelings, plus 14% "serious, pensive." It is not surprising, therefore, that this is one of the three top pictures in terms of positiveness of emotional tone, in Eron's ratings of stories.

Fleming classified stories in four main types:

Samples	Dreaming	Looking	Seeking inspiration	Relaxing	Other
Fleming's males	34%	26%	24%	14%	2%
Roe's artists	62%	0%	12%	0%	0%
Henry's businessmen	40%	26%	10%	7%	17%
Rapaport's highway patrolmen	27%	43%	4%	14%	11%
Fleming's women	32%	34%	14%	12%	0%

[3]But many of these written stories may have been ambiguous. When a college man or woman says "This boy . . ." it does not necessarily imply any perceptual distortion. There was no inquiry to clarify such points.

She reports the theme of suicide in no man and only one woman (2%); Eron reports it in 5% of his men and women alike. These figures contrast with the statements by authorities that this picture tends to bring out suicidal themes—only if they are there, in the patient, one may fairly safely conclude. For this reason, and because the deep black of the picture often has a shocking effect on subjects who are laboring with depressive feelings, it is mainly useful in clinical situations when one suspects suicidal thoughts or depression. Watch for reaction time and any unusual difficulty in getting started on a story, as well as exaggerated themes of light versus darkness symbolically interpreted.

—Otherwise, I have not found this a particularly useful picture, and it was given only middling ratings (for either an adult or child set) by clinicians in Hartman's study.

CARD 15

Murray's description: A gaunt man with clenched hands is standing among gravestones. (Woodcut by Lynd Ward in *Madman's Drum;* 3 in the old series.)

It is rare for normal persons to misrecognize the sex of the man: 4% of Eron's (1950) males and none of his females, 9% of the Kansas highway patrol, 4% of Murstein's men and 9% of his women, but no one in the psychiatric residents, biologists, or physicists did so. In the Murstein (1972) study, 6% of males and 17% of females called him "devil," "monster," or "other." Among other perceptual distortions, the commonest are seeing the hands as manacled or handcuffed (Eron's females, 8%; biologists, 11%; poorest residents, 7%; highway patrol, 4%; but physicists and best psychiatric residents, 0%) and seeing the gravestones as chairs (Eron's females, 2%; unfortunately not specifically tabulated in my normative groups, but may be included in "other comments" about gravestones, given by 11% of biologists, 13% of poor psychiatric residents, and 6% of the patrolmen). Grouping all "other perceptual distortions" together, Eron reports 9% among his mixed male group. This figure may, however, include calling the man a Negro, about which see below, or seeing other human figures at the top of the picture (listed as a distortion for 2% of his women, and given by 6% each of Roe's eminent physicists and our superior psychiatric residents). I do not think, therefore, that the last interpretation should be treated as a sign of impaired contact with reality, but rather of hyperalertness; a lot depends on what is made of it, since there are in fact two human-like forms there, though vague and inconspicuous.

In the miscellaneous normative data available, it is particularly difficult to make clean comparisons on this card. J. C. Coleman (1969) reports that among his English schoolboys, 6% of 10-year-olds and 33% of 13-year-olds saw the man as "an evil ghost or spirit, the Devil or someone practicing Black Magic." Kiefer also found a rising trend with age in the tendency to see him as "Death, Ghost, Image" from 16% to 32%; compare Eron's women, 12% of whom gave supernatural themes. Among my five normative groups of males, only 4% of Kansas patrolmen and 11% of physicists called him a supernatural being—ghost or dead person; we had no scoring categories to catch the other possibilities just mentioned, but they must be rare in normal men. Among schoolboys, 21% (age 10) and 10% (age 13) gave themes of criminal acts in the graveyard such as robbing the graves; 19% of Kiefer's Canadian girls and women called him a miser, moneylender, robber, or murderer, 4% (all adolescents) giving the plot "evil person robs or kills"; and 15% of Eron's women gave themes of acquisition, which include the ideas of miser, moneylender, and robber. Deficiencies of the scoring system used with our five male normative groups make it impossible to say how many men may have given such themes.

In any event, the commonest theme is that of a man praying, mourning, or contemplating the death of others (or his own impending death) in a graveyard. Some variant of this story was given by *all* of the best psychiatric residents and 86% of the poorest, by 51% of physicists, 68% of biologists, and 85% of the highway patrol. The specific theme of death of wife was given by half of the residents, 11% of scientists, 40% of the Kansas patrolmen, 34% of Eron's males and 22% of his females. Religious themes, especially that the man is praying, were given by 45% of English boys (age 10), 21% (age 13), 37% of Eron's males, 30% of his females, 18% of Kiefer's females, 24% of the highway patrol, 20% of psychiatric residents, and 8% of scientists. The last were almost unique in seeing his mood as contemplative or philosophical: 21% of biologists and 11% of physicists did so, only 2% of the patrolmen. About half (44%–59%) of all five of my normative groups saw him as sad or depressed; Kiefer reports only 12% of the feelings as "grief, sorrow" plus 25% "despair, lonely," 20% "fear," and 15% "guilt, remorse." Eron's samples attributed similar feelings: loneliness, females 18%, males 13%; guilt, females 15%, males 7%; sad reminiscence, females 12%, but "intraaggression" 30%, which seems to mean mainly looking forward to his own death. Guilt and self-accusation seem about equally common reactions of men; suicide is a rare theme for either sex (in normal groups, only 5% of biologists and 6% of good psychiatric residents).

The fact that this is a difficult card for many people is attested to by the frequency of complaints that the picture is unreal, "someone's dream" or the like, which were given by 14% of Eron's normal and psychopathological men and by 10% of his women; by other comments about the picture or the artist, given by 9% of hospitalized and 3% of nonhospitalized men and by 2% of his normal women; by stories with alternate themes (7%–9% of all his groups).

by confused stories (7% of hospitalized men only), or picture description in place of stories (2% of Eron's women). One way subjects try to cope with the stylized, nonrealistic look of the picture (and with their own unpleasant feelings and thoughts about death) is to tell abstract or symbolic stories in which the picture is taken as representing an idea, moral, or feeling. None of the Kansas highway patrolmen nor the good psychiatric residents did so, but between 5% and 16% of my other three groups did; also 8% of Eron's hospitalized veterans, 12% of his nonhospitalized men, and at least that many of Kiefer's women and girls.

Nevertheless, symbolic stories should always be examined with considerable care, with particular attention to the subject's reality testing. Highly educated and sophisticated persons (like Roe's scientists, about 10% of whom gave such stories) fairly easily deal with symbolism in a way that shows its literary derivation; among less educated persons, it is more likely to suggest a breakthrough of primary process thinking. You can usually tell conventional supernaturalism, likewise, from personally relevant and highly valent supernatural stories in which the central figure is not a man but an embodiment of some abstract principle like Death. Particularly malign are stories in which the hero is a dead man risen from the grave to stalk about the world of the living; this connotes pretty strongly the feeling of being dead inside that many schizophrenics speak of.

In the conventional story, another feature to look for carefully is the reaction of the hero to the death of his beloved. Is he able to find another love and to make a decent life for himself? Is he completely desolated and without any further inner resources? And note carefully whether there is any indication that he really loved the lost person or not.

This is another of the "black-shock" pictures, one which in addition has such a strong connotation of death that it characteristically gives somewhat slower reaction time.

My impression does not agree with that of several other authors to the effect that the figure who is dead is a "target of the subject's aggressions." As we have seen, quite often the dead person is the man's wife; since he is an old man, it could hardly be one of his parents, and the wife seems a very reasonable interpretation. Of course, wives are prime targets for hostility, but one does not learn a great deal by being told that again.

Occasionally, the dark color leads subjects to see the man as a Negro. I have seen this only in about a half-dozen cases, not enough to be sure whether or not the mere fact of seeing a Negro there implies prejudice; but of course any story in which a Negro is introduced gives an opportunity to judge the degree of ethnocentric prejudice.

—All in all, a useful picture for pulling certain themes and for suspected depression, but not usually recommended for a basic set (ranked in the bottom ten by Hartman's judges for both adult and child use).

CARD 16

Murray's description: A blank card.

Norms are a special problem for this nonpicture, partly because it has little specific "pull" but also because all of the available data were obtained with standard instructions. I have come to believe it very important to use special instructions; without them, it may be of little value, and with them it is often the most useful card in the set. I usually say: "This is a blank card. This time I want you to look at the card and make up your own picture, and then tell a story about it." Sometimes it is necessary after the subject has looked at the card for some time without saying anything to prompt him by asking "Do you have a picture? Why don't you start out by describing it to me?" And then it may be necessary in some cases to ask the subject to go ahead and give a story about the picture he has described.

Otherwise, some subjects attempt to cope with the difficult problem posed by this card through facetious, evasive devices like "two white swans caught in a blizzard." Incidentally, 8% of the men and none of the women in Fleming's sample gave facetious stories.

Even with the recommended instructions, intellectually limited subjects do have difficulty with this card oftentimes, and it may be of little value with them. On the other hand, it does no harm to try it, because one can quickly tell if the subject is going to be able to make anything out of it or not. In a way, it presents the greatest challenge of the whole series, because the requirement to make up one's own picture leaves the subject without the protection of the external stimulus on which to project his feelings; there is a greater danger that his own real preoccupations and his own feared impulses may emerge.

Whatever the instructions, this is the card with which autobiographical themes are most likely to emerge. Eron found that 24% of his hospitalized males, 13% of nonhospitalized men (college students and neurotic veterans), and 22% of his women gave autobiographical stories. Frequently, in my experience, the current life dilemma is what gets expressed.

The fact that there is a certain amount of picture pull from the whiteness of the card was shown by results of an unpublished study done by one of my students, Helene Kafka. She interspersed through a set of about a dozen pictures the regular white card, a red one, and a black one; there were striking differences in the kinds of stories produced. Available norms with Card 16 with quite diverse groups show surprising uniformities in their imagery. Kiefer's Canadian girls and women, for example, in 40% of the cases, told a story in which the setting was in the country, wilderness, or mountains; 12% of both Eron's male groups gave the theme "favorable environment"; settings in "the great out-of-doors" were likewise quite common among psychiatric residents. In the latter group, particularly striking was the frequency with which bodies of water (and to some extent snow) came into the story. A good sign of psychological health is the ability to tell a convincingly happy story to this picture, with a scene in which there is a strong element of vitality in the green grass, growing things, spring of the year, etc. Likewise, neurotically trapped persons frequently tell stories to this picture in which the scene is one of tedium, monotony, dullness, or desolation; schizophrenics often give particularly devastated landscapes as settings for their stories. Incidentally, as far as autobiography is concerned, I have the impression that neurotics are more likely to put the scene in their own past, and healthier persons to put the scene in their own future.

CARD 17GF

Murray's description: A bridge over water. A female figure leans over the railing. In the background are tall buildings and small figures of men. (Woodcut by Lynd Ward in *Madman's Drum;* F-12 in the old series.)

Misidentification of the woman as a man is rather common; 18% of Eron's female sample made this error as did 6% of Murstein's 110 college students. In addition, 5% of the Eron sample saw her as black, 2% failed to notice her, and 2% saw it as two different scenes. This is the only quantitative study of perceptual misrecognitions; Rapaport mentions as having occurred in his mixed clinical samples (many of whom were psychotic) "misrecognition of the bridge as a balcony of a house; perspectives misconstrued; the woman or the group of workers omitted; the woman seen as a man" (Rapaport, Gill, and Schafer, 1946, p. 407). The black sun bothers some patients, only a few of whom think of an eclipse as a reasonable explanation.

This picture is more likely to stimulate thoughts of suicide than any other; suicide was the commonest theme in Kiefer's group (27%; in half of the stories, the woman actually killed herself) and was tied for first place in Eron's group (32%, the other theme being "ordinary activity"). The woman's posture, leaning so far forward, makes it a thoroughly plausible interpretation; otherwise, she seems to be looking at or for something—curiosity themes were given by 18% of Eron's sample, while Kiefer reports that 26% of the themes were, "Watches dock activity with interest, sympathy, or unconcern." An additional 19% told stories about smuggling, mostly in which the heroine discovers it and either reports it or can do nothing; less commonly, she is the lookout for or a participant in some secret activity.

Other common themes are poverty and a frustrating, restricting environment.

The frequency of suicidal themes means that the cautionary comments given above in connection with card 3BM are relevant. If you suspect that a female patient is depressed and perhaps thinking about killing herself but has not brought forward pertinent material in responding to other cards, this is a useful one to present. Otherwise, it is not generally considered very valuable.

CARD 17BM

Murray's description: A naked man is clinging to a rope. He is in the act of climbing up or down. (Drawing by Samuel Thal after an unfinished sketch by Daumier, "The Housepainter," which was used in the old series as M-16.)

Sexual misrecognitions of the man in this picture have not been reported, they are so rare. Eron notes that other perceptual distortions occurred in 8% of his total male sample (mostly given by psychotics), but does not say what they were. The man's nudity was noted by only 10% of his men, so references to clothing may make up most of the distortions.

Up or down? Up, said 43% of Eron's group; down, said 26%. In light of such frequencies, it would be risky indeed to lay much interpretive weight on either interpretation. Also, since about a quarter of Eron's males commented on the muscles, the mere fact of such remarks cannot justify the inference of an unusual degree of latent homosexuality.

Coleman used this card with his British schoolboys; about a third of them gave stories with the theme, hero is "maintaining or improving physical fitness (e.g., in a gymnasium)"; 21% and 10% (of 10- and 13-year-olds) gave stories about a circus act, "(e.g., an acrobat or trapeze artist)." Compare Eron's figures for American men's themes: self-esteem, 23%; exhibition, 20%, approbation from peers, 10%; competition with peers, 15%. An athlete showing off his prowess is thus the most common story. Next comes the idea of escaping from some kind of danger, given by 17% of Eron's men, 15% of the 10-year-old boys and 38% of the 13-year-olds (adolescent rebellion?)—a significant difference. The man may also be climbing up for curiosity (e.g., to get a better view)—12%, Eron, or from aspiration—10%, Eron.

This card is mainly useful, therefore, to elicit stories having to do with achievement, narcissistic (or occasionally, latent homosexual) concerns with showing off, especially of the body, or escape from one's difficulties. On the whole, however, it cannot be recommended for routine use.

CARD 18GF

Murray's description: A woman has her hands squeezed around the throat of another woman whom she appears to be pushing backwards across the bannister of a stairway. (Drawing by Samuel Thal; F-17 in the old series, redrawn.)

One of Murray's main aims in getting this picture redrawn by Thal was to increase the ambiguity of sex of the person being choked. He succeeded better than the authors of standard texts seem to have realized. While only 2% of Fleming's female sample misrecognized the sex of the choking figure, 44% of them saw the figure being choked as male, and only 46% gave it as definitely female. There was also a great discrepancy in the age attributed to this peculiarly drawn figure, who was not infrequently called deformed, ill, or the like, but making it a child is hard to justify. In Murstein's study, 38% of his 61 college women and 74 college men described the two figures as something other than two females (usually, a woman and a man). Eron reports that a total of 28% of his normal women misidentified sex on this picture, also. Since 10% of Fleming's normal women commented on the "choker's" deformed or queer hands, that is not a deviant remark. The following perceptual distortions were given by only 2% each: beamed ceiling, no carpet on stairs, oil lamps.

Murray's description implies that the picture portrays an aggressive act, and the main controversy over this picture is whether one may assume that such a message gets through to everyone. It is true that the theme with highest frequency in Eron's norms was of a parent giving some kind of help (20%), and only a minority of Fleming's sample (just about one-third) saw this scene as an actual or attempted murder, with the emotions being violent, cruel, or "insane." A slightly larger proportion saw her as "holding ill or drunk person" (36%), 12% as comforting, 10% as arguing, and 6% as holding a dead person. Forty-two percent of the sample in all saw the ambiguous person as being dead or dying, with an additional 24% describing him or her as ill. (Allowances being made for a different coding system, the above frequencies seem consistent with Eron's other findings.) I agree with Henry's remarks, to the effect that even though most normal people do not describe it as such, it is reasonable to assume that the theme of interpersonal hostility is perceived and very commonly defended against. The implication is that you should not attribute to a patient more than a normal degree of denial, reaction formation, or defensive distortion in relation to aggressive ideas and impulses, just because she or he does not tell a story of a violent attack or fight. Likewise, since about one out of ten normal women see one or both characters as insane or crazy, that is no indicator of psychosis! In the study by Murstein, David, Fisher, and Furth (1961), this card was judged the most "hostile" by 100 psychology students, using Thurstone's method of equal-appearing intervals.

—A generally useful picture, with men as well as women, particularly when there is a question about the handling of hostility; this was ranked about 11th of the 31 for either an adult or a child set in Hartman's study.

CARD 18BM

Murray's description: A man is clutched from behind by three hands. The figures of his antagonists are invisible. (Drawing by Christiana D. Morgan; M-12 in the old series.)

There is little problem about the sexual identity of the man portrayed here; Eron reports no misrecognitions, and only one man in Fleming's study (2%) saw him as a "girl in disguise." (Murstein, however, claims that 8% of his 122 college men and women saw "two women"!) The problem posed by the picture is accounting for the three hands, their positions, and the lack of any visible owners. This fact, and the disturbing content implications, caused 14% of Eron's subjects to give alternative stories. Only half of Fleming's subjects (but 82% of Eron's) made no comment about the hands, 36% saying that they were confusing, and 16% calling them imaginary symbols (6% of Eron's men gave symbolic stories); but not a single member of the Kansas highway patrol gave that last interpretation, and only 2% of them said anything to the effect that the number of hands was confusing. The other big discrepancy between the patrolmen's interpretations and those of Fleming's more educated civilians was that 68% of the latter saw the man's expression as "anxious, desperate" while none of the patrolmen did. (It is possible that Fleming counted the number of times the man was called desperate or the like somewhere in the course of the story, most of which may not have been intended as describing the pictured expression—which strikes me as remarkably bland.) Though only 4% and 2% of these two samples actually described the man's expression as "tranquil," subjects do at times comment on the lack of an expression appropriate to his situation. It may be partly responsible for the high frequency with which the man is seen as drunk (from 36% to 38% in three samples, 49% in Eron's nonhospitalized group), unconscious (Fleming, 38%; patrolmen, 24%), dead or being killed (8% in both groups), or hypnotized (4% of Eron's combined sample).

In the usual stories, the hero is the victim of an attack by others (Eron, 15%; Fleming, 24%; patrolmen, 23%; English schoolboys, 49%); he is a criminal who is caught, arrested, and/or jailed (Eron's hospitalized subjects, 28%; nonhospitalized, 12%—a significant difference; Fleming, 20%; patrol-

men, 26%); he is being helped by others (Eron, 39%; Fleming, 24%; patrolmen, 17%; boys of 10, 21%; but boys of 13, 0%); he attacks others or tries to
(Eron, 12%; Fleming, 10%; patrolmen, 8%). The schoolboys saw the hero as
an aggressor in a robbery or attack in 24% and 41% of the cases (10 or 13
years). Suicide is a rare theme, being given by only one person (Fleming,
2%).

As Stein notes, the fact of an attack from the rear sometimes arouses
homosexual anxieties if they are present. This card may be helpful in
detecting schizophrenic thought disorder; latent or ambulatory schizophrenics' attempts to account for the three hands may lead to quite autistic
material. Because of the strong pull for such interpretations, it may be
helpful in cases of addiction or persons who fear or are tempted by alcohol
or other drugs. It is not generally used as part of a basic set, however.

CARD 19

Murray's description: A weird picture of cloud formations overhanging a snow-
covered cabin in the country. ("The Night Wind" by Burchfield.)

This is indeed a difficult picture (less so in its original colors), and an
unusual number of subjects have real problems in telling stories. They often
complain that the picture is unreal (Eron's males, 19%; his females, 17%),
give descriptions instead of stories (15% of his hospitalized males and 3% of
the nonhospitalized—a significant difference; 12% of his females), give
alternative plots (6% of males, 3% of females), symbolic or abstract interpretations (5% of males, 8% of females), or reject the card entirely (12% of his
nonhospitalized subjects but only 1% of the hospitalized and none of the
women).

The predominant interpretation is of a house, warm and safe inside,
while a blizzard or some evil force rages outside (given by 30% of Kiefer's
female sample and half of Eron's males). Eron codes it in more fragmentary
themes: aggression from the environment, which includes all kinds of attacks
on the house and its occupants, from snowstorm to spooks, given by 60% of
males and 70% of females; contrasting contentment inside, about 23% in
both samples. But Kiefer found (predominantly among adolescent girls) that
14% of her sample interpreted the scene as a seascape, the house as a ship, or
the like, as did 8%–9% of Eron's male sample. Ghosts, witches, evil spirits,
and other supernatural elements are common in women's stories for this
picture: Kiefer, 27%; Eron's females, 20%; his males, 15%; 18% of Murstein's 131 college students' stories contained supernatural figures. The least
frequent interpretation is a house in a flood, given by 8% of Eron's hospital-

ized males and 1% of his nonhospitalized sample; Kiefer unfortunately groups "flood" together with "storm" (15%).

I agree with Henry (1956, p. 265) that "The ability to tell a coherent story here usually reflects some security feelings, some independent thinking, and a good reality grasp." Note however that it is not just schizophrenics overcome by fantasies of eerie evil forces all around who have difficulty telling coherent stories; stereotyped, insecure people with little capacity for adaptive regression often do, too. I have had some success in helping people who seem about to fail the card entirely by suggesting that they tell a nightmare in response to this picture; it sometimes produces useful material that overlaps little with what comes out with other pictures.

—Not recommended for routine use.

CARD 20

Murray's description: The dimly illuminated figure of a man (or woman) in the dead of night leaning against a lamp post.

As Murray notes, the sex of this figure is indeed ambiguous. Only 3% of Eron's normal women but 12% of Kiefer's girls and women saw him/her as female; 13% of Murstein's did so or were noncommittal. In Eron's male sample, 7% of hospitalized and 20% of nonhospitalized men made this error (about half of them calling her a prostitute), while an additional 11% of the hospitalized (mostly psychotic) veterans were unable to decide whether to say male or female; 6% of Murstein's college males failed to call the hero a man. Other perceptual distortions are rare; one of Eron's women saw no character in the picture, and one saw a man without a head. Similar errors among his males were given by only two psychotics.

Again, the difficulty of the picture is attested by the frequency of alternative story possibilities instead of a single plot: 21% of hospitalized males, 11% of nonhospitalized men, and 8% of normal women (all Eron's samples). The predominant interpretation is that the man is loitering or waiting (75% of Eron's men, 38% of his women). Kiefer divides the most common stories into four categories: "lonely stranger or escapee wonders what to do," 24%; "waits for person, signal, or something to turn up," 21%; "man with problem walks, ponders, enjoys Nature," 21%; "guard, sentinel, caretaker, or crook stops to watch or listen," 12%. Loneliness and the wish to be accepted by others occur in 17% of Eron's males' stories, in 30% of his women's. Themes of crime, with the hero either the perpetrator or victim, are common among both men (24%) and women (30%), but men are more likely to see the hero as the victim of poverty (20% versus 3%). Nine percent of men and 7% of women describe the hero as drunk. Men are more likely to attribute guilt or remorse to the figure (5%); women, fear or worry (7% of Eron's females, but 20% of Kiefer's girls and women).

—I have not found this a particularly useful picture, especially not with subjects who have difficulty with such dark and perceptually vague stimuli. I doubt that it adds much that cannot be gotten from other pictures. It was in the bottom third of the pictures in Hartman's study.

4

The chapter that follows was presented at a conference on thematic apperception methods convened by Jerome Kagan and Gerald Lesser in 1959 (see Kagan & Lesser, 1961). I wrote it just before my disillusionment with metapsychology crystallized; indeed, my original plan was to present a metapsychological reconsideration of TAT rationale. I omit here the first few pages, which were a sketch of what such a treatment might look like and which now strike me as not worth republishing.

What remains is primarily a phenomenological contrast between fantasies and TAT stories, in which the framework of the metapsychological points of view as presented by Rapaport and Gill (1959) serves as a means of organizing the discussion. It was intended as a contribution to the understanding of the kind of human product TAT stories constitute, to the ultimate end of aiding interpretation. As the title emphasizes, they are affective as well as cognitive in nature. (That emphasis was lost in the original publication by a printer's error in omitting the word "affective" in the title.)

The Nature of TAT Stories as Cognitive-Affective Products: A Psychoanalytic Approach

The first publication on the TAT was a paper by Christiana D. Morgan and Henry A. Murray, Jr. (1935) boldly entitled: "A Method for Investigating Fantasy." It would be easy to cite many passages in that paper and in later publications (Murray *et al.*, 1938) where they used the terms interchangeably or spoke of "stories (fantasies)."[1] Since then, many others have written about

---

[1] In a personal communication (1959), Murray comments: "'A method for investigating fantasy' meant, of course, a method of educing story constructions which are susceptible of interpretation in terms of fantasies (largely unconscious). In 1936 what we had in mind for the TAT was to reveal (through interpretation) the kind of material—semi-conscious and unconscious imaginations—that analysts were dealing with. Fantasy was the only available, generally-accepted, word. The stories, according to our hypothesis, were not fantasies themselves but were molded or shaped by fantasies, *to some extent. But even here* it is hard to draw a sharp line, since most story-composers are aware of more or less vivid images and *imagents* (imagined events) preceding or

the TAT and related techniques, and have very frequently referred to them as methods of studying fantasy (Beier, Gorlow, & Stacey, 1951; Bell, 1948; Henry, 1956; Leary, 1956; Masserman & Balken, 1938; Symonds, 1949). I have just looked through the indices of the last ten years[2] of the *Psychological Abstracts* under the heading, fantasy, and have been surprised to find that a great majority of the American references—except for psychoanalytic, clinical contributions—have been papers or books on the TAT and related thematic tests.

Should we assume, then, that the word *fantasy* means nothing more nor less than a TAT story? Usage would not really support that conclusion, and of course the idea of the TAT as a test of fantasy would be a complete tautology. Let's see what the excellent psychological dictionary of English and English has to say about fantasy: "imagining a complex object or event in concrete symbols or images, whether or not the object or event exists; or the symbols or images themselves: e.g., a daydream.—Fantasy is usually pleasant and represents a sort of wish fulfillment. Originally synonymous with imagination, it is now distinguished by the fact that, if it represents reality at all, it is whimsical or visionary, not primarily either constructive or reproductive. Yet it is not necessarily delusive or pathological. Freud made distinction between dreams of fantasy and those showing dream work." A fantasy, then, seems to be a daydream; let's look at the definition of that term: "a reverie while awake.—Usually the unfulfilled wishes of the dreamer are imagined as fulfilled. Wishes are not disguised and fulfillment is imagined as direct, without repression. Daydreaming is not inherently pathological." So a daydream seems to be a reverie! English and English define reverie as: "a state in which the train of thought or of images is little directed purposively and in which one is relatively insensible to external happenings.—Reverie may have a single coherent object but does not have a theme: e.g., one may think about the old homestead, its discomforts, the joys one experienced there, how it has fared, etc., without these thoughts having a theme. In a daydream, there is said to be a theme, even when the objects change and even though the theme may be difficult to discern."

These definitions are not terribly enlightening (except perhaps for the fact that they say nothing about TAT stories!); they suggest that there is little clear distinction between these three concepts in general psychological use.

---

accompanying their spoken or written words. Fantasy, in my lingo, is an involuntary, undirected stream of images and imagents. Story composition is based on this, but involves direction (say, the intent to write a comic story and hence a little mental magnet attracting influxions of potentially comic elements), and evaluations of these influxions, rejections of some, acceptances of others, etc., etc." I am most grateful to Dr. Murray for this clarifying statement and for his permission to quote it. I also wish to acknowledge my indebtedness to parallel discussions of many issues treated in this paper, by my friend Dr. Leopold Bellak (1954a,b).

[2][That is, 1949–1958, before any of the major publications by J. L. Singer and his colleagues (summarized in J. L. Singer, 1966) and the book by Klinger (1971), none of which had appeared when this paper was written.]

Fantasy, however, seems to be the most inclusive term, and reverie differs from the other two in being restricted to wandering thinking that is not thematic and which moreover takes place in a less fully waking state of consciousness than a daydream.

When we turn to psychoanalytic literature, we do not find a great deal more clarity about definitions. Fenichel (1945) offers the following rather general one: "As long as thinking is not followed by action it is called fantasy. There are two types of fantasy: creative fantasy, which prepares for some later action and daydreaming fantasy, the refuge for wishes that cannot be fulfilled." Freud was not usually much concerned with precise and inclusive definitions, but in his introduction to Varendonck's book he goes into an interesting discussion of terminology. Bleuler (1951) had proposed the term "autistic thinking" for fantasy, but Freud said that this was not happily chosen. Varendonck's own suggestion, "foreconscious thinking," Freud thought "misleading and unsatisfactory" as a designation for the subject matter of the book, since daydreaming was not much changed in its character when it went on consciously, as it certainly did some times, and since directed thinking might be preconscious as well as conscious.[3] So Freud proposed that the mode of thought-activity involved in daydreaming should be called "freely wandering or fantastic thinking, in opposition to intentionally directed reflection. At the same time it should be taken into consideration that even fantastic thinking is not invariably in want of an aim and end representations." Here, as he had done in an earlier paper (1908a), Freud refers to the fact that there are no clear-cut, dichotomous types but many intermediate states and transitional forms between fantasy and other types of thinking, ranging from dreams, on the one hand, to directed, secondary process thinking on the other.

It should be apparent that when we talk about fantasy we are dealing with a broad range of cognitive processes and products, a somewhat chaotic and neglected realm that could use some systematization. The only book devoted specifically to the topic is that of Varendonck (1921), but as Rapaport (1951a, p. 451) points out, "he fails to distinguish among the varieties of fantasy-thinking, such as hypnagogic and hypnopompic reverie, daydream, etc."

Rapaport speaks with such conviction because he has made an intensive study of the phenomena in this realm, both as reported in the literature (1951a) and in a study of his own fantasying (1951b, 1958). For a total of eight weeks, Rapaport worked at recording his own thought processes during the time from retiring until deep sleep; he learned to do a kind of automatic writing which he could carry on up to states of dimmest consciousness or closely approaching dreaming sleep. Rapaport says of these records: "They: *First*—contain thought fragments which do not seem to differ from

---

[3]Nevertheless, Fenichel preserved the usage, speaking of "preconscious fantasy thinking" (1945, p. 46).

waking thoughts; *Second*—they contain segments about which I noted while recording that they are just like the daydream into which I occasionally drift off, interrupting my regular work, in the daytime, and their character—as recorded—bears this out; *Third*—they contain material which is introduced by comments to the effect that I am unable to continue recording, sleepiness is catching up with me . . . reveries or some of them 'hypnagogic hallucinations.' They vary greatly in length, and in character, some of them are like dreams, some quite unlike the latter; *Fourth*—these records contain dreams, but these also vary greatly in character" (Rapaport, 1951c; cf. Bellak, 1954a,b).

Despite the fact that he gives his experiences four names, Rapaport notes that there is a continuous series of phenomena, on which this four-fold scheme has been imposed. It gets to be very difficult, for example, to distinguish a hypnagogic hallucination and reverie from a dream. Let me cite a personal experience in support of this point. A few months ago, I was a subject for Dr. William Dement, in a trial of the technique he and Kleitman worked out of awakening people while they are dreaming, as ascertained by the presence of rapid coordinated eye movements (Dement & Kleitman, 1957). After a series of awakenings, in the middle of the night I started to fall asleep thinking of a forthcoming event about which I was a little apprehensive because it might disrupt my work. Suddenly I roused myself, realizing that I had begun to dream that the stack of out-boxes at my office in which I keep papers I am currently working on was toppling over. Here was apparently a perfect example of what Silberer (1951) called the autosymbolic phenomenon: the representation of an abstract idea—here, that my work would be upset—by a concrete hypnagogic image depicting it. According to my EEG, I was asleep, and it was in the middle of the night, yet this was the same kind of brief pictorial reverie that Silberer had reported slipping into after working during the day or early evening. Perhaps it makes little sense to try to impose a categorical order on an essentially continuous set of phenomena.

Since classification can take us no further,[4] let us turn to something more like a dimensional analysis. Rapaport (1951b) cites three major dimensions along which these fantastical phenomena vary, the last of which is subdivided into four.

1. *The amount of reflective awareness—the awareness not only of a content but of the awareness that one is aware (or the possibility of it).* This variable has a somewhat erratic relationship to the general level of awareness; in some senses, I think we would agree that we are at the peak of conscious awareness when we are so deeply committed and fully absorbed in some cognitive activity that we have no self-consciousness, no immediate reflective aware-

---

[4][I meant to imply that classification of types of fantasy is of limited value, not that Rapaport's taxonomy is exhaustive or definitive.]

ness, though in such a state retroflection (as Troland called it) is of course always possible. And at the other extreme, in dreams, surely we lack this consciousness most of the time; and yet we are all familiar with dreams in which there occurs the comforting thought, "this is only a dream." Rapaport points out the fact that this last experience is not a complete example of reflective awareness, but is something close to it. In general, in states under the broad heading of fantasy there is less reflective awareness than in usual realistic or directed thinking.

2. *The ability to exert effort, to "will."* Rapaport says of this variable that it is "rather vague" yet it is useful. "The more closely the dream state is approximated, the less it is possible to exert voluntary effort." Varendonck (1921) noted, as did Rapaport, during his recording of a daydream that as it started to approach true dreaming, the act of recording became more and more effortful and would be broken off.

3. *"The differences between these states show up in the formal characteristics of thought"* (Rapaport, 1951b, p. 394). This is the clearest respect in which these states vary, Rapaport says, and he goes on to subdivide these formal characteristics into the following four:

a. *Imagery versus words.* Varendonck (1921), Kris (1950), and Rapaport (1951a), all agree that as one regresses from directed thought through reverie toward dreams, imagery (particularly the visual) becomes increasingly prominent and words much less so. McKellar (1957) reports that most hypnagogic images are auditory, but in any event purely verbal imagery plays a small role. It is true, for many people imaging accompanies ordinary directed secondary process thought, yet somewhere down the line an important transition takes place: memory images or imagination images give way to a qualitatively very different hypnagogic or dream image, which is a great deal closer to a hallucination. Such hallucinatory images are very rarely found in states of full waking awareness, and then usually under states of considerable stress or deprivation (McKellar, 1957), or in psychosis. A good deal of to-do has been made about the emergence of such "hallucinations" in so-called sensory deprivation, a condition in which subjects' reality contact is artificially disturbed. As I have argued elsewhere, some of these phenomena closely approximate hypnagogic images, which are appropriate to the altered state of consciousness (Goldberger & Holt, 1958; see also Holt, 1964b).

b. *Implication versus explicitness.* A characteristic feature of waking thought, Rapaport says, is the explicitness with which representation takes place, whereas in dreams and dream-like forms of thought implication is common. For example, Rapaport cites a fragment of a dream, in which he is with his father and knows that his father is satisfied with him; the record adds, "I do not know how I knew that: there was no external expression on him to show that." A closely related point is the difference in continuity between waking and dream-like thought. In the latter, there is no need to make explicit the transitions from one image or concept to another, whereas in waking—especially in communicative—thought, a great deal needs to be spelled out that would otherwise be left unsaid.

c. *Rational versus autistic logic.* In dream thought, Rapaport (1951b, p. 395) says, the place of correct logic "is taken by forms like *'pars pro toto,' 'post hoc ergo propter hoc,'* 'What holds for the little, holds the more so for the big'— that is, by participatory, syncretic, animistic forms; the so-called dream-mechanisms, or mechanisms of the primary process: condensation, displacement, substitution, prevail here." And of course symbolism too. As is true of the other variables, the difference is not absolute; waking thought is sometimes illogical and autistic, and dreams vary a great deal in this respect. Studies of dreams in our laboratory have consistently shown that the fantastically dream-like dream is not a very usual phenomenon (though of course the method of obtaining data may be partly responsible); many reported dreams are quite prosaic accounts of events that might really have happened, in which there is no disturbance of the logical straightforwardness of the events. Indeed, there are numerous famous examples of the solution of mathematical problems in sleep (Hadamard, 1945). In an unpublished study of dream-diaries kept by field-dependent and field-independent adolescents, Carol Johnson (Eagle) found frequent reports of dreams that differed in no respect from ordinary, simple wish-fulfilling fantasies, for example: "I dreamed that we had an examination and my paper had the highest mark in the class." The dream-work mechanisms that are so characteristic of dreams and reveries may also be seen in the conscious waking thought of normal subjects taking the Rorschach test[5] (Holt, 1970c).

d. *Sophisticated versus primitive syntax.* The verbalization corresponding to or taking place in the various states studied by Rapaport in himself varied a great deal in its syntax. From the deepest levels, the language was primitive and incorrect.

Therefore, as Rapaport makes quite clear, there are no perfect correlations in this field between any of these characteristics and the level of awareness or type of fantastic thinking, yet there are strong general trends of the kinds pointed out above.

There are several other dimensions that may be implicit in the above but are worth making explicit. First, there is the degree to which thinking is *directed* as against "freely wandering." This may be conceptualized as the degree to which sets or anticipations, which usually guard thinking and keep it from straying away from the point, are operative. One of the striking characteristics of fantasy thinking is the chain-like way in which it wanders from the point at which it started, often proceeding by means of what Freud called "unessential" links or principles of association. This is perhaps the

---

[5]This is not to say that they operate in the same ways; the differences between dreams and Rorschach responses are surely more impressive than the similarities. Yet one can observe condensations, symbolic responses, and even autistic logic in nonpatients' Rorschachs.

basic point underlying one of the two continua that Kris (1950) saw in this kind of thinking, the one "reaching from problem-solving to dream-like fantasy." (The other was words versus imagery.) That is, in order to solve problems, thinking has to be kept at the task by guiding sets.

Another obvious dimension of fantasy is the degree to which the images and events correspond to reality. The dream-work mechanisms of course play a large role in producing fantastic deviations from reality, but there also may be unrealistic conjunctions in fantasy, like anachronisms—imagining oneself to be present in a remote historical era—or unrealistic turns of events, in which condensation, displacement, and symbolization play no apparent role.

A third additional dimension is the degree of narrative structure. A usual concept of the daydream is that it is a kind of miniature drama or story, with some kind of at least minimal plot or sequence of events. Yet fantasies and related types of thinking vary all the way from long drawn-out, highly complicated narratives, to wandering thought without any plot or narrative connection, to single images unconnected to anything else by any sort of continuity.

Finally, an important dimension of variation is the *affective* involvement of fantasy-thinking. Some daydreams (especially in isolating persons) have a poverty of affect, being almost purely cognitive events; in most others, however, strong affects (e.g., anxiety, lust, hatred) suffuse the thoughts and images.[6]

[At this stage of our knowledge, it is in fact difficult to say where to draw the line between emotion and fantasy. Surely they are intimately and complexly interrelated. I believe that all but the simplest emotional experiences of direct reaction to what is pleasing or painful require the capacity to *imagine consequences,* a process that is the heart of fantasy. Only after this basic cognitive ability is developed in infancy do we begin to see evidences of the dreadful experiences usually leveled down and mislabeled as anxiety— terror, panic, rage, and desolate grief. These are states of the whole person faced with the believed imminence or actuality of certain kinds of terrible losses (of life, of bodily integrity, of loved parents, or of other vital supplies) and forced to imagine frightful scenarios of consequences. The fact that normal persons so seldom experience these overwhelming, disastrous states is no accident; they are the true motors of defense. But in the defenses against the shattering affects, emotional fantasies play a large part. I remember a catatonic patient whose hands had become rigid and distorted by being unrelentingly clenched as he acted out a fantasy of clinging to something which he feared was being taken from him (or so his attending psychiatrist told me). Many a neurosis is the enactment of a desperate myth, an irrational conviction that safety against some feared disaster can be found only in the

[6] I am grateful to Dr. Roy Schafer for calling this point to my attention.

strategic retreat of the symptom. The human vulnerability to neurosis and psychosis may lie in the gift of imagination, the capacity to construct possible futures which arises long before the ability to evaluate them realistically.]

If we pause and look at the above mentioned points about types of fantasy from the standpoint of the metapsychological points of view, most of them turn out to be economic and structural considerations. As yet unemphasized is the obvious *dynamic* one, that many fantasies tend to be obviously wish-fulfilling. Yet this is a dimension of difference too, for surely there are many kinds of fantasy in which no obvious or easily discernible wish-fulfillment takes place. Let me give another personal example: one night not long ago as I was lying in bed just about to go to sleep I had a hypnagogic image of a rooftop with a dragon lying across it, the scales of the dragon being beautifully lacy, dark green ferns. This was a momentary presentation, like a lantern slide flashed on for a second or so and then taken away. I would accept it as a matter of assumption that this image occurred for some psychological reason, and it is of course possible to make a symbolic sexual interpretation of it, which may be valid. The point, however, is that any wish-fulfillment that is involved is quite disguised and obscure, as compared to the "typical" daydream. As Smythies (1953) says, hypnagogic images are often "without any *apparent* connection, emotional or volitional, with the aims, interests or feelings of the person concerned." (Italics mine.) Doubtless Smythies may be overlooking the role of defense and of the obscuring symbolic language of the primary process; nevertheless, the degree to which wish-fulfillment is *apparent* in the product is a clear dimension of variation.

There is a large category of fantasies in which wish-fulfillment is not evident, but in which the apparent opposite is very clear: daydreams in which anxiety or guilt play a large role. In such a fantasy, for example, a person may picture himself being subjected to all kinds of dangerous and harrowing experiences even including images of his own death by torture. The psychoanalytic explanation of these phenomena is essentially the same as the explanation of nightmares: they are defensive phenomena, in which an unconscious fantasy of some direct instinctual gratification is covered by a defensive presentation marked by anxiety and unpleasant events. The role of the superego and guilt over drive-gratification is clear in many such phenomena.

But defensive fantasies do not always take this nightmare-like form; they are quite various. It's interesting that in his first recorded discussions of fantasies,[7] Freud spoke of them as "defensive structures, sublimations and embellishments of the facts [which] at the same time serve the purpose of self-exoneration" (1887–1902, p. 196). In several of his later published papers (Freud, 1899a, 1906a, 1908a) he described the defensive role of daydreams and other fantasies, and other analysts (see Fenichel, 1945) have

[7]Letter to Fliess of May 2, 1897.

cited many examples of defensive fantasy: those involving or in the service of denial, identification, projection, etc.

Next, some *genetic* considerations. Putting together pieces from various psychoanalytic sources (Fenichel, 1945; Ferenczi, 1913; Freud, 1900a, 1905d, 1905e, 1906a, 1907a, 1908a, 1908e; Rapaport, 1951b) I arrive at the following account: fantasy begins with the first psychic activity, which according to the psychoanalytic primary model of thought is a hallucinatory experience of gratification following a frustration. Thus, fantasy is the oldest form of thought, one that continues throughout life. As Fenichel (1945, p. 46) says, fantasy "is merely the undifferentiated predecessor of thinking, in which all characteristics of the primitive ego are still to be seen." As childhood advances, it is increasingly displaced from consciousness by secondary process thinking and is made unconscious by the defenses as they develop. Except when the infant is in a state of what Wolff (1959) calls alert inactivity, when he is able to respond realistically to his surroundings, psychoanalysts assume that he is fantasying much of the time that he is awake.[8]

As the infant matures into a toddler, gaining motor skills and ability to manipulate his surroundings, he also develops more specific desires, by canalization (Murphy, 1947) of his originally diffuse urges. The more wishes, the more fantasies; for example, when a boy's sexual desires are turned toward his mother he may try overtly to win her away from her spouse, but the Oedipus complex is basically, and largely remains, one big affect-laden fantasy. One of the most notable things about childhood is the emergence of play. Surely, in part, play is merely the pleasurable exercise of the sensory-motor apparatus, as Piaget (1936) has pointed out. At the same time, however, the maturation of the effector apparatuses (i.e., motor skills) makes it possible for the child to act out his fantasies, which gives rise to dramatic play. Indeed, play may be looked on as a necessary consequence of the fact that both fantasy and motor skills develop before inhibitions and other defenses do. The child is not yet sophisticated enough to see through the transparent charades of his play nor have his defenses developed to the point where the acting out of his fantasies would be much hindered. So long as the child is not occupied with serious adaptive tasks, like going to school or being put to work, he is free to translate his inner fantasy into the external

[This paragraph shows how confidently I assumed, in the 1950s, that the psychoanalytic theory of thinking was sufficient and valid. I took it for granted that the years I had spent studying it made it unnecessary for me to read cognitive-developmental psychology, most notably the work of Piaget. Only when I tried more systematically to reconsider the development of thought in the terms of metapsychology (Holt, 1967d) did I begin to see how internally inconsistent and factually misleading the preceding account is. I now believe that we know very little about fantasy in young children, that it is safer to infer the properties of preverbal thinking from Piaget's theories than from Freud's, and that there is little reason to assume much fantasying— or even much wishing—during the first two (largely preverbal) years of life (see Holt, 1976a, where I have elaborated on the connection between fantasies, wishes, and fears).]

act of play. Freud (1908e, pp. 144, 145) noted that "This linking [of play to reality] is all that differentiates the child's 'play' from 'phantasying.' . . . the growing child, when he stops playing, gives up nothing but the line with real objects; instead of *playing*, he now *phantasies*. . . . I believe that most people construct phantasies at times in their lives." (Emphasis is Freud's.)

Fantasy is thus originally preverbal, proceeding by means of images which are doubtless nonvisual as well as visual. (Indeed, we often forget the extent to which a purely visual image is a symbolic shorthand for the full sensory reality of an experience; it is a first stage toward the development of concepts.) Ferenczi (1913) describes the preverbal stage of magic gestures, which are presumably part of the development of fantasy, but notes the great economy of effort that the learning of language introduces.

Adolescence is a time at which fantasies greatly burgeon, and many adolescents spend large amounts of time in daydreaming. Since the adolescent is adult in his sexual equipment, and has enough intelligence and knowledge to picture various possible roles in an adult world of work and amusement, yet is barred from participation in most of these activities, it is natural that he live them out in a trial or preparatory way by means of his daydreams.

A few *structural* considerations remain to be specified. Freud notes in a couple of places the fact that fantasies differ considerably in their esthetic pleasingness, and that the fantasies reported to him by some subjects are esthetically beautiful. This suggests the role of *abilities* in the genesis of fantasies, something that is not often mentioned because it plays a rather inconspicuous role. Since fantasies rarely involve much problem-solving, intelligence and resourcefulness need not obviously be drawn upon in their construction. Bleuler (1912, p. 432) wrote: "For the realistic function there is only *one* correct result, [but] autism has 'endless possibilities' (Jung) and its goals can be reached in the most varied ways. Thus the differences between good and poor functioning of the latter do not appear great even when they are most extreme. While there is a difference in principle between correct and false inferences or arithmetic calculations, the tale of a child and that of a genius are equivalent as far as autistic purpose and subjective fulfillment are concerned." Rapaport (1951a, p. 432n) comments on this statement: "It would seem that there is a radical difference between the tale of the child and the genius. The latter, besides being subjective fulfillment, is deliberate action, planned for in character, and communicative in aim. The role which the ego plays in bringing it about and shaping it from an impulse or inspiration is different from that in the child's tale." Though Rapaport, in taking up the term "tale," seems to be talking more specifically about storytelling than Bleuler was, it still seems likely that his remarks would apply to some uncommunicated daydreams of highly intelligent persons. Certainly one is struck by the ingeniousness of some of the daydreams Varendonck and Rapaport report having had, and in the history of scientific discovery there are many instances of creative solutions to difficult problems during fantasy-thinking.

Freud points out another structural factor when he says that fantasies are "built up out of and over the childhood memories" (1906a, p. 274). Speaking about the memory materials on which fantasies draw, he wrote:

> We must not suppose that the products of this imaginative activity—the various phantasies, castles in the air and daydreams—are stereotyped and unalterable. On the contrary, they fit themselves in to the subject's shifting impressions of life. . . . Mental work is linked to some current impression, some provoking occasion in the present which has been able to arouse one of the subject's major wishes. From there it harks back to a memory of an earlier experience (usually an infantile one) in which this wish was fulfilled; and it now creates a situation relating to the future which represents a fulfilment of the wish. What it thus creates is a day-dream or phantasy, which carries about it traces of its origin from the occasion which provoked it and from the memory (Freud, 1908e, p. 147f).

I omit from this discussion any but the briefest mention of the role of fantasies in psychopathology. In order to understand hysterical fantasies and the patterns of acting out in character disorder, it's necessary to assume unconscious fantasy. Transformations of fantasies play important roles in the symptoms associated with a number of mental illnesses. For example, an obsession is an ego-alien fantasy (or fragment thereof) that insistently presents itself in awareness; a delusion is from one point of view a transformed fantasy that is accepted as a reality.

The *adaptive* point of view is perhaps represented to some extent by my remarks above about realism, but Hartmann (1951, p. 372f) has attacked this issue much more directly. "What are the adaptive elements of fantasy life? . . . Varendonck (1921) . . . is of the opinion that the biological significance of fantasy-thinking, in sharp contrast to dream-work, lies in its attempts to solve problems of waking life . . . it is generally known that fantasy can be fruitful even in scientific thinking, which is the undisputed domain of rational thinking. . . . Another example in point is the auxiliary function of fantasy in the learning process. Though fantasy always implies an initial turning away from a real situation, it can also be a preparation for the reality. . . . It may fulfill a synthetic function by provisionally connecting our needs and goals with possibilities of their realization." Finally, Hartmann cites the adaptive function of some fantasies in increasing our insight into our own intrapsychic life, which may lead to increasingly effective mastery of the external world. Yet obviously this is another dimension of variation; it could hardly be maintained that all fantasies have equally adaptive implications.

I deliberately saved for last a point that belongs under the consideration of the adaptive aspects of fantasy: the relation of fantasies to literary products. In his paper on this topic, Freud (1908a) made the best case I know of for the parallels between fantasies and stories, and although he was talking about the popular products of published writers, his remarks apply almost equally well to TAT stories. I have summarized his points and added to them a little in Table 4.1. By way of discussion of that table, let me quote from this delightful little paper of Freud's.

First, stories of the kind he is talking about all have "a hero who is the center of interest, for whom the writer tries to win our sympathy by every possible means and whom he seems to place under the protection of a special Providence" (p. 149). The hero, we know as we read, cannot really come to a bad end no matter how severe his trials. "It seems to me, however," Freud adds, "that through this revealing characteristic of invulnerability we can immediately recognize His Majesty the Ego, the hero alike of every day-dream and of every story" (p. 150). In novels, all women fall in love with the hero, which is hardly realistic but quite usual in daydreams. (Incidentally, these last two qualities of invulnerability and irresistibility are not so prevalent in TAT stories, or in contemporary novels as in the popular romances of Freud's day.)

Second, in popular stories, there is little characterization, as in fantasies: people other than the hero are either "good guys" or "bad guys."

Third, in this paper, Freud stresses the common element of wish-fulfillment in fantasies and in stories, though to apply the point to TAT stories one has to generalize it a little bit more, as I have in Table 4.1. This point really boils down to the fact that fantasies and stories are motivated quasi-creative products in the production of which most aspects of the total personality may play a role. This is not to deny, however, that all of these factors may not show themselves somewhat differently in fantasies than in TAT stories.

Freud was quite clear about this last fact: "We are perfectly aware that very many imaginative writings are far removed from the model of the naive day-dream; and yet I cannot suppress the suspicion that even the most extreme deviations from that model could be linked with it through an

Table 4.1.   Similarities Between Fantasies and TAT Stories

1. Both tend to follow the general narrative format, with a central figure or *hero* who has various adventures.
2. In both there tends to be little characterization of persons other than the hero; they are just auxiliary and supplementary figures.
3. The goals and activities portrayed in both derive from S's personal goals and wishes; likewise, abilities, personal memories, defenses, information, sentiments and attitudes, patterns of interpersonal relations, personal style and many other aspects of personality are used in the construction of both.
4. Both exist in a variety of forms, using various mixtures of primary process and secondary process.

uninterrupted series of transitional cases" (p. 150). Note that Freud is only drawing parallels, while maintaining the distinction and recognizing important differences; he does not say that stories and similar products of creative imagination *are* fantasies. Later, he notes another difference: to hear another person's fantasies gives us no pleasure, they "repel us or at least leave us cold." But the products of a man of literary talent give great pleasure, "which probably arises from a confluence of many sources." Specifically, the writer "softens the character of his egoistic day-dreams by altering and disguising it, and he bribes us by the purely formal—that is, aesthetic—yield of pleasure . . . to make possible the release of still greater pleasure arising from deeper psychical sources" (p. 153). Thus, Freud makes it quite clear that there are striking and essential differences between fantasies and stories, as well as similarities.

Nevertheless there is one more similarity I have listed in the table, in an attempt to put down every resemblance that seemed defensible: the fourth point. It is one, however, that could be made about almost any other cognitive product, and does not particularly differentiate the TAT and daydreams from anything else. It's worthwhile to notice, however, that TAT stories exist in quite a variety of forms and, in part, overlap with fantasies on the dimensions we have seen above on which fantasies differ one from another.

In the paper cited, Freud (1908e, p. 151) says: "If our comparison of the imaginative writer with the daydreamer . . . is to be of any value, it must . . . show itself in some way or other fruitful." He proposes, therefore, that the works of authors may be studied in ways learned from the analysis of fantasies. Specifically, he suggests that in a creative work, "A strong experience in the present awakens in the creative writer a memory of an earlier experience (usually belonging to his childhood) from which there now proceeds a wish which finds its fulfilment in the creative work. The work itself exhibits elements of the recent provoking occasion as well as of the old memory. Do not be alarmed at the complexity of this formula," he adds, "I suspect that in fact it will prove to be too exiguous a pattern. Nevertheless, it may contain a first approach to the true state of affairs. . . ."

With reference to the other kind of writing, which uses readymade material, Freud makes the canny suggestion that the writer's individuality "can express itself in the choice of material and in changes in it which are often considerable." Much of such material—for example, myth—is itself to be considered "distorted vestiges of the wishful fantasies of whole nations."

This was an idea that had appealed to Freud ever since 1897, and he had used published works as a source of inferences about the personality of their authors several times earlier (1900a, 1907a). Many other analysts, notably Hitschmann (1956), took up the suggestion and applied it with great eagerness to the works of many famous writers. Because of this psychoanalytic tradition, therefore, it is easy to see why Morgan and Murray decided to elicit stories from their subjects and to try to learn from such material about the subjects' fantasy life.

On the whole, the similarities between TAT stories and fantasies or daydreams are not particularly far-reaching or impressive. How about the differences? Let us see what they are and what their implications are for an understanding of TAT stories.

The list in Table 4.2 is much longer than in Table 4.1, and indeed it could have been extended. Notice that the dimensions of fantasy cited above are mostly included in Table 4.2.

The first difference, in the quality of consciousness, is based on the first dimension mentioned by Rapaport. Even though there is some range, daydreams (the type of fantasy that is closest to the TAT story, and therefore the fairest subject for comparison) typically take place in a special state of consciousness. Miller (1942) calls daydreaming unconscious in the special sense of being "unresponsive to stimulation" and says: "subjective report puts it midway between waking and dreaming, and it can easily shade off into either one."

Table 4.2. Differences Between Fantasies and TAT Stories

Fantasy	TAT Story
1. *Quality of consciousness:* Produced in a dreamy or abstracted state of consciousness; little reflective awareness.	Produced in full waking state of consciousness, with reflective awareness.
2. *Spontaneity versus effortfulness:* A passive cognitive product: arises spontaneously, with a feeling of drifting rather than one of responsible effort; self-imposed.	An active cognitive product: produced by an act of conscious will or deliberation, in response to an externally imposed task.
3. *Imagery versus verbalization:* May be nonverbal, in whole or part made up of sensory images.	Always verbal in nature (though imagery may at times play a subordinate, ancillary role).
4. *Implication versus explicitness:* Continuity and transitions often implicit, also connotations or attributes of persons.	Continuity, transitions, etc., usually explicit; less use of implicit connotations.
5. *Primary versus secondary process (formal aspects):* May use formal properties of primary process openly in the finished product.	Product rarely shows evidence of primary process, or does so only under shelter of various conventions.
6. *Memorability:* Often unnoticed, repressed, or otherwise unavailable to recall.	Typically receives full attention and is easily remembered; seldom fully repressed.

Table 4.2. (*continued*)

Fantasy	TAT Story
7. *Narrative structure:* Little plot, loose structure; little modeling after literary forms.	Externally imposed narrative structure, with plot, suspense, and other literary devices copied from culturally given models.
8. *Role of motives and defenses:* Content generally dictated by rather direct wish-fulfillment or by anxiety and defense; wishes expressed may be infantile or unsocialized.	Content much less obviously dictated by these aims; wishes expressed are generally more socially acceptable.
9. *Involvement of affect:* Usually accompanied by strong affects, which are often crude.	Affects involved are rarely strong, usually more differentiated and mature.
10. *Role of external reality (press):* Sometimes set off by an external press, but latter may play no real role in the product, which need not be responsible to it.	Always set off by a complex press (picture, setting, etc.); S is under pressure to respect and use reality of picture.
11. *Role of abilities:* Since there is little adaptive challenge or relevance, abilities often play little role.	Abilities play a large role in shaping the product; adaptive challenge is always present.
12. *Relation to action:* Merges into planning; may be followed or accompanied by acting out (or living out).	Has little relation to planning; does not lead to acting out (or living out); only minor acting out accompanies it.
13. *Self-relevance:* Egocentric and obviously self-relevant; S typically appears as main figure (hero).	S rarely appears in story; self-relevance often not obvious to S; less egocentric.
14. *Role of communication:* Rarely communicated; if so, usually to an intimate; considered highly private.	Always communicated, to a distant, professional person; relatively public.
15. *Range of subject matter:* May be repetitive, stereotyped, dealing with a narrow range of problems, situations, persons, needs.	The TAT pictures force S to deal with a substantial variety of basically important situations, types of persons, needs, problems.

It is fairly obvious that, except under the most exceptional conditions, TAT stories are told in a state of full waking awareness. The level undoubtedly fluctuates somewhat from moment to moment during story-production, but still within rather narrow limits. If, as Rapaport contends (1958), the level of consciousness has a marked effect on the organization of thinking that goes on, this may be the most crucial and fundamental difference between fantasies and TAT stories, one from which a number of the others proceed. The state of our knowledge about states of consciousness and accompanying modes of thought-organization is as yet too scanty and unbuttressed by research to permit definite causal statements. But it seems quite likely that the state of consciousness heavily determines the role of imagery (#3 in Table 4.2), memorability (#6), and the roles of external reality (#10) and of communication (#14).

Second, spontaneity versus effortfulness, or passivity versus activity (see Rapaport, 1953): one of the most strikingly characteristic things about typical daydreaming is that it is not done deliberately, but rather one feels that he has been "drifting" when he suddenly comes to his senses and realizes that he has been deep in a fantasy. Fantasy has an almost ego-alien characteristic in this way; occasionally, of course, we deliberately lose ourselves in daydreams, but for the most part they come upon us unwittingly—often even at times of such high seriousness as listening to a paper in a scientific conference! If you were wool-gathering during the past few minutes, for once you may be comforted by the fact that you were only illustrating the point made in the paper.—Thus, we can call a fantasy a *passive* cognitive product, one in which the deliberating ego plays a small role. Very occasionally, one may encounter a subject who tells TAT stories in an almost equally effortless way. Most characteristically, however, it is an *effort* to tell a story; one must search about for materials; the effort takes some time and is punctuated by gaps while the subject tries to think of something to say. Surely a daydreamer never had to pause and think up something to say to himself! The very fact that a reaction time of anywhere from a few seconds to several minutes intervenes between the presentation of the picture and the beginning of the story is in itself impressive evidence of the effortful, active character of storytelling as a cognitive act. A slightly different aspect of the same point is the fact that no one tells you to daydream—you do it of your own nonvolition; whereas a TAT story cannot by definition arise spontaneously but must be elicited by an externally imposed obligation.

Third, the role of imagery and of verbalization: fantasies may be partly or entirely nonverbal, whereas TAT stories by definition are made up of words.[9] Especially as daydreams verge on hypnagogic reveries, as we have seen, they may become more and more entirely pictorial, like dreams, words appearing only as speeches of the pictured figures; or they may be made up of vivid auditory imagery rather than visual. Of course, a daydream may be as purely verbal (especially in people who have predominantly nonvisual, but verbal imagery) as a TAT story, and in some stories the influence of imagery

[9]For this reason, I have not attempted to make use of Rapaport's interesting point about syntax. There may well be important differences between the linguistic usages of fantasies and stories but the situation is confused by the fact that fantasies must be verbalized to be studied, and they are usually put into words in a state of consciousness different from the one in which they were produced.

can at times be divined. After a particularly vivid bit of description of a scene other than the card, I have sometimes inquired and found that the S had developed the story partly in terms of visual imagery. And when Card 16 is handled in the way I have found most fruitful [see Chapter 2, above], the S is *asked* to create a visual image and then make up a story about it. This point is closely related to the next one, since a reverie may be made up entirely of images without any connective tissue for continuity.

Fourth, the issue of implication versus explicitness in the finished daydream or story. As we have seen, fantasy needs no explication of transitions, personal connotations, or the bases of associative chaining; this is closely related to the thirteenth point, the role of communication. Since the daydream is for strictly personal consumption, much that would need elaboration and explanation can merely be stated. In addition, however, images or thoughts may have the property Rapaport described, as in dreams, so that you *know* something about a person or thing without its being spelled out.

This last property is strange to the TAT story, which must live up to social standards of intelligibility. Therefore, unexplained transitions and gaps in continuity are rare in stories.

The fifth difference bears on the role of the primary process in the reported product. The daydreams we have to study (and perhaps even more so, the ones we don't get our hands on!) are often marked by contradictions, sudden unrealistic transitions in time and space, condensations, displacements, symbols, and other formal characteristics of the primary process. Since the daydream is responsible to no one, is usually unreported and perhaps even is usually unavailable to conscious memory, it has little need for secondary revision and the conventions of the secondary process. Nevertheless, most reveries that we know about are somewhat more orderly than dreams, probably due to the fact that they are produced in a state of consciousness marked by greater vigilance.

TAT stories, however, rarely show much evidence of the primary process in the reported product. Even though the primary process may have played a great role in the silent development of the story, the finished product is generally orderly, with no obvious, tolerated contradiction, autistic logic, or blatant unrealism. Rarely, I should add, *unless* we ask the subject to regress in the service of the ego by telling us a fairy story, dream, or the like, and then only certain flexible and well-controlled subjects are able to introduce much primary process.[10] When the primary process obviously shows

[This statement demands modification in light of the subsequent work of Eagle (1964). After adapting my manual for scoring manifestations of the primary process in Rorschach responses to narrative materials, she obtained dreams and TAT stories from the same subjects and scored them independently. To our surprise, the highest density of primary process scores occurred in TAT stories given with the instruction to tell a nightmare, the second highest in stories after a request to tell a fairy story, and actual dreams had only a few more primary-process characteristics than ordinary TAT stories. The effect was general and did not depend on the presence of a few highly creative or "flexible and well-controlled" persons in the sample, which was made up, however, of unemployed actors.]

itself in the TAT story of a normal person, it is usually under the shelter of the "once upon a time" convention of fairy story, science fiction thriller, or the like.

The sixth difference listed in Table 4.2, the memorability of the product, is closely related to the first point, the quality of consciousness. The fact is that a daydream is fragmentary, fleeting, and generally unreportable. Taking place as it does in a special state of consciousness, it may receive relatively little attention and thus may not be available to deliberate recall. Since I have started writing this paper, I have been paying a great deal more attention to my own daydreams, and—possibly for this very reason—I have found them annoyingly wispy. There is rarely any kind of story development, sometimes only a single image of gratification or a wished-for state of affairs. One is often uncertain whether this fragmentary recall is due to the fact that a bit of it has appeared above the surface, available to reflection.

Parenthetically, at this point, I'd like to remark that Dr. Leo Goldberger and I are currently carrying on an experiment in reality deprivation, in which we cause our subjects to lie upon a comfortable bed and to do nothing for eight hours, their eyes and ears being prevented from taking in meaningful stimuli by means of experimental devices that produce a homogeneous, monotonous field.[11] What better invitation to daydream? We systematically inquire about fantasies at the end of the eight-hour period, and the remarkable fact is that most subjects deny having had any. Although they sleep a good deal of the time, they *are* aware of having been awake, of not having been thinking about anything in a directed or rational way, yet they cannot report what their "freely wandering thoughts" have been. This is in spite of the fact that by the time subjects have gone into this situation we know them fairly well, they have written intimate autobiographies for us and have been subjected to many hours of testing and interviewing, so that one would hardly expect a great deal of ordinary reticence. We doubt that the lack of reported daydreams is due to conscious withholding, therefore; it seems more a matter of the intrinsic difficulty of catching hold of a fantasy and recalling it.

TAT stories are of course sometimes rather fragmentary, but in a different sense. The brevity of a TAT story usually results from the inability of the storyteller to get started at all; he almost never gives you only a bit of the beginning or a single scene from the end of a possible story; instead, he simply describes the picture and stays very close to the pictured scene. Whether long or short, the TAT story (being produced in full conscious awareness) receives focal attention and is available to direct recall. When doing the Self-Interpretation (Luborsky, 1953) one very rarely finds it

---

[11]It is quite possible that the conclusion reached here is specific to the kinds of young male subjects we have used. [The work was later published; see Goldberger (1961). I verified the observation in a self-experiment (Holt, 1965c).]

necessary to read back the story to the subject. He usually has it in mind and if requested can repeat it substantially unchanged. (I'm aware of the fact that there *are* changes and occasional loss of an entire story, and that a whole technique may be made out of getting a subject to recall his TAT stories some time later and noticing the discrepancies. That does not destroy the basic point.) If it were not for this memorability, the valuable technique of Self-Interpretation would be impossible [see also Rock, 1975].

The seventh point of difference deals with the degree of narrative structure. Daydreams are characteristically loose and fluid in organization hence, incidentally, less memorable than stories). They do not follow a set model such as the one suggested by the TAT instructions; there may be no clear-cut beginning nor end; and the fantasy may dwell upon the situation of gratification much longer than is characteristic of stories. Many fantasies have little suspense and little plot. An unstudied but potentially very interesting question would be the extent to which fantasies of different persons incorporate delay or simply plunge directly into gratification. Casually, it would appear that as people become older and more sophisticated, up to a point, their conscious fantasies are less infantile and direct, incorporating more story-like properties. The fantasy does not need to be much affected by literary models, though as a person steeps himself in literature his own daydreams *may* take on somewhat more of a literary cast.

When we turn to TAT stories, we find that the instructions, in whatever variation, always incorporate a demand for a description of the scene depicted in the picture, events leading up to it, thoughts and feelings of the characters, and an outcome. Most examiners also ask for a plot, a dramatic and interesting story. In doing so, they are implicitly telling the subject that he is to follow the model of the short story, a literary form that is characteristic of our own era. Hardly anyone can help but draw on schemata that have been laid down by the many stories he has first had read to him and then later on read himself. One of the main features of plotting is suspense. In the Broadway model, a plot means "boy meets girl, boy loses girl, boy gets girl." In the daydream, the middle part is generally dispensed with, and often enough even "boy meets girl" falls by the wayside; "boy gets girl—right into bed" may be the principal scene. Then too, many subjects give their characters fictional names or introduce dialogue, descriptions, trick endings, and other literary devices that are little found in daydreams.

The eighth difference has to do with the nature of the motivation expressed. Despite the fact that the same subject may at one time daydream and at another time tell TAT stories, and remain the same person with the same basic needs and interests, still the way that those motives are expressed will differ in the two media. The fact that the daydream is private and uncommunicated, that it is a regressive and often not recalled kind of thinking, makes it possible for the fulfillment of wishes to be relatively direct and for the wishes themselves to be unsublimated and close to the hypothetical state of original drives. If someone has annoyed us, we can easily imagine killing him, or inflicting on him tortures we would not even consider witnessing in reality, much less carrying them out ourselves. This is not to say that all daydreams deal exclusively with raw sex and aggression; many of the examples Varendonck gives in his book deal with such relatively sublimated matters as his anxieties about his doctoral thesis.

The wishes expressed in TAT stories, by contrast, are generally less blatant and less obviously related to direct, "instinctual" aims. The exigencies of communicating the story to an examiner cause most subjects to stick to what is "decent" or "reasonable" or "socially acceptable." Their own wishes, which may indeed be mirrored in the stories, are much more indirectly and inferentially involved than in the case of daydreams. A man may express his heart's desire in his fantasies, but keep such precious thoughts to himself while taking the TAT.[12]

The ninth difference is closely related to the preceding one. Perhaps because of the unsocialized nature of the wishes implicated in fantasies, the latter tend to incorporate more affect than TAT stories do. Again, there is a good deal of overlap; as was noted above, some fantastical thinking involves little emotion, and many tellers of TAT stories do put a good deal of affect into their productions. Yet there remains a difference in central tendency, so that we note it as a significant loss of distance when the subject gets appreciably angry, sexually excited, or anxious while telling a tale, even one in which such emotions are appropriate—but to the characters, not to the author. As this last distinction is much more blurred in fantasy, intense and less differentiated affects are appropriate and typically occur to a greater extent than in storytelling.

The tenth difference bears on the role of external reality. Quite often it is possible to find a meaningful aspect of a person's environment—a press—that has set off a train of fantasy thought. Varendonck reports a number of such in his book. On the other hand, a good deal of fantasy thinking takes place at night when we are in bed in a state of relative stimuluslessness; at such times, and at others, a fantasy may take off from any chain of thoughts. Thus, at the end of the day we may reflect on a number of the impressive events that have happened to us and perhaps have delayed reactions to them in the form of daydreams. One could argue that, in such an instance, the fantasy is in fact a delayed reaction to an external press; indeed, it is hard to imagine a fantasy without *some* reference to press. The point, however, is that a fantasy need not take off directly from anything in the person's situation, nor need it include any particular representation of the press if one

---

[12][In his discussion on this paper at the conference, Tomkins reminded me of his paper (1949) on the relation between fantasies and TAT stories. It included the case of "a young graduate student in mathematics at Princeton, who spent almost six hours a day repeating a fantasy which took from an hour to an hour and a half to go through because it was so complicated. In the TAT, there was no evidence for it as far as I could see" (Tomkins, 1961, p. 47).]

does incite it. Daydreaming is under no pressure to include or pay attention to anything external at all. A TAT story, on the other hand, is directly constrained to include in a responsible way a description of the picture, the immediate press that has evoked it. The instructions, the general attitude of the examiner (that this is a serious business) and the setting, all conspire to impress this requirement on the subject.

By way of a slight digression, I find it interesting to note that the old tradition at the Harvard Psychological Clinic, where the emphasis was so heavily on motivation, was to pay little attention to perceptual distortion or stories in which the subject took liberties with the reality of the picture. If he asked what the object was on the floor in 3BM, for example, S would be encouraged to interpret it any way he wished: "It can be anything you'd like." In this setting, perceptual distortions are not mentioned by Murray (1938) except as indicators of the strength of needs. It is only fair to point out, however, that in a relatively nonpathological population of college men, such formal features were relatively unimportant (cf. Wyatt, 1947; Holt, 1958b). By contrast, Rapaport, Gill and Schafer (1946), working with a variety of psychiatric patients, explicitly recognize the role of picture and instructions in constituting an adaptive requirement and thus a situation in which reality testing can be studied.

The eleventh point follows from the last one: if there is an adaptive challenge, then abilities play more of a role in the product than where there is none. In reveries, except those that verge on planning, the principal starting point is wish rather than reality: hence, adaptation plays very little part, if any, in many fantasies. In the productive daydreams of inventors or of people who develop scientific theories or solve mathematical problems, the fantasy may deal with an internalized reality, but this is the exception rather than the rule. The ordinary, garden variety, wool-gathering reverie pays precious little attention to reality, and abilities have little relevance to the task of producing a satisfying imaginary gratification of some wish. If the wish is forbidden by defenses and if direct gratification cannot be allowed even in fantasy, then the daydreamer may unconsciously use abilities and defenses conjointly in devising ingenious by-passes. And in the more sophisticated fantasies of people who characteristically think in terms of reality, and who may pose themselves problems that must be solved in accordance with a definite internalized[13] set of rules, abilities will play an increasing role in the final product.

In TAT stories, which are produced in response to an examiner's request and which involve accommodation to a usually well-structured stimulus card, abilities typically play a considerable role. Henry (1956) has shown

[13][I have let this term stand here and elsewhere, but following Schafer (1976) I do not mean internalization to imply some spatial transfer of substance but a person's learning something— here, a set of rules—and integrating it with more general value premises that form part of his/ her identity.]

that intelligence can be estimated from TAT stories with a significant and rather high degree of accuracy (r = .85), and surely we are not entirely disingenuous when we tell the subject, "this is a test of imagination." The *ability* to be imaginative, to express one's thoughts in vivid and well-structured language, the ability to enter imaginatively and empathically into the inner lives of other people and thus to create convincing characters in one's stories, the ability to take hold of a rather complicated set of instructions and to hold together a coherent train of thought over a period of quite some minutes without external prodding—all of these are abilities in the true sense, and such abilities are displayed, to a larger or a smaller extent, in all TAT stories.[14]

The twelfth difference bears on the relation to action. A consequence of the relative lack of control and defense accompanying drive expression in some people's fantasies is that they sometimes lead to a direct acting out of the wish in question. To take a prosaic example, if I get thirsty working at my desk on a June afternoon, I may have a fantasy about drinking a delicious bottle of wine, and may stop by at a liquor store on the way home to dinner. In this respect, fantasy shades off into planning. Another kind of fantasy—generally unconscious—accompanies acting out. For example, typical displacements, in which we take out our anger on persons who are safely below us in a social hierarchy, are usually accompanied by a fantasy (perhaps unconscious) of getting even with the person who is really bothering us.

TAT stories are very rarely accompanied or followed by any obvious acting out. Despite the fact that my focus so far has been entirely on the stories themselves, I agree with Schafer (1954) that *test behavior* is an integral and equally important aspect of the TAT. When a story containing themes of succorance—dependence on older and wiser persons to bail the hero out of his difficulties—is accompanied by requests to repeat the instructions, and followed by the subject's asking if it wasn't a good story, we see the same need that is expressed thematically being acted out in the relationship to the examiner. Indeed, such congruences between interpretations based on behavior and on content (and on formal aspects of the stories, too) are among our best ways of checking and verifying our inferences. Yet this kind of acting out remains rather pale and insignificant compared to clinical examples from the histories of character disorders. For instance, Ehrenreich (1959) describes the hypnotherapy of a man who had committed a bizarre, impulsive murder in a dissociated state. The reconstruction makes it very plausible that he was acting out a fantasy of retaliation against a woman who

[14][In terms of Guilford's (1967) useful Structure of Intellect model of abilities, at least the following are prominently required of a person to tell good TAT stories: cognition of behavioral units, relations, and implications, and divergent production of both semantic and behavioral units, relations, systems, and implications. Indeed, there is hardly a cell on the semantic and behavioral planes of his model's cube that does not enter into the performance to some degree.]

had traumatically seduced him in his childhood (and against several other women), and then in his cutting the lungs out of the body and trying to blow them up, he was enacting an unconscious fantasy of bringing back to life his dead sweetheart. Of course this is an extreme case in all respects, but I trust it makes the point.

The thirteenth point has to do with self-relevance. To be sure, it is true as Murray has pointed out that both TAT stories and fantasies are anthropocentric and have a figure of dominant interest, a hero. But fantasies are typically egocentric, imaginary events in which the daydreamer himself takes the leading role. It is an unusual TAT story in which the teller is presented as the hero. Because of this self-involvement, it is plain enough to anyone that his own daydreams are relevant to an understanding of his personality, that they express something important about him. One of the central points of Murray's rationale for the TAT is that the process of projection enables a subject to express a great deal about himself in a TAT story without any awareness of this fact. The point is easily verified in routine clinical practice with the TAT, if one follows Murray's original practice of inquiring into the sources of stories, or if following Luborsky (1953) one asks for a self-interpretation. Using either method, one quickly discovers that a large proportion of patients have great difficulty in seeing much if any self-relevance in the great majority of their stories.

The fourteenth difference in Table 4.2 is in the role of communication. As Freud (1908a, p. 160) remarked, "day-dreams are cathected with a large amount of interest; they are carefully cherished by the subject and usually concealed with a great deal of sensitivity, as though they were among the most intimate possessions of his personality." Because a daydream is such a regressive kind of cognitive-affective product, it may seem childish, silly, or nonsensical, the feelings too strong and the expressed wishes too self-indulgent or embarrassingly direct to be told—except to someone to whom one is very close. The fact is that psychoanalysts are the ones who hear the most reports of fantasies, and then often at the cost of much struggle with resistances. Outside of analysis, we are more likely to tell our daydreams to our closest friends or our wives than we are to casual acquaintances.

TAT stories, on the other hand, are typically told to an examiner who does not in reality have a very intimate relationship to the subject; they are quasi-public utterances. This fact, and all of the other attendant circumstances under which testing takes place, may have a very considerable effect on what is communicated to the tester; the effect may take place partly in conscious censorship and to a large extent through a less conscious molding of the response process itself. The point needs a little qualification, for "in many circumstances under which testing is carried out a relatively strong fantasy relationship may also be present—the tester as therapist, as parental figure, etc." (Schafer, 1959a).

The fifteenth and final point of difference between daydreams and

TAT stories deals with the range of subject matter touched on. Since fantasies are spontaneous, indulged in due to an inner urge, there is nothing to stop them from being monotonously stereotyped and repetitive, while the variety of situations presented in the TAT cards tends to stimulate discussion of different subject matter. It takes a powerful preoccupation indeed to produce a set of stories with identical themes told to a set of cards as varied as the TAT, though in profound emotional states like a depression even this effect can be achieved, as Tomkins (1947) has pointed out. Theoretically, we could dispense with pictures entirely, and simply ask the subject to tell stories. Aside from the advantage of standardization that the pictures introduce, and the fact that they make it easier for people who are not particularly creative to get started, the pictures have the distinct advantage of presenting the S with a series of situations of varied emotional significance with which he must deal; the pictures confront him with persons of both sexes and various ages, in given configurations, and strongly suggesting types of problems—any part of which a given S might prefer to avoid, and could fail to touch on in his spontaneous fantasies. In this way, the TAT enables us to take stock of many departments of personality, which might otherwise be locked to us.

You may have noticed, by now, that most of the differentiating characteristics of fantasies listed in Table 4.2 *may* be true of TAT stories, too. We have all encountered stories in which the S himself appeared, or loosely structured ones, or fragmentary or bizarre stories rich with formal indications of the primary process. Stories sometimes do contain "raw, instinctual" themes—and so forth. Certainly a TAT story *may* be and sometimes is very much like a fantasy, far down the continuum toward the dream, just as some dreams are quite reasonable, prosaic, and pedestrian.

Why are stories not more often like daydreams?

We get a hint at the answer by noting that when they are, the teller is usually quite a disturbed person. Fantasy is a regressive kind of thinking, and a good deal of our mature personality structure has been set up to enable us to think in a more effective, orderly and realistic way. The emergence of regressive thinking indicates a decompensation of these controlling structures and thus a loss of ego autonomy—or else a controlled, playful relaxation of defenses by a person who signals his intention by saying, "This is going to be a ghost story," or who has been asked to tell a fairy story. The whole point is that the nature of the TAT calls for secondary process thinking with only a little, well-controlled admixture of primary process for life and color. For this reason, we can easily recognize the uncontrolled emergence of primitive thinking and can make diagnostic use of the fact.

Now that we have gone through all these differences and have agreed— I hope!—that a TAT story is *not* a fantasy, it is fair to ask, Was this trip necessary? Is all of this distinction-making more than a terminological quibble? I think it amounts to a good deal more, and this is the reason I concentrated at such length on the differences. There would be little harm in simply defining the word "fantasy" as meaning "TAT (or other thematic test) story" if it were not for the fact that the term has its own meaning, in general as well as in psychological usage: that is, a product of uncontrolled imagination, a daydream or reverie. This last is unwanted semantic baggage you must carry if you stick to the familiar misusage; you must constantly make it clear that when you speak about fantasy you do not mean it in the sense most people will assume.

The other danger is that if we call stories fantasies, we will overlook or forget all the important aspects of TAT stories that make them what they are. This is the implication of the tradition that says the TAT is a test of motivation, while the Rorschach tells us about personality structure. Of course, the first approaches to TAT interpretation were focused entirely on content analysis, and for many people this is still the whole story. Such a narrow conception may lead to missing the boat diagnostically and to an impoverishment of what the TAT can give us generally. As you will recall from the Englishs' definitions (quoted above), the general concept of both fantasy and daydreams is that they represent "a sort of wish fulfillment" and that "wishes are not disguised and fulfillment is imagined as direct, without repression." This view stated in these definitions is an extreme one, of course, but it highlights the traps one can fall into by considering stories as fantasies. Parenthetically, I'd like to observe that this tendency—to consider the TAT as a test of fantasy and to look at the stories from a primarily motivational point of view—looks very much like a hangover from the early days of psychoanalysis, before the days of ego psychology. Before 1923 was the heyday of id-analysis, in which defenses and other ego-structural factors, and adaptive considerations of all kinds were ignored. Psychoanalytic theory and practice have come a long way since then, and since the work of Sigmund and Anna Freud, Hartmann, Rapaport, Kris, and several others. Must TAT workers lag, and confuse themselves with anachronisms? Certainly we don't *have* to.

I propose, however, that one of the TAT's *strengths* is the fact that it elicits the kind of material it does, with some aspects or elements of fantasy, but many differences. Mostly the differences are related to its being a set task with adaptive requirements, and mostly one sees the effects of these features through the formal aspects of the performance. They indicate not only gross pathology, as already indicated, but also various specific types of disorder. For example, one sometimes picks up paranoid trends through fantasy-like content, such as themes of persecution; much more often, however, they may be seen in stories with ordinary content but the characteristically litigious formal feature of deriving everything by tortured reasoning from the picture itself. Here is a useful diagnostic indicator that we would not have had if the TAT really opened up a door into a hypothetical store of unconscious wishes through which fantasies might pour out.

The example is not an isolated one. Most of the inferences about personality structure that we can draw from the TAT depend on these nonfantasy aspects, as I have tried to argue (Holt, 1958b [Chapter 5, below]) and as Schafer (1958a) has so beautifully shown.

The similarities between TAT stories and daydreams that exist enabled Murray and Morgan to treat stories much as if they *were* fantasies, and to analyze them in the same way, with considerable validity. Two factors may be distinguished in their (perhaps misleading) success: first, they were dealing with Harvard undergraduates who were normal in the sense that they were not seeking help, and lacked the kind of psychopathology that produces the most dramatic formal features of stories, but who were highly nonnormative in their verbal creativity and flexibility. These boys could really make up stories, imaginative ones that had much of the feel of a fantasy; I still recall my shock when after some years at the Harvard Psychological Clinic I started using the TAT clinically—the meagreness, the flatness of the stories I got contrasted sharply with the ideational riches of the Harvard student. The other factor was Murray's and his co-workers' great interest in what is loosely called *dynamics* to the virtual overshadowing of other aspects of personality. Despite the fact that *Explorations* contains scores of nonmotivational variables covering most of personality, the principal concept of the book is the *need*, and the need-press combination of thema seems to be a close second. Now we have seen that even dynamically, TAT stories differ from fantasies, but the differences in this respect are not too great: after all, the stories *do* contain goal-strivings, just as fantasies do, and even if they are not the same goals, it is not easy to tell the difference.

Let us take it for granted that a thematic test story is quite a different cognitive product from a typical daydream. What *is* the relation between the two? We have already spoken of one relation, a formal one: at their extremes, these two types of thought products are adjacent and even overlap somewhat with respect to a number of continua (such as that from primary to secondary process).

A more substantial and intimate relation was originally suggested by Morgan and Murray (1935): that TAT stories draw on fantasies for their material. It fairly often happens that to Card 16 Ss tell obviously wish-fulfilling stories, sometimes in the first person. In the Self-Interpretation, such Ss frequently say, "This is a favorite daydream of mine," or the like. Any person's repertory of fantasies is likely to contain a fairly innocuous candidate for this kind of display; for example, themes of occupational success or of a pleasant vacation in beautiful surroundings. Yet the blank card is a special case in several respects; it offers the S no reality to cling to but forces him to fall back entirely on his own resources. Thus, it fails to have a number of the characteristics listed in Table 4.2 as typical for the TAT, and *ought* to stimulate the most fantasy-like stories. But how about stories told to the other cards? It probably happens quite rarely that the storyteller, when given one of the typical pictures, produces a ready-made daydream and offers it as a story after making a few elementary changes, as from the first to the third person.

Nevertheless, Ss may draw on ready-made material from fantasy when dealing with structured pictures too, under certain conditions. *First,* there must be a pre-existing fantasy relevant enough to the picture to be brought to mind by it (not necessarily consciously). *Second,* the S must have flexible enough defenses so that he has access to such material, which in many persons is kept under strict repression. *Third,* the S may draw on fantasy for a story if some other, nonfantasy material (such as personal memory) is not even more relevant, ready, and suitable. The story is a product of many determinants and conditions, in addition to and in interaction with the fantasies that are touched off. The latter must ordinarily undergo many changes, therefore; requirements of social communication may expurgate them, requirements of fitting the picture may truncate them, the whole apparatus of anticipations, abilities and models may take bits of several fantasies, remold, transform, revise, and elaborate them—and all of this silently—so that the teller himself does not recognize much similarity between his own fantasies and the finished product. It is easy to see that many circumstances can change the role played by each of these nonfantasy sources: the relation between E and S, the nature of the situation, increase in motivation or conflict, decompensation of defenses, and so forth—all could change so as to let fantasy play a larger role. They may also, in other variants, keep it out entirely. Thus, if the fantasy material suggested by 13MF is so strongly repressed in a very inhibited young man that any hint of it is proscribed by his defenses, he may block completely, merely describe the picture, or draw on some extrapersonal material such as newspaper stories, novels, friends' adventures, or the like, none of which may give more than an indirect hint about his own sexual fantasies.

If the relation is so uncertain, how have we gotten away with calling TAT stories "fantasies" for so many years? I have talked glibly in my own test reports about "the characteristics of the patient's fantasy life," meaning nothing but what his TAT was like. Why could we? Because *nobody checks.* The resident on the case is going to assume automatically that when the psychologist talks about fantasy the latter knows more than he does; the analyst who does know about the patient's fantasies just skims through the jargon in the report looking for what he can use; and the personality researcher, if he is interested in fantasy at all, accepts the TAT as a measure of it and never thinks to *test* this assumption. Is it not remarkable that in the first twenty-five years of work with the TAT only one comparative study of the daydreams and TAT stories of the same person has been published (Tomkins, 1949)? It is high time for more such research.

5

At the Harvard Psychological Clinic, the work of Fred Wyatt (1947) on formal aspects of TAT stories caught my interest even though it turned out disappointingly. A couple of years later, perhaps that was what made me more interested than my peers in the structural components of the TAT which, David Rapaport taught us, were so useful diagnostically. The accompanying paper tells the story of my persistent belief in this approach, despite the discouragement of small and fluctuating correlational validities. (A rationale for this seemingly irrational belief is given in Chapter 5, Vol. 2.)

Recently, I dusted off the old manual for scoring formal aspects of the TAT for two of my students, Ronald Naso and Jean Cirillo, who are incorporating parts of it into a method of scoring level of ego development in TAT stories. The chapter that follows is, then, an interim report.

Formal Aspects of the TAT—A Neglected Resource

An often-encountered fallacy is the statement that "the Rorschach is a test of the structure of personality, the TAT a test of its content." I have even seen a question on a preliminary examination for the Ph.D. in clinical psychology, which required the student to accept and justify such a statement. The trouble with this formulation is that it is incomplete; it is a half-truth, which would read just about as accurately the other way around. For certainly research and clinical practice in recent years has shown that Rorschach content can teach us a great deal about strivings, preoccupations, conceptions of self and of others, and other "content" aspects of personality [see Chapter 11, below]. The purpose of this paper is to present arguments and facts to support the position that much can be learned about the structure of personality from the TAT, primarily from a study of its formal aspects.

Actually, the point is not specific to the TAT. As we have progressed from the era of "psychometrics" to that of diagnostic evaluation and assessment of personality, our conception of tests has changed. In its original meaning, a test was (or was intended to be) a quantitative measure of a specific psychological variable. Thus, it was reasonable to approach any new instrument by trying to narrow down its sphere of relevance as much as possible. As psychologists learned to use projective techniques and related methods they began to grasp the fact that they were dealing with what Cronbach calls "wide-band" instruments: not tests of precise functions, but devices that elicit broad, characteristic samples of behavior in more or less standardized ways. And it has become gradually clearer that records of such behavior could be subjected to almost as many different kinds of analysis as there are theoretical propositions about personality.

Therefore it has become inappropriate to criticize a projective technique for not having an agreed-upon scoring system, even though some people still reject the TAT on these grounds. There can be no one set of scores for an instrument like Murray's, which draws forth such a rich and multidimensional output. Rather, there can be as many different scoring systems as there are types of variables that may be discovered in it.

Methods of clinical assessment like TAT, Rorschach, interview, autobiography, play sessions, etc., have in common that they pose a task that cannot be satisfied by a simple adaptive act, as can an arithmetic problem. Rather they confront the subject with a requirement to produce something from himself in as creative a way as possible, yet within the guiding framework of some general adaptive requirements. Thus, as compared to free association, the TAT requires that the subject attend to the picture, interpret it with a degree of realism and produce a story with certain structural features. It is far from an "unstructured" requirement, just as the pictures themselves are mostly rather clear in their major import, but there are enough degrees of freedom so that the subject can express countless variations on the basic themes that are suggested (e.g., parent-child relations) and can meet the adaptive requirements in his personal idiosyncratic ways. The usual clinical interview poses a similar kind of adaptive requirement with plenty of leeway for personal expression, and most other projective techniques likewise. Whether we choose to attend to content themes or to the formal properties of the performances depends in each instance on *us*, the interpreters, not on the material. The question is whether or not we have the conceptual lenses that enable us to see a person's defensive style as well as his resolution of the Oedipus complex when we interview him about his parents, or study his Rorschach or TAT responses. Human productions of this degree of freedom and richness can always be analyzed for formal properties as well as for content.

When we approach any clinical material, then, including TAT stories, we can conceivably direct our attention toward any of its infinite number of aspects, and must choose on some basis. Our choice is determined, usually, either by a theoretical proposition or by a practical requirement. As we shall see shortly, it makes a good deal of difference to the usefulness of a set of variables just what theoretical or practical considerations the psychologist has in mind. When we draw a general distinction between form and content, however, we are orienting our analysis of data toward different spheres of personality. For the same general distinction can be made in the realm of personality itself. Consider for a moment how we reach conceptions like need for aggression, introspectiveness, or reliance on reaction formation, as personality variables. We do so by generalizing from many particulars of just the kind we find in projective tests. Is it not likely, therefore, that we should be able to generalize best about the particular motives, sentiments, identities, conflicts, and personal-historical themes in a personality from the *content* of responses to assessment? By the same token, if we mean by structure of personality persisting regularities in the *how* rather than the *what* a person thinks, feels, wants, strives, etc., we can find the particulars from which structural generalizations are made by attending to the ways he copes with the demands of a TAT as well as a Rorschach or a WAIS.

Murray and Morgan were primarily interested in producing an instrument by which they could study the motivational ("dynamic") aspects of personality, which were the ones that mainly interested them. Consequently, Murray concentrated on developing a scoring method that focused on content—needs, press, and themas. But he had builded better than he knew. The TAT was so designed that it struck a happy balance between freedom and control; not only was it an unrivaled source of dynamic hypotheses, but it allowed a useful variety of formal features of performance to emerge at the same time. It remained only for persons who were mainly interested in the structure of personality to exploit the structural resources of the test performance.

So far, I have been using the terms *form* and *content* as if their meaning were perfectly obvious and did not need definition. Indeed, the distinction between manner and matter, or style and substance, is as old as criticism in the arts. But when you get down to specifics, it is not so easy to say just what the defining principles are, and where dividing lines should be drawn. Unambiguous examples come readily to mind: when we single out the fact that the little violinist in Card 1 likes his instrument and enjoys playing, we are surely attending to content. When we take note of the fact that the story is neatly finished without the examiner's having to intervene or prod, it is certainly a formal feature that engages our interest. Consider, however, a general variable like Adequacy of Hero—is this an aspect of content or of form? It touches closely on a feature of plot; surely part of the substance of a story is the success of the hero in achieving his own goals. But note that we are not talking about any particular story, nor any particular way of being adequate: one subject might get a high rating for a story in which a religious man succeeds in mastering his impulses so he can successfully contemplate the kingdom of heaven, and another could get the same rating for a hero who succeeded in killing his rival for the possession of a woman. Such a generalized property of content seems worthy of being kept separate from thematic material of the usual, concrete kind. Another way of looking at it is to ask *what inference we draw* from the abstracted part of a story. If it has been caused by and enables us to infer the presence of some value, attitude, purpose, preoccupation, or type of present or past personal relationship, it should be considered content.[1] In this case, however, the fact of consistently adequate heroes suggests primarily an inference about ego-strength: the capacity to delay impulse and strive successfully for long-range goals, sustained by self-confidence. By this token, the general quality of stories referred to in the variable, Adequacy of Hero, can be considered a formal aspect.

Concretely, we might make the distinction as follows. Let us take a story in which the hero, a student of the violin, enjoys the instrument, works hard to perfect his artistry, and becomes a great virtuoso. The fact that the hero succeeds in this particular way enables us to make a *content* inference: strong need for achievement. But the general fact of adequacy, taken together with the success of heroes in other stories in reaching other, nonachievement goals, leads to the *formal* inference of ego-strength.

In what follows, therefore, I shall use content in this sense: particular meanings referable to analogous meaning-contents in the teller's own life. It is convenient to define formal aspects residually, as everything else[2] about stories except content, since it is hard to do it any other way, just as it is remarkably difficult to produce a useful definition for the term, personality structure.

SOME HISTORY[3]

There have been two main approaches to formal features of the TAT: test-centered and person-centered. From almost the beginning of TAT work, some people have recognized that there *were* formal aspects to the

---

[1]K. M. Colby (1955) has coined the word *meantent* (a condensation of *meaning* and *content*) to stand for all these matters, because it is a little awkward to speak of the "content of personality."

[2][Following Schafer (1954), I now find it desirable to distinguish, within this residual realm, between test behavior and formal aspects of the stories themselves. All nonverbal aspects of the *S*'s performance comprise test behavior, a distinction which likewise appears simpler than it turns out to be in practice.]

[3]This historical sketch is far from complete, and omits mention of some TAT workers who have published research on formal aspects (e.g., Balken & Masserman, G. Lindzey) or whose published method of interpretation includes considerable use of formal aspects (e.g., M. Stein, S. Rosenzweig). But the fact is that the great majority of TAT interpreters have emphasized content almost to the exclusion of formal features. For example, of the 15 "experts" included in E. Shneidman's (1951) *Thematic Test Analysis,* the great majority worked almost entirely with content (M. Arnold, B. Aron, L. Eron, R. Fine, W. Joel & D. Shapiro, S. Klebanoff, S. Korchin, J. Lasaga, P. Symonds, R. K. White), a few made some use of formal aspects (L. Bellak, J. Rotter & S. Jessor, H. D. Sargent), while only A. A. Hartman in addition to myself [see Chapter 6] used formal features extensively. Hence the title of this paper.

performance and that they were being neglected by Murray and Morgan's content-oriented approach. In 1940, Frederick Wyatt began elaborating a system of formal aspects, proceeding largely from a logical but story-centered approach and covering such qualities as the following (see also Wyatt, 1947):

1. Linguistic analysis (e.g., type-token, adjective-verb ratios).
2. Modes of presentation (e.g., general sentiment of the story, major emphasis of presentation, setting in time and space, quality of plot, development of the story, introduction of figures, character of imagery, etc.).
3. Comprehension of stimulus (e.g., relationship of figure and background, details utilized, shock-like effects, etc.).
4. Subjective reactions (e.g., expressions of like or dislike as to the stimulus, explanatory remarks and comments).

He and Marianne Weil applied these categories to the TATs of 11 Ss who were being intensively studied at the Clinic at that time, rating their stories as objectively as possible on these dimensions. They then performed a syndrome analysis, emerging with clusters of co-varying formal aspects, and correlated both the syndromes and the original variables with the many rated variables of personality that became available from the Diagnostic Council in 1941.

The results were so disappointing that they gave the whole cause of formal aspects a setback. The correlations were meager, did not fall into meaningful patterns, and suggested that the features of TAT performance under study were not determined to any large extent by important dimensions of personality.

In retrospect, it is possible to see two reasons for the failure of this pioneering effort: first, the selection of formal variables was made on rational rather than clinical grounds—it grew out of an attempt to catalogue all major aspects of the stories rather than to find measures of important aspects of the persons who told them—so that many of the myriad possible formal aspects were not used. Second, the set of personality variables in use at the Clinic was Murray's latest revision of the system described in *Explorations in Personality* (Murray et al., 1938); and though it was by far the most imaginative, broad, and comprehensive set of personological variables in existence, it did have a weakness: in the realm of personality *structure*. The system had after all grown up in the same fertile brain that had produced the TAT and the need-press approach to its analysis. Murray's first and most dominant interest was in motivation: the current needs, the fantasy themes and the residues of infantile experience that determined the goals for which men strove in reality and in dream. He did not ignore structural components, such as defense mechanisms, traits, and abilities; these were all studied and rated. With the exception of the general area of introversion-extroversion, however, Murray was not deeply concerned with these features of personality and his approach to them was more summary, less differentiated and less founded on extensive clinical observation than was his orientation to dynamic aspects of personality. Therefore, the structural personality variables that probably determined the formal features of the TAT were relatively neglected, and so could not be discovered in Wyatt's study. It remained an open question whether such undiscovered causes might have large significance.

The other main figure whose approach to what he called the *variables of form* was an essentially story-centered one is William E. Henry. In his book, *The Analysis of Fantasy* (1956), a chapter is devoted to these variables, and in his case studies one can see the sensitive and imaginative ways he uses them in the actual analysis of the TAT. A listing of Henry's main variables of form shows their relatedness to Wyatt's, and their origin in the study of logically possible features of the stories themselves. In addition, however, the list also clearly shows that some variables originated in a deliberate attempt to find analogs of Rorschach scores.

1. Amount and kind of production (e.g., length of stories; amount of introduced content; kinds of introduced content; vividness and richness of imagery; originality versus commonness of imagery; rhythm and smoothness of production; interruptions of story production; variations in all of these from story to story).
2. Organizational qualities (e.g., presence of the four basic parts of the story; level of organization; listing, description of relations, imaginative elaboration; coherence and logic; inclusive whole concepts; manner of approach to central concept; variations in these).
3. Acuity (e.g., of concepts; observations and their integration).
4. Language usage.

Aside from the fact that he worked with a slightly different set of variables than Wyatt, Henry achieved some success with formal features for several reasons. I do not mean to be snide when I say that one reason was that he did *not* begin by putting his variables to a rigorous statistical validation, as Wyatt did. With a clinical instrument, it is undoubtedly wise— perhaps even necessary—to subject the method to intensive clinical trial and development first, and only after this informal process of revision and hunch-forming to test hypotheses or look for correlates. At any rate, Henry did develop his system in the more usual clinical fashion, while subjecting it to indirect tests (e.g., Henry, 1947) which seemed to support its general validity.

In my judgment, Henry's variables are an improvement over Wyatt's, but they still leave something to be desired. They do not get at aspects of personality that are as clinically significant as one might wish.

The other approach, which by contrast might be called person-centered, was followed by Rapaport, Gill, and Schafer (1946) and Schafer (1948). They began by giving the TAT to patients of all kinds, in a diagnostic, not a research context. They approached the study of the stories with definite ideas about certain features of personality structure—particularly the defenses and signs of their decompensation. Notice in the following partial summary of their findings that Rapaport organizes his variables by the aspect of personality or pathology they refer to, not in terms of the stories themselves.

> Affective lability: exclamations, interference of affects with story production, the content shaped primarily by affective response to the picture.
> Depression: paucity of production, over-elaboration or perseveration of the theme of happiness versus sadness (verging on content).
> Obsessiveness/compulsiveness: circumstantial descriptions of pictures, fragmentation with doubting, intellectualizing, awareness of own thought processes, compulsive criticism of picture, pedantry.
> Paranoid trends: deducing motives of E, elaborate inferences, perceptual distortions, cryptic statements.
> Schizophrenia: over-elaborate symbolism, bizarre or delusional qualities, peculiar verbalization or story development, vague generalities, disjointed or mixed-up organization, arbitrariness, continuation of same story from one picture to another.

Schafer (1948) has added a number of other formal features to this list, formed in the same way. He lists, for example, formal aspects that are found in character disorder: facetiousness, attempts to shock the examiner, over-casual attempts to shrug off emotionally touching topics, etc. [See also Schafer (1958a).]

A FEW DATA[4]

No one will have any trouble seeing that the Rapaport-Schafer approach to formal aspects is the one that seems most fruitful to me. Shortly after I first learned it, I began work with Lester Luborsky and David Rapaport on a research project in which we were trying to learn how to predict competence of psychiatric residents during their training (see Holt & Luborsky, 1958). We tried various tests, and of course the TAT was one of them. We decided to see how well various specific aspects of content, and general formal features of the stories, could be used in this predictive task (as well as aspects

[4]The research reported here was supported by the Veterans' Administration, the New York Foundation, and the Menninger Foundation, and was carried out in collaboration with Dr. Lester Luborsky.

of Self-Interpretation; see Luborsky, 1953). Consequently, we set to work collecting such indicators (or as we called them, cues) and looking for them in TAT stories from selected samples of residents who were judged by their supervisors and by their fellows to be the best and the worst of the first group of residents.

Going over the 20 sets of stories from good and poor residents, I tried to list all of the formal features that distinguished the two groups; these were the nucleus of a manual that ultimately grew to a single-spaced typed document of 54 pages. This manual grew by a process of applying the variables to various sets of stories, rewriting, adding qualifications and examples to sharpen the discrimination of better and poorer residents. The manual was organized, following Rapaport, in terms of various features of personality thought to be relevant to functioning as a psychiatrist.

The manual was subjected to its first cross-validation when the stories of 34 applicants to the class that entered the Menninger School of Psychiatry in 1948 were analyzed blind. Then at the end of the first year of work by the men who were accepted and entered the school, we got their supervisors' ratings of their over-all competence as psychiatric residents (the criterion). The predictor was the *cue-sum*, the total number of times each positive variable was recorded as present in one of 12 stories told by a subject, minus the number of times negative variables appeared in his stories. This score was correlated significantly[5] with the criterion, at around *.4;* the score from the content manual did at least as well, and the sum of cues from the two together was correlated approximately **.6** with our preliminary criterion! This figure was obtained by including two men who had dropped out of psychiatry and assigning them minimal criterion scores, a somewhat dubious procedure; when they were omitted and when a final criterion was available after the men had finished their three years of training, the correlations with supervisors' evaluations of psychiatric competence for the remaining 32 men were not nearly so exciting: for the Formal manual, .24; Content .31; total, *.38.* By that time, however, we had already revised the manuals in light of the findings on the first cross-validation, and were well launched on a second.

In this final predictive study, the *N* was nearly twice as large: 64. The manuals had been brought to a condition of high polish, and were applied blind once more, this time during the course of a design too complicated to go into here (see Holt & Luborsky, 1958). Our criterion measures were as good as could be obtained; measures of Over-all Competence had an internal consistency of better than **.9,** and were based on close contact with a man's actual psychiatric work.

Three psychologists applied the TAT manuals to the dozen stories told

[5]Correlations in *italics* are significant at the 5% level, those in bold type at the 1% level. Two-tailed tests are used throughout.

and written by each subject. Unfortunately, there was not enough time for careful training of the other two raters in the use of these highly judgmental variables, and the degree of agreement in scoring was poor. The coefficients of observer agreement for the cue-sum from the Formal manual were **.42,** **.34,** and *.23*—all significantly better than chance, to be sure, but quite inadequate for reliability.

It should be no surprise, therefore, that in this second cross-validation the scoring of only the judge who had written the manual retained significant validity as a predictor of general psychiatric competence. His (my) cue-sum was correlated .22 with Over-all Competence as judged by supervisors, and .25 with the same criterion variable as judged by a man's peers (a sociometric criterion). Though this was a meager result, there was hardly any cross-validation shrinkage (from .24 to .22), while the validity of the Content manual, no matter who scored it, regressed to zero.[6] If we look at validity not in terms of correlation but in practical terms, of hits and misses through taking men who scored above a critical point in the earlier study and rejecting those who scored lower, we find that the formal manual in my scoring held up quite well: there were significantly fewer misses than would be expected by chance ($p = .04$), and there were only 4.5% extreme errors (predicting top performance for a man who was inadequate, for example), which is slightly better than the base rate of 18% ($p = .10$).

An additional result gives a clue to the indifferent success of the formal manual's cue-sum as a predictor of Over-all Competence. The formal cue-sums of two judges were correlated over **.3** with Supervisors' Evaluations of *Spontaneity versus Inhibition.* This aspect of psychiatric residents' behavior was not as relevant to ratings of general competence as many others (criterion evaluations of Spontaneity were correlated **.63** with Over-All Competence; only two others of the 14 specific criteria had lower correlations with this, our principal criterion). Consequently, the reserved, quiet, self-contained man who did well in his psychiatric work might have been erroneously rejected if the formal manual had been put into operational use.

So far, we have been talking about the group of formal variables as a whole. Let us look at them individually in some detail.

First, the formal aspects that ended up by having little validity as predictors of psychiatric competence. (This does not necessarily mean that they are not valid indicators of the constructs they were supposed to measure, for in some instances, the latter turned out to be less relevant to psychiatric work than we had thought.) *Comments on the mood, spirit, or connotations of the picture:* this was included as a measure of Cultural Wealth, a

---

[6]This time the validities of the two manuals were not additive, as they had been in the first validation; the total cue-sum for both manuals correlated positively but insignificantly with the criteria. The content manual was quite reliably scored, but had no validity in either this study or in the study of labor mediators. The validities of the Formal cue-sum are significantly different from zero at $p < .10$.

variable that in the end had only a slight and tenuous relationship to the criterion. A negative cue, *Vulnerability to unpleasant mood of picture* (a measure of Inadequate Emotional Control), was not scored very often and did not differentiate well. *Expressions of intense inadequacy feelings* (a sign of low Self-Confidence) did not get scored more than once or twice, and so could not demonstrate any validity in this study; we had earlier seen clear manifestations only in men who left the field of psychiatry. A cue to poor Clarity of Thought—*Vagueness, overgeneralization, or disjointedness of organization*—did not work, probably because it was not scored strictly enough, for mild degrees of this quality are pretty widespread, even in men who turn out to be quite adequate psychiatrists. Stereotypy of Thought is another personality variable that showed very little relation to the criterion of competence in this sample; one of our measures of it, *Stereotypy of story or content*, had no validity. The other, *Originality of Story*, did quite well; in my scoring, for example, this one cue was correlated *.26* with Over-all Competence and *.27* with Diagnosis.

But to return to the less successful cues: *Arbitrary story developments* seemed to be a measure of Emotional Inappropriateness, but did not work very well—probably again because it was not scored strictly enough. I still feel that arbitrary turns of events, forced and unprepared endings, and the like, are good indicators of a lack of sensitivity and appropriateness in emotional expression. *Sensitive descriptions of cards versus perceptual distortions:* this cue was one of our main measures of Perceptual Sensitivity, a variable that was completely unrelated to the criterion. Apparently the kind of interpersonal sensitivity needed in psychiatry is unrelated to sharp versus distorted observation of test pictures. Finally, I thought that *Self-references* indicated low Self-Objectivity, which was a relevant enough variable. But although in earlier samples, self-referent remarks had been given predominantly by the poorer prospects, this cue did not work in our final sample.

The list of formal variables that had continuous validity as predictors of psychiatric competence throughout the various trials is not large. The following tended to discriminate better from poorer residents in the scoring of at least two of the three judges in both validity studies, though only my scoring of Originality was correlated significantly with Over-all Competence. *Originality of story* also tended to be correlated from .23 to *.26* with several specific aspects of proficiency. Indicators of Psychological-Mindedness were also good—*Degree of characterization of figures* in story, and especially *Complexity of motivation or of interpersonal relationships* in story. The former had no significant correlational validities, but the latter predicted Spontaneity versus Inhibition ($r = .29$). Genuineness versus Facade was measured by signs of *Facade:* pretentiousness, pollyannaish concealment of conflicts, or ungenuine behavior by hero (acceptable to teller). Finally, *Evidences of zest and enthusiasm versus automatism or compulsion to repeat errors* held up fairly well, but was not correlated well with the criterion rating of Spontaneity versus

Inhibition, though it was supposed to be a measure of Adequate Emotional Control.

We also rated *Adequacy of Hero* on most of the cases, though it was put back into the picture after the final predictive study had begun and so was not added in with the sum of formal cues. Taken alone, however, it had even better validity. One other judge scored it as well as myself; our coefficient of agreement was **.78,** which is not bad. In my scoring, it was correlated *.31* with Over-all Competence (Supervisors' Evaluations, $N = 53$) and .23 to *.28* with four other criterion variables. As scored by the other judge, it was correlated significantly only with the residents' evaluations of competence in Management (*.30*) and ward Administration (*.33*); my scoring was correlated *.28* with this last criterion, too. It seems reasonable to assume that the self-confidence measured by this TAT variable is particularly useful in running a psychiatric ward smoothly.

So much for the data from the selection of psychiatrists. Finally, I want to cite some further validating data from an independent and quite different study.[7] I had a visit in 1954 from a psychologist at the New York State School of Industrial and Labor Relations, Henry Landsberger, who was planning a study of the personalities of labor mediators. He wanted to use projective techniques including the TAT, and having got wind of the fact that I had developed a method of scoring Formal aspects for the selection of psychiatrists, wanted to try them out on his labor mediators. Rather skeptical that anything would come of it, I nevertheless lent him a copy of the manual and worked a little with Dr. Joan Havel, training her in the scoring of the categories, which she did for him.

A while later, I was quite surprised to hear from Dr. Landsberger that he had completed the testing of 18 labor mediators, and had gotten independent criterion evaluations of their work from people who were closely acquainted with it. With his kind permission, the principal results of the TAT scoring are presented in Table 5.1. (See also Landsberger, 1956.)

Although the sample is small, there are ten significant correlations in this little table indicating relationships of some size. It is almost embarrassing to report such good validities from another study, when my own failed to produce any correlations as large. But it is encouraging that in general the variables were correlated best with criteria the meaning of which was closest to them. Thus, *Stereotypy of story and sentiments* are best correlated with Originality of Ideas, while the three remaining variables (all of which bear on a person's capacity for interpersonal relationships) are best correlated with the interpersonal aspect of mediators' work, expressed in the criterion variable, The Mediator as "One of Us."

[7] I am very grateful to Dr. Henry Landsberger for permission to cite his findings. Dr. Landsberger adds a caution that the various criteria he used were intercorrelated, as were the TAT scores, so that there are strictly speaking not as many independent results as one might think at first glance.

Table 5.1. Validities of Formal Aspects of TAT Against Criterion Ratings of 18
Labor Mediators (Landsberger's study)

	Criterion Ratings					
TAT Variables	Overall Competence	Originality of Ideas	Intellectual Grasp	The Mediator as "One of Us"	Liking for Him	Control of Feelings
Stereotypy of story and sentiments	.42	.51	.41	.39		
Emotional inappropriateness	.35			.41	.25	.35
Genuineness versus facade	.49		.29	.52	.50	.46
Complexity of motivation	.42		.25	.44	.37	.24

Note: Italics indicate significance at the 5% level. Coefficients of .41 and larger are significant at the 10% level.

In addition to the variables listed in the table, *Vagueness and overgeneralization, Characterization,* and *Originality* were also used, but without significant findings. Landsberger correlated two other criterion variables with the formal aspects scoring but without finding any significant relationships. It seems odd that *Stereotypy of story and sentiments* should work so well for mediators and not Originality, whereas the opposite was true for psychiatrists. Perhaps the difference is that we distinguished between *good* and *bad* originals in the psychiatric study, giving negative scores for stories the originality of which was due to psychopathology, whereas both good and bad originals were scored positively in the study of labor mediators.

CONCLUSION

Test variables of the kind described here are suitable primarily for construct validation (Cronbach & Meehl, 1956); the data given here constitute the beginnings of an attempt to establish construct validity for a few formal aspects of the TAT. The approach of construct validity is slow, and one cannot expect high correlations. If the figures cited here were taken literally as the only basis for paying attention to formal aspects of the TAT, most clinicians might well be forgiven for deciding that they are simply not worth the effort.

Projective techniques have not yet reached the state of development, nor have research methods for validating them, where we can give up that treacherous but indispensable crutch, clinical experience. As I have used the TAT over the years and as I have tried to teach it, I have become more and more convinced that not what is told but how it is told can teach us most about personality, particularly in its structural aspects. Certainly in diagnostic testing we can be of most assistance to the referring psychotherapist, psychiatrist or psychoanalyst by concentrating on personality structure rather than by trying to reconstruct development or interpret symbols. This is not to deny that we can learn a great deal from content; but if the TAT had only its formal aspects to offer us, this vigorous offspring of a great psychologist would still be indispensable for psychodiagnosis and the experimental study of personality.

6

On various occasions, I have characterized blind diagnosis using a single test as a stunt. Such an exercise is not representative of good clinical practice, and it does not validate a test or a method of analyzing it; indeed, it does nothing more than show what one person can do with one kind of data—a performance that says little or nothing even about that person's clinical prowess under normal circumstances. Yet the fact remains that it subjects a diagnostic method to a searching test, and if the method can give rise to judgments that are independently verifiable, a presumption of validity is created more quickly than in any other way I know . Because I believed that much more could be done with the TAT than most clinicians seemed to think, I agreed to take part in two such blind diagnostic demonstrations, with the understanding in advance that the reports and results of independent clinical diagnostic studies would be published. Both are reprinted here (as Chapters 6 and 7). I have gone out on this kind of limb on about half a dozen occasions (the others not published), and none has proved a disaster. The number is not large, but at least the two examples that follow are representative of this small population.

These cases are not presented, I want to reiterate, as evidence of the TAT's validity, nor can the degree of success and failure attained in them be directly attributed to the approach described in the preceding pages. Rather, they illustrate concretely a way to analyze data and to synthesize a portrait of a person in trouble, in which the influence of my teachers—particularly, Henry A. Murray and David Rapaport—will be apparent. (I presented and exemplified it in a somewhat different way in my 1972 book, Assessing Personality.)

I have a special feeling for the case of John Doe, because it initiated a friendship of several decades with a delightful and creative psychologist, Ed Shneidman. He asked me (largely on the basis of having read my chapter in Anderson and Anderson, 1951, here reprinted as Chapter 2), along with 16 other proponents of scoring systems and other methods of working with the TAT, to apply our techniques to a TAT and a MAPS test, which he had given to a 25-year-old male subject. We were asked to begin with an account of our method of thematic test analysis, followed by full working notes or scoring sheets, and ending with an integrative report. I omit here the MAPS test protocol (which I did not examine until I had finished analyzing and writing up the TAT) and my analysis of it. It differed largely in being filled with much more blatantly schizophrenic material, wild and bizarre ideas presented with an exhibitionistic flourish.

Though I have altered the text of my notes and interpretative summary only to make minor corrections, the format is different. It seemed that the reader's task would be *simplified if the working notes were printed immediately following the stories to which they pertain. Some material on "the clinical story" concludes this chapter, to give you an idea of how John Doe appeared to those who interviewed and treated him.*

A Blind Interpretation of Doe's TAT

To the extent that I could be said to have a method, it consists in reading over the stories and making notes on aspects of form and content that strike my attention as being deviant or as fitting together with impressions from other stories or from other tests. (In clinical work I always use a battery of tests.) These notes, which are more or less copious, depending on the time pressure under which I am working and on the purpose for which the TAT is being used, are quite similar to the ones reproduced here. They consist mainly of three types of material: notations of significant formal aspects of the record (where I depend heavily on Rapaport), rather unsystematic skeletonizing of content in terms of need-press themas (where my debt to Murray is most clear), and speculations about the symbolic and dynamic significance of anything in the record. I try to be free and undisciplined in these speculations (which derive mainly from what knowledge of psychoanalysis I have) but keep a watch on the extent to which I am projecting myself, and treat them only as speculations until they are corroborated.

After these notes have been made, I read them through again, often making additions, and collate them with similar notes from any other material I have about the subject, in pretty much the usual way: looking for repeated themas, for congruences and overlaps between different stories and between different tests.

In diagnostic studies, I believe very strongly in the position argued most clearly by Schafer (1948), that tests allow us to make inferences about aspects of personality and the organization or disorganization of thought and affect, *not* directly about diagnostic categories. From the picture of personality that emerges out of the interpenetrating mosaic of these immediately inferred features, it is usually possible to form a diagnostic impression, couched in the terms of whatever nosology one may be currently using.

So far as I know, no one has reported anything very helpful on the final process, the synthesis of all one's more or less scattered ideas and impressions into a unified, more or less self-consistent picture of a personality. Here is where experience and knowledge of psychopathology are usually invoked, to help explain the more or less creative process that goes on, but I do not think that it contributes much to an understanding of thematic analysis to fall back on such truisms. Trying to introspect, I am inclined to think that it is a kind of hierarchic structuring of the material, really concept formation, in which implications of the raw data are grouped into first-order abstractions, and these in turn are related to each other leading to synthetic emergents, and so on. But this may well be an intellectualized rationalization of an essentially unconscious process. When we learn someday to study, understand, improve, and teach this aspect of TAT analysis, I think we shall be getting at the heart of the matter.

Here are the TAT stories of John Doe, each of which is followed by my working notes.

TAT RECORD

DOE, John   Male   Age 25   Single

1   This child is sick in bed. He has been given sheet music to study, but instead of the music, he has come across a novel that interests him more than the music. It is probably an adventure story. He evidently does not fear the chance that his parents will find him thusly occupied as he seems quite at ease. He seems to be quite a studious type and perhaps regrets missing school, but he seems quite occupied with the adventure in the story. Adventure has something to do with ocean or water. He is not too happy, though not too sad. His eyes are somewhat blank—coincidence of reading a book without any eyes or knowing what is in the book without reading it. He disregards the music and falls asleep reading the book.

1. *Sick in bed*—unusual (never saw it before). Perceptual distortion, *self as sick*—(p Affliction → p Gratuity). Also some of the usual p Imposed task, but with an almost perverse twist: question of *malingering?* Sees score as such—not very usual, and violin as a novel—very unusual perceptual distortion.

General *ease and freedom* in telling story—spontaneously gives quite a lot. Therefore, not a simple uneducated sort—especially with his vocabulary (coincidence, thusly), but probably college level. See also references to being "quite a studious type," regrets missing school.

Impression on first reading—intelligent, rather intellectual schizophrenic, probably paranoid, not very long duration (because of productivity, and freedom, lack of flatness).

Inappropriate flavor, complete *arbitrariness* of—"Something to do with ocean or water" (breakthrough of own preoccupation), *peculiar* statement beginning with "coincidence"—also *delusional-like idea*, "knowing what is in the book before reading it"—*delusions of being able to read minds,* or of having own mind read? Paranoid is supported by inferential tone, especially in second sentence.

Has to bring up *fear of parents* only to deny it. Flavor of masturbation conflict: (a) no violin: denial of phallus? (b) alone in bed doing something he should fear being caught at by parents—adventure?—water?

Suggestions of affectless *bland front* in "not too happy, not too sad"— especially in "His eyes are somewhat blank."

Stays fairly picture-focused—doesn't stray far into an independent story—*obsessive-compulsive* structure, also supported by evidence for studiousness, and especially the ambivalent statement, "not too happy, though ,not too sad," and similar *balance between statement and denial throughout* story.

Idea of coming across a novel while confined to bed is loose and thoughtless—not very reality-oriented. I'm still puzzled by distortion of violin into novel. Speculation: violin = penis = books, intellectuality as phallic superiority ruse, compensation?

Adventure theme also very unusual here—a personal preoccupation (escape fantasies?). Cf. heightened dramatic tone throughout.

Conception of parents: rather harsh, unloving, inconsiderate; sick boy is given music to study, which he apparently doesn't want—(his disregard is an indirect and passive-resistant counteraggression) and they would be angry at finding him reading something pleasurable *even* when he's sick, instead of "work." Severe discipline is suggested, against which he probably reacts passively. An elaborate tissue of indirect hostilities between parents and child is suggested.

"Coincidence of reading a book *without any eyes*": last phrase a strikingly peculiar way of saying without looking, or with eyes shut or the like. Strongly suggests castration: not just anxiety, *feeling of being castrated* (cf. no violin).

Negative content: lack of any interpersonal relations—not too unusual, though hero-centered to a degree that is characteristic of quite narcissistic people.

Facade: based on slightly pretentious tone of verbalization—use of "thusly," not idiomatic, and stilted (see also next-to-last sentence). Ability to communicate with others beginning to break down (schizoid peculiarities).

On basis of this story alone, I feel certain that there is a schizophrenic process present, even though not necessarily a pure schizophrenia. Slightly pretentious, facade tone, helped along with basic fact of perverse refusal to acknowledge presence of violin, strongly suggests that he *does* see violin but consciously thinks that he's being "clever" or "original," or is out-tricking the examiner (whom he might see as trying to trick him) by ignoring it or seeing it as a book. That he is aware of it on some level is suggested by the fact that the basic theme, p Parental Imposed Task→ n Auto Resis, passive Aggression, comes through. Consistent also is statement at the end: he *disregards* the music. Not a psychopath trying to act smart—too schizzy.

Sick in bed as a child may be an autobiographical theme. He's almost certainly "sick" (that is, psychotic) now, and so that may be enough explanation for it. But most psychotics don't [see the card this way]; therefore it becomes plausible that he may have had long illnesses as a child, cutting him off from other kids, and→to fantasy escape—dreams of travel and adventure.

Sentence 3 may also describe his overt behavior: nonchalant, seemingly "at ease," really frightened underneath.

Above are almost all hypotheses, to be confirmed or excluded by later stories.

Strong passivity throughout—especially in outcome. Also suggestion of *flight* and *avoidance* of very passive sort—drastic enough to include denial of threatening aspects of reality.

Nothing holds his interest long—not even adventure novel. Hero soon withdraws into *own* fantasy, to conviction of knowing what's in book without reading it even though "took a chance" to read it, and finally withdraws into sleep.

> 3BM   This is a girl in a cell and she has been jailed because she was found guilty of prostitution. She is in this position in the picture because she is very ashamed, not because of being arrested, because she is quite familiar with the police, but because of the fact that her picture and a newspaper write-up was being sensationally spread across the country. She knew that her sister, who was a nun, would suffer from it, and it made her feel very badly because she, at one time, had a chance and an opportunity to follow her elder sister's example, but it was too late now. She grabs a concealed knife from under her blouse and stabs herself.

3BM. Girl in a cell—ordinary apperception.

"Girl" only slight evidence for feminine identification; enough empathy with girl in thoughts and feelings to strengthen it, though.

"Jailed because she was found guilty of prostitution": *sex is something very criminal* for him, more than in reality. Implies intense sex-guilt.

Note that she feels *ashamed,* not guilty, and that it's not so much because of well-internalized values but because of external consequences. Implies *poorly internalized superego.*

Shame about tremendous p Cog suggests *unconscious need, against which there are reaction formations, to exhibit and look* (cf. implied fear of p Cog in 1, concern with eyes). Suggests possibility of *delusions of reference.*

Knew sister would suffer—confirmation of *passive aggression.* This time, through dragging self down, family members can be hurt; supported by other *intragression* (suicide carried through). So his techniques of aggression are *passive resistance plus self-destruction,* destroying poorly internalized family members (unconscious of it: "made her feel badly").

Sister—an unusual introduced figure. *Sibling rivalry?* And/or just a classic *sacred-profane* split (nun and prostitute). Latter split confirms externalization tendencies, consistent with paranoid developments. Moralism, superficial religiosity, suggested by *nun,* lost opportunity to identify with her.

Knife, not gun, a slight distortion, though not very unusual.

Note no real regret for the hurt to the sister: heroine feels badly because it was too late for *herself* to be saved the same way. Narcissism supported, *basic isolation, lack of true self-love.*

Story has a fair (better than average) degree of coherence and smooth dramatic development. Sounds as if told fairly easily and smoothly. (Would help to have times, also indication of technique of administration: how story was recorded.) (In story 1, inquiry would have helped.)

Suicide theme not unusual, though going through with it a little more indicative of something personal. Still not at all depressive.

4   The girl in the picture is half-caste. She is in love with the man who is going to leave her and return to his wife. They have spent quite some time together in intimacy. She is pleading with him to stay with her or help figure some way to plan for the coming of the child she is going to bear. She is in poor circumstances financially, and he tells her she should make arrangements to conclude the birth and thus everything would iron out because he is definitely determined to leave as the affair in his mind is at an end. She is very broken up by it. She pleads for him to spend one more night which he agrees to, and in the middle of the night she sets fire to the house, thus solving the problem of all concerned.

4. Half-caste—suggests *ethnic prejudice, projection* of lust onto outgroup members. More *sexual preoccupation,* but probably seems somewhat ego-alien (because of above). Abortion is unusual theme—(even though expressed in stilted words; "conclude the birth")—suggests *raw, unsublimated nature* of his sexual fantasies. [*N.B.*: Date of testing was 1947.]

Man is *callous,* shows no regard for woman with whom he has lived for some time "in intimacy": *no capacity for real love,* a genital object relationship. Same sacred-profane (wife versus mistress) split as before. Lust, enjoyment of sex, is something unworthy, indulged in by morally bad people who must be harshly punished for it. So far, it's women who are crassly lustful, and they must destroy themselves for it (projective again).

Notable feminine identification here: almost all is from the woman's viewpoint, the one he naturally seems to adopt. But since women are so *bad,* his feminine side is probably ego-alien, repressed and projected. (Was his mother self-destructive too?)

Note concern with *pregnancy* (cf. water in story 1).

Sex is dangerous to the man: he spends the night and gets burnt up.

Final comment is too *bland or flip*—seems content with this very sudden, violent outburst of destructive aggression. This kind of sudden inappropriate aggressive ending (in no way suggested by the picture, as suicide in story 3BM was), especially when so blandly passed off, is another schizophrenic indicator. Something especially infantile and unmodulated about this aggression; setting fire to the house—destroying *everything*—self, lover, and house too. Suggests hatred of whole family, whole world; possibly world destruction fantasies.

6BM   This is a scene in a play. The two characters are on the stage, one is a famous elderly actress, who has a son about the age of the young man appearing opposite her. The dialogue in the play has suddenly taken a new meaning for her. She sees now that the play which was written by her son, has an entirely different meaning, in this scene in the picture. The boy is telling the mother that he has just committed a murder. She understands now that this was her son's way of conveying to her the terrifying facts that this is actually what had happened. In the play, as her son had written it, the climax comes when the mother calls the police. But the famous actress decides to put her own climax into action after the play is over. She calls her son and says, The climax of your play will have to be changed. She says, I think the audience will prefer this one, so here she draws a revolver and shoots him. (*What kind of murder was it?*) Oh, a girl. Motive primarily to do with sexual. She had been unfaithful.

6BM. Traumatic relationship with mother is "too hot" to be approached directly—he must avoid, make it irreal. (All the avoidance and callousness suggest some *character disorder features. Also glibness of verbalization—may have catatonic features*—cf. "blank eyes" of story 1. *Acting out?* Possibly denial, through acting out, of own ego-alien femininity.)

Stage—famous—note repetition of exhibitionistic-voyeuristic theme. Some *preoccupation with external rewards (money, fame) as a substitute for love?*

Theme basically same as in last two: indulgence in sex→ death. Now mother is definitely the punisher. Again, the "shocking" ending: sudden murder of a socially particularly unacceptable kind: mother shoots son in cold blood, and quite unnecessarily. And what a cold, inexorably moralistic mother!

Note that the defense isn't successful: the fear and hatred of the mother breaks through anyway.

Paranoid note in the second and third sentences. Some hint of contamination or confusion in the last spontaneous sentence: "so *here* (i.e., in the pictured scene?) she draws a revolver and shoots *him*"—whom? the young actor or the son?

External superego: "the *audience* will prefer this." Mother, not father, is the punisher. Cf. in story 3BM, not much concerned about police (father-figures)—it's a woman who administers the final punishment in each case so far.

Dramatic quality in rather *phony*, trumped up, shocker endings (facade). Nevertheless, the imaginal flow is remarkable, as is the originality (even though latter is primarily pathological in origin). Suggests a person of some real talent and creativeness, at least potentially, before illness (though probably never enough inner resources ever to produce much).

> 7BM   This would be a man and his son. The son is very depressed over his health. The father is telling him that as a young man he too had the same illness, and that it can be cured if the son has the will to cure it. The father tells the young man that he himself alone can cure it. The son believes that there is no hope, but replies that he will go away for a little while and think it over. The father replies, You are not doing a favor to me by saying that. I am thinking about your getting well for the simple reason that you have a wife and children to support, and in the event of your being bed-ridden, the responsibility for your family will be put entirely upon your mother and I. The young man finally concludes that he will take his wife and family with him and try to make things go better in a healthier climate. (*What kind of illness did he have?*) T.B. (*Did he get better?*) No, I don't think he does. After a few years he dies and the children are old enough to support mother or perhaps he left insurance. Never contacted father again. No correspondence. After not having heard from each other for a long time, the old man dies and leaves the children a large estate. This is his way of having repented.

7BM. Concern over health again (cf. story 1). *Hypochondriacal* features to be expected, especially before the break (if any). (This so far sounds like a rather acute phase of paranoid schizophrenia.)

N.B.: hero is *more nearly adequate in relationship to father than in relationship to mother.*

Moralistic advice from father—probably the kind of talk he got himself about his complaints when without organic basis. Yet, implication that father was doing something wrong in applying coercion to son, because he "repented"—perhaps for having been concerned with the son's health only because it bade fair to force him to support daughter-in-law and grandchildren. *No love between father and son, no nurturance from father* stimulated by son's illness: *conception of parents as moralistic pressures, not loving and supporting persons.*

Note *sustained pessimism* (no hope . . . doesn't get better)—not a happy ending yet, only neutral retreat of story 1. This man lacks capacity either to break away from either parent or to enjoy himself at all.

Father had same illness: unclear significance as yet.

Still somewhat *preoccupied with money and material support.*

Son's reaction to father's pressure: *submit, go away, passive rejection and aggression* in never contacting father again: repeated, no "correspondence."

> 11   This is a fantasy. This highway cuts over an arched bridge. The people on the road are black and wearing capes. There are perhaps two pack animals carrying supplies. About the middle of the picture there is a prehistoric animal with just his serpentine neck showing and a web foot. He has been waiting for these

travelers until they came into sight and then, when he saw them, he started rolling huge boulders across their path. However, they must have been predestined to reach their goal, because the boulders have fallen short of the highway. They are evidently the first travelers to get this far because it is presumed that the black area to the right of the beast is a pit full of lost human souls. However, the beast looks as though he will race ahead of them and in some future spot along the road send them to whatever fate has for them in the future. (*Fate?*) Looks like wicked people trying to escape or something, and this seems to be going deeper into more of a dark place than from where they came from.

11. Note beginning: this is a fantasy. Still *can* recognize the difference between reality and fantasy, wants it clearly understood that he recognizes it when he goes off the deep end.

Extremely good perceptual sharpness here—in striking contrast to story 1!

Strongly *fatalistic* tone: the outcome is never in the hands of the people themselves, but is a matter of "predestination" or "fate"; implies *low self-reliance* (later on denied, see story 16), projection of responsibility.

Note obsessive/paranoid "reasoning" quality appearing again: "must have been . . . because" (sentence 5); "evidently . . . because it is presumed that . . ." (sentence 6). Note verbal usage—on a consistently high intellectual level—with some of the slight formalism and stiltedness of the obsessive. Also, rather *excessive balance and counterpoise of ideas:* attack, but escape; fated to get to goal, but beast will run ahead and get them; they are fated to be (destroyed?). (Note vocabulary: serpentine; predestined; it is presumed.)

Moralistic flavor: wicked going into darkness—pit full of lost souls, no escape for the wicked. Unusual ending: particularly strong self-destructiveness, can't let self escape.

Beast is a superego force, aggression directed against the evil self.

Note escape theme—slight addition to previous.

12M   This is a young artist in Paris who is badly off financially; so badly in fact that, because he hadn't sold a painting in over a month, he is prostrate from starvation. But the painting he had sold for a loaf of bread had somehow gotten into the home of a wealthy patron of the arts who had seen great magnificence in it and had turned it over to the director of an art institute. The picture was sold for a large sum. The director, after great pains, had finally located the artist and was standing over him now trying to get some response, trying to tell him that he was to be commissioned to paint for the wealthy woman for a large retaining fee. But, however, it was too late. The picture that had brought the director to his bedside had had too great an effect on the artist. It was a picture of a loaf of bread.

12M. Note financial preoccupation again. Starvation—loaf of bread. *Deep oral cravings*—fear of starvation underlies the superficially anal-sounding concern with money.

Something of the previous fantasy of acclaim, fame, etc., here. Continued tragedy and failure, self-defeat is even nearly explicit. *Fantasy of the good parents* (mother and father) who will appreciate him, feed him, support him. But it's only a fantasy: would come too late.

Slick O. Henry quality again—supports the character-disorder flavor of *glibness.*

> 13MF   These two people have come to a strange city and taken lodgings in a middle-class hotel. They both met while riding on a bus. The girl approached him first by saying she was a stranger and had no place to stay. The man too was a stranger and welcomed the opportunity because she did not appear to be just a common pickup. They registered as man and wife and retired to their room, where the man in the glaring bright light of the room saw the girl for the first time. He saw in her the very thing he had come to this town to get away from. She was the same in proportion, in color, and even in manner as the girl he could not have at home, because the girl at home had died. Overcoming this feeling by turning off the light, they had relations, and now with the lights on again, a feeling of shame has come over him and he leaves. This girl was morally a different girl from the one that had died. He could never get the other girl.

13MF. Same sacred-profane split, sexual preoccupation, moralism. Voyeurism—denied in turning off light so he *can't* see her. Only a girl who doesn't permit any sex is really any good.

Note that girl is *initiator sexually*—man is passive and compliant. Note that he leaves—sex is something kept isolated from love—forcibly (sentence 8). He leaves this girl, and the other one died. *No stable sexual relationship.* (In 7BM, hero had a wife, but only as an attribute for purposes of the story—no relationship was described.)

> 13B   This doesn't say much to me. This scene is of a very poor farmhouse in an isolated part of the country. The little boy has just been told that he is going to have a little brother. However he can't quite figure it out. He has been told to stay out of the way, and some other small children have told him that they have had little brothers too, and since they have arrived the mother has not had so much time for them. The little boy in the picture is thinking all this over, and since he cannot get much affection from his father who is too busy working in the fields to even be kind to him, the boy, in his small mind, comes to the conclusion that it's a hopeless case. He looks behind him into the black room which only accentuates the fact that his case looks black also. He decides to leave home and just then his mother calls him, the baby is going to arrive and he must rush over to get Mrs. Smith, the nearest neighbor. The mother tells him that she thanks God that she has a son like him to help her now, which makes him feel very elated and he decides he will never leave home. He had really done more than his father had in doing this.

13B. First half is keyed by statement, "this doesn't say much to me." Not much involved. *Theme of pregnancy* again. (Schizophrenic fantasy of rebirth?)

Only happy ending to date, and after a usually pessimistic view; "it's a hopeless case." Elation. Oedipal fulfillment—note final statement.

Repeated theme of flight, rejection of parents as a counter to feeling of being unloved, rejected.

The ending is probably a wish for what never was, and should have been. Of course, he never *has* left home really.

Sibling rivalry theme again (cf. 3BM)—seems like something real.

"Black room—case looks black"; schizophrenic flavor, physiognomic thinking, fluid.

14   This is a photograph that the man has taken while exploring a deserted house. Directly after taking this picture he had turned his flashlight to the floor and discovered a mutilated human body. This was the only possible suspect, the figure in the picture. He could, with imagination, almost put together characteristics of the figure shown in the picture. As this man lived in a small town not frequented often by visitors, he knew who this figure was seen leaving the window, but he being a minister, was not sure he should divulge the identity because between the time that the murder was committed and the time that the police discovered it, the suspect had confided in the minister what had occurred. The man in the picture had told the minister that it was in self-defense; that he had been startled by an intruder who had suddenly sprung upon him. However, the minister believed that it was the other way around and did notify the police who found out actually what had happened. The man in the picture was hiding because earlier he had robbed a jewelry store and been followed by the victim.

14. More sudden uncalled-for crude aggression: *"mutilated* human body." Really sadistic aggressive wishes, but quite ego-alien. Has the sound of a frequent fantasy.

Opening statement, an attempt to make a slick mystery out of it.

Note minister (cf. prayer in last)—suggests a good deal of religious content (probably derived from mother, through identification).

Robbery→ pursuit→ kills, mutilates (note: mutilation never satisfactorily explained—a sadistic flourish)→ discover, confession, retribution.

Note that a *moralistic father-figure can't be trusted*—confidence isn't respected so that he may be punished. Superego is inexorable, implacable.

16   This is a great plain where there used to be a settlement not so long ago. It is very hot and dry on the plain and the people who had been inhabitants had suffered a great deal from the heat, lack of water, and even outside influences. They were entirely reliant upon themselves and no one was reliant upon them. Because of the reason that they were alone was also the reason that they came to their doom. If they had had one line of contact, one way of conversing, even a telepathic touch with the outside world, they could have perhaps been saved. Now nothing is left except ruins and destruction of something that had once been evident as at least having been here. We know that it must have been there because of the ruins, and yet no one is sure because no proof is offered in either having had contact or having seen. It could all be imagination.

16. (Cf. Earnst.[1]) Barren environment thema—*oral deprivation*. Cf. story 12M, starvation. Really fierce oral cravings from a loveless (= milkless = waterless) infancy. A really schizophrenic utterance: paranoid ideas of "outside influences," narcissistic withdrawal ("entirely reliant on themselves"), utter loneliness and sense of death, yearning for human contact while convinced it's unattainable. World destruction fantasies more clearly hinted at; their nature as a projection of inner deadness and emptiness clear. Note growing tone of slight confusion, breakdown of verbalization into near-peculiarity. Line between reality and fantasy very thin and easily lost (last sentences.).

TAT INTERPRETATION

Diagnosis. The young man who tells these stories appears to be suffering from a paranoid schizophrenia of relatively brief duration, which is probably not now in an acute efflorescence, although an acute break has probably occurred. This diagnosis is based upon evidence in the TAT of: (a) distortion of perceptual contact with reality (especially story 1); (b) pathologic loosening of orderly thought processes (seen most clearly in stories 1, 6BM—where there is a suggestion of contaminated thinking—and 16); (c) delusional ideas (e.g., telepathy); (d) occasional breaking down of the ability to communicate with lapses into autistic use of language; (e) extreme narcissistic withdrawal from interpersonal relationships; (f) preoccupation with raw sexual and sadistic fantasies, suggesting that primitive wishes are breaking through prepsychotic defenses; (g) paranoid ideas of reference and malign influence; (h) desperate but hopeless yearning for love conceived in very infantile, oral terms; (i) moralism and religiosity; and (j) emotional inappropriateness and blandness. These aspects of personality taken together are consistent only with the presence of a schizophrenic process, and make the diagnosis of a full-blown psychosis quite likely.

It is very likely that almost any test given this patient would yield evidence of schizophrenia; establishing the degree to which the illness has progressed, however, is more difficult and uncertain. To begin with, a long-standing, deteriorated condition is virtually ruled out by the substantial degree of coherence, liveliness, and realism of most of the stories, indicating that many areas of cognitive functioning are relatively intact. None of the grosser and more obvious hallmarks of schizophrenia is to be seen. The fact that verbal peculiarities are few and not particularly striking argues that the disease is not of long duration, or at least that there is considerable retention of a "social front." (This line of reasoning, incidentally, also supports the

[1][This story reminded me of the Case of Earnst, by R. W. White, in Murray *et al.* (1938), because of the prominence of two major themas in the formulation of that personality—an "Oral Succorance Thema" and a "Provision Quest Thema," presumed to have developed from infantile oral frustration.]

diagnosis of *paranoid* schizophrenia.) The liveliness and productivity of fantasy of which the subject is capable are hardly consistent with the flatness and stereotypy to be looked for in chronic schizophrenia; they suggest rather the "diseased fancy" of a mind that is suffering an acute or near-acute psychosis. Some emotional inappropriateness is present both in the flavor of the verbalizations and in inappropriate, arbitrary story events; nevertheless it is not rampant. Delusional thinking seems to be present, likewise, but it does not crop out a great deal. This is not to deny that the patient may be very much deluded, even hallucinatory; but in acute paranoid schizophrenia these secondary symptoms of the condition are very often in the background in a TAT. The words with which he begins story 11, and the cautious inferential approach adopted in several of the stories, show some of the suspicious self-control with which the paranoid often is able to conceal his psychosis in testing and other brief, relatively impersonal encounters. Further, the fluctuating nature of his controls, now letting through pathologic ideas, now maintaining an appearance of rational coherence, is characteristic of the acute phase. This phenomenon may be seen most strikingly in the contrast between the gross perceptual distortion of story 1 (violin = book) and the unusual perceptual sensitivity and accuracy of story 11. It would be rare indeed for a chronic schizophrenic to turn in such a brilliant performance as his description of the figures on the rocky path.

If the psychosis seems not to be chronic, could it then be in a very early stage, say a very schizoid personality on the verge of a break? The strong indications of world destruction fantasies in stories 4 and 16, along with all the evidence of a process that has "broken through," furnish evidence that things have gone much further: that the world of the prepsychotic adjustment has been destroyed, and that the restitutive efforts of a psychotic personality are what we see now principally.

Personality structure. What *was* the prepsychotic adjustment? Signs of intellectualization, ambivalent balancing of possiblities, and the somewhat stilted choice of words from a wide vocabulary suggest some obsessive elements; the occasional tendency to "prove" the story from observational details does not go far enough to support the conclusion of an ingrained paranoid personality structure. Rather, this degree of inferential approach is further evidence for obsessive defenses. At the same time, aspects of character disorder are suggested in the many manifestations of avoidant defenses, the pretentious facade, and some callousness (as of the man in stories 4 and 13MF) that does not sound like simply blandness, but an attempt to shock.

Consistent with this personality structure, we might expect that the illness has at times been complicated by hypochondriacal complaints and perhaps by catatonic-like features. Acting out (perhaps sexual promiscuity, in an attempt to deny his femininity) may have been prominent. I would expect to see him going around with an air of nonchalant sophistication, talking rather glibly and with pseudo self-assurance that hides a devastating sense of inner emptiness, longing, and even deadness. Self-centered and aloof, he is incapable of giving any kind of love to another and of expecting any love from anyone else. He probably is insufferably narcissistic and exhibitionistic, affecting poses designed to attract shocked (and, he hopes, admiring) attention. For all of his intellectualization, he has very little insight.

These personality traits just described may in the past have raised a differential diagnostic problem involving psychopathic personality or severe narcissistic character disorder, but the schizophrenic quality must have shown itself nevertheless in clinical observation.

Intellection. The vocabulary, verbal usage, and general imaginal productivity show the patient to be a man of at least bright normal, probably superior intelligence. He has a kind of originality that is distinctly pathological, arising partly from perversity, but suggesting that he can with some justification consider himself talented, though he lacks the drive, the capacity for sustained interests, and the self-confidence to have produced anything much. Probably he has had some college training but no degree. What ability he has is held back by a deep self-destructiveness that cannot tolerate success.

His thinking, which can be very sharp and clear, is at times broken by arbitrariness and physiognomic associations, as his over-valent preoccupations break through the smooth flow of thought. Raw, unsublimated sexual preoccupations, ideas about pregnancy, and sadistic fantasies probably make up a good deal of his thought content. His pretentious use of a somewhat intellectual way of talking may obscure the clinical observer's perception of these defects in thought organization a good deal of the time.

Motivation. Although the patient may have had a number of transitory sexual affairs, he has undoubtedly never had a stable heterosexual relationship. He longs desperately for a human contact, yet feels unable to establish one. There are clear indications of a strong feminine identification, implying latent homosexuality, but whether or not there has ever been any overt homosexual experience is impossible to say; at any rate, continued accepted homosexuality is very unlikely. Despite his sophisticated front, he has intense feelings of guilt about masturbation and other manifestations of sexuality, even a conviction that he must die because of his sexual sins.

In the face of his overpoweringly destructive aggressive impulses, the patient feels helpless and struggles to keep them (like his sexual urges) ego-alien. Feeling rejected and unloved, he rejects the world, but apparently can rarely be directly hostile. Passive-resistive techniques, and striking at others through self-destructive behavior seem to be his preferred modes of aggression. His poorly internalized superego is savage and infantile, directing much of his aggressive potentialities against himself. One manifestation is in his ingrained, hopeless pessimism. He feels that his battles are lost: he may in a sense feel already castrated, already dead (though these are speculative conclusions from slight evidence). Another form the pessimism takes is fatalism, the feeling that he is unable to guide his own destinies, that everything is in the hands of the fates.

As is often true of persons who have not been able to form (through identification) a personally meaningful, integrated set of values, the patient is quite moralistic, with a good deal of superficial religiosity. The projective mechanism is used a good deal, probably expressing itself in ethnic prejudices as well as in more patently paranoid forms. Another manifestation of his moralism is his classically dichotomous conception of women as either good or bad (nun versus prostitute, sacred versus profane love). He seems to see women as the lustful, morally bad ones, while men are passively involved with them or righteously reject them. Shame, fear of external consequences, and "what people will think" are more than usually important to this man. Consistent with this emphasis on externals is the repeated concern in the TAT stories with money, fame, and other external rewards—as substitutes for the love he cannot get, one feels.

Underlying much of the patient's behavior are ragingly intense oral and passive cravings. He feels starved, deprived of the oral gratifications of infancy that were rightly his. There are some superficial reaction formations against these hungers, probably some show of pseudoindependence and self-reliance in an attempt to embrace the necessary, but his passivity and dependence on others easily show through.

A minor theme already mentioned is a voyeuristic-exhibitionistic need, which is again probably ego-alien and projected. It may be manifested in the content of some of the patient's delusional ideas, as well as in exhibitionistic behavior.

Historical reconstruction. There are a number of leads in the TAT stories which tempt one to make some genetic hypotheses. First of all, the parents are clearly depicted as moralistic, punitive, cold, and demanding persons, from whom the patient feels he never received love and support. The mother seems to have been the more frustrating and the more feared (consistent with his having identified himself with her more than the father). She was probably a harsh, religious, rejective person, from whom he vainly longed to hear loving words. The hatred of her that developed is so strong that he may be aware of it; his fear of her is so great that he may not be able to go against her will openly. At the same time, guilt-laden incestuous fantasies do not seem to be far from the surface of consciousness. His father he sees as weaker; in relationship to him he feels more adequate, though the patient very probably resists him passively rather than overtly. In fantasy he longs for good, kind, loving parents, but knows that it is impossible to find them.

A few indications of sibling rivalry conflict suggest that an added difficulty imposed on the patient as a child may have been the necessity to share the tiny amount of affection available in his family with one or more other children. More than this it is difficult to say. The unusual theme of illness in story 1 raises the possibility that his dependence, escape into fantasy, and isolation from companionship may have been exacerbated by protracted childhood illnesses.

Prognosis. This patient would probably be very difficult to deal with psychotherapeutically if one were not ready and able to give him great quantities of undemanding love for the long time that it would take to convince him that it was not a trap. Only then would it be possible to begin building the capacity to love others and the basic self-respect that he so totally lacks underneath his narcissistic lacquer. Despite the many defenses against the close interpersonal relationship of psychotherapy that exist, there are assets in this man (intelligence, an active and original mind) which might make one hopeful for a fair prognosis, if a sensitive and talented therapist wanted to devote himself to the difficult task of salvaging a potentially creative and useful human being. Without therapy, the outlook is dark indeed: the best one could hope for would be some uneasy remissions, which would bring the patient little happinesss, followed by final relapses into chronic psychosis.

ADDENDUM: THE CLINICAL STORY

From a 35-page section of *Thematic Test Analysis* I have excerpted and summarized the clinical essentials, with the kind permission of the editor, Dr. Shneidman.

John Doe came to the VA Neuropsychiatric Hospital in Los Angeles on January 24, 1947, requesting admission and treatment. What follows is the psychiatric case history abstract written shortly thereafter by Dr. W. L. Unger, who later was Mr. Doe's first psychotherapist.

Present Complaint: Patient is a 25-year-old white single male who entered voluntarily with the following symptoms: insomnia, palpitation, night sweats, trembling when people observe him, and feelings of inadequacy. He states his difficulties began about six months after being in the Navy. He was in the medical corps and was a corpsman in the "psycho unit," later stationed on a hospital ship. Since his discharge, he has been unable to maintain a job because of the above symptoms. He dreads people watching him. His concentration is quite poor and this has become more intense within recent weeks. He is in good contact.

Family History: His father, a pharmacist by profession, was 60 years old at the time of his death from tuberculosis. The patient says that he did not have very close contact with his father because of the tuberculous condition. At the time of his father's death, the patient cried for eight hours and says that he regrets that he had not been able to put his arms around his father. The patient was 12 years old at the time of the father's death. The father is described as being moderate tempered, cool, and aloof.

The mother, age 63, is in good health. She is generous with people. She is emotional and demonstrative. It was necessary for her to work while the husband was still living. She is, at present, living in an apartment which she shares with the patient. A sister of the mother also lives in the same apartment, but at one time, neither spoke to each other for a period of five years. She is described by the patient as being solicitous and sympathetic, yet, she has frequently told the patient, "I never want to tell you what to do." When the patient goes out with friends, the only thing he talks about is his mother. He speaks of how beautiful and how wonderful she is, and calls her up many times during the evening while he is out.

Siblings: A brother, age 41, has a history of many attempts at running away from home. He has been married twice and frequently has been found drunk by the patient. This brother frequently had altercations with the father while he was alive and the patient felt sorry for the antagonism caused by this brother. He is opinionated, but "wrong 99% of the time."

Another brother is 18 months older than the patient. This brother was closer to the patient all through their school years, but the patient says that this brother always wanted his own way, wanted to be the leader. He is now married, has three children, and has a responsible job. He was described as having a genuine interest in the welfare of the patient.

Personal History: As a child, the patient bit his nails and sucked his thumbs. He describes himself as being quite meticulous as far as habits were concerned and liked to keep things in order. He was always jealous of his toys and was afraid of wearing them out. He had enuresis until the age of 12. As a child, he frequently dreamed of being chased and not being able to run away. He was usually caught and would wake up frightened. At the age of seven, the patient was in an automobile accident in which the mother, father, and the oldest brother were seriously hurt. The patient was not seriously injured. At the age of eight, he was accosted by a man he describes as a "degenerate," who attempted to kidnap him. This had a profound effect on him and he frequently thought of this traumatic experience. As a child, the patient was frightened by the eldest brother who would grimace and make peculiar noises outside the bedroom window of the two younger boys. He was always afraid of the dark and did not like to be left alone.

Military History: Patient enlisted in 1943 and was discharged in 1946 with a diagnosis of psychoneurosis, severe. While in the service he befriended another corpsman with whom he spent a major part of his service. One incident that the patient relates took place while riding cross-country on a hospital train. They had gotten off the train for a stretch during a ten-minute stopover and he urged his friend to look at some souvenirs being displayed on the station platform. The train began to pull out and as the patient was able to run faster than his friend, he had gotten on the train, but the friend slipped and fell beneath the wheels of the railroad car. The patient says he did not go to the aid of his friend but sat down in a chair and prayed that his friend was not killed. . . . He later learned that an amputation was necessary and he visited his friend in the hospital. He says that he did not feel guilty any longer but felt badly for some time after the accident occurred.

* * *

Schooling: During his school years he always received good grades and A's for effort. His memory was remarkable and he memorized an entire play in three days while in high school. . . .

Social History: The patient states that he has the desire to meet people, but cannot stand to have them look into his face because he believes that people will think he is strange. He preferred elderly people because he says "they will understand my condition." At the age of 20, he went with a girl of the same age but never had the intention of proposing marriage. He had sexual relations with the girl and believes that she was the source of his present luetic infection. He states that he had frequent sexual contact with pickups while in the service, but never felt gratification.

Present Illness: The patient relates a recent incident wherein he went to a motion-picture theatre in the afternoon of a weekday when the house was relatively empty. He decided to visit the washroom before going to his seat and walked upstairs to the men's room. However, when he wished to take his seat, he could not walk down the stairs because he would have to face the manager, several ushers, and the popcorn girl as he descended. He remained upstairs in the washroom for five hours and descended only when he was able to walk behind an old man. He also states that he frequently waits for people to gather at the corner where he wishes to board a bus because he cannot get into a bus alone. He admits compulsive behavior in that he frequently counts steps, blocks in the linoleum, and squares in the ceiling. He says that the hair on the nape of his neck bothers him and he frequently shaves his back.

Mental Examination: The patient is always very tense and evades giving history of his luetic infection. He states that he feels relieved now that the interviewer knows his condition and is anxious to have treatment for it. He has been preoccupied with pains in his chest, and believed something was wrong with his heart. He was greatly relieved when he was told that the electrocardiogram was negative. He receives interpretations willingly and states that he is anxious to make an adjustment. He feels that he owes his mother support, but is anxious to make a life for himself. He has good insight and is well oriented in all spheres. He denies any hallucinations. On the ward, he is described by his ward physician as being rather facetious and playful and enjoys occupational therapy.

The diagnosis on admission in January 1947 was "psychoneurosis, anxiety type, acute and severe." Mr. Doe was admitted to an open ward, where he took part in general ward activities including group psychotherapy. The psychiatrist's initial note about his participation in the latter was " . . . tense. . . . Verbalizes freely, but not wholly accessible." He suspected homosexual panic; a psychiatric consultant a week later said that the "diagnosis lies between obsessive-compulsive neurosis, anxiety-hysteria, and schizophrenia. Most likely appears to be obsessive-compulsive." Another consultant in April reaffirmed the psychoneurotic diagnosis. By June, he had become "somewhat upset and confused in past several days," and the question of schizophrenia was again raised. Psychological testing was begun, but the TAT was not administered until August. By mid-June, his physicians had begun to feel that he was "an incipient schizophrenic," and he was given insulin coma treatment over a three-week period. He took the TAT two days after his sixth and last insulin coma. The psychologist reported, after studying the Rorschach, Wechsler-Bellevue, Bender-Gestalt, Make-A-Picture-Story Test, MMPI, and Draw-A-Person, that "the overall impression is that of a schizoid personality subjected to strong emotional conflicts and attempting to adjust on an obsessive-compulsive level in order to prevent a schizophrenic break." The patient was transferred to an open ward again and was given psychotherapy for a month. On September 18, he was discharged at his own request because he did not feel he was being helped and continued therapy at a VA Mental Hygiene Clinic for eight sessions during the next two months. The discharge diagnosis from the hospital was "anxiety reaction."

The following is the final "summary evaluation" of John Doe by the woman who was his last psychotherapist.

> The patient, a 25-year-old single man, is a tall, slender, young man, who gives the impression of boyishness. He seemed suspicious, indecisive, and unable to relax. There seemed to be considerable effeminate mannerisms in his behavior. He showed his anxiety by smoking considerably, moving about in his chair, and speaking constantly. The history of this patient indicated that this is a person who had never been able to make secure object relationships. One got the impression that his mother had been a very seductive, over-solicitous, overprotective, inconsistent person. Apparently, she had always been conscious of her appearance, acted as if she were younger than her actual age, and, in general, seemed to be a very narcissistic and controlling person. The patient reacted with violence to her use of alcohol. He considered her to be a very nagging, complaining person, who frequently irritated him. He described instances where his hostile impulses were so great that he was unable to control himself and thus had blackened her eyes and threatened to kill her. He talked also of wishing to strangle her. He recalled his resentment toward his mother for her keeping him away from his father with whom he wanted to have a close relationship. The patient felt that his mother's dependency on her family for support, since the father's death, had been one of the reasons why he had undergone insecurity and disturbance. This was particularly true, he said, in the way she required the patient to cater to her family in order not to alienate them. The father seems to be a hazy person in the patient's life. The patient resented his father's tuberculosis and death as well as his mother's prohibitions in permitting any kind of relationship. He recalled the way in which everything had to be sterilized. He could not even sit on his father's chair. With much feeling he also talked of not being allowed to go to the funeral of his father. He used to blame his father for everything that had happened to him since but now does not do it any more. He was ashamed of having no father and would envy people who had fathers. From this, it seemed quite obvious that this patient lacked male identification and that he not only had hostility toward the father-person, of whom he was deprived, but also felt that his mother kept him from having a father.

Patient has two older brothers with whom there seems to be no close relationship except in terms of rivalry and resentment. Patient talked of the way in which his brothers would scare him, tell him ghost stories, and tease him. The oldest brother is apparently an alcoholic, whereas the second brother seems to have made the best adjustment of the three.

The patient's childhood, from his own description, seems to be a turbulent one. Apparently he was very fearful and withdrawn from early childhood. He was always meticulous in his clothing and was unwilling to share anything with others. Somehow, religion seemed to play a great part in his life and apparently a source of security to him was Catholicism. He was drawn toward religion and toward priesthood because he felt that he would receive protection and security there. At an early age he wrote a story and an autobiography which revealed his loneliness and his hope that Catholicism and priesthood would be the way out. In adolescence, although extremely religious he was too guilty to consider entering the priesthood. Obviously, some of this guilt is in relation to his sexual drives, masturbation, and probably also in relation to incestuous feelings that he must have had toward his seductive mother. There seems to be considerable guilt in relation to his own hostility. He has established some defenses against this through obsessions but these defenses are cracking and he fears that his hostile impulses might become so great that he would be unable to control them. It is probably quite true that this man's reality world has never been too kind to him, that it is hostile to him and that he fears he cannot control his reactions to it.

Prior to his going into the Service, the patient was able to hold a job, although it was quite obvious that he had difficulty with authoritative figures and was very sensitive to other people's opinions of him. Military service for him was a very difficult experience, especially having to live with so many people. It was a very traumatic affair for him when his buddy was run over by a train. It was in Service, too, that the patient must have had considerable homosexual panic since he was constantly with men. He told of a relationship with a WAVE who was unattractive and at the same time a girl whom he used to test constantly. The patient has considerable fear of women and has the feeling that they are somehow superior to him. He also told of an attraction to a girl with bleached hair, very well groomed, and apparently somewhat theatrical. In this description one got the feeling that perhaps the patient was also describing his own mother and that this kind of girl was also an incestuous relationship for him.

The patient seemed obsessed with thoughts about death, homicide, and suicide, and apparently these thoughts have been with him even before adolescence. Since Service, the patient has had numerous fears, which actually seem to be fears of his own impulses. There was depersonalization, many ideas of reference, and a considerable amount of hostile fantasies. It is felt that this patient is a paranoid schizophrenic who is still able to maintain control over his hostile and destructive impulses, although this control is very tenuous. He is suspicious of any relationship, male or female. His use of obsessive ideas and compulsive actions has gradually broken down so that one now sees remnants of them. As long as he can live a withdrawn and sheltered life perhaps he can continue to functon outside of a hospital; however, in the face of frustration he may become an active psychotic with homicidal and suicidal impulses.

In December, 1949, twenty-five months after Doe's last psychotherapeutic session, Dr. Samuel Futterman, the chief psychiatrist of the Mental Hygiene Clinic, sent John Doe a letter, asking him to come in to discuss his plans "either of continuing [therapy] or of other arrangements." He came in promptly and was interviewed by Dr. Futterman. He expressed a wish for help but reluctance to seek it at the clinic because of fear he might be assigned to a therapist who had once made him wait; he knew that "he would have to blow up at" this psychiatrist. He told of constant fears, reference ideas (fear that others were staring at him or would find out something bad about him), many somatic symptoms, delusional religious ideas, and feelings of depersonalization. "He is afraid to walk in the streets because of the crowds," the psychiatrist wrote in his report. "They might do something to him. He might do something to them." He was living in a remote area with his mother and getting along well with her, but "constantly apprehensive during the day. He goes to the bathroom to urinate twenty to thirty times a day."

In conclusion, Dr. Futterman wrote: "Clinically, this is a case of schizophrenia, paranoid form, with almost preconscious self-destructive or outward destructive tendencies. The outward world is hostile and he himself feels that he must react to it by his hostility, but so far has not really acted out on it." So far as we know, he still has not done so.

7

There is only a little to add to the introductory remarks before the preceding chapter. It was again Ed Shneidman who persuaded me to do a public exercise in blind diagnosis, in 1952. John E. Bell had organized a successful symposium for the annual meeting of the Society for Projective Techniques at the APA meetings three years previously, and this time Shneidman followed the same format: each of a number of tests was interpreted by a presumed expert who had only a couple of scraps of orienting information in addition to the test protocol; the data were published in time for members of the society to study them before attending the symposium, where the test mavens read their reports aloud, after which came a presentation of the clinical story, life history data, and official diagnosis.

This time, there was no request for working notes to be published. Nevertheless, I kept mine and used them when I made a teaching case out of Jay for the course on the interpretation of the TAT, which I taught for a good many years. I have included them here, only slightly edited; I had to resist the temptation to correct and enlarge them in the wisdom of aftersight, for there are a number of matters I passed over too lightly—particularly, evidences that a psychotic break might have already occurred. They lack a good deal, also, in system and order, being a mixture of notes on divergent material and inferences, the latter usually expressed without appropriate qualification. I hope that they will help, however, in suggesting some of the steps I went through in getting from the stories to the finished report.

I did not edit out, either, my testy remarks about the way the TAT was administered, though I apologize to Ed Shneidman for them. (We were both a good deal younger then.) If I had known, I would not have liked the fact that Jay's first testing session opened with ten cards of the TAT, the other eight being given at the beginning of the second session, and such standard starters as a Wechsler intelligence test not being given until the third session. Still, none of this might have made any great difference; I would not have guessed the important unknown determinant of Jay's unusual passivity—the fact that he had been hospitalized primarily for pulmonary tuberculosis, an enervating disease for which complete rest was traditionally prescribed.

A Blind Interpretation of Jay's TAT

As a kind of control, I decided to set down, *before* looking at the TAT, some of the truisms and clichés that are found in most test reports, and that can be fairly safely said once you know someone is a patient of Jay's age and sex.

ESP INTERPRETATION

I guessed that since Gregor[1] was schizophrenic, Jay would probably be neurotic, and since symptom neuroses are so rare these days, I decided to call it a character neurosis. Here is my ESP personality description. The core of the patient's neurotic problem is to be found in difficulties in relationships with other people. At the age of 32, he has been unable really to find himself, to know where he is going in life. He has failed to achieve up to his potentialities (his intelligence is definitely better than average). At times, anxiety and tension drive him to act out in ways that are ultimately self-injurious. He is troubled by his inability to find satisfaction in life, especially in sexual relationships, which lack mature intimacy and mutuality, due to an unresolved Oedipal fixation. He is, in fact, psychosexually immature, with noteworthy latent homosexual trends and oral-passive needs. Further, he has difficulty in expressing hostility appropriately, with respect to intensity and object. This difficulty is particularly apparent in his relationships with father-figures. There are indications of some unconscious castration anxiety lying behind this last-mentioned problem of adjustment. Despite his front of relative maturity, he is in many ways essentially a child emotionally, never having wholly freed himself from dependence on his parents. He does have some ego-strength, however, and pretty good contact with reality most of the time. With analytically oriented psychotherapy, the prognosis is fairly good; without treatment, prognosis for his finding happiness in life is distinctly guarded.

And now for my interpretation of Jay's TAT. [The stories follow, just as they were given to me. I later learned that Dr. Shneidman had administered the test, tape-recording the responses, and that he usually asked for each story to be given a title.]

FIRST TAT SESSION

Subject: Jay   male   32 years old   white, Protestant

1   I feel that the boy plays the violin. He . . . he is a musician. He has just used the instrument and perhaps he has been moved by his performance, that is he put the instrument down and is more or less lost in contemplation of the music he has just played. Perhaps he is contemplating the form of the violin. He impresses me as being a European child. I feel that he comes from Central Europe someplace and that the picture was taken there . . . I mean he's not . . . he's an alien person. I play the piano myself, and I feel a certain dislike for the violin . . . and mention that here. However, I think that he feels no dislike for it. I think that's what I have to say about this. (Title?) Reverie, or something like that. That's the predominant mood, I think.

[1][The reference is to the pseudonymous subject of another, similar demonstration of blind diagnosis in a symposium organized by Bell (1949).]

1. Sentience, esthetic interest, and feeling are expressed. Possibly some obsessiveness in the "perhaps"es.

Contemplating the form—stalling, doesn't know how to go ahead.

Some effort to reason from close scrutiny of the picture, implies obsessive-compulsiveness. Some perceptual sensitivity. "An alien person"—why? Dislikes violin.

Self-reference: piano, not violin (self-centered).

No story development—but then, poor inquiry; also, no reaction time, no total time. It may be because of depression, low mood. Doesn't sound like a primitive person—plays the piano.

No evidences of psychosis.

2   My first feeling about it was that it was much in the style of Henri Rousseau's paintings . . . it has a very stark and primitive quality . . . I'm impressed by the fact that the man and woman are back to back, that is they are . . . a feeling of estrangement . . . The woman is carrying books and looks intellectual, that is, she . . . they are. . . thoughtful books. The woman at the right is carrying the child. . . There is a sort of biblical feeling about the picture, that is, the . . . the externals are modern but the . . . something simple and direct about it, it has a kind of biblical feeling for me. No one is particularly interested in anyone else in this picture. They are each lost in a kind of individual or personal world of their own. I think that's all I can say. If I were going to title it, I would call it. . . well, I don't know. I have a feeling of . . . it would be . . . Apartment, if I may say that of the people that impresses me most. I think that's all I have to say about it.

2. Artistic reference—he knows something about art, though it *isn't* like Henri Rousseau! Picks up general feeling qualities—likely to give CFs and rather diffuse reactions to color: an impressionistic approach, not a systematic one. Yet he started in both this story and the preceding from an instantaneous W, not very differentiated.

Note again, *feeling of estrangement* (compare "alien person" in 1). A projection of his own feeling of being estranged from people. Continues an associative, ruminative, allusive way of talking. (Obsessive but not compulsive—not one to get things done efficiently.)

"Intellectual . . . thoughtful books"—these are aspects of his own identity and interest. Estranged particularly from parents. Note condensation in the way he develops the sentence; but in the acceptable range.

Peculiar title: Apartment; compare schizophrenic implications of "each lost in a kind of individual or personal world of their own." Many references to his *feelings* about it—more a feeler than a thinker (hysterical elements?).

No story development. Is this passive aggression, resistance to the *E?* or only the effects of poor administration?

No warmth and family solidarity in his background—cold, distant parents, not supportive.

3BM   I am immediately reminded of Matisse, another painter. Very bold linear quality about it. It is a painting, I think. It might be a sort of retouched photograph but . . . It's a, very interesting as a painting, I think. The feeling, of course, is one of dejection or despondency and I am made sort of uncomfortable by the position of the woman, the raised shoulder and the crooked neck. The object on the floor is apparently a gun . . . I'm not sure of that . . . but I make a gun out of it, but I like the composition of it very much. If I were to give you the title . . . it has some bearing on the despair of this woman but . . . (Could you say what led up to the situation in the picture?) If she has been rejected or disapproved of I think . . . she feels the loss of someone . . . which is what rejection means to her. I don't know what specific incident . . . happened . . . but someone close to her has left her. And, of course, even as I speak her sex changes almost as I'm looking at this and she becomes more of a man and so I suppose more like myself. In that I identify with men more easily than with women and I can understand rejection as felt by a man, or at least I feel that men have my feelings and women I don't understand, and I never can quite comprehend that feelings that women have are like feelings that I have.

3BM. The reference to painters is pretentious, particularly when as inappropriate as this. He might be a sensitive but not well-educated, arty homosexual; his esthetic potentials are not well developed. Throughout, he stays entirely too close to the picture, using it as a "resistance"? External compliance but inner listlessness and unwillingness to cooperate with parental figures.

Quite an empathic description, but of the *vulnerable* kind. Yet able to maintain esthetic distance. There's something soft, effeminate, too arty about him.

Lacks appropriate distance from or perspective on the task, in his effort to figure out what "really" happened; he doesn't grasp and hold well in mind what he is supposed to do. His persistent failure to tell stories resulted, at last, in some inquiry.

p Loss → rejection → despair (cf. 1 and 2). p Disapproval.

Note narcissistic self-references. Now the fluctuating sexual identity is clearer. He protests about women's having different feelings from his own. But obviously, feelings, and empathic feeling contact with people, are important to him (he wants them).

4   I feel that I don't like to criticize these from the standpoint of art, but I am impressed by the vulgarity of this picture. Just from the standpoint of its quality as illustration opposed to art. I don't mean to say that any emotion or feeling expressed is vulgar, but the artist's rendering of the people involved doesn't show feeling to me, I mean, it's just skill and has the quality of magazine illustration about it . . . and yet although I say the feelings expressed are not vulgar, I have no feeling about what is expressed there. The man is pulling away from the woman. He is fixed on something else. She seems to be trying to hold him. She seems to be puzzled by what he is doing. There's something vaguely disquieting or unappealing about it to me. I don't know how to express it any more than I already have.

(Could you go on and say who they were?) No, I . . . nothing occurs to me as to who they might be. First my parents have gone through a situation like this, but I can't identify these people with my parents . . . they were like that, somehow. (What might you call this story?) Well, it's the look of entreaty on the woman's face that seems to predominate here . . . so I would call it Entreaty, or something of that nature.

4. Again, the atmosphere strikes him, the vulgarity. Note inability to criticize without apologizing. Continues to have almost intuitive sensing of the emotional undertone of the situation without a conscious rational analysis of it.

Woman entreats, man pulls away. No more story than that! Reference to parents implies difficulty between them, maybe separation.

6BM   Well, again the thing that I remark is that the people are not looking at each other. The mother, presumably she is the mother, has taken offense at something . . . she wishes to hold the son. She wishes to keep this young man in the . . . he is undetermined about it . . . about what to do. She has made it a point to play on his filial devotion to her to keep him with her. There's conflict in his mind about whether he wants to stay or ought to stay or to leave and . . . make a life for himself. And the indecision of the man is most pronounced to me. (What occurs, could you say?) Well, I can only say there are hard feelings all around. I don't know what the man will do. It's his decision, however, not the mother's. It's up to him but I don't know what he will do.

6BM. People not looking at each other: cf. 1, 2, broken relationships in 3 and 4. He is still describing pictures, not telling stories.

Mother wishes to *hold* son (as woman wanted to hold man in 4); yet she rejects him: has taken offense. Guilt ("filial devotion"). She's not got a bit of consideration; implies Jay's own mother was a cold, manipulative woman.

Pronounced indecision of the man—cf. obsessive doubts and immobility. I'll bet he doesn't do anything—no push, and can't decide: "I don't know what he'll do."

"Hard feelings all around"—a bleak and loveless world he lives in!

The conflict is dependence versus independence; does he project onto mother?

7BM   The young man has heard some unpleasant news. Some information has been imparted to him by the kindly looking old gentleman. I don't think of them as being father and son. I think of them as teacher and pupil or a relationship of that sort. The old man has told him something that the young man must come to understand. I don't know just what it is . . . Something that the old man recognizes isn't unpleasant although it seems to be to the young man now. The old man is resigned to waiting, knowing that the young man will eventually have a more balanced outlook in the matter. It's just a momentary setback for the man but he will . . . The young man's feelings have been hurt. That is, his pride suffers a blow, I think that the feeling of again indecision . . . no, not indecision . . . yes, the wavering the man feels in respect to this news that he has just heard is the predominant feeling of the picture here. Again it's Indecision.

7BM. Unpleasant news; nothing cheerful yet. It only seems so—wisdom of the older man shows it isn't really unpleasant.

p Inf → n Intragg, Ego Ideal (hurt pride).

Indecision over indecision a classic! Intense ambivalence. Perhaps he has the feeling that sometimes older men are well-meaning, but even then there's little they can do. Things have to be suffered through—moral masochism.

Not father and son—old man is kindly (and his father isn't?). Vagueness continues; unable to think of specific ideas.

8BM   This one seems very heterogeneous to me, that is that nothing relates much to anything else. A man has apparently been wounded. He's undergoing an emergency operation of some sort, probably to remove a bullet from his abdomen. The operation is being performed under a rather haphazard and makeshift circumstances. The young man in the foreground seems completely out of place and so I wonder whether there isn't some sort of symbolism meant to show the discrepancy often between the promise young people show and the harsher reality that comes out of it. That is, the young man is also the man on the operating table as an older person. [Pause] I would really be stumped for a title to this one. Well it would be the attentiveness of the men who are doing the operating that seems to afford the only relief I see in the picture. I don't particularly like to look at the other parts. It's the way they are engrossed in their work that is the most pleasing to look at. So I would say I feel better looking at their attentiveness rather than at any other element in the picture.

8BM. Same dominant impression: nothing related to anything else (isolation). It shows a latent wish that they should be, however, and perhaps some latent tendency to try to combine, integrate, but it is held back by the neurosis (also related to wish to keep parents apart).

Note vocabulary: "heterogeneous." But he's a dilettante.

He first focuses on the man being operated on—his passive identification. Something is being done *to* him, Jay. The young man in front identifies himself with the operand, not the operators.

He is critical of the circumstances of the operation: not an easy fellow to please, he has a sharp eye for the incongruous, and easily thinks things are out of order.

Symbolism—a sophisticated outlook. This is almost surely a college-trained fellow. He's too limp to have attained his sophistication any other way than by having been exposed to and able to soak it up from an environment.

Self-concept of early promise—"prodigy"? but later reality is harsh.

Takes on as self-imposed the task of finding a title after having been asked only twice (or was it also part of the original instructions? If so, a mistake with a guy like this, because it gives him something static to obsess about, and adds nothing.)

Note that the only thing he likes about this picture, which many find inspiring, with heroic action of a nurturant sort going on, is the most passive receptive thing the operators are doing: attention. The one aspect that he can identify with. He likes to see people absorbed, engrossed—part of his ego ideal, or "good identity."

Vulnerable to the pictured aggression.

> 11   This one has a romantic nineteenth-century quality about it. There's a strange form that appears to be going in two directions. One to cross a bridge and another one . . . another direction to return by the path it has presumably taken to arrive at this point. It's threatened also from up above in the canyon wall by some kind of . . . some sort of . . . I-I-I . . . weird animal of some sort of strange nature here. As I look closely the scale changes, I see two or three small persons there, at least a man and woman, before . . . I'm saying that this is a man and this is a woman with long Grecian robes. Whereas before, it seemed like two bison-like animals with their . . . a head on each end . . . the body and sort of pulling in opposite directions there. I am also aware now of a figure crossing the bridge. Running, that is, the arms are extended forward and backward, leading the way here. Once again I'm faced with the job of what to call this. I don't know what the predominant mood of it is. The natural beauty of the picture is impressive. I don't necessarily feel that the people are endangered even by this . . . monster up above them. First it seemed so, but the monster himself now looks rather gentle and curious as to what is happening down here below him. The road across the bridge seems to be leading nowhere. It seems to go into the sheer face of the cliff. However, it seems to be bright back in there. The road probably curves around the face of the cliff and out into the light again. Even though the people there at the bridge are very small compared to the rest of the composition they hold the attention strongly. The light and dark contrast there is great, of course. Since I don't know the feeling of the people, I don't know which way they are going; it's merely the transitional quality of the situation that impresses me. I think that's all I have to say about it.

11. Same sensitivity to atmosphere; likes "the natural beauty of the picture." His ambivalence and indecision take visual form as something "going in two directions," forward and back—health versus further decompensation? Is he decompensating? This gives the impression of being a static state, of a man who has always been passive, obsessive, and schizoid.

"I-I-I"—does he have a speech defect? Probably not; more like faithful recording of normal hesitation.

As before, he reports a change in the percept as he looks closely: introspective, brooding kind of fellow. Also a projective quality to it, as if external reality were changing and he is only reporting. His perceptual grip on reality doesn't seem firm, though he actually perceives quite accurately.

Monster at first dangerous, now "gentle and curious"—parallels own reaction formations? Compare curiosity attributed to monster and the attentiveness in 8BM. There may be some thematically related symptoms (voyeurism, exhibitionism, ideas of reference, paranoid over-alertness).

His own static, stalled attitude in "road leads nowhere" but up against a stone wall.

He has an analytic turn of mind: ruminates out loud about *why* the people stand out so, the brightness contrast. He's something of an intellectualizer.

Transition—his own state? (Because of the administrative technique, we get little besides the defenses.)

> 12M   Well this reminds me of some very early experiments with hypnotism. The man on the couch . . . the boy on the couch has just been successfully hypnotized by the man bending over him. [Pause] There isn't much more I can say beyond that point. The . . . the right hand of the man bending over the fellow is . . . is characteristic gesture of benediction or blessing but I don't feel that that alters the story of what is happened here. It is still a hypnotic experience. [Pause] Since I mentioned one hand, I might as well mention that the other hand seemed menacing to me in some manner . . . in its being held tight to the side there is something that doesn't portend any good for the person hypnotized. I think that's all I have to say about this one. For a title, Hypnotic Experiment or something of that sort. (Could you say anything about who they might be?) Well, if I'm to identify with any one I would be the person on the couch who has been hypnotized, possibly because it was always my wish to be hypnotized, when we would experiment this way, and never succeeded. In that event I can identify the other man as the person who conducted these experiments with me. A friend that I grew up with. But I feel no menace to me from that person. I might say no blessing either. I think that's all I have to say about this one.

12M. The hypnosis is *successful*. Old man again seen as kindly—gesture of benediction, yet other hand seems menacing: *ambivalence* toward father. [A classic instance of paranoid inference from detail.]

Clumsy inquiry; Jay is psychologically minded enough to take this as, 'With which one do you identify yourself?' Naturally, with the boy; tells of experiences of trying, wanting to be hypnotized. This is a rather poorly sublimated passive homosexual wish—a wish to submit to the will of a man. Also some of his masochism is in it, especially in seeing menace in the other.

> 13MF   Well, the man has either just attempted . . . sexual intercourse with this woman or realizes that it is out of the question and is consequently grief stricken at that. The woman is indifferent, but well, I think. I feel that it is the woman who has

... it doesn't make her indifferent if I continue this way ... it is the woman who has developed this situation, that is, she has led the man into it. She is probably a little provoked by its failure and therefore not indifferent. One of the two is bookish, I would say the man probably, since I associate bookish people with a certain indifference to sexual intercourse, or other manifestations of sex. Not really, I mean in some cases I do ... I feel that books are related to the situation however. I do feel that it's through a failure to consummate this thing that the man is feeling ... probably a mixture of grief or humiliation ... inadequacy. Of course, it would be with the man that I would identify here. The worst part of this whole thing is trying to give titles to these things. It seems useless to me. I don't know what to title this one either. I don't feel much sympathy for the man either, I will say that! May I stop here rather than try to think of a title for it? (What would you say their relationship might be?) Well they are friends rather than lovers and they are not married or not related. Possibly they are related, I mean the first instantaneous thing that I thought was that they were brother and sister. I mean there's a truer feeling about it than anything I have said since. I keep wondering whether in these ... the ease with which I identify with these pictures makes me wonder if there is a set for dark men and a set for blond men ... because I notice so many dark men in all of them. The man is leaving I might say. He isn't just standing there and he's going to leave the room. If the people are lovers, then it's humiliation he feels. If they are brother and sister then the feeling is one of shame. So it depends. I don't know what their relationship is. I think that exhausts this.

13MF. Note contrast between woman's indifference and man's despair.

He's passive as usual: hero is seduced but ineffective; Jay is heterosexually impotent.

Woman is indifferent in the sense of callous disregard of his feelings, only put out because she didn't get laid. This is a very hostile view of women; sounds more and more like a homosexual. (Some of his underlying, pervasive doubt is about his own sexual identity.) The man is sensitive, refined—feminine qualities; the woman is the opposite.

Reasoning from detail—bookish. Projection of own intellectuality: "I associate bookish people ... intercourse." Denies, as if it's becoming too obvious, that he speaks about himself.

Heterosexual failure leads to grief, inadequacy feelings. Oddly gratuitous remark that he identifies with the man. This is pure denial (negation) of feminine identification. But it also shows his great pliancy—he is so eager to please (though also passively negativistic) that he transfers to this story his understanding expressed in the last one, of what the E wanted. He probably watched E like a hawk in other tests for the least signs of whether he was doing right or wrong—maybe.

The complaint about titles is a beautiful example of this combination of passive compliance and passive hostility.

Thought of brother and sister is never quite explicitly related by Jay to the other, sex story, but comes pretty close: shame. Not clear whether he meant to leave it that way—these characters with those events. It's pretty unusual to come so close to an incest story; suggests either a fixation on sister or on a young mother or stepmother. Incest barriers would account for inability of the hero to go through with it. How does this fit in with the hypothesis of his homosexuality? (Often, homosexual men can't touch women because they are taboo, identified with mother or sister.)

Intensely introspective and self-observant, self-critical. Watches own feelings, gauges the degree of their validity in a way very characteristic of intellectual, schizoid obsessives. But the brother-sister business may be a blind—an intellectualization?

Note projective implications of "set for dark men"—sees it all as self-referent. Over-alertness again.

SECOND TAT SESSION

14   Well it's morning and the man in the picture has just awakened and has gone to the window and is looking out on . . . at the sunlight. He's alone in the room. He's a painter, I think, there's the quality of the Paris garret about this picture. He's not reaching for anything, he's just supporting himself there with his outstretched arm . . . and presently will turn away from the window and leave the room, go down into the street for breakfast, something like that. His feelings are . . . well he's untroubled, there's no particular feeling that he has. He . . . is just pleased by the sunlight and the view of the city that he sees. That's all, I wouldn't title it either. It's just as I said.

14. On this day, Jay seems to feel a little brighter in mood, less heavy and static.

A painter; more atmospherism; more rumination.

The only activity: looking, then go eat. Pleased by the view, untroubled.

Happiness—mainly absence of trouble, not much positive feeling to it. Comes from solitary absorption of visual scenes.

15   I don't have much feeling about death, or really very much sympathy for people who have been bereaved and I regret this. I mean I feel that it's a fault with me. My aunt died about a week ago and I had to write . . . felt I ought to write a letter to my uncle and I was surprised at the difficulty of getting any real feeling into the letter. I have something of that feeling here. I can't understand this man's grief. I don't know what it is like to love someone so much that they would be missed a great deal. And of course that is my loss. Maybe someday I can regain that feeling I once had about death which whether it's good or bad at least it was strong and that's the thing that I would like to have, this strong feeling. I have nothing to say about this man.

15. More denial (an important defense for him, apparently).

Typically narcissistic beginning—about his feelings about death, etc. He doesn't take the task of telling stories very seriously (maybe because pictures are more important to him than literature) but is quite willing to reveal himself. There are quite a number of direct self-statements in this TAT—a fair amount of personality description could be made from them alone.

His feelings are very largely isolated; he can summon up very little affect. Anything so threatening as death particularly calls on this combination of denial and isolation: no feeling. He has difficulty in empathizing unless something touches him directly.

No story—talks only about self. Confesses he has never loved anyone much—feels it as a loss, or says so! Misses, longs for, strong vivid feelings.

> 16   Well, I see a circus, a childhood situation where there is a great deal of activity and color and excitement. A merry-go-round in the right foreground, I imagine that. A lot of balloons and cotton candy and a carnival atmosphere throughout the whole thing. There are lots of people, of course, there. No one is . . . no one predominates in the situation that I see, just a lot of people. I'm present there in my present capacity of just looking at it, I don't see much myself in the picture. I suppose there is a sideshow tent or something on the left here and the movement is into the picture between the merry-go-round and the sideshow back into more of the customary circus attractions. There is no narrative in this either. It's just a thing that I have experienced before perhaps although I don't recall ever having been to the circus. It's a static picture, I mean, one in which a story is developing even though there is movement, a great deal of movement within that static picture, but nothing involving me except as an onlooker. I'm merely observing. I guess that's what I see (Title?) Well, Circus or something like that would be a nice antiseptic title.

16. And here it is: in childhood, there was a time when he had vivid feelings. Interesting that it was on an occasion when his senses were particularly stimulated, *just looking.* Note references to color, excitement—emotion. *Candy.* Carnival atmosphere. Sideshow—things to look at. No narrative.

But he says: "I don't recall ever having been to the circus"! Some sense of humor. Ambivalence again in the balance: movement, yet a static picture.

> 17BM   There's a painting by Daumier, I'm sure this must be copied from it, called The Housepainter . . . and whenever I see that painting I think they painted houses differently in those days. I suppose it's significant to decide whether this man is climbing the rope or lowering himself and having said that it sort of puts me in a position where I am unable to answer it, and become again conscious of . . . or self-conscious about it, I mean . . . [Pause] I have nothing more to . . . feel that I want to say about it. (Can you tell me anything about the person?) Well, the feeling of lifting one's own weight is a good feeling, and of course, he is feeling that here. He supports himself. [Pause] He is apparently looking at something in the distance. That is, his mind isn't strictly on what he is doing here, and he's apparently absorbed in what he is looking at. And I think the expression on his face is one of pleasure. And I think that's all I have to say about him.

17BM. Correctly identifies this as a copy of a Daumier. Gives irrelevant personal associations. Correct insight (sentence 2) leads to paralysis of decision, self-consciousness.

"The feeling of lifting one's own weight is a good feeling"—some striving for independence. "Supports himself" is a good.

Pleasure again is the result of looking, not doing. Never says if hero is going up or down; fair enough—Jay isn't doing either. He's staying put, his will paralyzed.

18BM   Well, it has a very weird surrealist quality about it. There are three hands visible in the picture and none of the hands can belong to the man in the picture here. He's being restrained by at least two people who are not at all visible. The man himself seems to be insensible, that is he doesn't . . . he isn't aware even that he is being held back or held up. He has the appearance of a sleeping man or a drowning man. It's a very serious picture from the standpoint of design and content. I don't like it, that is, I don't have a good feeling about it, but yet I think I would like to have it around. It annoys me or irritates me in some way. There's something puzzling about it and it has a real dreamlike quality to it. (Could you tell a story about it?) [Pause] It doesn't belong to any realistic order of things that I'm familiar with. It could be a scene from a movie or a play or a ballet. It has a certain sort of Cocteau quality about it, disembodied hands wafting around in the air. It's effective art and it doesn't touch me any place with respect to its possibilities for happenings in the world I'm living in. It's simply curious. That's all I can say about it.

18BM. Atmospheric comment. Again refers to art—rather recherché (Cocteau). But makes empty comments like "a very serious picture from the standpoint of design and content." He knows a fair amount about art, and likes to show it off, in his identity as sensitive bored esthete. Pretentious.

Hero: completely passive, being *restrained,* though he's asleep or drowning. Thus, he perceives well-meaning efforts to help and support him as restraint. He wants independence, probably intellectually rejects all dependence (the pride of the lone artist), but he is emotionally and probably financially dependent on his parents or someone—but has to protest against it in order to accept it.

Continual marked ambivalence about almost everything.

Refuses to try to make up a story, via a long intellectualization. His character defenses against doing anything are very strong.

The homosexual attack implication is repressed, comes out only in the reference to the homosexual Cocteau. Tries to make it distant by saying "dreamlike . . . doesn't belong to any realistic order of things."

18GF   Well, as in many of these, the artist has been quite skillful in creating an expression that is extremely ambiguous. It could be either two possibilities. In this case the mother might be kind of loving or there's a certain menace I see in her

face, too. I suppose that's what the test is for, to see specifically what my interpretation is, I'm sort of just pulled between the two, her hand is extremely unpleasant as
far as art goes, I think. It has . . . sort of . . . well, deformed isn't what I mean . . . it
has something of the characteristic of an animal, a pig or something of that sort.
The person she is addressing is apparently a woman. The whole scene is very
unpleasant to me in some way. There's something sinister in the action. The older
woman is standing so that presumably a mother and daughter relationship
between them. (Can you tell what might be happening?) The daughter is being
reprimanded or restrained in some manner. Perhaps the feeling of the mother's
jealousy or envy, something of that nature. It's not a situation where any love is felt.
(What finally happens?) Well, I don't know. I only hope that the mother is
thwarted. I don't know what happens. (Title?) [Pause] Well, names pin things
down so much. It's just a scene of a continuing situation and if you name it you
emphasize it so much that it makes it false or pulls it out of context too much, that's
why I just don't want to name it and so I won't.

18GF. Continual paranoid sharpness in probing for the artist's intent,
and taking it as self-referent. He has to figure things out; his self-esteem
depends not on doing, but on being able to look with a piercing eye, discern
the intent of anyone else, and thus disarm any probing attempts. By *seeing
through* the other fellow, he can feel superior. In it, he displays quite a lot of
skill, incidentally.

Ambivalence about mother—both "kind and loving" and menacing.

Sharp eye for the distortion in the picture of the woman's wrist. (He
should do well on Picture Completion, though might miss items like "lip-
stick.") Uses it as an opportunity to *degrade* the woman.

Constantly narcissistic reaction, which is paradoxical, in that he's so
intellectualized and isolated, yet he reacts primarily in a feeling way to
pictures. Instead of an objective attitude (what *is* the picture?) or a constructive attitude (what can I make with it?), he has a purely subjective attitude:
what does it do to me? After a glance, his eye turns inward to read the dials
of his sensitive reactivity, and he reports this as if it were the most interesting
and important thing he could say—which it is, to him. So he's an extremely
narcissistic, self-centered guy.

Mother again is *restraining*—the great evil, in his eyes. His defense is an
odd one; it lets him see the atmosphere accurately, get the main feel of a
threat, but prevents him from getting any more concrete in his perception.

Mother is *jealous* or *envious* of daughter: this is unusual. He mentions
love to deny it. Is the good father the focus of these feelings?

Petulant refusal to be pinned down—typical intellectualizing avoidance
of the real issue, escaping into formulations. (He might have given more if
told that autobiography was *not* wanted, but imagination.)

It's obvious that this is an obsessional person, with strong isolation,
probably some paranoid trends, and very strong latent homosexuality.

strong feelings of inadequacy. A languid, flaccid, torpid quality. He can't throw off this heavy feeling that lies on him (because all of his energies are taken up in neurotic defenses). A lot of artistic knowledge and sensitivity without any taste. Quite shrewd and psychologically minded, an almost paranoid dwelling on the *purpose* of the test. He *hates* to pin things down 18GF)! A pretty clever rationalizer.

Most impressive thing about these stories is a heavy, static, passive tone that hangs over them. All action seems paralyzed by indecision. Certainly a textbook example of obsessive doubting and indecision. What is he defending against so hard? Aggression, partly—difficulty in recognizing it in 18GF. This is a passive, receptive attitude extended to almost a logical extreme—his antennae are out, he drinks in all sorts of global, diffuse, yet rather sensitively accurate impressions of the world. Superior IQ yet underattainment. An esthete, with a very feminine, intuitive, and would-be empathic approach. Not good at organizing things—he breathes in W-qualities, doesn't integrate but differentiates to some extent—takes a situation apart and then is unable to get it back together. Rather severely decompensated.

Identity: An *artist.* An esthetic sensitive, one whose main business is using his eyes to take things in. An *intellectual,* bookish, one who knows about things, understands, can make passing references to matters about which the common herd don't know at all. A thoughtful person, with deep interests, curiosity, a need to understand. An *individual*—a lone wolf, an independent person, living in his private world, who wants not to be restrained.

He wants to be a feeling person, intuitive, empathic, but is quite limited in this, and recognizes it.

A man, to whom a woman's feelings are remote and not understandable. A critical person, with high standards; yet a man with filial devotion. A *proud* person, an unusual and gifted person, far above the common herd, who once showed great promise but hasn't been able to realize it. (Possibly, also, a homosexual.) "Gentle and curious"? Indifferent to sex, rather aloof from people. Sophisticated, psychologically aware—one who is not taken in easily.

(Not a person who had at all a normal childhood of play with other boys, sports, girlfriends, circuses, or indulgent and permissive treatment by parents. Instead, it was a chilly and remote family, parents separated or not congenial, few friends, little contact with girls, lonely and bookish.)

TAT INTERPRETATION

In writing up this case, I had a conflict between using my contribution to say all that I could find in the TAT about Jay, to show the limits of what the test can give us, or to present some of the main features with indications of the evidence and reasoning involved in discerning them. I decided to do the

former: partly because the evidence in the TAT for so much of what I have
to say is obvious, partly because it is a less demanding task.

Diagnostic Considerations

My best guess about Jay is that he suffers from a severe character
neurosis with obsessive, narcissistic, schizoid, and paranoid features (in order
of their prominence). It is not inconceivable that he is psychotic, in which
case it would be a paranoid condition of relatively short duration, but I think
that he is not. There is only one real peculiarity in the test; the paranoid traits
of reasoning from detail and looking for the (usually self-referent) hidden
meaning or intent of things do not in themselves indicate psychosis, and his
perceptual contact with reality while taking the test was generally quite
adequate, on both occasions. There is a very real question, however, whether
or not he may be an overt homosexual. Certainly the evidence for a confused
feminine identification and strong passive homosexual needs is overwhelming, but all of this is to some extent ego-alien, and the whole problem could
conceivably be quite unconscious. My hunch is that Jay has a conscious
conflict over homosexual thoughts, that he has not adopted a homosexual
way of life even though he may have engaged in some perverse acts. And I
call it a character neurosis because the mixture of pathological trends seems
to be interwoven with a distorted personality structure, in which overt
symptoms are not as important as (ultimately self-destructive) character
defenses. Furthermore, there is little evidence of any conscious anxiety,
instead, we see avoidant defenses directed against Jay's having to face his
problems. He seems to have a kind of chronic low mood, but this is not so
much a depression as an expression of the way he is bound up in neurotic
conflicts and defenses.

Ego-Identity

As a first approximation to a fuller picture of what kind of man we are
dealing with here, let us see what kind of identity he has worked out for
himself, as mirrored in the TAT. To begin with I do not think that he has a
very stable sense of identity. Certainly he has more or less unconscious
doubts about his masculinity. He seems to feel that he is still in transition
toward a truly mature and independent self, though at times he must fool
even himself with his facade. He has chosen an identity that cuts him off
from the group support of the culture, a defiant way that thinks itself the
more superior when it is rejected by the majority. He is a sufferer, almost a
martyr. He is, or would be, an *intellectual esthete;* a knowledgeable, sensitive
sophisticate; an individual in the true sense, proud to be a lone wolf, proud
to be different, to live in an aloof private world. Apparently this identity
stresses receptive artisitic sensitivity and perceptiveness rather than creativity

or being productive. It is enough to be thoughtful, curious, informed, with high critical standards, and superior abilities even if one's early promise has not yet been fulfilled in work. This role requires complete independence more than he has been able to attain; it may exclude the "filial piety" that is the conscious representative of his dependence on his parents. It requires that one be invulnerable: never taken in by people, and indifferent to the allurements of sex. For some people, a similar identity may be viable, but Jay cannot really find any happiness through it. The main rewards of this way of life are not fully available to him: free love (remember his aloofness to sex), a rebellious kicking at the props of the conventional world (but Jay is still bound to his mother), and a richly sensuous, feelingful mode of experiencing life—but Jay's obsessive mechanism of isolation shuts off great areas of feeling. It is a pretty nearly bankrupt identity, yet he clings to it, apparently knowing no other except perhaps that of a frightened, dependent child.

Abilities and Thought Organization

The vocabulary and the wealth of artistic references in these stories let us know that Jay is a man of distinctly superior native endowment (verbal Wechsler-Bellevue IQ somewhere around 130). [His Verbal IQ was actually 134, Total IQ 142.] He is capable of keen and sensitive observation, but with the following limitations. He grasps quickly the main flavor of a situation, being something of a specialist in atmospheric nuances, but is less good with practical details. At the other end of the scale, he has a projectively sharpened alertness to small significant details that may tip him off to what is going on behind the scenes. His is a more impressionistic and analytic than synthetic mind; he breaks a problem down, tries to figure it out, but overvalues understanding at the expense of action; he leaves it to others to put things together again, or to carry out solutions. Rather than feeling free to let his fantasy go, he plods along or is able to produce almost nothing.

Jay has not subjected his good intellectual ability to enough discipline to have made it pay off in much by way of intellectual achievement. I suspect that he has been to college and may have graduated; he may dabble with one of the arts, but it's hard to believe that he is capable of enough hard effort to produce any mature work of art. Furthermore, his constant references to painters are not only pretentious, they are not wholly accurate (Leon Kroll does not have much in common with Henri Rousseau), and his further comments indicate that he does not even have particularly good taste. (Compare his admiring remarks about the TAT pictures to the scathing commentary of outstanding artists; Roe, 1946.) He is arty without being artistic. This is further evidence of the superficiality and lack of application of his mental approach. He skims the surface, in a facile way, catches the main note and doesn't trouble himself with thoroughness; he relies on his ability to drink in impressions, to pick up catchwords, to "talk a good game."

Because he is so clever, he has probably been able to get through school this way and to impress a fair number of people. But such habits of work are a shoddy foundation for any kind of vocational success or for real self-esteem.

A principal basis for the conclusion that Jay does not accomplish anything is the obsessional paralysis of the characters in his stories, and of himself in telling them. He hates to be pinned down, and can find plenty of rationalizations for not making up his mind about almost anything. This is one reason for the heavy, static, torpid quality that hangs over this TAT like a pall. It expresses a languor, a flaccid passivity that pervades all of his personality. The obsessiveness also makes his thinking ruminative and associative; he rambles, rather than going to the point.

A more positive feature is Jay's psychological-mindedness. He is quite aware of and interested in the psychological dimension of human life, and readily thinks of events in terms of their motivations. This is an asset for his undertaking psychotherapy, though its value may be nearly nullified by his intellectualizing defenses. He is intensely introspective, brooding over and fascinated with his own reactions to things, which are much more interesting to him usually than is the external reality itself. In fact, a great deal of his thought content is organized around *himself,* his own likes and dislikes.

Motives, Conflicts, and Defenses

An impression of far-reaching passivity is given by Jay's TAT, which is about as extreme in this way as any I have seen. A number of varieties may be distinguished: there is oral-receptive passivity, the passive submissiveness of moral masochism, and of latent homosexuality; we see also indolent passivity, an almost neurasthenic drooping quality of immobility; there is the passivity of dependence, and there is a curious mixture of passive compliance and passive hostile resistance. It is hard to imagine Jay's doing anything, just as *he* cannot imagine anyone doing anything more active than looking or attending. Since Jay places high value on supporting oneself, being beholden to no one, there is a continual conflict between his dependent and independent needs. It seems characteristic of him not to solve his conflicts, but to remain waveringly ambivalent about them. He wants help and support, yet he cannot get close to anyone, and sees every kindly hand stretched toward him as bearing chains with which to shackle him. Even in story 18BM, where he says that the man is asleep or drowning, he still sees the three hands as *restraining* this utterly limp figure.

Jay seems to have a number of the attributes of a dilettantish arty homosexual, including a conception of women as consistently hostile, callous, unsympathetic and generally alien creatures. But in his very insistence on his inability to understand a woman's feelings—he goes out of his way twice to remark that he identifies himself more easily with men than women—he seems to be protesting his masculinity. In his story to 13MF he projects a strong feeling of heterosexual inadequacy, apparently covered by a front of indifference to such vulgar and carnal matters, yet the attitude is not one of repugnance or fear. I think therefore that these straws point toward a lot of conflict about sex, with passive wishes to be overwhelmed by a man underneath it. It is unusual to have a nonpsychotic patient introduce a theme of brother-sister incest, even though not consummated, as openly as he does, but I feel quite cautious in interpreting it. No doubt Jay, like everyone else, has incestuous impulses and conflicts of greater or less strength, but just how great a role they may play in his illness, and whether it is mother rather than sister who is really involved in his unconscious fantasies, I do not feel prepared to say. At any rate, Jay tells us directly that he has never been in love and he has undoubtedly never had any satisfactory sexual experiences.

Passive resistance as an expression of hostility has been mentioned. It appears that it is very hard for Jay to express any aggression in other than indirect ways, such as consistently failing to tell stories in a storytelling test, criticizing and complaining, though often in a half-apologetic way. It is difficult for him even to perceive a directly aggressive act as such in picture 18GF, though he frequently notes a vague awareness of *menace*. In fact, this is an example of one of his idiosyncratic defenses; it lets him catch the atmosphere, the general feel of a threat, but prevents him from getting any more concrete in his perception. It seems perfectly safe to reiterate my foregone conclusion: that he has great difficulty in expressing hostile feelings in appropriate amounts and toward the right persons. An elaborate structure of defenses has been set up against any aggressive impulses: denial, reaction formation, projection, turning against the self and obsessive thinking all can be traced in these stories. The isolation of feeling seems to play a particularly important part, in relation not just to hostility but to all emotions. Jay complains of inability to feel deeply; he knows he is missing something, and keeps a careful finger on his own emotional pulse, scrutinizing the validity of each conscious affective state. At times he may even feel somewhat depersonalized. Despite this armor, he is vulnerable to hurts, and perhaps also to depressing external circumstances.

One of the most striking things about this TAT is the concentration of the characters on looking, watching, and seeing. Curiously enough, despite his narcissism, Jay says little about audiences, praise, or being looked up to and at. He is somewhat exhibitionistic, of course—he is quite willing to reveal himself to the examiner—but the voyeuristic need seems very much stronger. There is not much evidence that it is involved in conflict; it may be that Jay has really achieved some sublimation of this motive in his artisitic interests.

Interpersonal Relationships

The most striking thing about the relationships between the characters in Jay's stories is their remoteness, coldness, and aridity. Even his relationship to the examiner, we feel from the tone of the stories, is formal and rather distant. The patient apparently feels that he has little in common with most people and is unable to empathize with them. His way of understanding a person is to see through him and to feel superior for it. He is likely to be passive in relation to women; if he has any sexual interest in them, he hopes to be the pursued rather than the pursuer. His relations with everyone seem to be marked by pronounced ambivalence, though perhaps the negative pole is less prominent when he is dealing with men. Women in general and maternal figures in particular appear to Jay as binding, perhaps even castrating, while older men may seem more benign.

The historical background for these relationships would seem to have been a family in which there was not only little love, but not even much contact between the members. Indulgence, permissiveness, warmth, emotional support? Not in Jay's family. He seems to have grown up as a lonely, bookish little boy, not taking part much in ordinary play with other boys and girls, nor enjoying any of the perquisites of childhood. "I don't recall ever having been to a circus," he says, after presenting a wishful image of a world bright with color and gaiety in which he was not participating—just looking on from the outside.

Such is the picture of Jay as it comes out in his TAT. He is a young man so bound up in a variety of pathological character defenses that he can hardly move, and can conceive of happiness only as the absence of trouble, to be sought in the solitary absorption, through eye or mouth, of some of the world's goods. Let us hope that he uses some of his excellent intelligence and psychological sensitivity in exploring, with the help of a therapist, better ways to a more positively defined happiness.

ADDENDUM: THE CLINICAL STORY

The following notes were made by the examiner on Jay's general test behavior; they were not (as I advocate) included as part of the test protocol.

After an initial description of Jay as tall, well-built, and handsome, the examiner noted that he holds himself erect and "does not sway or 'mince' when he walks."

> He is well groomed; he is neatly shaven; his hair is combed; and his fingernails are filed and clean.
>
> He speaks very softly, almost gently; his voice is cultured and refined. He is pleasant to work with and unfailingly courteous. (He asked after the examiner's health, complimented the examiner on his necktie, etc.)
>
> There are no tics or mannerisms, although his gestures with his hands are noticeable; he often—when holding a Rorschach or TAT card, for example—held his little fingers out and bent as though he were holding a teacup. He held his hands in an "artistic" manner, poised and graceful.

He seemed to have unimpaired reality contact. His speech was coherent; his affect was appropriate (Shneidman, 1952, pp. 331–333).

Presenting problem: Jay's medical record contains the following summary:

Patient was first discovered to have tuberculosis in 1945 while in the Service. He was hospitalized for eleven months. He had a three-stage thoracoplasty done on the right chest. Subsequent to this surgery he received a maximum hospital benefit discharge. He was again hospitalized in 1947–48 and was readmitted to a hospital in 1950 when the presence of the disease was again noted (p. 334).

To understand his transfer to a VA neuropsychiatric hospital, it helps to review some of his sexual history. At about the age of 15, Jay became aware that he was sexually interested in men, not women. "He felt that his homosexuality was an unusual power—to be able to love a man. He felt that it should be written in a book. He then began to sense the feeling that people had about homosexuality" (p. 340). He had his first overt homosexual experience at age 18, and became sexually quite active during the next few years before joining the Army in 1942, just after Pearl Harbor, when he was 22.

He was in the Service for four years. He served in clerical and administrative capacities and was a top-grade non-commissioned officer. He was overseas. He recalls no traumatic incidents in the Service. During his stay in the Service, he had no sexual relations. He did not seem to feel any urgent need for relations at that time.

Toward the end of his time in the Service (1945) it was discovered that he had tuberculosis and he went directly into a Service hospital (*Ibid.*).

Shortly before his third hospitalization for TB, in 1949, Jay

entered the University majoring in design and art. In his art work, he was able to see sex symbols all through his pictures; female forms (not male forms) and copulation. He used to tear up his own work when he realized that sex symbolism was in them. He felt that perhaps his reading in psychoanalysis had something to do with his seeing this symbolism but did not know to what extent.

At the University he met Bob, his best friend. Bob is a young married student. Jay became aware that he was in love with Bob. It was different. They saw things the same way. He and Bob spent much time together. Between Jay and Bob all sexuality was implicit. He does not know if Bob knows he is a homosexual . . . There had been one very close embrace. Jay felt that Bob had initiated it. He asked Bob about this and Bob said that he did not. Jay feels that he may have hallucinated it. He wishes it had never happened . . . It upset them both; it frightened Jay badly.

Bob is like Jay in many ways; they have many of the same likes and dislikes and this is reassuring to Jay. He feels guilty about coming between Bob and his wife. He wants Bob to be a normal husband . . .

In many ways Bob reminded him of his father. "I feel I am trying to reach my father through Bob."

After Jay had attended school for a year it was discovered that his TB had returned. Bob brought Jay to the hospital. There was a tearful farewell at the hospital. Soon afterward Jay received a letter from Bob in which Bob quoted from The Book of Acts. Jay interpreted this to mean that Bob was God and that he, Jay, was Jesus Christ. He feels now that he was looking for a father. Bob said so, too.

A second letter from Bob was also very confusing to Jay. The letter caused him to feel that he must see Bob, and let Bob go free. He left the TB ward that evening and began to arrange for a hundred mile taxi ride. He was stopped from doing this by the nurse and doctor.

The next day he was asked to see the psychiatrist at the hospital. He was terrified. He was afraid that he was losing his mind. He had no accurate sense of the chronology and even later could never remember the whole incident well (Shneidman, 1952, p. 343f.).

The following excerpts come from the psychiatrist's report of the interview:

He was cooperative in the interview, well oriented and gave evidence at least clinically of being a very intelligent individual. There were no definite delusions or hallucinations elicited. The main difficulty appeared to be in the fields of trend and content of thought, reasoning and judgment. His trend and content of thought are rather difficult to follow throughout. He does a lot of vague verbalizing which he, himself, describes as "verbalizing." Most of his ideas show a trend toward paranoid thinking, a trend toward depersonalization, escape from reality, even at times toward grandiose ideas . . . he relates that he receives delightful bodily and emotional sensations from the shape and design of things, such as a cup, a dish, the lines on a wall. To relate further some of this type of thinking, he says that he now is going to get well, that is, cured of his tuberculosis, by his own efforts alone without the aid of streptomycin. He may have difficulty in remaining here, in following the routine, because he becomes so agitated by things, so thrilled, so to speak. Also, he says that he is going to get well because in helping himself he will be helping others. He goes on to explain that he feels that he will help others because others love him. He says that he does not believe in God, therefore he must assume in his own mind the characteristics that others would think of as God . . .

It is my opinion that we have here a paranoid schizophrenia developing in a rather typical textbook manner, beginning with lifelong homosexual drives, the unresolved conflicts of same, and now the early development of unreality reactions, self-punishment and guilt feelings, such as death wishes, indirect suicidal ideas and early grandiose thinking. His actions of last night—his calling a taxi—certainly manifest psychotic thinking. His reasoning and judgment are definitely schizophrenic in type (pp. 333–334).

A few months later, in September 1951, he was transferred to a neuro-psychiatric hospital, where, in February 1952, he began psychotherapy; it was mainly supportive, with only a little interpretation. The psychological tests were given and the history was taken (by Dr. Shneidman) in April 1952. The following excerpts are taken from that life history interview.

Family constellation
Jay's family consisted of his mother, father, sister, and aunt.
  A. Mother
  Jay's mother is still alive. She is a large, medium to heavy-set woman.
  He was his "mother's child"; his younger sister was his "father's child." His mother was very strict but he was very fond of her. He compared his mother unfavorably with the neighbor who was lenient and whose home was always in an uproar; at his own home he was never permitted to romp.
  He always felt that he never got the appreciation he wanted from his mother or father. He was discouraged in many things that he tried to do. For example, when he was five he tried to develop a marionette theater in his basement, but his mother felt that it was in the way.
  When he was six, his mother said that because of his enuresis—which he had until he was ten—she would "break him." He remembers interrupting her and begging her not to "break him," although he did not know exactly what she meant by this, but viewed it as some kind of threat.
  His mother had lots of headaches. She used cold rags on her forehead to alleviate the pain; he had to wring the rags out and renew them.
  He had a way of getting around his mother. He felt she was nervous. He could always escape to his neightbor's house or to his aunt's house. On the other hand, mother would let him (and his sister) bake and play in the kitchen.
  When Jay was ten, there was talk between his mother and father about separation two years prior to their divorce. He remembers his sister and himself crying loudly urging his father to stay. When their crying began to diminish, his mother urged the children to cry anew. Jay was twelve at the time of his parents' divorce. He remained with his mother. He has never been able to accept the divorce. He never told any of his friends about it. . . .
  After the divorce his mother never married again. Her reason was that she did not want the children to have a step-father. Jay now wishes she had married. He feels that she is now his responsibility.
  His mother is now very apologetic about her past actions, and he finds this behavior in her very distasteful. She now wants to take the blame for his nervous breakdown.
  At present Jay says he loves his mother but in a sort of way he cannot describe. He says that one is supposed to love his mother so he loved his.
  He is now very reluctant to speak of his mother, because of his homosexuality. He is unable to say why this is so.
  B. Father

Jay's father is living and in good health. He is a successful contractor in Jay's home town.

He feels that his father believed Jay was illegitimate when he was born. He does not know how long his father believed this. Jay felt there was a neighbor woman in love with his father from an early age; Jay wanted to communicate this information to his mother but never did. He wanted to spy on his father and get proof of this.

His father had spent a lot of time teaching Jay to read and write. He recalls sitting in his father's lap and learning the alphabet and simple words. He felt annoyance at age seven when father wrote out the word "incomprehensible" and sent him to bed because he could not pronounce it. His father always gave him presents such as atlases, books, or microscopes. At the age of five, he was given an encyclopedia by his father. He feels that much of his present interest in learning came from these gifts. Father also provided for music lessons.

He associates to "being punished" that his father once drew blood by accident on his (Jay's) cheek. Jay felt this was a punishment to his father. He remembers that, at the age of six, he once quarreled with his sister over who would sit next to the window in the car. His father asked him if he wanted to walk and he said yes. He was put out of the car. He got scared but his father was frightened too that he would go through with it. Along these same lines, when he was ten, he broke his arm riding a bicycle. His father took him to the doctor. His father was very upset about it. The broken arm did not hurt Jay, but seemed to hurt his father very much. It was characteristic for his father to be more upset than Jay.

He remembers his father as one who *never* spoke to his mother; the father gave her "the silent treatment." The father would play solitaire then go down town. . . .

Jay has visited his father and stepmother occasionally. When he visits he has no communication with his father but he gets along fine with his father's wife. He is sure that his father loves him but there is something wrong between them which Jay must work out.

C. Sister

His sister—his only sibling—was born when he was two years old. There were many arguments with his sister, some over who would sit by father. It was usually Jay, but his sister claimed that privilege. He was once spanked by his father with a hairbrush over this.

When he was ten years old, a girl friend of his and his sister devised a game whereby they exposed themselves to each other. He felt embarrassed for his sister.

His sister outgrew him physically and reached her full size before he did. At one time, she was a full head taller than he. She would take advantage of her size to intimidate him. He was afraid of her yet he was aware of how much he loved her. He and his sister used to fight a lot with bare hands. He was concerned because he knew how viciously he was attacking her, but he justified this by telling himself how much larger she was. He wanted to apologize, yet he did not because he felt it would indicate weakness on his part.

At present his sister is married and has moved from Jay's home town. She and Jay correspond occasionally, but he has seen her only a few times in the past several years.

D. Aunt

His maternal aunt kept Jay with her much of the time. She was twelve years older than his mother and had no children of her own; her husband was a factory representative and traveling executive. Jay spent much time with his aunt up to adolescence. He remembers spending a lot of time with the aunt in her yard with her flowers. . . .

This aunt was very solicitous and brought him up as a sickly child, giving him many vitamins and pills and treating him as though he were delicate. He was made to feel like a semi-invalid. . . .

He is reminded of his aunt by his present (male) doctor to whom he is unable to express any displeasure because of his awe of authority, for it was his aunt who had taken the responsibility for his health early in his life—and who then demanded expressions of affection from him (Shneidman, 1952, pp. 335–337).

Current Attitudes and Goals

A. Occupational Goals: Role of Art

He had a plan last year of studying art in Paris. . . .

He said that he was very interested in art and that he could never really live without it. He could share feelings with fellow artists that he could not share with anyone else. This feeling was often not expressible in words. His art work satisfies him; he can express himself in art. He believes that he can ultimately resolve his sexual needs in sublimation in art work.

B. Attitude toward Therapy

After two months of psychotherapy he said he had definitely undergone some change of attitude in that he was much more eager to continue now than he had been before. (However, there was no real show of feeling.) He stated: "I am curious to know how it will come out."

He had read in a popular psychology book that an artist did not need psychotherapy unless he was blocked. He feels that he may be blocked but he fears therapy because it may interfere with his art. He feels that he needs something—something that art is supplying. He fears that therapy will remove that need so that his art will no longer be necessary.

C. Outlook toward Marriage and Sexual Adjustment

He spoke about marriage as a goal. He felt that he ought to marry for the sake of companionship, yet he felt that he never could.

He spoke of a nurse he knew at a previous hospital who, he felt, expected him to propose to her. This particular nurse reminds him of his sister. He had been quite a favorite among some of the nurses there.

There is, however, a girl to whom he felt attracted. He does not want to marry her but feels that he must make a decision. This girl is not physically attractive; she is rather short, a little fat, and sloppy in her dress. She is, however, the kind that needs to be looked after.

He said that he often felt that his change from being homosexual to being normal would have to be the eventual solution, but he felt some misgivings about such a goal.

He stated that his social inhibitions were the result of his inability to accept his homosexuality. In addition he cannot accept other homosexuals and he feels this is because he cannot accept his own homosexuality.

He feels he is cheating people who think he is normal, yet realizes he cannot or should not reveal his true sexual status because they will reject him if he does. He wants to associate with normal people who will know him and accept him for what he is.

He feels that he must eventually solve the problem of marriage. He believes that he could never attain his ideal position in life unless he married but he realizes that he just could not do it that simply. He has seen men who were married and homosexual too and he has admired this ability, but felt that it was beyond him and that he must solve the problem differently. He is willing to give up his homosexuality as long as it does not mean giving up his art work at the same time. He feels that it is a very involved and complicated problem (Shneidman, 1952, pp. 344–345).

The Rorschach

8

Chapters 8 through 11 have to do with the Rorschach test, approached in a more focused way than the preceding treatment of the TAT. As I write these words, I realize that it was just about 25 years ago that I began work on what is still an unfinished task, converting Rorschach's familiar inkblot test into an operational measure of primary process thinking. The story may be pieced together from the chapters themselves, though they do not make explicit the many changes in the scoring method as it grew from a one-page checklist to a mimeographed document of over 200 pages (50 of which, a manual for scoring form-level, are primarily the work of Martin Mayman). Obviously, the main change has been accretion, but I have also had to recombine and reorganize categories as experience taught more intelligible ways of presenting them.

Working on this scoring manual and the research in which it was used has been both a spur to theoretical clarification and a means of achieving it. Most of my work on psychoanalytic theory has been published elsewhere, and the bulk of it is collected in a book which I hope will appear shortly after the present one. In line with my paper on motivation (Holt, 1976a), I have substituted "wish" (or "motive") for "drive" in a good many places. Because of all these changes, technical and terminological, I have had to make a number of minor editorial revisions in this paper and to delete material concerning categories I no longer use. Nevertheless, these small changes having been made, it still remains a good general introduction to the primary-process scoring method.

Gauging Primary and Secondary Processes in Rorschach Responses

When Rorschach gave us his test—his blots, his way of administering the experiment, as he called it, and interpreting the results—he also left us a system of scoring the responses. Essentially, this was a way of abstracting from a complex performance four or five important dimensions—dimensions which hundreds of Rorschachers since have found most useful. Hermann Rorschach was perfectly open in pointing out the intuitive and heuristic nature of these scoring categories. One of the first points he made in his monograph was that the theoretical basis of the test was almost nonexistent.

Since Rorschach's death, other hands have worked to expand and perfect the scoring, but mostly this has meant increasing its differentiation and making explicit the criteria for assigning the particular scores. Attempts to work out a theoretical rationale of the test, or to construct new scoring systems on a theoretical basis, have been few indeed. It seems that the majority of workers have followed Rorschach himself in working mainly within the framework of some kind of psychoanalytic theory in their thinking about personality, yet only rarely has this led to attempts to set up new scoring categories.

With the help of a number of assistants and colleagues,[1] I have been trying to develop such a theoretically based system of scoring. Rather than taking existing categories for classifying Rorschach responses and asking (either via theoretical analysis or empirical correlation) what they mean, we have started with the psychoanalytic theory of thinking and have sought to find aspects of the test performance that concretely embody the concepts and phenomena to which the theory directed our attention. In the present preliminary report, my intention is primarily to give an example of a way that Freud's thinking may be able to make an even greater contribution to the usefulness of the Rorschach method than it already has. The scoring system described here is at present being used in research only, and it does not try to capture all that is important to score in Rorschach responses. Rather than competing with conventional systems (with which it slightly overlaps), it supplements them.

Specifically, it is limited to the problem of finding operational definitions for the psychoanalytic concepts of primary and secondary processes. It is rather remarkable that these are among the least-known and least well understood of Freud's concepts, considering the basic place they hold in the theory, and the fact that his account of them was first published over 55 years ago, in the *Interpretation of Dreams* (Freud, 1900a). The reason probably is that the seventh chapter of that book, where the concepts are introduced and most fully expounded, is about the toughest going in all of Freud's output, and before the *Standard Edition* no good translation was available.

Psychoanalysis popularly has the reputation of being a voluntaristic, antirational theory, one that portrays thought as the plaything and creature of man's impulses. Actually, of course, Freud did *not* deny that logical, rational, realistic, and efficient mental processes exist, or even that they make

[1] I am grateful to many persons who have helped in various ways with the work reported here. Marilyn Brachman and Anthony Philip have been able research assistants; Joan Havel's contribution to the manual is more extensive than anyone else's and was invaluable. Roy Schafer and I exchanged ideas constantly while he was writing his book on the Rorschach (Schafer, 1954) and I my contribution to another (Klopfer, Ainsworth, Klopfer, & Holt, 1954), and often thereafter; he and his colleague, Justin Weiss, have improved the manual by many valuable criticisms and suggestions. To David Rapaport, I am indebted for many things, perhaps most of all for a point of view from which this work is a natural outgrowth.

up a great part of conscious mental life, a part which his therapy aimed to enlarge. He grouped them under the conceptual heading *secondary processes*. The term *secondary* was a warning, however, that another type of thinking preceded it genetically and had priority for our understanding of the unconscious. In his studies of neurotic patients, he found that their dreams and symptoms were not the random coughs and sputters of a faulty engine, but intelligible and highly meaningful products of a peculiar kind of mental operation. This he called the *primary process*. He found evidences of its workings in the slips of the tongue and other errors, in jokes, in the thinking of primitive people, children, persons under extreme stress and strong affect, and in the creative processes of artists. It disregards considerations of time; logical contradictions abound; when the primary process holds sway, ideas shift about, lose their identities through fusion or fragmentation, become concrete and pictorial, and are combined and associated in seemingly arbitrary or trivial ways. The course of thinking and of remembering is dictated by the instinctual drives, while realistic considerations are disregarded and the distinction between wish and reality is lost. Truly, the picture of a mind wholly in the grip of the primary process deserves the image of the "seething cauldron," which Rapaport (1942) has used to describe it.

One needs only to imagine such a state of affairs to realize that it is an ideal conception, rather than the description of an empirical possibility. Just as the rational man of the Enlightenment was an ideal type never to be encountered, likewise his opposite, the Id incarnate. In much of what Freud wrote about these concepts, it is fairly clear that he did not think of them dichotomously, but as defining the extremes of a logical continuum. Any actual thought process, even that of a baby or a deteriorated schizophrenic, has to be located somewhere in between the poles. Rapaport (1951b), Hartmann (1950), and Kris (1952) are quite explicit about this way of viewing primary and secondary process.

Out of the many points that might be made in discussing these concepts, I want to emphasize three. First: the more primary the thinking, the more wishful it is. In contemporary psychoanalytic ego psychology, motives are conceived of as a hierarchy, ranging from the most uncontrolled libidinal and aggressive urges to the most controlled and relatively autonomous interests, values, highly socialized desires, and the like. As we go higher in tl˙s schematic structure, originally raw, blind urges are increasingly tamed by controlling structures; in metapsychological (economic) terms, the energies are *bound,* and (in Hartmann's term) *neutralized,* or sublimated. A motive belonging anywhere in this hierarchy can control a train of thought, so it follows that the less neutralized the wish and the closer its aims are to those of the hypothetical instincts, the more primary will be the mental process.

Second: primary thinking can be recognized not only from its preoccupation with instinctual aims. It also has certain peculiar *formal* characteristics. These include autistic logic instead of straight thinking, loose and nonsensical types of associative links, and distortion of reality in numerous ways. But the most notable formal deviations of primary thinking were described by Freud as the mechanisms of the dream work (1900a). *Condensation* is a process resulting in the fusion of two or more ideas or images. *Displacement* is a shift of emphasis or interest from one mental content to another (usually a less important content in terms of relevance to conflict or instinctual aims). *Symbolization* is the replacement of one idea or image by another, always a concrete visual presentation which may have various formal features in common with what is being symbolized but which disguises the latter's dynamic significance. In fact, all of these mechanisms may be used defensively, since they produce changes that usually conceal the original meanings of the material on which they exert their effects. Thus, in the formation of dreams they transform the dream thoughts in ways that make these "hot" materials acceptable to the censoring influence of the Superego.

On the next higher level of generalization, in terms of metapsychology and the libido theory, the essential operation in all of these mechanisms is the *free mobility of cathexis*. According to Freud, every active idea has an energy charge, or cathexis attached to it. In the secondary process any particular idea's cathexis is bound to it. A thing is reliably itself; an orderly, stable, realistic view of the world becomes possible. In the primary process, on the other hand, the aim is to re-experience situations of gratification by the most *direct methods* possible, even if it means arbitrarily pushing ideas and percepts around so that contact with reality is lost. In energy terms, this means that an idea and its cathexis are easily parted.

The operations of condensation, displacement and symbol-formation are by no means confined to the production of dreams and neurotic symptoms. They are conspicuously present in the language of schizophrenics; indeed, schizophrenia has been described as a state in which conscious mental life is dominated by the primary process instead of the secondary. Any weakening of control may result in the emergence of primary thinking: in reverie states, under the influence of drugs, in slips of the tongue, humor, and so forth.

Third: the final point I want to underscore about the primary process has to do with humor and other enjoyable sides of life. It is one of mankind's great gifts to be *able* to abandon reality voluntarily for a little while; to shake free from dead literalism, to recombine the old familiar elements into new, imaginative, amusing, or beautiful patterns. Among modern psychoanalysts Kris (1952) has been particularly interested in the functioning of the psychic apparatus in artistic creativity and humor. As he puts it, the ego of a mature and healthy person can at times relax, abandon secondary process standards in a controlled and recoverable way, and *use* the freedom and fluidity of the primary process productively; this he calls *regression in the service of the ego*. A person who is not asleep and dreaming may therefore fragment and recombine ideas and images in ways that flout the demands of reality on either of two bases: because he cannot help it, due to a temporary or permanent ego-weakness; or because he *wants* to, for fun or for creative purposes, and is able to because he is not too threatened by his unconscious wishes. Thus, the third point is that we find primary thinking in conscious subjects either out of strength or out of weakness. In the former case, it is more likely to be accompanied by pleasant affect, and a playful or esthetic frame of reference. If, on the other hand, primary thinking emerges in a breakthrough, the subject may feel anxious or threatened and is likely to act defensively.

But why should the Rorschach test performance lend itself to analysis in terms of primary and secondary process? First, if one accepts the idea that thought processes may be arranged in a continuous series from the most primary to the most secondary, then we can apply these concepts to *any* sample of mental activity. We know, however, that anything obviously primary in character is exceptional when we are dealing with people who are not patients, so something more than an appeal to the general continuum principle is needed.

Taking the Rorschach is a situation with a number of more or less unique features that favor the emergence of primary modes of cognition. First of all, the subject is called on to produce a series of visual images. This is a preferred mode of operation for the primary process: without the requirement (which the TAT imposes) to produce a connected narrative, there is less demand for organizing and synthesizing and less necessity for secondary process thinking. Moreover, the ink-blots offer complex stimulus configurations, richly enough varied to evoke and support almost any kind of image that may be latent in the viewer's mind, yet without actually and unmistakably representing anything in reality. The permissiveness of the situation allows a person to produce percepts with any degree of fancifulness or realism, depending on his own internal standards of what he should be doing—and on what he can *allow* himself to produce, or fail to *prevent* himself from perceiving. The result is a task that one could hardly improve upon if he set out deliberately to maximize primary process influences on waking thought and perception.

Like many other clinicians I used these concepts unsystematically in diagnostic testing for some time, but it did not occur to me to devise a scoring scheme to measure primary process until 1951 when I was preparing my contribution to *Advances in the Rorschach Technique*. At that time I was struck both by the lack of attempts to systematize the application of psychoanalytic theory to the Rorschach, and by the suitability of this part of the theory of thinking to such a purpose. The first lead came via the first point just emphasized about the primary process: the wishfulness of primary thinking. A passage in an article on ego-psychology by Hartmann (1950, p. 87) set the wheels to turning. Discussing neutralization, he said that it meant not only "different modes or conditions of energy" (a notion that is difficult to make operational), but also "the degree to which certain other characteristics of the drives (such as their direction, their aims) are still demonstrable." As a first approximation, therefore, it seemed reasonable to suppose that a thought product was neutralized to the extent that evidences of any kind of libidinal or aggressive aims were lacking in it. Accordingly, I set up a rough scoring scheme and tried it out on a number of Rorschach protocols. A response was scored if the content itself or anything about its verbal elaboration involved any libidinal or aggressive aim. The ratio of all such responses to the total number of responses given was considered to be an "index of drive-directedness" (wishfulness) of thought—one manifestation of the pervasiveness of the primary process in thinking.

The next step was to find an empirical application for this index, to see if it was measuring what I supposed that it did: what Hartmann has called "the conflict-free sphere of the ego." I have described elsewhere (Klopfer, Ainsworth, Klopfer & Holt, 1954) how the attempt to understand the preliminary empirical results led to the idea of adding another scoring dimension, now embodied in the section of the manual on Control and Defense. It was essentially a recognition of the third point above, about regression in the service of the ego. To distinguish between primary process material that was in the Rorschach because it intruded in a threatening, ego-alien way, and that which entered in a controlled and often pleasurable manner, it was necessary to score indications of threat and of enjoyment, and also the use of humorous, artistic, and other "sublimated" controlling contexts.

Further reflection and reading on the theory of the primary process led to the next major addition: the formal categories, corresponding to point two in the preceding theoretical discussion. The material I first used in framing concrete scoring categories was a group of thirteen Rorschachs that had been given by subjects in an experiment by my colleague, George S. Klein (1954). He was studying the influence of need on cognitive processes in people who had different types or styles of cognitive control. There were eight with *flexible control* and five with *constricted control.* Judging by the differences in their performance on various experimental tasks, it seemed reasonable to assume that flexible control would be correlated with a capacity for controlled and creative use of the primary process.

The protocols were scored blind for content and the few control categories available at that time, but after the identity of the cases was revealed, I searched the Rorschachs for differences in formal manifestations of primary and secondary processes, finding enough to warrant a cross-validation study with blind scoring of a larger sample (Holt, 1960c [Chapter 9, below]).

Beginning in December 1954, Dr. Joan Havel worked fulltime for several months applying the manual to a mixed group of patients' Rorschachs, revising and expanding the scoring categories, especially those pertaining to control and defense. By now[2] the manual is in its fourth revision and runs to about 40 single-spaced typewritten pages, which is

[2][I.e., in 1956. For a more contemporary description, see Holt (1977a) or Chapter 11, below.]

obviously too long to reproduce here, even if it had attained enough stability and proved usefulness to be worthy of publication. After we have completed the cross-validation study just mentioned on flexible versus constricted control, there will undoubtedly be further revisions, some of them necessitated by an accompanying study of observer reliability. The manual will then be subjected to various tests of validity.

The present preliminary report will not present any data, therefore, only a little more description of the method and some of the problems that have been encountered in working with it.

CONTENT

Twenty-two[3] different categories are used in the scoring of content; all of them are presumably indications of primary-process thinking. It is assumed that if none of these categories is scored, the content of a response is mainly determined by secondary-process thinking (although such responses may show formal deviations).

How does one decide where to draw the line when classifying content? Once we have adopted the view that there is a continuum from primary to secondary process, we can hardly say about a single response that it either does or does not involve "the primary process." Perhaps a logical consequence of the continuum point of view would be to rate every response on a continuous scale for the *amount* of primary as against secondary process involved in it. Even this expedient would not take into account the phenomenon that Schafer (1954) has pointed out, that of "spread" along the continuum from primary to secondary. Some responses are in every way crude, poorly organized, and wishful (they would have very little spread along the continuum and would be located near its primary end); others may contain some wishful content, and perhaps may have some of the formal features of the primary process, while at the same time being highly organized, accurately perceived, and cleverly rationalized (intermediary position on the continuum with a wide spread).

A kind of scaling complex enough to represent all of these considerations would be unmanageable and most probably unreliable. I decided, therefore, not to strive for any such precision, but to make do with some rough approximations. An inescapable minimum of arbitrariness entered into the cut-off points, and I shall not be surprised if some readers feel that certain kinds of responses have been unjustifiably omitted and others included without adequate reason, since it has not been possible to include here much explanation of the decisions that were made.

We started with the observation that some kinds of content, within any one qualitative category, seem more primary than others of the same oral,

[3][In the original text, 25; it included a small group of "affective drive derivatives," which I have dropped. The oral categories have been subdivided into oral-receptive and oral-aggressive.]

anal, etc., type. So Dr. Havel and I decided to distinguish a Level 1, closer to the primary-process pole of the continuum, and a Level 2, closer to the secondary pole, although still patently wishful. The distinctions between the two levels may be generalized as follows.

First, there is involved a primitive versus civilized dimension: the more that the type of motive described or implied is socialized and discussion of it is appropriate to social communication between strangers in a professional situation, the more the thinking concerned is secondary, and we score Level 2. Conversely, the more direct, intense, raw, or blatant the drive-expression, the closer to the primary process, and we score Level 1. The second criterion has to do with the degree to which the response focuses on the wish-relevant aspect of a larger percept, such as a particular organ. In addition, Level 1 actually includes a good many pathological fantasies, which differ from simple direct references to the form of gratification in question in that their "blatancy" is probably a function of defensive exaggeration. Perhaps also Level 1 responses combine aggression and sex more often than might be expected in hypothetical conditions of direct instinctual gratification.

Some examples may make these distinctions clearer.

Libidinal

Level 1
Oral: 'Breasts'; 'an open mouth.'
Anal: 'A pile of feces'; 'a person's backside with hemorrhoids.'
Sexual: 'Female organs'; 'intercourse.'
Exhibitionistic-voyeuristic: 'Human figure, nude.'
Homosexual (sexual ambiguity): 'Some sort of symbol—phallic; not phallic, sexual—guess I'd say vagina'; 'men with breasts.'
Miscellaneous libidinal: 'Menstruation'; 'birth'; 'urine.'
Level 2
Oral: 'Two dogs kissing'; 'men, a little drunk, over a punchbowl.'
Anal: 'A woman—she has a big fanny.'
Sexual: 'A bride and groom standing, holding hands.'
Exhibitionistic-voyeuristic: 'Woman with a transparent dress on'; 'a face, leering up at something.'
Homosexual: 'Two men, holding ladies' handbags.'
Miscellaneous libidinal: 'Ovaries'; 'embryo'; 'Cupid.'

Aggressive

Where possible, these responses are subdivided into subject-oriented (sadistic) and object-oriented (masochistic) types.[4]

---

[4][For the present terminology and way of classifying aggressive responses, see Chapter 11, below.]

Level 1

Potential; subject: 'Something with snapping jaws—there's his hot breath coming out to get you' (*oral* scored secondarily); *object:* 'frightened figure—menaced, nightmarish.'

Active; subject: 'Witches tearing a woman apart'; *object:* 'sharp instrument going through the penis.'

Results: 'Animal, looks like it's been in a horrible fight—all torn up'; 'decayed flesh.'

Level 2

Potential; subject: 'People arguing, swearing at each other'; 'cat's face, snarling'; 'a fist'; *object:* 'shield'; figure—looks afraid of something.'

Active; subject: 'People fighting or conspiring'; 'bomb bursting'; 'bull's face, charging'; *object:* 'an unhappy person—looks like he's being bawled out.'

Results: 'Blood'; 'man with a wooden leg'; 'dead chicken'; 'blackened trees after a fire.'

Anxiety and Guilt

Level 1

'Man tied, falling into space helplessly.'

Level 2

'The Inferno'; 'devil'; 'a pile of rocks, about to topple over.'

The manual contains definitions of each category, with many more examples than the above and discussion of borderline cases to be scored or not scored.

FORMAL ASPECTS

Primary-process thinking was first defined in terms of certain formal characteristics. In considering how these might appear in responses to the Rorschach we thought first of the formal characteristics of dreams—condensation, displacement, symbolization. But there is obviously a considerable difference between Rorschach thinking and dream thinking. The Rorschach, being anchored in consciousness, provides only a very crude equivalent to the dream process. We cannot fully know—without associations and without some knowledge of the subject—what is condensed, what displaced, what symbolized in a Rorschach response; nor can we always know when such processes have occurred. Sometimes the work will have been so skillfully finished off by secondary processes (e.g., secondary revision in the dream) that condensation and the like will be completely concealed. But we can catch those instances where the tool-marks of the primary process *have* been left on the finished product. Moreover, it seems reasonable to suppose that a person's failure to cover up the traces of the primary process in his thought and perception is a significant fact about him, in light of the general cultural pressure to "make sense," to see and think realistically and logically. Conceivably, *all* Rorschach responses may involve some elements of primary process thinking, but our concern is not to track them all down: only to identify the amount that a person allows himself to express (or expresses in spite of himself) in the interpersonal relationship of the test situation.

In constructing the formal section of the manual we did not limit ourselves to a search for the types of formal deviations described for dream processes, though this was its starting point. With this general orientation, we tried to derive the scoring categories from the unique situation presented by the Rorschach. These categories refer both to the perceptual organization of the responses and to the thought process that underlies giving it. They attempt to measure deviations from the logical, orderly thinking grounded in experience with the real world that characterizes the secondary process.

The manual contains twenty-seven[5] categories under the heading of formal aspects. Because they are less self-explanatory than the content categories, it would take a good deal more space to make them intelligible. Without the expectation of being completely convincing, therefore, I shall present several of the formal rubrics briefly and with an example.

The main aspect of condensation that one finds in the Rorschach I have called image-fusion: the failure to keep images separated in the way demanded by a realistic view of the world. Seven varieties of image-fusion have turned up. In four of them, the fusion comes about when more than one idea arises with respect to a single area of the card and the subject fails to suppress, at least temporarily, all but one image. In three types, the fusion comes about between adjacent areas and the subject has difficulty in delimiting a single percept.

Fusion of Two Separate Percepts: No example will be given, since this is the familiar *contamination* response.

Internal-External Views of Something: 'Could be part of a woman's breasts with a bow in between . . . this might be the lungs . . . she might be wearing the bow around her neck.'

Partial Fusion of Separate Percepts: 'Here we have what appears to be a French motif—French poodle—trimmings of the poodle or trimmings of the female—brassiere—high-heeled shoes' (Card III).

Unrelinquished Percepts: 'It's supposed to be something in the cat's mind, but to me it looks like a ball of yarn.'

Composition: Parts from two or more percepts are combined to make a new, hybrid creation: 'A rabbit with bat's wings'; 'dogs—kind of antennae for a tail.'

Arbitrary Linkage of Two Percepts: 'Women, sort of stuck together' (VII—attached at lower center).

---

[5][The number is now 40. Some of the types of image-fusion listed here are now given the same score, and a few others have turned up.]

Arbitrary Combinations of Separate Percepts: Impossible—'Two animals holding a bridge in their mouth.' Improbable—'An idol, and music notes; a twelve-piece orchestra in back of him.'

We also operate on the hypothesis that *Arbitrary combinations of color and form* are an attenuated form of condensation, in which the fusion takes place between two modalities rather than within one: 'Red bears'; 'green clouds.'

Just as the failure of ideas to maintain fixed identities in the primary process show up in condensation, so too it may logically result in the breaking up of natural perceptual units. It is tentatively assumed that the usual *Do* response (seeing a part where most people see a whole person, animal, etc.) represent this kind of *Fragmentation.*

Another guise that the assumed free mobility of cathexis may take is *Fluid transformation of percepts,* such as occurs when the S describes one thing as turning into another before his very eyes: 'An Indian with a hide over him . . . now he's beginning to transform; as his hide droops down,' it becomes two enormous feet. . . .'

We assume that the dream-work mechanism of symbolization is represented in the Rorschach by *Visual representation of the abstract. Color* may be used to stand for an abstract idea as in the following: 'two dogs—the red makes me think of violence'; or 'the red is nature in the raw'; or *spatial relations* may be used similarly: 'intercourse, or union—I didn't think of a specific picture, everything is just united.' Finally, a general idea may be represented by a *concrete image:* 'An explosion, could represent anger.'

The failure of thinking to be logical is one of the hallmarks of the primary process. We score such failures only when the verbalizations are cast in a somewhat syllogistic form, and when the logic used is fallacious. Following Rapaport, we call this *Autistic logic:* 'Everything is so small it must be the insectual kind of thing.' The *DW responses* may be considered a subtype of autistic logic, since in the classic example of 'cat' for Card VI, 'because of the whiskers,' the implied syllogism is: cats have whiskers, this has whiskers, therefore this is a cat.

Illogical thinking leads to contradiction, which is tolerated in the primary process. We score three types: 1. *Affective contradiction:* 'Witches—could be a diabolic dance or chanting their chants—a very pleasant picture—could be music or love and enjoyment.' 2. *Logical contradiction:* 'Pagoda god—a peaceful evilness.' 3. *Inappropriate activity:* 'Mice—sitting back in armchairs with a cigarette.'

Rorschach workers are accustomed to see the primary process operating in a characteristic way that we call *Autistic elaboration.* This is a response verbalized in such a way as to indicate a great increase or loss of appropriate distance between the subject and the blot to which he is responding; it is essentially the same thing that Rapaport and Schafer call confabulation, but since that term is also used by many Rorschach workers to refer to the DW response, I am avoiding it altogether. 'That looks like maybe some Aztec god—a double-faced god, and it has been carried to a climate or placed in a refrigerator—and the nose is all frozen up and ice has built over it and settled on it.'

After running across some examples of *Verbal condensation* (portmanteau words, like 'diaphragram,' a condensation of diagram and diaphragm), we decided to include the scoring of autistically distorted language in general. Following Rapaport, we distinguish *Peculiar* and *Queer verbalizations* and *Verbal incoherence.*

Finally, in a Rorschach response, one occasionally sees evidence of *Loosening in the conceptual organization of memory:* 'A bat—the winged bat, a bird, and I hate bats.'

CONTROL AND DEFENSE

It is evident that two people, giving the same Rorschach response, may have vastly different subjective experiences in doing so. One may, for example, show considerable discomfort in giving a response that juxtaposes two incongruous elements; another may be quite pleased with its fancifulness. Also, essentially the same kind of content may be presented by two persons in ways that indicate quite different degrees of control over the impulse represented in each. There seems to be a constantly fluctuating relationship between the two forms of thought, which must be kept in mind for the proper evaluation of primary versus secondary thinking.

These considerations led to the development of a group of variables focused on the subject's attitude toward the test and toward his own productions, and the extent to which he is master of or is disturbed by the primary-process elements in his thinking. These variables are grouped into the *Control and Defense* part of the manual; they are based on the *way* in which the subject gives a particular response. Each response that is scorable in terms of either the content or formal variables outlined above is considered with respect to the kind of control or its absence that goes along with it.

There are more control categories than any of the other kinds. Moreover, they require even more discussion and exemplification to make it clear just how they are used, so I shall give a few in some detail and then merely indicate generally the other kinds of things that are covered.

The *context* in which a response is placed can do a great deal to make its primary process elements intelligible and acceptable as communications in the testing situation. Historically, man has developed certain specific contexts in which wish-related content or primary-process manipulations of images or ideas may be expressed and accepted socially. Consider the *aesthetic context*, for example. The taboo on nudity is lifted for paintings and sculpture; thus, the voyeuristic impulse directly expressed in a response like 'a naked woman,' if given with no further justification, appears to be under some sublimatory control when the response comes out as 'the Aphrodite of

Praxiteles.' Likewise, many bizarre image-fusions are found in the paintings of Hieronymus Bosch[6] or Brueghel or in some of the modern surrealists. If a subject sees a composite figure in which human and animal features are condensed, therefore, but says that it is like one of the devils in a Bosch painting, he has found a place in social reality for an otherwise autistic creation.

Sometimes the attempt to control a response by putting it in an aesthetic context is so forced and unconvincing that we felt it desirable to distinguish between successful attempts (such as the ones just quoted) and unsuccessful ones, like the following: 'Witches of Macbeth, two more witches boosting them into a kettle.' There are, of course, witches in Macbeth, and the reference would have served to control the frightening implications of this image, if it were not for the elaboration—Macbeth's witches did not push other witches into cauldrons, so the aggressive impulse that emerged in this response was not really controlled by the attempt to refer it to an aesthetic context.

Similarly, we distinguish successful and unsuccessful use of *cultural* (e.g., anthropological), *intellectual,* and *humorous* contexts.

Another kind of controlling or defensive maneuver is scored as *Negation,* when the content or formal element is presented in negative form: 'Lions, they don't look fierce'; 'if it's supposed to be a sex organ I fail to see it.' The last response also contains elements of *Projection,* another relatively ineffective type of attempted control.

The other categories[7] include *Introspection* (efforts on the part of the subject to remove himself from the responses by observing or thinking about his own thought processes), *Criticism of response* (a verbalized awareness that something is wrong with a response), *Vagueness of percept* (a complaint after response is given that it can't be clearly seen), *Reaction formation and denial* (following a threatening or unpleasant response by qualifications that try to undo or prettify it) and *Delay* (scored when the content or formal deviation of the response emerges only in the inquiry).

The type of organizational control scored as Z by Beck I have included (following Friedman, 1953) under two headings: *Combinations* (responses to discrete areas are brought together into a larger unity), and *Integrations* (differentiation of a blot area that is frequently seen as a unity, followed by a recombination of the dissected parts).

A couple of categories are devoted to sequential effects, which take into account the modification or replacement of one response by another that is either more or less primary in nature.

A basic consideration in evaluating the degree of cognitive or intellec-

---

[6][Erika Fromm (1969) has published an interesting application of the primary-process scoring system to Bosch's paintings.]

[7][A good many more Control & Defense categories are now scored; see Chapter 11, below.]

tual control in the Rorschach has traditionally been the scoring of form level or accuracy. Likewise, some recent research by Friedman (1953) has shown that some of Heinz Werner's concepts may usefully be applied in a type of form-level scoring that differs slightly from the traditional distinction between F+ and F−. Friedman found that his categories distinguished both children and schizophrenics from normal adults. We have, however, adopted the basically similar but more differentiated form-level scoring of Mayman (1956; see also Lohrenz & Gardner, 1967).

CONCLUDING REMARKS

There can be little novelty in an attempt to apply psychoanalytic concepts to Rorschach testing; Rorschach himself was influenced by what he had read of Freud, and his collaboration with Oberholzer helped to give Rorschach interpretation a psychoanalytical orientation from the beginning. Many readers will feel that the sorts of considerations outlined here have been for years familiar parts of their regular clinical practice with the test.

What my colleagues and I have done has been to take the application of psychoanalytic theory to the Rorschach out of the clinic and make it explicit and orderly enough for systematic scoring. We are, of course, using this system only in research at present. It seems not unlikely, however, that this attempt to apply a number of Freud's most fruitful concepts as rigorously as possible may some day return to the clinic a tool with increased precision and incisiveness.[8]

---

[8][A final word about theory: In this paper, I attempted to *apply* Freud's concepts, not to examine them critically. They were useful in guiding the development of the primary-process scoring system, the structure of which shows the influence of Freud's metapsychology. Therefore, aside from some minor terminological adjustments, I have left the theoretical part of this paper unaltered even though I have come to believe that metapsychology should be abandoned and replaced with philosophically and scientifically more defensible concepts and propositions.]

9

In the spring of 1957, word came of a special convocation to celebrate the 30th anniversary of the Harvard Psychological Clinic, and to mourn the imminent destruction of the dear old frame building at 64 Plympton Street which had been its local habitation most of those years. The invitation to present a paper galvanized me to complete an attempt I had begun a few years earlier to find relationships between Rorschach primary-process scores, on the one hand, and an interesting dimension of cognitive style developed by my close colleague George S. Klein from the work of a Dutch psychologist Stroop (1935).

I recall with great pleasure the June weekend in Cambridge when the convocation was held. It was a reunion of old friends and an occasion to become acquainted with a number of the gifted younger people who had had the opportunity to work with Harry Murray and Bob White after my time and to catch from them the lasting excitement of studying lives in progress.

The Clinic had been my true alma mater, *one that had sheltered George Klein too during his brief stay at Harvard before coming to NYU as my first recruit for our Research Center and eventually its formal co-director. For the rest of our joint working lives (ended by his tragically premature death in 1970), we strove to recreate in a very different physical setting some of the intellectual ambiance of that richly stimulating Clinic on Plympton Street.*

The pages that follow contain the text of my presentation at that warm and nostalgic occasion. The footnotes were added for publication in an Indian journal, the editorial board of which I had recently joined, and I have as usual slightly retouched the text to bring the theoretical vocabulary up to date.

Cognitive Controls and Primary Processes

During this anniversary year, I have had the great pleasure of realizing a dream that had been with me throughout the 13 years since I left Harvard. At the Research Center for Mental Health in New York University, we have finally gotten under way a program of interrelated researches[1] cast in a

[1][Subsequently reported in several papers and a book (Barr, Langs, Holt, Goldberger, & Klein, 1972).]

familiar mold: a sizable group of experimenters, some of them graduate students, some more elderly types like George Klein and myself, who are directing the work, all carrying out our personological researches on the same small group of subjects, who are intensively studied and assessed (see Murray *et al.*, 1938). When someone invents a better general model for research in this area, I hope I shall not be so much blinded by sentiment and nostalgia as to be unable to adopt it; meanwhile, the old model seems to have plenty of power and mileage left in it.

Our researches cluster around three major themes, all of which are related by the kind of psychoanalytic ego psychology that we profess: the problem of perception and cognition without awareness (e.g., Klein, Spence, Holt, Gourevitch, 1958), the problem of the structural organization of cognitive processes (e.g., Gardner, Holzman, Klein, Linton, Spence, 1959), and the problem of their relationship to motives and to primitive, archaic modes of thinking (e.g., Pine & Holt, 1960 [Chapter 10, below]). In a more telegraphic style, we speak of these as the problems of preconscious cognition, cognitive controls, and primary process.

The work I want to describe briefly includes both of the latter two themes. It began with the decision to try to make Freud's concepts of primary and secondary processes concrete and operational enough to work with them experimentally. The familiar defense mechanisms and a few other concepts had been explored and exploited frequently in the laboratory, but none of these was as central to psychoanalytic theory as this neglected pair of basic concepts.

Let me remind you briefly of some definitions: the primary process is thinking that is dominated by wishes, rather than by fidelity to reality and logic; and it is characterized by certain formal properties, chiefly the dream-work mechanisms of condensation, displacement, and symbolization, and autistic rather than rational logic. The secondary process corresponds more closely to the official version of human thought promulgated by logicians and philosophers, as the realistic exercise of reason. It is purposive, organized for effective goal-striving instead of being wishful. This contrasting pair of definitions is intended to bring to mind an image of a continuum defined by its idealized poles, not a simple dichotomy.

Freud never offered a concise, pointed definition of the primary process: rather he provided us with a number of somewhat heterogeneous descriptive characterizations (e.g., Freud, 1900a). And, in fact, others after him have found it difficult to state any single, simple defining principle that would include everything recognized by analysts to be part of this ancient common heritage of mankind, shared by sage and savage, child and madman alike.

Nevertheless, if we want to take a more or less standard sample of cognitive behavior, such as the Rorschach performance, and make a microscopic scrutiny of the protocol for evidences of the primary process, Freud's writings and those of other analysts offer many concrete and helpful guidelines. This is just what I did in setting up a primary-process scoring system. I took quite literally what I found in the psychoanalytic literature, translated it into the terms of Rorschach percepts and verbalizations, and came up with a set of scoring categories. This method is embodied in a four-part manual which describes 25 content categories, 28 formal aspects, 46 types of control and defense associated with primary-process manifestations, and an over-all rating of the S's emotional reaction to taking the test.[2] To use this method, you read each response of the Rorschach record, keeping in mind all these possibilities, and whenever you recognize any of the manifestations of primary process specified under the content or formal categories, you record the corresponding score on special scoring sheets.

You will recall that in defining the primary process I distinguished between its wishfulness and such formal properties as the dream-work mechanisms. The scoring system contains corresponding divisions into content and formal categories. Reasoning that a person who is taking the Rorschach test is not pursuing any obviously sexual or aggressive goal, I have assumed that if imagery of these kinds appears, it reflects not purposive goal striving but wishful thinking and, as such, is primary in nature. The manual lists the usual libidinal "partial drives"—oral, anal, exhibitionistic-voyeuristic, etc., and also subdivides aggressive contents into images conveying potential aggression (such as "a tiger crouched to spring"), active aggression ("people fighting"), and the results of destructive action (e.g., dead or injured persons or animals).

In addition, all of these content categories are divided into the more blatant, primitive expressions, called Level 1, and more socially acceptable, toned down, and derivative expressions, called Level 2. For example, a Level 1 oral response would be "a huge gaping mouth"; a Level 2 oral response would be "a dish of ice cream."

The formal aspects of primary-process thinking are more heterogeneous and harder to summarize. They include signs of condensation, displacement, symbolization, fragmentation, loose and fluid associations, autistic logic, contradiction, and other miscellaneous features of primary-process thinking. The formal variables are divided into two levels also, Level 1 being those that are closer to the primary-process pole, Level 2 those that are further up toward the secondary end of the continuum.

Every response that is given a formal or a content score must also be

[2][This statement was written at a time when an earlier version of the manual was being used. In the current revision (Holt, 1969d), there are 20 content categories, 40 formal scores, and 44 controls and defenses. In addition, there are now four ratings to be made for each response in lieu of the overall rating: form level, creativity, defense-demand (i.e., the degree to which the response would be unacceptable as a communication in polite society, without some kind of cushioning or modification), and defense-effectiveness (how well the defenses used to satisfy the response's defense-demand). The last takes into account the Control and Defense categories scored, the form level, and the S's affective reaction to his response, which we elicit by a special "affect inquiry" along with the usual inquiry on determinants, etc.]

considered for the degree of control that is built into the percept or its communication. We score seven major types of controlling and defensive devices, in addition to form level or accuracy: the context of responses (intellectual, esthetic, etc.), reflections about them (criticism of the response or introspection about it), their sequence, the degree of remoteness or distance built into the response, delay of response (for example, bringing out the idea that two people are fighting only during the inquiry), and a few miscellaneous (mostly pathological) defenses.

At this point, I imagine that you may feel slightly bewildered by this brief description of a complicated scoring system, which requires a 40-page manual to be made reasonably clear.[3] If you do, your reaction speaks for the complexity of the phenomena that we denote by the deceptively simple term, primary process. It refers to a *class* of related types of cognition. There is every reason, therefore, to expect to find individual differences in primary-process functioning. And I am not just referring to variations in the content of individual experience—the fact that, for example, various symbols for any one theme may exist; I want to suggest rather that perhaps some people's primitive thinking relies heavily on symbolism, while others may be pervaded by condensations, still others are characterized by wishful imagery, and so forth.

As soon as I start to speak about characteristic individual modes of thinking, I recognize that my ideas owe a great deal to my friend and co-worker, George S. Klein. He has developed the concept of cognitive controls and styles to conceptualize the types of consistency found in perceptual and other cognitive behavior, and has experimentally isolated a number of specific principles of control. A cognitive control is a structure, in the sense that it refers to a relatively stable and enduring aspect of the personality that guides response and may incidentally give it an individual flavor and contribute to its efficiency or inefficiency (Klein, 1958). It is therefore a part of the ego; but the primary process is usually referred to the id, when it is spoken of in terms of the tripartite model. It might seem, therefore, that the two would be quite separate, and that individual penchants in conscious and in unconscious cognition might be unrelated.

We know, however, that the id and whatever is unconscious are known to us only via the (conscious) ego, and certainly in the Rorschach we are limited to communicated conscious cognition, no matter how much primary process we may see in it.[4] It seemed to me, therefore, that people with contrasting cognitive controlling principles might be expected to differ in their primary-process manifestations, particularly if these cognitive controls had been shown to be relevant to modes of dealing with wishes.

Operationally, a cognitive control-principle is defined by a specific task,

[3]The manual is now much longer.
[4][For this reason and a good many others (Holt, 1975b), I no longer use the tripartite model.]

usually one that does not involve any obviously conflictful or emotionally relevant content. But what is an analogy of wishful thinking that is relevant to motivational control and yet relatively conflict-free? Experience with the Rorschach test (among other considerations) suggested that the presence of color poses such a problem to the perceiver. Colors act as if they were the perceptual equivalents of affects even when they are presented relatively abstractly, and people differ remarkably in their ability to handle colors smoothly in interpreting the Rorschach blots.

A separate and independent task was required, however, and the Stroop Color-Word Interference test seemed admirably suited to the purpose. It consists of, first, a list of color-words (e.g., red, blue, green, yellow), typed in regular black ink and repeated in random arrangement enough times to make up a double-spaced typed page (Stroop, 1935; Klein, 1954). At a signal, the subject reads these off aloud as quickly as he can. Next he is given a sheet on which are typed clusters of asterisks printed in different colors of ink, the same number of clusters as words on the previous page, and similarly arranged. The subject now names the colors of the inks as rapidly as he can. Finally, he must read as rapidly as possible the colors of the inks from a third sheet with the same number of typed words, like the first except that the color words are typed in nonmatching inks—for example, *blue* in green ink, to be read as "green." Everyone finds it more difficult to read the third series than the second, but there is a wide range of performance times, on both the second and third series.

At first glance, there may seem to be a considerable difference between the nature of this task and the dependent variables from the Rorschach. Note, however, that in most general terms, the primary process is to ordinary waking communicated thought what noise is to an informational channel. The Color-Word Interference test puts in another kind of noise and requires the subject to perform as efficiently as he can in spite of it. Partly the interference comes from the colors themselves, and the necessity to perform the unaccustomed act of naming them as quickly as possible. For most persons, however, the main noise in the system is the overlearned habit of responding to a word in terms of the meaning denoted by its pattern, which must be disregarded in the final, critical series of the Stroop test. Naming the colors of the ink in which the words are typed, when the words are shouting at you to say the wrong color name, requires a constant inhibition—or a capacity to achieve an odd kind of dissociation.

At any rate, it seemed to me quite possible that performance on this task might predict the handling of primary-process material in the Rorschach. In brief, it does. Comparing subjects (Ss) who do well with those who do poorly on the Color-Word test, I found a heartening number of statistically reliable differences, using two nonparametric tests (Fisher's Exact test for 2 × 2 tables, and the Mann-Whitney U-Test).

Let me say next a few words about the samples from which I have chosen extreme Ss. I began with a small handful, 13 in all, who had been Ss for George Klein in his Harvard thirst experiment (Klein, 1954). He was good enough to let me use their Rorschachs, and I got my first hunches from an intensive study of these few cases. Since then, both the Color-Word test and the Rorschach have been given to about two dozen freshmen in the New York University School of Education, and to 60 very assorted Ss in Topeka, including some college students, nurses, aides, and wives of staff members at the Menninger Foundation, plus a few patients. Pooling all of these 97 cases, and applying certain criteria[5] uniformly to all of them, I have selected 15 who performed with consistent ease on all parts of the test, and 20 who did badly on both naming colors alone *and* the critical third series—the interference task. These results derive from three quite different samples; therefore, they are a certain kind of cream skimmed from a large pool. I think that if relationships emerge through the heterogeneity of these assorted groups, they may be assumed to be relatively free of sample bias.

We find, first of all, that subjects who do poorly on the Color-Word test—let's call them Distractables[6]—find the Rorschach something of an ordeal, typically. They tend to give fewer responses ($p = .05$), with less color ($p = .02$) and less movement ($p < .05$), than their opposite numbers, but with

[5]The criteria actually used were multiple, considering simultaneously scores on Part II (colors alone), Part III (the critical interference series), and the ratio III–II/II, the measure used by Klein (1954). I adopted the more complex criterion because I noticed that some Ss in the extreme groups on Klein's measure were interfering with the general trends. On closer scrutiny, some of these turned out to have very high ratios because they did unusually well on II and moderately poorly on III, while others had low ratios because they did poorly on II and not particularly badly on III. So for the undistracted group, one of the following conditions had to be met: the performance on II (colors alone) was under 61″ and that on III (interference) under 90″, while the ratio was less than .55; *or* the score on II could be up to 63″ (III still being under 90″) if the ratio was .30 or less.

For the Distractable Ss, one or the other of the following conditions had to be met: the reading time for II had to be over 61″, that on III over 105″, and the ratio (III–II/II) greater than .70; *or,* II could be as low as 46″, III 105″ or more, if the ratio was 1.20 or higher.

There is therefore some overlap between the groups on part II, colors alone, though in general the groups are well separated. The means are:

		II	III	Ratio
Undistracted	$(N = 15)$	56.5	80.6	.43
Distractable	$(N = 20)$	65.3	125.8	.94
Total group	$(N = 96)$	59.46	99.17	.678
(ranges)		(41–82)	(61–153)	(.29–1.37)

The scores for the S who is discussed at the end of the paper were *not* included in the above means and ranges for the total group.

[6]I am not following the terminology I suggested to Klein (1954) for his extreme groups (flexible versus constricted control) because somewhat different criteria are involved in his and my selection of extremes.

more sighing, squirming, nervous laughter, and other signs of tension. Yet they are not markedly constricted; the median R is 27.5, median ratio of movement to color 3:3. The comparable figures for the Undistracted group are: R, 40; M, 4; sum color, 5.

Keeping in mind these general trends, let us look at the evidences of the primary process in the Rorschachs. To hold the effect of differences in R roughly constant, the total number of responses containing primary-process content and evidences of unrealistic modes of thought (formal signs of primary process) are expressed as percent of R. When we do this, we find that the Undistracted group has a somewhat larger total proportion of primary process ($p < .10$). Their Rorschachs are especially distinguished from those of Distractable Ss by having many Level 1 (more extreme) *formal* signs of the primary process ($p = .05$). For example, Undistracted Ss significantly ($p < .05$) more often gave responses in which the image is a composite that does not occur in nature: people with wings, a bear with two heads; often they made these more socially acceptable, so to speak, by taking advantage of culturally given composite images, such as centaurs, or many-limbed Hindu gods. Surprisingly, the only other single formal category to differentiate the groups significantly ($p < .05$) is Fragmentation—the *Do* response, which was found only in the Undistracted group, the ones who did well on the Color-Word test.

In terms of Content, the groups did not differ significantly in the proportion of responses that express aggresion in its various forms, but the Undistracted Ss gave more responses with libidinal content ($p < .005$). In particular, they were more likely to allow themselves obvious and blatant expression of oral wishes ($p < .05$). In one content category, however, the Distractables gave a higher frequency of response than did the Undistracted Ss: those representing anxiety without any libidinal or aggressive reference—mostly percepts of things falling or tumbling down ($p < .02$).

Turning now to the realm of Control and Defense, we find only one category that was used frequently enough to differentiate the groups significantly. When an Undistracted S gave a response with Level 2 primary-process material (either formal or content), he was more likely than a Distractable S to follow it by a neutral response to the same blot—that is, to shift back to the secondary process level of functioning ($p < .05$). It is as if the more Distractable Ss were the captives of their primary processes: they were less likely to allow such material into awareness but once it had begun to emerge, they were relatively unable to stop, except by ceasing to respond to the card entirely.

In summary, Ss who performed smoothly and relatively undistracted by the perceptual "noise" of the Color-Word Interference test also met the situation of taking the Rorschach easily and showed fewer signs of being afraid to let primary process show up in their responses. Comparatively speaking, they were more responsive to the test in general, took it more calmly, with fewer indications of anxiety and disturbance or occasionally with positive enjoyment, and were able to give more responses with libidinal content or unrealistic formal elements, while having less difficulty in returning afterwards to a more secondary process level of responding. The fact that Fragmentation (Do) responses occurred only in this group suggests that at least a few of them may have done well on the Color-Word Interference test by a kind of dissociative breaking-up of the perceptual experience. Performance scores on the Color-Word test, then, are related to a person's capacity to use and feel comfortable with his primary process, and not to become so much threatened by it that he has to exclude it rigidly from conscious cognition, or to become disturbed if it emerges. More abstractly, it may be said that experimentally measured cognitive controls are related to the quantity and types of primary-process manifestations, at least in the Rorschach test.

I want to conclude by telling you briefly about an extreme case, a 14½-year-old boy who on the whole was more disrupted by the Color-Word Interference test than anyone I have seen. He took two minutes to read the second series, naming the colors of the asterisks, which is about twice the average speed of college students. On the third, critical series, he stumbled along, making many errors (which he mostly corrected) and finished in 3 minutes 40 seconds, a full 100 seconds longer than he had taken on colors alone. He took this test and the Rorschach in the same spirit of trying to be a good sport, but having obvious difficulty.

His first Rorschach response gives dramatic expression to some of his pressing conflicts: "This is a person in the middle, being pulled on by these two big people on the side, like they're trying to pull him apart. Looks like these people are pointing away at the same time, or maybe they have wings." There was no other response to the card. The response is scored for content—active aggression, Level 2 (it would have been Level 1 if the person in the center were seen as being actually torn apart); it also gets the formal score Composition, Level 1, since it contains a fused image of man and bird, unbuffered by any mythological or other reference to a socially shared image, like that of an angel. On Card II, he saw a couple of rock and roll dancers, commenting that "the red spots in it don't mean anything." On Card III he saw the usual human figures and again remarked on his inability to interpret the color; he described the human figures as disturbing to him, because they seemed all mixed up, they didn't know who they were or what they were doing: "They want to do something they can't do, reaching for something they can't get at." (This is an example of a response scored under the Anxiety category.) To quote only one more response, Card IX: turning it sideways, he saw the green area as "An Indian, riding a buffalo—looks like he's holding on, riding for life or death" (another response indicating anxiety). In the inquiry, when he again stressed that it was a buffalo, not a horse that the Indian was riding, I was vividly reminded of Freud's famous analogy of the id as headstrong horse and the ego as its uneasy rider.

This boy was indeed having trouble controlling his powerful impulses, which had almost literally run away with him. He was being tested because he had impulsively stolen a car and run away from school, trying to get *to* his parents, who lived across the country. He was an adopted child of a vain, beautiful, and wealthy woman who had had several husbands during his brief lifetime, had adopted several other children and had seen very little of them herself, leaving them to the care of servants and hired parent-substitutes. The boy grew up confused about who he was, where he came from, what he belonged to, rejecting his mother's "high-society" values while longing for some human contact with her and never having a stable father figure with whom to identify and to help him build a sense of identity. With the onset of adolescence, he shot up to 6 ft. 2 in. and a muscular 180 lbs.—a man's body with a man's desires, and stunted resources with which to manage them. He started acting out—fighting, running away, and finally the car theft. Yet in the hospital, where he was tested, he spent much of his time in fantasies of how to organize his days and control his life; he spoke wistfully of his desire that someone give him a set of definite rules and make him follow them. One could hardly ask for clearer clinical evidence that he was on poor terms with his impulses and his primary process, struggling to maintain control. And in this extreme subject, the same qualities were faithfully reflected in his performance on the Color-Word test and the Rorschach. If all our cases worked out that neatly, we should be spared a great many of the headaches, but perhaps also a lot of the gratifications, of research in personality.

10

For about five years, one of the most gifted young staff members of the Research Center for Mental Health was Fred Pine. He came to us as a postdoctoral research fellow, and left as an Assistant Professor and sorely missed member of our team, who had decided that his true interest lay in work with children. He had since made himself a distinguished career in that field.

One of his first interests when he began work with us was my approach to measuring primary-process manifestations in Rorschach responses. He learned the manual, attempted (in vain) to devise a quicker method by making up a multiple-choice format, and made a lasting contribution in his suggestion of a special "affect inquiry." That consists of asking the respondent, during the inquiry period as the examiner goes over all the responses checking on their location and determinants, how he felt when giving them—amused, playful, upset, anxious, indifferent, or whatever. I had previously tried to pick up indirect signs of such affect and to infer it; the direct approach worked much better, and added clinically useful data as well in many cases.

The distinction had become rather critical as my students and I realized the importance of a major distinction: was primary-process thinking apparent in Rorschach responses because of a psychopathological breakdown in the defending and controlling strategies that usually kept it out of awareness? Or was the subject enough undisturbed by illogical and wishful percepts and thoughts to be able to use them constructively, as in humorous, artistic, or scientific creativity? The present paper was one of the earliest attempts to test Kris's (1952) hypothesis that regression in the service of the ego—which I prefer to call adaptive regression—was necessary for creative work. Since its publication, at least ten other tests of essentially the same hypothesis have appeared, using my Rorschach method to assess the independent variable, all with at least some positive results when male subjects were used—except for Pine's (1962) attempt to replicate this study with a group of male actors. (See, however, the data from those same subjects presented in my 1970c paper, where I have discussed the issues addressed here at greater length, summarizing the similar work of a good many other investigators.) The astonishing correlation reported here was of course a fluke, and has not been equalled in other work. Yet it is remarkable, I think, that others have repeatedly reported the same sex difference we found—positive results for males, and no relationship (or a considerably lower one) between creativity and Rorschach measures of adaptive regression for females.

This paper was published with Dr. Pine as its senior author. Though he has kindly given permission for me to reprint it here, I have not felt free to change the terminology as I have done in other papers of this vintage. Hence the prominence of the concept of drive (which I have examined and rejected in a recent theoretical piece [Holt, 1976a]).

Creativity and Primary Process: A Study of Adaptive Regression

Beginning with Freud (1911b, 1907a), but especially since Kris' explorations of creative processes (Kris, 1952; also Pappenheim & Kris, 1946), psychoanalytic theorists have described relationships among creativity, primary process (Freud, 1900a), and a particular kind of ego control that permits adaptive use of primary process. The concept "regression in the service of the ego" (Kris, 1952; see also Schafer, 1958b) refers to a momentary and at least partially controlled use of primitive, nonlogical, and drive dominated modes of thinking in the early stages of the creative process. The present study is one of the degree to which characteristic individual modes of expression and control of primary process in the Rorschach test are related to the quality of productions created in a variety of experimental tasks.

The study of creativity can begin from at least three different standpoints: the process, the product, and the person. Kris' work centers primarily though by no means entirely on the creative *process,* on the dynamic events surrounding the creative act itself. At the moment of creation, thinking is more fluid and often more drive dominated and less logical than usual; it is generally pervaded by intense emotionality—feelings of omnipotence, intense pleasure and/or pain (Milner, 1957). Thinking closer to the primary-process type is thus involved, but in the service of a productive act geared eventually to the creation of a communicable and socially valued product. The oft-described phases of creativity (Kris, 1952; Rapaport, 1951c) reflect this total process: the more primitive thinking characterizes the "inspirational" phase while the more controlled thinking characterizes the "elaborative" phase.

In a recent research, Pine (1959) studied the *products* of creative activity, employing the concepts of drive expression and drive control. The quality of productions—of essentially uncreative subjects (Ss)—in a literary task (TAT) and in a task of scientific hypothesis formation varied with the amount and control of drive content in the product. Not only did the better productions include more drive content, but in addition such content was better controlled than in the poorer productions. Controls were reflected in the effective integration of the drive content into the total created production as well as in modulation of drive intensity and socialization of drive aim.

By contrast, the present study approaches the problem of creativity— and uncreativity—from the standpoint of the *person,* the creator. It involves a number of assumptions, from which three hypotheses were generated. We assume, first, that it is possible to score quantitatively evidences of the primary process that are apparent in a finished thought product—in the present case, in Rorschach test responses. Further, we assume that people differ in the degree to which they permit their responses to the Rorschach test to manifest recognizable signs of the primary process, or are unable to prevent its emergence in their responses (phenomena which we call, for short, the expression of primary process) and in the effectiveness of their control over such expressed primary-process content. Finally, we assume that a score taking into account both the amount of expression of primary process and the effectiveness with which it is controlled constitutes an operational measure of adaptive regression (Kris' regression in the service of the ego). What we cannot assume, however, and what this study undertakes to explore, is the extent to which styles of expression and control of primary process on the Rorschach test are generalized and apply to a variety of tasks not all of which seem to require primary-process modes of thinking.

Hypothesis 1. S's tendency to express more or less primary process is unrelated to the quality of the productions he creates in various tests of imagination.

Hypothesis 2. S's tendency toward effective control over expressed primary-process material is positively related to the quality of his created productions, effective control being associated with higher quality.

Hypothesis 3. S's tendency toward adaptive or maladaptive regression to primary-process modes of thinking (based on an evaluation of the combined expression and control tendencies) is positively related to the quality of his created productions, adaptive regression being associated with higher quality.

These hypotheses stem from an assessment of the relative significance of control—in contrast to expression—of primary process for creativity. Amount of expression per se takes no account of the control processes required for creative work. It is expected that Ss who produce a good deal of primary-process material on the Rorschach test with consistently good control will give the highest quality productions in the tests of imagination (Hypothesis 3). It is expected, further, that individual differences in control over primary-process expression will be related to the quality measures, even apart from consideration of the amount of expression (Hypothesis 2). This is because almost all Ss express at least some primary-process content on the Rorschach test, because the tests of imagination that were used by and large do not require a capacity for expressive thinking comparable to that required for the production of, say, a major work of literature, and because we did not expect our sample of college students to contain many persons who would regress pathologically.

In testing these hypotheses, the study has one additional aim: to provide validation for Holt's system for scoring expression and control of primary-process material in the Rorschach test (Holt, 1959e; Holt & Havel, 1960). Previously, this system has been shown to provide an effective predictor of response to perceptual isolation, particularly in terms of the operation of primary-process thinking during isolation procedures (Goldberger, 1961; Goldberger & Holt, 1961a).

METHOD

Subjects. Ss were 13 male and 14 female undergraduates at a large urban university. They were a group of volunteers who were intensively studied through clinical and experimental research techniques by numerous investigators for about one year. Ss had been selected for the research program on the basis of *(a)* approximate indications on the MMPI of emotional stability, and *(b)* intelligence (upper 60% of entering college freshmen) on the Ohio State Psychological Examination. They have no particular excellence in creative arts or science nor, with two exceptions, do they have any professional commitment to these areas. Ss are the same as those used in Pine's (1959) related study. The present study focuses on seven tests administered to all Ss. "Creativity" scores were derived from each test, but the nature of this score varies with the particular test; in aggregate they are referred to as the "quality" scores.

Thematic Apperception Test (TAT). The TAT was used in investigating the quality of literary productions. The test was administered individually. Standard instructions were given and Ss were told to take about 5 minutes per story and, on Card 11, to "tell a fairy tale such as you might tell a child." Nine stories per S were considered here, those given to Cards 1, 4, 11, 13MF, 16, 2, 18GF, 19, and 18BM (males) or 15 (females). Stories were recorded verbatim, the first five tape recorded and the last four written out by S.

The stories were rated on 12 attributes that were expected on a priori grounds to reflect the *literary quality* of the story: length, figures of speech, vocabulary, variety in sentence structure, naming characters, use of direct speech, characterization, time perspective, unity and continuity, genuineness, originality, and specification.[1] Fuller descriptions of these variables are given elsewhere (Pine, 1959); an attempt was made to control for length as much as possible in the latter 11 variables. Each of these story attributes was rated by one rater; five raters were used in all.[2] Although it was necessary to

---

[1] We wish to acknowledge our indebtedness to D. J. van Lennep, whose work in this area suggested some of these variables for analysis.

[2] One of the authors (FP) and four other raters carried out these ratings. Only FP knew anything about Ss' scores on the other creativity tests, and he rated only the objective variables on the TAT (length, number of stories with direct speech, number of stories in which characters are given names). One of the TAT raters had some share in the ratings of the independent Rorschach variables. Although this rater had only a part share in rating the TAT (rating 2 of the 12 variables) and only a part share in rating some of the Rorschach protocols, correlations between the TAT quality scores and the Rorschach independent variables for handling of primary process were carried out with her ratings of the TAT excluded from the TAT score to check on any possibility of rating contamination. The correlations obtained did not differ in pattern or in statistical significance from those described below (Table 10.1) for the total TAT score.

We wish to express our acknowledgment to the many members of the staff of the Research Center for Mental Health who carried out various rating tasks.

use each rater for more than one rating, only ratings which were unlikely to be confused with one another (e.g., variety in sentence structure and characterization) were assigned to one rater. Ss were ranked on each of the 12 story attributes and final ranks were derived by summing the 12 for each S and reranking the totals. The final combined ranking was used in all data analyses. The scoring reliability of the final literary quality scores was determined by the intraclass correlation technique (Ebel, 1951) applied to the 12 rankings; reliability of the mean score was .82 for the total sample.

The Science Test. The Science Test consisted of two problems, each posing a scientific dilemma which S was asked to resolve. One item (#2) was drive related and was generally felt by Ss to be far the more fanciful while the other (#1) was more neutral. Ss were required to write out three theories to account for each hypothetical situation. Instructions were to make the theories complete and realistic (i.e., probable) and to use imagination in a down-to-earth scientific manner. There was no fixed time limit, but no S took longer than one hour. The test called for skill in forming imaginative hypotheses; analysis and synthesis of information were only minimally involved and hypothesis testing was not involved. The problems were as follows:

1. A general idea of the way that coal forms is first that trees fall and decay; then owing to certain upheavals of the earth, land gets on top of them and over time the pressure of the earth turns the original material into coal. There are no trees in Antarctica, yet I want you to assume that coal has been found there. How could this be accounted for?[3]

2. It is known that the differentiation of male and female sexes came about fairly early in animal evolution. That is, even in the lower animals male and female sex organs are in different individuals—there are separate male and female sexes. I want you to assume that recently a very advanced animal species, almost like the human species, has been found in which all individuals have both male and female sex organs. How could this be accounted for?

Ratings for *quality of theories* (on a four-point scale) were based on the specific theories given by S as well as on the general modes of scientific thinking (parsimony, a questioning attitude, use of known facts, etc.) reflected in the response. To test interrater agreement, Spearman rho between scores derived from each of the two raters' ratings was used; rho was .89 for males and .62 for females.[4] Findings from this two-item test can be regarded as suggestive only; the internal consistency of the test is nil

---

[3]This research was completed before the actual discovery of coal deposits in Antarctica.

[4]Both Science Test items were rated by one of the authors (FP) and one other rater. These two raters also rated the Brick Uses and Consequences Tests (to be described below). Although the author in all cases knew which S had produced which response, the other rater never knew this and had no way of extending a halo effect across his several ratings. Ratings were carried out by the two raters working independently and final scores were obtained through discussion and reconciliation of differences. In no case did either rater have any knowledge of the ratings of the independent variables on the Rorschach.

(interitem rho on the quality scores is .05 for males and −.34 for females), and findings are presented for each item separately.

The Humor Test. The Humor Test consisted of 15 cartoons for which Ss invented captions. It was administered individually with no time limit. Ss were asked to write out responses and to make the captions as funny as possible. Captions were rated on an eight-point scale for *humorousness.* Five raters rated the captions given by female Ss and these five plus two more raters rated those of male Ss.[5] Each rater's 15 ratings for each S were summed to give a final score. Interrater agreement by the intraclass correlation technique (reliability of the mean rating) was .86 for the males and .87 for the females.

The Animal Drawing. Each S was asked to draw a "fantastic animal," making it as unusual as possible. Two judges independently ranked the drawings on *drawing ability* and on *originality.*[6] Interrater reliability (rho) for drawing ability was .90 for males and .84 for females; for originality, agreement was lower (rho .29 for males and .42 for females). Disagreements were discussed until a final ranking was achieved for each variable. The final ranks for the two variables are statistically independent (rho −.01 for males and .22 for females).

The Brick Uses Test. The Brick Uses Test (Guilford, Frick, Christensen, & Merrifield, 1957) required S to list as many uses as possible for an ordinary brick in 5 minutes; scores were based on the number of shifts in the type of use given. Guilford's scoring manual permits derivation of a score having high loading on his *spontaneous flexibility* factor. Interrater agreement in the present sample was 89%.[4]

The Consequences Test. The Consequences Test (Guilford *et al.,* 1957) consisted of four items, each describing some hypothetical event (for example, the sudden destruction of all books). S's task was to list possible consequences of the event (time limit: 5 minutes per item). Guilford's manual gives a score having high loading on his *originality* factor. Interrater agreement here was 86%.[4]

The Rorschach Test. The Rorschach Test was used to derive Rorschach creativity scores as well as rankings on the independent variables: expression and control of primary process.[7]

[5]The seven raters (none of these the authors) were all unaware of which Ss had produced which responses (and even of which responses were given by a single S). Although three of the seven had rated other creativity tests, the Ss' names had been removed and there was no possibility of halo effect. One of the seven raters had a partial share in rating some of the Rorschachs, but no contamination was possible since he did not know which S he was rating on the Humor Test.

[6]The two raters (not the authors) were each ignorant of the Rorschach scores and of which S had produced which drawing. These raters each contributed to the ratings of the Humor Test but to none of the other tests.

[7]Ratings of these three Rorschach variables were carried out as follows: Each protocol was scored for all variables by two raters working independently and then coming to a consensus. The two raters varied from protocol to protocol, in each case selected from a total pool of seven raters. Any problems they had in arriving at a consensus were later discussed with one of the authors

The creativity rating: Each Rorschach response was scored on a four-point scale. The rating is based upon a composite of statistical infrequency, sensitive use of determinants, good form level, appropriate elaboration, and a quality of richness (see Holt, 1959e). To avoid contamination with the primary-process scores, the *creativity* ranking in the present sample was based on the average rating of only those responses that received no primary-process scores.

Amount of expression of primary process: Holt (1956b; Holt & Havel, 1960) has described a theoretical rationale and an extensive scoring manual for scoring primary-process manifestations in the Rorschach. All reponses that have aggressive derivatives, libidinal derivatives, anxious content, or various nonlogical or bizarre formal qualities are scored. The final ranking for amount of primary process is based upon the proportion of S's responses that have scorable primary-process elements, double weighting for extreme instances (Level 1 as compared to Level 2 in the scoring manual). Holt and Havel (1960) report interrater agreement well into the .90's (rho) for over-all scores on amount of expression of primary process.

Effectiveness of control over primary process: Holt and Havel (1960) describe procedures for rating the "defense-demand" and the "defense-effectiveness" of each response scored for primary process. Defense-demand, rated on a six-point scale, is defined in terms of the acceptability of the response in ordinary social communication; thus, for libidinal content, for example, the response "two people holding hands" requires almost no special controls while "two people having intercourse" does. Defense-effectiveness, also rated on a six-point scale, is defined in terms of the success of the controlling factors associated with the primary-process material. Such things as the form level, the associated affective response of S, the intellectual or esthetic context of the response, and S's evasiveness or confusion are considered. Thus, the composition, "This part looks like a horse but the rest makes me think it's a man" is a less effectively controlled formal primary-process response than "a centaur," which refers successfully to the social reality of a myth, puts the response at a safe distance, and makes a condensation-like response sensible. Interrater reliability of the mean defense-

---

(RRH) in a meeting of all seven raters and a final decision reached. Although the Rorschach creativity scores were derived from only those responses where primary process was not scored, it is apparent that one cannot argue that these were uninfluenced by primary-process scoring in the same protocol. The Rorschach creativity score turns out to be one of the poorest correlates of the independent Rorschach variables for handling of primary process, however, and makes no significant contribution to the results (see Table 10.1). The two primary-process ratings (expression and control) were not independently rated although they turn out to be statistically independent (see below). Of the pool of seven raters, five (including RRH) did no other ratings for the study. One was one of the seven raters for the Humor Test (where he was "blind" as to S) and one was one of the five TAT raters (and, as described in Footnote 2, omitting her ratings made no difference in the results).

demand and defense-effectiveness scores was computed for the male sample; rhos were .84 and .74, respectively.

Final scores for each S were derived from the defense-demand and defense-effectiveness scores by a procedure developed by Goldberger (1961). For each S, responses where defense-demand was high and defense-effectiveness was good were tabulated; similarly, responses where defense-effectiveness was poor, whatever the defense-demand, were tabulated; responses with good defense-effectiveness but low defense-demand were omitted. Final individual scores, which were then ranked, were based on the ratio of well-controlled responses (high demand, effective defense) to poorly controlled responses (ineffective defense, whatever the demand).

Adaptive versus maladaptive regression: This score is based on the combined amount of expression and effectiveness of control scores described above. It was developed and used with good predictive success by Goldberger (1961), and is described in detail by Holt and Havel (1960). In brief, it produces a ranking as follows: at one extreme are Ss who are high on both amount of expression and effectiveness of defense (controlled or adaptive regression to primary-process modes of thinking); at the other extreme are Ss who are high on amount of expression but low on effectiveness of defense (uncontrolled or maladaptive regression to primary-process modes of thinking); in the middle are Ss who are low on amount of expression (constricted control).

RESULTS

Before studying the hypotheses of the research, we examined some of the characteristics of the rankings of Rorschach primary process. Rank correlations between the measures of expression and control of primary process were computed. The rhos were negligible (.01 for the males and .24 for the females). These correlations indicate the statistical independence of the two variables as measured here; below, we treat them as independent in correlating each separately with the quality scores. The low correlations cannot, however, be taken to reflect functional independence in the individual. Rather, we would expect that expression and control of primary process would generally be integrated in some way in an individual's functioning—but in an idiosyncratic way. It is just these idiosyncratic possibilities in the relation between the expression and control of primary process that permit statistical independence in measurement.

The combined (adaptive regression) Rorschach score is correlated far more strongly with the control score component (rho is **.90** for males and **.79** for females) than with the expression score component (rho is .11 for males and .13 for females). Thus, on methodological grounds alone, one would expect findings for the control and the combined scores to be more similar to each other than either is to findings with the score for amount of expression. We cannot, therefore, make independent tests of Hypotheses 2 and 3 but can only look to see the directions of change (if any) in the findings for the control score when the score for amount of expression is combined with it.

Hypotheses 1, 2, and 3 state that the quality of a person's created productions is unrelated to his tendency to express more or less primary-process material on the Rorschach but is related to his tendency toward more or less effective control over expressed primary-process content and to a combined score (adaptive versus maladaptive regression) taking both amount of expression and effectiveness of control into account. Thus, it was expected that the quality scores on the various experimental tests would be correlated with the control and with the combined scores but not with the score for amount of expression alone. Results are presented in Table 10.1.

As indicated in Row 1 of Table 10.1, an over-all creativity score derived for each S was correlated significantly with the control scores for both males and females ($p = .06$) and with the adaptive regression score for males; the correlations with the amount scores, though positive, are negligible. The

Table 10.1. Rank Correlations Between Test Measures of Creativity and the Rorschach Scores for Primary Process

Creativity Score	Males ($N = 13$)			Females ($N = 14$)		
	Amount	Control	Adaptive Regression	Amount	Control	Adaptive Regression
Total Creativity: over-all score	.13	**.80**	**.90**	.21	.52	.28
TAT: literary quality	.05	**.74**	**.83**	.59[a]	.27	.26
Science (neutral): quality of theory	−.17	.19	.08	−.32	.34	.24
Science (drive): quality of theory	.11	.43	.40	.64[a]	.11	.01
Rorschach: creativity	.17	.27	.31	−.22	.21	.22
Humor Test: humorousness	−.03	.13	.19	.32	.10	−.13
Animal Drawing: originality	−.14	.55	.49	.22	.38	−.05
Animal Drawing: drawing ability	−.04	**.69**	**.68**	.24	.39	.33
Brick Uses: flexibility	.24	.36	.48	−.02	.44	.18
Consequences: originality	−.04	.59	**.74**	−.16	−.02	−.03

[a]Contrary to hypothesis. Significant at 5% level; two-tailed test. Figures in *italics* indicate significance at the 5% level; figures in **bold face** indicate significance at the 1% level.

over-all scores were obtained by summing the ranks for each S on eight of the nine individual test measures and reranking the totals; to avoid double-weighting the animal drawing, and since the ratings of originality had poor interrater reliability on this test, only the ranking of drawing ability was used in computing the over-all scores. In view of the variations in the subtest correlations with the Rorschach scores for the female sample (to be described below), there is some question as to the representativeness of the over-all scores for the female sample. The validity of these scores was therefore investigated.

Staff members used qualitative data from tests and life histories to Q-sort all Ss on various personality variables, which were then subjected to a syndrome analysis (Horn, 1944); syndrome scores were then converted to normative ranks (cf. Block, 1957). These rankings are partially contaminated since two of the eight component tests making up the over-all score (the TAT and the Rorschach) were used in evaluating Ss for the Q-sorts. With recognition of this qualification, three rankings were selected on a priori grounds to check the validity of the over-all scores. For the females, the over-all creativity score was correlated with "creativity: needs for achievement, creative construction, love of novelty, sentience" (*.63*), with "clear and effective communication versus blocked and uncommunicative" (**.73**), and with "vivid imagery versus minimal and stereotyped fantasy and clings to reality" (*.56*); the corresponding correlations for the males were *.61*, **.80**, and *.58*, respectively. All these correlations are significant at the 5% level or better (two-tailed test). Thus, the over-all scores have some measure of validity. Be this as it may, valid test differences may still be obscured by these over-all scores.

Correlations between the Rorschach variables on the one hand and the quality scores on the individual tests on the other are presented in the remainder of Table 10.1. For the males, the correlations test by test parallel those with the over-all score. In each of the nine measures, the quality score is correlated more highly with the Rorschach control score than with the amount score. In four instances, the correlation with control is significant and in all cases it is positive; in five instances, the correlation with amount is negative and in all cases it is negligible. The score for adaptive versus maladaptive regression tends to give slightly higher correlations than the control score; the correlations are significant in three instances. There is little patterning among the tests that do and do not produce significant correlations; tests as different as the TAT, the animal drawing, and the Consequences Test give the highest correlations.

For the females, there is much more variation in the separate test correlations. Only two correlations are significant, and these—surprisingly—are both with the amount of primary-process expression. Correlations with control and with the adaptive regression score are higher than those with amount in only about half of the cases.

Since other data available on this same female sample suggest that the adaptive regression score is not a meaningful one for this particular group (see Holt and Havel, 1960), and since this score produced no significant correlations in the present sample, we focus then on the two simpler (and independent) Rorschach scores, amount and control, for the females. The major difference in results between males and females is in the correlations with the amount score. For both groups, the correlations with control tend to be consistently positive (except for the Consequences Test for females) although the correlations for the females are smaller; that the females had less variation in their control scores may account for some of this difference. The wide range in correlations with amount in the female group, from strong positive to moderate negative, sharply differentiates the two groups.

The correlations nevertheless seem to fall into a pattern for the females. The tests which, at least in appearance, permit more open-ended and expressive verbal responses, and in particular permit more drive expression in the responses, are just those where the correlation for the female Ss is higher with the Rorschach score for amount of primary-process expression than with the control score. This category includes the TAT and the drive related Science Test item (and perhaps the Humor Test).[8] Why should it be that, for our college girls, individual differences in amount of primary-process expression are at times better predictors of the quality of imaginative productions, and individual differences in control over primary-process expression are consistently the better predictors of the quality scores? A critical point here, we suggest, is that people vary in their automatic (not necessarily thought out) approach to a task in terms of the implicit assumptions they hold regarding what the task and the experimenter require of them. Thus, for tests taken in an experimental situation and in a university setting, Ss may implicitly "direct" (or "set") themselves to give highly controlled imaginative productions; in this case, individual differences in the capacity to exert effective control over imaginative productions would get reflected in the quality of the finished product. In contrast, given such tests as the TAT, and in spite of the university surroundings, Ss may at times approach test tasks as though the appropriate response were to give a fanciful and freely expressive response, even if the response would not be too well controlled; in this case, individual differences in the capacity for fanciful expression would be reflected in the quality of the finished product. In our data, it is as though the males consistently had the former (control) response set while the females had at times the former and at times the latter response set.

Why these college girls might have demonstrated such duality in their

[8]On the face of it, the Rorschach test is also such an open-ended test and permits drive expression. It was not used in this analysis, however, because the Rorschach creativity score is based on only those responses where primary process is not scorable in the response and because a control factor (form level) is built into the rating criteria.

implicit approach to the tasks is of interest, and may reflect a greater field dependence (since they vary with the ostensible task "demand"), or a bimodal identity including both more expressive and more controlled aspects (feminine-masculine) with neither being consistently more dominant. Be this as it may, these speculations led to some expectations regarding the data. If the males responded to even the more fanciful tests in a way reflecting the effectiveness of their controls, and if the females responded to these tests in a way reflecting their potential for fanciful expression, then there should be two ways to get high (or low) quality scores on these tests: either by effectively (or ineffectively) controlled imaginative productions or by highly (or minimally) expressive productions. The males should tend to give the former, and the females the latter; but this should not be the case for the tests which "demand" more specific and controlled productions. Some indirectly relevant data were available for two of the more expressive tests (TAT and drive related Science) and for one of the more controlled ones (neutral Science). Ss had been ranked for the *amount* of drive content in their TAT and Science productions and also for the degree of *control* over expressed drive content (see Pine, 1959, 1960); control was reflected principally in an integration of the drive content into the core of the created product. These ratings of expression and control of drive content are not identical with the ratings of expression and control of primary process on the Rorschach because of test differences and because the Rorschach ratings included formal as well as drive indices of primary process (although the latter predominated); however, what is more important, they do reflect expression and control within these created productions themselves and thus provide a better test of the hypothesis that there are two kinds of productions which could get high scores. It was expected that the quality scores on the TAT and the drive related Science items would be correlated more highly with control of drive for the males than for the females and more highly for amount of drive expression for the females than for the males; this difference was not expected to appear in the neutral Science item. Correlations (rho) are presented in Table 10.2.

Correlations with amount of drive are higher for the females than for the males on the TAT and the drive related Science item but not on the

Table 10.2. Rank Correlations Between the Quality Scores and Expression and Control of Drive Content in the TAT and Science Test

	TAT		Science (drive)		Science (neutral)	
	Amount	Control	Amount	Control	Amount	Control
Males	.60	.42	.09	.05	.12	.06
Females	**.77**	.28	.52[a]	.04	−.36	.64

[a] p = .06.

neutral Science item. Correlations with the control scores are higher for the males than for the females on the TAT but the reverse is true on the neutral Science item. (Throughout, larger group differences appear in the Science items than in the TAT.) Thus, there is some indirect support for the proposition that the females achieved high (or low) quality scores on the more open-ended, expressive tests in a somewhat different way from the males; individual differences in drive expression were more significant in the females than in the males on these tests.

The correlations shown in Table 10.2 are also of interest for their parallel to the correlations of Table 10.1. In both, for the male sample, the TAT produces a significant[9] correlation with the control score (although the correlation with amount is higher in Table 10.2), while the two Science items produce no significant correlations. The variation in the correlations for the females found in Table 10.1 is repeated almost exactly in Table 10.2. In the TAT and the drive related Science item, all correlations are positive and the correlation of the quality score with amount is much higher than with control; in the neutral Science item, the correlation with control is positive and with amount is negative. Thus, with amount and control scores derived from the TAT and the Science productions themselves as well as with the parallel scores on the Rorschach test the same sex differences and patterning of correlations are obtained. These findings support the validity of these patterns of difference in the present sample.

DISCUSSION

The results are suggestive in several ways. First, the way in which primary process material is handled on the Rorschach test is related to the quality of imaginative production in a variety of test situations. That control over primary process expression, rather than gross amount of expression per se, is related to the quality of created products is indicated by all of the data of the male sample and by results with the over-all creativity score for the females. These results give general support to the hypotheses of the study, and they indicate further that Kris' concept of regression in the service of the ego can be subjected to empirical study—that predictions generated by this psychoanalytic concept can be studied with operationally defined scores and quantitative techniques.

The data for our male sample, where scores for adaptive regression and for controlled primary-process expression could predict quality scores on tests of imagination even where primary-process thinking was not evidently

[9][Throughout this paper, one-tailed tests were used originally, which amounts to our having adopted an alpha (or significance) level of .10. Moreover, it must be admitted in retrospect that we freely interpreted nonsignificant *differences* between correlation coefficients, heedless of our small sample size.]

required by the tests, are of additional interest. The tests used here have certain parallels to the model of primary-process thinking: thus, the TAT requires a "make-believe," nonliteral kind of thinking and also the use of drive content (for motivation of characters); the role of primary process in humor has been discussed by Freud (1905); even with the Brick Uses there is a parallel to primary process in that high scores are attained by *shifts* in the direction of thinking, by a style that contrasts with the directed thought of the secondary process. But these parallels between the test requirements and primary-process thinking are at best tenuous in most or all of the tests used. We would argue, in contrast, that primary-process thinking is not directly implicated in the production of responses to these tests, but rather that modes of expression and control of primary process (perhaps beginning in early childhood) become generalized as broad cognitive styles (Klein, 1950) which are reflected in all areas of thinking. Thus, where tests require flexible and original thinking, and where the control style permits this, thinking can be flexible even apart from the (hypothesized) original relation of control directly to primary-process thinking.

But there is an important caution to be drawn from our results. The subsample differences indicate that there are limitations to the extent to which we can generalize from these data. Kris' discussion of the relation of regression in the service of the ego to creativity can be viewed as a broad approximation—an approximation subject to important differences in samples that vary as to age, sex, the absolute level of creativity of the Ss involved, and the nature of the creative production. The most we can say from our data is that expression and control of primary process are relevant to an understanding of the creative process, but that the specific nature of the relationships involved may vary and awaits much further research for detailed specification.

The sex differences in our data are of interest for their implications regarding the relationship between "creativity" on the present test measures and creativity as it is more naturally found in the productive arts and sciences.

First: Do the two significant correlations between quality scores and *amount* of primary-process expression (rather than with effectiveness of control) indicate that some highly rated productions were quite expressive but seriously lacking in controls? This would contrast to an "ideal" of creative productivity as both personally expressive and sufficiently controlled to be communicable and potentially socially valued. Whether or not some truly creative productions can be really uncontrolled, or whether the nature of controls in some areas (e.g., painting, dance) is simply different from and perhaps more subtle than the intellectual verbal controls required by most of our tests, the essential point is that our data do not really suggest that some high quality productions here were uncontrolled. The Ss who gave these results were "normal" college girls. It can be assumed that some control factors were included in *all* of their expressions of primary process, and the Rorschach scores support this assumption. Furthermore, these girls are obviously all sufficiently well controlled to function effectively in school and generally, and presumably they would be able to impose control when the adaptive requirements of a task require it (as in the tests of imagination) even if some of them could relinquish control somewhat on the Rorschach.

Second: The introduction of the idea that our male and female *S*s had implicit but differing response sets which led them to approach the various tasks differentially requires comment. Certainly this concept is relevant for our present sample where sudden "inspiration" had little or no part in the production (upon demand) of imaginative products and where varying expectations and goals were likely to be activated by the entire experimental setting. But does such variation in approach to productive work, variation in terms of more expressive or more controlled responsiveness, apply in the creative arts and sciences? The concept certainly does not seem applicable where creative experiences come in off-guard moments, during sleep, or when the sudden inspiration is experienced as though coming upon the person from outside without his being responsible for it (Ghiselin, 1952). But there is a way in which individual preferences for more expressive or more controlled productivity are relevant for the broader realms of creativity: in the way in which people, consciously or not, gravitate toward areas conducive to differing kinds of productivity. Thus, as the girls in the present sample may have responded with more or less fanciful and idiosyncratic expression in tasks that permitted such expression, so there seem to be differences in western culture in the areas where males and females have made their greatest contributions. A Sappho existed long before a Madame Curie, and it is probably still true that there is a greater proportion of women in the arts than in the sciences. Thus, alternative areas open for productive work in a particular social milieu may provide room for differing individual styles of creativeness.

11

Around 1960, with the help of an excellent research assistant (now Dr.) Lester Alston, I began gathering together for normative purposes a large group of Rorschachs that had been scored according to my primary-process system. It was a slow business, assembling the samples, making sure that they were scored and tabulated uniformly, coding the scores and organizing them for machine processing, and finally getting the tabulations and intercorrelations, with the considerable help of (now Dr.) Philip Halboth. The analyses reported here were completed just in time to be incorporated into the paper I had been invited to give at the 1966 Nebraska Symposium on Motivation.

Measuring Libidinal and Aggressive Motives and Their Controls by Means of the Rorschach Test

The psychoanalytic theory of motivation is today in a state of flux, not to say confusion. Its fundamental concepts (psychic energy and tension reduction, and the passive reflex model of the organism) are bankrupt, and more evidence is piling up daily that a different set of basic assumptions must be chosen as the starting-points of a tenable theory. Yet the clinical discoveries of Freud, his formulations of so-called personality dynamics, the indirect and disguised effects of unconscious motives and defenses on behavior—these seem to me of indisputable value for the practicing clinician and personality researcher, poorly supported by hard data though many of the relevant propositions may be. The consequence of this anomalous state of affairs for my own work is that I am simultaneously criticizing various aspects of the metapsychological model (Holt, 1963a; 1965a, 1965c; 1967e) and working with a psychoanalytic system of scoring drives or wishes in the Rorschach which seems to me as fruitful as the theory seems barren. A group of my colleagues and I are beginning to see some ways we may be able to develop a more tenable psychoanalytic model of man (Holt, 1967b), but it is too early to go into that [see, however, Holt, 1976a]. All I want to do here is to indicate my general feeling about the psychoanalytic theory of motivation, which is one of hope and respect mingled with exasperation, and then spend most of my time talking about some data.

I shall beg your indulgence, therefore, to speak freely and casually about libidinal and aggressive wishes without commitment to what Freud and other analysts have hypothesized about the libido theory or death instinct. It is rather curious, but perhaps instructive, how my method, which began as a deliberate attempt to apply to test data Hartmann's concept of the neutralization of drive energy, now seems to me to stand by itself and to be quite unaffected by the telling blows that have been dealt to Hartmann's notion by such critics as White (1963) and Rubinstein (1965, 1967) [and Schafer, 1976]. All I need to borrow from psychoanalysis at the moment is a framework for classifying imagery as relevant to a set of motives, and a precedent for adding certain things together (as in some sense equivalent) though they might not appear to common sense to be relevant to each other.

One other general preliminary: my method of scoring the Rorschach started as an index of neutralization (the degree to which motives are socialized), but then grew into a way of measuring manifestations of the *primary process* and the means by which a person tries to control it and defend himself against the anxiety its emergence presumably entails. Motivationally relevant material is scored only because the theory of the primary process calls for it; indeed, in my manual (Holt, 1963c; see also Holt, 1977a) I express reservations about the degree to which the Rorschach may be used as a way of measuring the intensity of motives. On the strength of the invitation to participate in this symposium, however, I decided to reopen this question and pull together what data I had, examining just what kind of measuring instrument for motivational variables I had created, almost inadvertently.

Psychoanalytic theory hypothesizes two ideal types of mental functioning, primary and secondary process, the latter of which refers to mature, civilized, rational, and realistic thinking which is effective in helping us attain our goals. The primary process is not just ineffective thinking; it is positively defined, in two seemingly unrelated ways: it is wishful—that is, dominated by the seeking for the most immediate gratification of sexual and aggressive desires; and it is magical—that is, it has formal properties of violating the dictates of logic and reality in specifiable ways, which I need not go into here. Quite aside from the tenability of the theory, it is a fact that in several large and quite different samples (e.g., VA schizophrenics, normal college students, unemployed actors, disturbed adolescents) scores of these two kinds, which I call content and formal aspects of primary process, tend to be positively and very significantly correlated, at a level of about .5 *after* partialling out the effect of R, the total number of responses.

Despite this empirical basis for keeping the content and formal measures together as a measure of a single, complex construct, primary process, I am not going to say much more about the formal aspects of the primary process as such, but concentrate on the measures of motives.

There is a bit of a jump from defining primary process as cognition dominated by the wish for immediate gratification and taking the emergence of libidinal and aggressive content in the Rorschach as manifestations of primary process. A basic psychoanalytic assumption is that *all* thought and perception is organized by wishes to some extent, as well as by the given requiredness of external reality or the logical structure of ideas. To identify signs of the primary process, then, we must ask not *whether* wishes are involved in cognition but *how* they enter the cognitive process: to what extent there is a seeking for unrealistically immediate gratification, as against seeking it through organized, goal-directed, and purposive behavior (which would be secondary process). It is a sign of primary process when wish *dominates* cognition, despite considerations of logic and reality.

A subject's response to a Rorschach blot is based, in varying proportions, on the imagery he brings to the task (Schafer, 1954), on the properties of the ink-blot itself, and on his definition of what is expected of him in the test situation, including his understanding of what it is appropriate for him to communicate to the tester. As an initial simplification, I have assumed that everything in this array of determinants—besides the subject himself— remains constant. By definition, all subjects are in the (presumably standard) situation of taking a test when they produce the responses that we are dealing with, and this situation is not one in which there can be any realistic striving for the direct gratification of wishes; therefore, any wishful imagery found there is presumably *not* a part of adaptive, purposive behavior. Hence I can assume, on discerning some evidence of "instinctual" relevance in the manifest content of a response, that wish is organizing the response in primary-process fashion.

A pretty good a priori case can therefore be made for using the Rorschach test as a way of measuring motives, despite its bad reputation in many scientific circles for its lack of clearly demonstrated reliability and validity, and for the imprecise if not actually untestable interpretations given it by many clinicians. The TAT was in the same boat a dozen years ago, yet thanks to the persistent efforts of McClelland, Atkinson, Clark, and Lowell (1953), Atkinson (1958), and their collaborators, it has developed into quite a respectable and widely used measure of needs for achievement, affiliation, power, etc. As Atkinson (1954) told this Symposium over a decade ago, imaginative thought is a good place to look for measurable manifestations of motives. Since the Rorschach was even earlier in the field as a clinical technique of assessing motivation based on the elicitation of a kind of imaginative thought, it is surprising that so few efforts have been made to develop it in a manner comparable to that of McClelland.

The first well-known attempt to use the Rorschach to measure motivational variables quantitatively was that of Elizur (1949), who published a method for scaling anxiety and hostility in the manifest content of Rorschach responses. I have found several subsequent attempts along similar lines, all of which refer to his work; if they use it at all, however, these later investigations introduce modifications (Walker, 1951; Storment & Finney, 1953; Murstein, 1956; J. R. Smith & Coleman, 1956). Interestingly enough, everyone seems to get positive results (or perhaps only those who publish), but nobody replicates anyone else's study! Holtzman and his co-workers (1961) have perhaps the most thoroughly worked-out synthesis of several of their predecessors' scales of hostility, particularly that of Murstein, and since Holtzman made his hostility scale part of the standard scoring of his own ink-blot test, he has been able to persuade others to use it without apparent tinkering.

The criticism leveled against the Elizur system by a couple of later workers was that it scales each Rorschach response on only three points of intensity: each manifestation of hostility (of which he lists a good many) is scored as strongly present, present, or absent. Murstein (1956) by contrast provides a seven-point scale for the intensity of hostility in each response.

My system differs from these others in one principal way in addition to a few minor ones, such as the fact that it measures libidinal as well as aggressive manifestations, and allows for either Elizur's type of measurement or Murstein's. (That is, one can simply count aggressive responses, which is what I have usually done, weighting the weak manifestations of a type of hostility half as much as the full; or, the DD ratings—explained below—provide a six-point scaling of the blatancy or intensity of the drive-manifestation, which as I shall demonstrate some investigators have made good use of.) When I first read Elizur's paper, some years before beginning my work on my scheme, it struck me that he was adding together all *kinds* of hostile responses, and even though the correlations he reported with independent measures are impressive, I suspected that one could get better results by maintaining certain qualitative distinctions. In particular, I felt that it would be useful to distinguish responses with a sadistic implication from those connoting masochism, so I subdivided responses according to the implicit identification of the responder, whether with the attacker (which is called *subject* aggression) or the victim[1] (*object* aggression). Further, the responses seem to fall into another natural division, according to whether the aggression is a *potential* threat or is seen as *actively* going on. Combined, these two distinctions yield four categories (P-S, P-O, A-S, A-O), but leave out a thematically inevitable final type: the aftermath or *results* of aggression: images of destruction, death, injury, or affliction. Though these have a masochistic tinge, they also have long been clinically considered to connote on the one hand castration anxiety, and on the other hand depression and a

---

[1][The subject-object terminology has been confusing enough so that I have recently decided to replace these terms with Attacker and Victim. The introduction of Overtness control scores, also, made it redundant to distinguish Potential and Active Aggression. I have not made corresponding changes here, however, because so much of the treatment of the data depended on the old four-fold distinction.]

sense of inner decay or loss of vital powers; so it seemed desirable to keep them segregated. It is of course always possible to recombine things that have been scored separately.

Like Elizur, I originally had a further category for Anxiety, on the theoretically rather shaky ground that images permeated with helplessness, uneasiness, and insecurity signaled the threatened emergence of some drive the exact nature of which could not be determined from the manifest content. In working on the reliability of scoring, however, I found that these categories were constantly being confused with various manifestations of aggression. In the end, therefore, I made the simplifying assumption that if a person was seen as falling helplessly, foul play could be suspected, or if a child was visualized as looking terrified, the implicit threat in the respondent's mind was probably a hostile rather than an erotic one. Therefore, most of the kinds of things both Elizur and I had scored under anxiety made their way into the object-aggression categories; in addition, some of Elizur's and others' (e.g., Holtzman, Thorpe, Swartz, & Herron, 1961) anxiety responses turn out to be images of overtly aggressive threats. Thus, usually I score as Ag 2 P-S the monsters, witches, wild animals, and poisonous spiders that are scored under anxiety in other systems.

One obvious reason for the lag in the development of the Rorschach as a measure of motives is that the data it yields have been thought unpromising: the responses are mostly isolated images, which rarely have any thematic elaboration. By comparison, stories appear to be much more likely media for the expression and development of needs, strivings, longings, and the like; motivation is the very stuff of narrative literature. A Rorschach response is more like a painting, a static representation of a scene which may at times be dramatic but which need not be wish-relevant, in the way that is almost inescapable for an interesting story.

By this very token, if motives show themselves where they are not called for, one can be all the more justified in the inference that they are having a peremptory effect on thought. The standard Rorschach testing situation surely lacks sexual or aggressive provocativeness; the skilled examiner refrains from being either seductive, insulting, or frustrating. In this bland, permissive atmosphere, repeated reference to images of gratification or threat must strike the examiner as suggesting some degree of preoccupation with the motivational theme in question. Thus, in the Rapaport tradition of Rorschach scoring to which I was exposed, Sex and Anal were regular content scores, and we always made marginal notations such as *agg*, and *homo* (homosexuality), without however trying to quantify the underlying motives: a massing of any of these indications was taken as a sign of a corresponding preoccupation.

When I decided to make a systematic scoring scheme out of these beginnings, the influences of classical Freudian theory and of Hartmann's doctrine of neutralization combined to restrict the purview of the system to rather direct manifestations of aggression—the five types I just described—

and of the so-called partial libidinal drives: oral, anal, exhibitionistic-voyeuristic, homosexual, and sexual in the narrow sense, to which was appended a miscellaneous category for such minor themes as the urethral.

The resulting 11 types of motivational scores were each subdivided again, into two *levels,* or, so to speak, degrees of primariness. For despite the fact that Freud's terminology and many of his discussions suggest a dichotomous view of primary and secondary process, the theory actually assumes a continuum: pure primary process is a fiction (as Freud put it; 1900a, p. 603) or an ideal type, defining one hypothetical extreme, while secondary process is the other pole, equally unattainable in reality by mortal man. Properly speaking, therefore, there is no gap in this continuous series where one can set up a boundary marker for *the* primary process. In practice, counting is a more reliable method of measuring than intensive scaling, so I decided on the purely heuristic device of defining one type of response, called Level 1, about which there could be no doubt that it represented marked predominance of primary process, and a Level 2 type in which a case for primary process could be made, but more admixture of secondary process was clearly involved.[2]

In approaching the necessarily arbitrary matter of establishing boundaries, the defining points at which to say, for example, "Now here we can definitely begin to see that an oral concern is organizing the perceptual-associative process of responding to the blot," I relied upon two main criteria. The first is itself a continuum, from raw, shocking, direct, blatant, or primitive forms of the kind of wish in question, constituting Level 1, to civilized, socially acceptable forms that are more appropriate to social communication between strangers in a professional situation, which make up Level 2. The second criterion has to do with the degree to which the response focuses on the wish-relevant aspect of an image, such as a specific organ; it is useful primarily for libidinal responses. When a certain part of anatomy is seen in isolation, it is scored on Level 1 if one or both of the following effects would result from placing it in the context of perceiving a whole body (or a whole face): (a) going from part to whole image implies a more socially acceptable type of content, in the sense that it is, for example, more permissible in polite society to praise a woman's figure than to speak specifically of her breasts; (b) the whole is a better Gestalt than the part, in the sense that it is not natural to see certain bodily details in isolation as units. Lewis Carroll had this latter criterion in mind and made good use of it in the passage where Alice saw the smile without the Cheshire cat. Third, in the

---

[2]Parenthetically, I might remark that I am less convinced today than I was only a few years ago that this was a fortunate decision; a more differentiated scaling now seems not only possible but desirable. Perhaps I should have foreseen that Levels 1 and 2 would be mistakenly identified with primary and secondary process, too (an error made by Zimet and Fine, 1965, in an otherwise useful demonstration that these two levels of content differentiate reactive from process schizophrenics).

realm of aggression, the arbitrary dividing line between the two levels was set at the point of death: when hostility becomes lethal, I assume that it is safe to say that it is taking an extreme, primitive form. Nevertheless, whenever the aggressive image has a palpably sadistic, gory quality, it is scored Level 1 even if murder is not obviously involved.

Later, this binary scoring of levels began to seem too crude, and I introduced a six-point scale of *Defense-Demand* (DD), a rating of the shock-value of the underlying idea of the response. Its lowest extreme is the DD of 1, for responses referring to matters that could be discussed without a ripple at a polite tea party; for example, the oral responses "a cookie" or "a teacup"—perfectly innocuous, but clearly relevant to oral wishes. It ranges to the shocking extreme of the following (anal and aggressive as well as oral) response, scored DD 6: "Looks like the rectum of a dead person after it has been partly eaten by worms." The more you shudder or palpitate when you read a response, the higher its DD rating. An example at an intermediate level is "breasts," rated 3 on the DD scale.

As I remarked above, the DD rating is the same no matter how a response is verbalized as long as the "underlying idea" does not change. For example, if someone picks out the top central rare detail on Card I, often seen as breasts, and denotes it "a lady's chest," or "a pair of mammary glands," it gets the same DD of 3 as if he had said "a set of tits." Yet there is obviously a difference, which can hardly be disregarded in any assessment of primary process. This difference is in the way the person responds to the implicit social demand and provides some defensive cover as the underlying idea is put into the stream of communication. My manual therefore includes about four dozen categories in which to score methods of control and defense associated with the wish (or other primary process) aspect of the response.[3] The "chest" response was an example of Euphemism (scored Eu−, because its nicey-nice attempt at prettification only calls attention to what is presumably being hidden); the "glands" response was an example of the intellectualizing defense, which I call putting the response in an Intellectual Context (Cx I+ or −, depending on how successful it is in making a topic discussable without actually boring us stiff).

In addition to the intellectual, there are scorable Esthetic, Cultural, and Humorous contexts, various ways of making motivational content remote (such as by attributing it to animals, or by making it distant in space, time, or level of reality), control by reflection on a response, and a variety of more pathological defenses like projection, evasion, and negation. And then the response as a whole is rated not only for its Defense Demand, but also for the effectiveness of the controlling and defensive processes that are employed, another six-point rating called DE. This rating starts from an evaluation of

[3]A number of these were suggested by Joan Havel, during the brief but fruitful time when she collaborated with me on the development of the scoring system.

"form level"—the accuracy of match between the concept of the response and the shape of the blot area chosen; in assessing form-level, I use the finely graded system of Mayman (1960) and his helpful scoring manual. Then the affect accompanying the response is considered, and the nature of the scored controls and defenses; disgust or anxiety will usually move the rating down, as will strained and ineffective defenses, while appropriate positive affect or well-applied controlling efforts will raise it.

Let me conclude this brief introduction to the scoring method by considering an example. Suppose someone says, on looking at the first card, "Ugh—a horrible vampire bat! It looks almost as if it was flying right at me." In the inquiry, she points out the usually seen details, adding that it makes her think of the story of Dracula. The conventional scoring, which my system does not supplant but supplements, would be something like W FM A P; and by most systems form-level would be considered F plus. In Mayman's scoring, all popular and near-popular responses are Fo (for "ordinary," acceptable accuracy). On my scoring sheet I would first record the response number, then the form-level, Fo, often followed by a rating of the Creativity of the response on a five-point scale; as a popular, somewhat but not remarkably elaborated, this would get a 2. Next, the content is scored. In this instance, the concept of a vampire bat, a blood-sucker, is an oral-aggressive threat, which would be scored L 2 O (libidinal, level 2, oral) and Ag 2 P-S (aggression, level 2, potential and subject rather than object—the vampire is not seen in the act of doing its dirty work, but is a potential aggressor, while no victim is seen). [It would now be scored L 2 O-Ag.] Now we record the control scores: R-(an), R-fic s+, and Cx E+; that is, the orality and aggression are less threatening because they are attributed to an animal, and the response gains additional remoteness from the appropriate reference to a specific fictional character, which is invoking an esthetic context.

Next, we consider the response again, asking whether or not there is any formal manifestation of the primary process, like condensation, symbolism, or contradiction. There *is* something autistic about the response: it is treated as if the subject had lost sight of the fact that the bat was only her interpretation of an ink blot, and was considering it magically aimed at *her;* this we score as a Self-Reference (S R 1). But it has a control in the way she verbalized it: by use of the words, "almost as if," she gains some distance and does not commit herself to the deviant idea. The relevant score is R-cond: remoteness, conditional.

Finally, we must rate Defense-Demand and Defense Effectiveness. DD is 3, near the midpoint of the scale; that is given by the manual. To estimate DE, we start with the assumption that a response with such good form-accuracy must be potentially near the top of the scale, +1.5, but since negative affect is expressed, it moves down a notch to +.5. The controls scored do not change the rating, since they are appropriate for that level.

The scorer still has the option of raising or lowering the rating one point for considerations that are not specified by the manual, but which his clinical judgment tells him are relevant. By reference to scored examples in the manual, we find that this response has the same general feel as others that are rated plus .5, so that becomes the final score: it is still on the positive side of the zero point, indicating that the primary-process manifestations that come into awareness were well enough coped with so that the response can be considered a regression in the service of the ego (Kris, 1952) or, as I prefer to put it, adaptive rather than maladaptive regression (DE: $-.5$ to -2.0).

Reliability. It should be clear to a reader who has had any experience in working with projective techniques, or with content analysis in any other context, that a good deal of judgment is required by this scoring system. The rater has to hold in mind a great many possibly relevant categories, some of which (like Self-Reference) occur quite seldom; moreover, since the overall ratings of DD and DE are each contingent on several prior decisions, they are bound to suffer from a cumulation of errors and cannot be expected to enjoy a very high level of rater reliability. Moreover, I have not been able to restrain myself from tinkering with the system, deleting categories from time to time but usually adding even more new ones, trying to improve definitions and clarify concepts. The result has been that my manual is now in its tenth revised edition and is still unpublished.

The degree to which two people agree depends on many things other than the nature of the scoring system and the manual that embodies it— notably, their levels of ability, training, and motivation, and the size and range of the sample of Rorschachs rated. But if graduate students of clinical psychology are interested enough to learn the system by studying the manual and scoring a few records under supervision, and if they discuss their differences after independently scoring some others, they usually attain a satisfactory level of reliability. At least, that is, for the kinds of overall summary scores that have been used in most research with the system. The number of responses containing any scorable manifestations of primary process (which we call, for short, Total or Σ Pripro) has enjoyed reliabilities of .90 and .98 in four studies with an aggregate N of 134. But since this measure is highly correlated with R, the total number of responses ($r = .78$, in 121 normal Ss; .75 in 81 schizophrenics), the apparent reliability is somewhat inflated; that .98, for example, shrank to .91 when R was held constant by partial correlation. As Cronbach (1949) has pointed out, simply expressing a Rorschach score as a percentage of R does not necessarily hold constant this very large source of variance, but in the case of most of the percentage scores I am going to discuss it does happen to work. In the standard sample of 81 schizophrenics, the correlation with R is virtually zero when summary scores for total pripro, the sums of Level 1 or Level 2 responses, of Content or Formal aspects, are expressed as percentages of total responses. In the normal reference sample of 121, the resulting correlations with R are low negative, on the order of $-.15$, except for % Formal which is $-.28$.

Here, however, I am mainly concerned with the Content scores, which are the measures of libidinal and aggressive drive-derivatives. The percent total Content has had a very good reliability, fortunately: in one study McMahon (1964) got an interrater agreement coefficient of .94 ($N = 20$); in another, Rabkin (1966) also reports an r of .94.

When we come down to the individual scoring category, product-moment correlation coefficients are no longer an appropriate way to express agreement. It becomes a complicated matter, and one not intrinsically interesting to most nonpsychometricians, to find a meaningful way of expressing agreement on the scores; if you are interested, you can find a discussion of the issues and some data in the introduction to the scoring manual (Holt, 1963c). On the whole, there was good agreement on the motivational content scores between two graduate students who were working with me in 1956 on the fourth edition of the manual; it ranged from perfect agreement in the case of L 1 E-V (which occurred, however, only once in 1089 responses given by 30 Ss), to complete disagreement on L 2 S, which was scored only once by one rater, while the other gave the response L 2 M. Yet in terms of the total percentage of agreement, the fact remains that both scorers made the same decision for 99.9% of the responses. Each of them had an awesome number of decisions to make. It we consider the 22 content categories alone, they had to make nearly 24,000 decisions to score or not to score, further complicated by the fact that any one score could also be recorded as weak or full. In 412 instances, one or both of them decided to use a content score—which means that 98% of the decisions were agreements that the score in question was not present. If we consider only those 412 instances, there was perfect agreement on the specific category and its strength in 50%, plus another 25% where the only disagreement was the quantitative one of the half-step difference between a full and a weak score. Even in the remaining 25%, the disagreements were often between closely related categories, as when one would score Level 1 Oral, the other Level 2 Oral, or between one and another form of Ag 2.

In the case of the data I am going to present, the scoring was originally done for another study in which interest was focused on the safely reliable overall scores like % total pripro. Therefore, I cannot assure you with any degree of confidence just how reliable the scoring of specific categories was. On the basis of past and present investigations of scorer reliability with other samples, however, I feel confident that the level of agreement on the individual category is about that of traditional Rorschach determinants, about 65% (Voigt and Dana, 1964). These findings should be viewed with some healthy skepticism when they are based on single samples and not very large groups of Ss. Wherever possible, I have sought to test their trustworthiness by looking for replication, or at least for as close parallels as possible in other samples. I am encouraged by the findings I have been able to pull together, because results from independent studies tend to support one another, and the agreement with psychoanalytic theory is often impressive.

INTRATEST CORRELATES

Before I present some data on concurrent validities of the content scores, let me briefly report on some interrelations among them and certain other scores derived from the Rorschach itself. Since this is a progress report on a sizable attempt to review and evaluate the scoring system preliminary to publishing it in full, it will be regrettably but necessarily fragmentary. As of this writing, I do not have available a matrix showing the intercorrelations of all the primary-process scores yielded by my manual, because the computer available to me did not until too recently have a capacity large enough to produce it. At present, for example, I do not know how the libidinal and aggressive categories are interrelated in my two principal samples.

The first correlations I shall present derive from two composite samples, one normal and one schizophrenic. The constituent subsamples are a pooling of subjects from my own studies plus those of five friends and colleagues, four of whom were graduate students of mine. I am very grateful to Drs. Douglas Heath (1965), Benjamin Lapkin (1962) James McMahon (1964), Theodore Saretsky (1961), and Lloyd Silverman (1963; Silverman, Lapkin, & Rosenbaum, 1962) for permission to borrow and make this use of their scored Rorschachs.

The great majority of the 121 normal subjects are males, and most of them undergraduate students at Haverford College and the New York University School of Education; but 50 are unemployed members of New York Actor's Equity. Of the 81 schizophrenics, 61 were chronic cases, middle-aged men in VA hospitals, the remaining 20 being adolescents of both sexes from a residential treatment center in New York. I have no particular brief for these as samples of any very meaningful populations; the best that can be said for them is that they are available, and the basic Rorschach data are good, having been collected and scored by persons I trained and can vouch for. The scoring is so time-consuming that it is no easy matter to build up large samples.

Let us take a look now at Table 11.1. This presents the intercorrelations of the raw totals for all the libidinal categories, the numbers above the diagonal deriving from the normal sample, those below the diagonal from the schizophrenics. In addition, correlations of each variable with R are presented, and mean frequencies per record at the far right. It may be helpful to get an orientation by considering the means, first. Notice that there is a very considerable range of frequency, some categories occurring

Table 11.1. Intercorrelations of Libidinal Categories (Uncorrected Frequencies) 121 Normal Ss *above* Diagonal; 81 Schizophrenics *below* Diagonal

	Libidinal Level 1						Libidinal Level 2						No. of R	Means	
	O	A	S	E-V	H	M	O	A	S	E-V	H	M	R	Normal	Schiz.
L 1 O	x	.27	.33	.17	.08	.07	.26	.01	.24	.18	.07	.35	.45	.60	.15
L 1 A	-.02	x	.30	.14	.21	.00	.06	.10	-.08	.01	.11	.17	.11	.17	.11
L 1 S	-.05	-.03	x	.16	.57	.25	.18	.09	.32	.27	.18	.21	.10	.86	.40
L 1 E-V	-.06	.08	.28	x	-.10	.25	-.09	-.01	.05	.08	-.11	.08	.03	.07	.02
L 1 H	-.05	-.02	.19	-.02	x	.29	.22	.11	.28	.11	.01	-.25	.04	.12	.01
L 1 M	-.03	-.03	.38	-.03	.36	x	.12	.02	.30	.12	.06	.02	.18	.10	.06
L 2 O	.32	.25	.05	.02	.04	.01	x	.17	.34	.32	.13	.24	.35	3.28	1.10
L 2 A	-.03	-.04	.38	.09	-.06	.07	.22	x	.01	.13	.12	.18	.14	1.03	.24
L 2 S	.13	-.04	.03	.21	-.03	-.06	.05	-.06	x	.17	.19	.11	.19	.16	.09
L 2 E-V	-.07	.01	-.01	-.05	.08	-.08	.03	-.02	-.01	x	.09	.15	.39	1.90	.83
L 2 H	.03	.04	.09	-.04	-.09	-.07	.04	-.05	-.02	.35	x	.07	.19	.82	.36
L 2 M	-.04	-.02	.07	-.02	-.01	-.02	.11	-.06	-.03	-.08	-.08	x	.36	.40	.01
No. of R	.10	.07	.10	.06	.06	-.04	.53	.24	-.04	.27	.13	.16	x	39.6	18.6

fairly often, others almost never. Such Level 2 Oral (L 2 O) responses as food, smoking, or emphasis on the mouth in describing a face have very little social taboo to overcome, while direct references to anal anatomy or feces, scored L 1 A, just as obviously are strongly barred from ordinary polite conversation betwen strangers. The rarest category of all seems to be Level 1 Exhibitionistic-Voyeuristic, scored only for references to nudity. Since that is not such a shocking thing in itself, the low frequency may have several other causes: perhaps this motive is not an important one in our culture (which seems doubtful if you have passed a newsstand lately; see also the substantial frequencies for L 2 E-V); or it may be a reflection of the meager opportunities the standard ten blots offer for visualizing nudists. The role of differential "card pull" is difficult to assess, but it must be there to some extent.[4]

Why not aim for simplicity as well as higher mean frequencies by combining Levels 1 and 2? I must confess that the figures in this table do not encourage me in such a step: in no instance is the Level 1 form of a wish more highly correlated with its Level 2 version than with anything else, except for orality in the schizophrenic sample. Maybe I have not chosen the best set of dimensions for this realm altogether, though I have exercised no originality here but have followed the rubrics suggested and supported by the clinical experience of many psychoanalysts. In any event, I hope that a factor analysis will help provide some suggestions for a possible reorganization. In that connection, let me call your attention to the fact that the one variable that is most consistently and highly correlated with all of the others, in both samples, is L 1 S. Perhaps the general factor that is clearly present in the positive manifold of the normal sample will center on Level 1 Sexual responses; that would be an unexpected confirmation of Freud's insight in classifying all of these partial drives as libidinal or sexual.[5] Finally, the central position of L 1 S is *not* attributable to its being highly correlated with R, the number of responses; by contrast, many of the interrelations among the Level 2 libidinal categories seem to be mediated by their common relationship to R, since when the number of responses is partialled out, all of the latter correlations fall below significance except those of L 2 O with L 2 S (**.30**) and L 2 E-V (*.21*).

---

[4]In the particular case of L 1 E-V, a good many responses that may come about because of strong and unsublimated interest of this kind may not be so scored: seeing sexual acts or organs, which are scored Level 1 Sexual; the substantial correlation between L 1 E-V and L 1 S in the schizophrenic sample tends to support this hypothesis, though I have no idea why it does not occur in the normal Ss. But then, L 1 E-V is uncorrelated with anything else in this table except for L 1 M, a miscellaneous category including images of menstruation, urine, birth, and contraceptives.

[5]The one with which it has the most negligible correlation in the normal sample is L 2 A, yet the two are strongly related in the schizophrenics. The reason, I believe, is that L 2 A includes, in addition to responses like "dirt" and references to buttocks, in which I have some confidence, two other subclasses of very dubious meaningfulness: references to the tails of animals, and rear views, which are the kinds of responses mainly responsible for the relatively high frequency of L 2 A.

The pattern of interrelationships for the schizophrenics' data is rather different, there being many more negative and insignificant correlations. Yet L 1 S is central there too, and a similar pattern of interrelatedness exists among L 1 S, L 1 H, and L 1 M, again quite unmediated by *R*. I do not believe that this particular triad would have been predicted from psychoanalytic theory, though clinical experience teaches us to expect persons with strong homosexual motives to give many overt sex responses.

If we turn to the aggressive categories, in Table 11.2, we notice first that there are many fewer significant correlations and less obvious evidence that any one variable is central. This is rather surprising, when you reflect that aggression is considered by most psychologists to be a more nearly unitary realm than the libidinal (as defined by psychoanalysis). Among the normal *S*s, the central variable appears to be Ag 2 A-S, despite the fact that it is only the third most popular in terms of mean frequency (but note that it has the highest correlation with *R*). As with the libidinal variables, I find it striking that the highest coefficients obtain within Level 1: perhaps this fact bespeaks a stylistic tendency to go "all out," and if you start being outrageous in one way to "let 'er rip," across the board. There are very few cross-relations between subject and object aggressive scores, however, within Level 1, while the two object-aggression categories are correlated, as expected, with Ag 1 R. It seems, therefore, that even though it is very rare for any extreme images of murderous or gory destructiveness to occur at all in normal *S*s, when they do it is in either a sadistic or masochistic pattern—which is conspicuously absent in our schizophrenic sample. Remember that these psychotics are mostly VA patients, generally chronic cases without florid secondary symptoms; it is appropriate to the usual metaphor applied to them, "burnt-out," that the aggressive category with the most correlations, for them, is Ag 2 R, the results of aggression. In a sample of fulminating, acutely psychotic cases, I should expect much higher incidence of Level 1 Aggression; it is noteworthy that these men, who averaged about ten years older than the normals, had even fewer Ag 1 responses. The only explanatory comment I can offer about the highest coefficient in the schizophrenic matrix, the **.53,** is that the two variables involved are both of the object, or passive, masochistic variety—but I have no idea why just these two (Ag *1* P-O and Ag *2* A-O).[6]

Two factor analyses have been done with some of the grosser summary scores from my Rorschach manual and a miscellany of other measures of personality (see Table 11.3). There are remarkable convergences between these two independent analyses, though none of the non-primary-process variables were the same, and strikingly different samples of *S*s were used.

Heath (1965) factored the intercorrelations of eight primary-process

---

[6]It may seem surprising that Ag 2 P-O is uncorrelated with any other aggressive score, in either sample; most of what little gets scored here used to occupy my Anxiety category, being images of frightened or endangered people or animals. Ag 1 A-O has been omitted from the schizophrenic matrix because of an error in the computer program.

Table 11.2. Intercorrelations of Aggressive Categories (Uncorrected Frequencies) 121 Normal Ss *above* Diagonal; 81 Schizophrenics *below* Diagonal

	Aggressive Level 1					Aggressive Level 2					No. of R	Means	
	P-S	P-O	A-S	A-O	R	P-S	P-O	A-S	A-O	R		Normal	Schiz.
Ag 1 P-S	x	−.02	**.59**	−.03	−.05	.07	.17	.16	.03	.01	.02	.06	.03
Ag 1 P-O	−.03	x	.22	−.01	**.49**	*.19*	−.04	.07	−.04	−.02	−.04	.004	.03
Ag 1 A-S	−.03	−.04	x	−.04	.10	.07	.03	.22	−.03	−.00	.06	.10	.06
Ag 1 A-O*				x	**.33**	−.05	.06	.22	.08	.02	.02	.02	
Ag 1 R	−.02	−.02	−.02		x	.17	.04	*.19*	.02	.14	−.01	.18	.01
Ag 2 P-S	.15	−.08	.20		−.10	x	.10	**.28**	*.19*	*.25*	**.33**	4.10	2.26
Ag 2 P-O	.18	−.07	−.08		−.05	.06	x	−.04	.00	.09	.22	.26	.12
Ag 2 A-S	.02	.16	.03		.04	**.29**	.14	x	*.20*	.10	**.39**	1.63	.65
Ag 2 A-O	−.03	**.53**	−.04		−.02	.12	−.07	.15	x	.03	.21	.21	.05
Ag 2 R	.01	.11	.09		−.03	**.39**	−.02	**.30**	.26	x	**.37**	3.48	1.43
No. of R	.08	.18	−.02		−.07	**.53**	.11	**.34**	**.43**	**.51**	x	39.6	18.6

*Through a mechanical error, this variable was omitted from the schizophrenics' matrix.

Table 11.3.   Comparison of Two Factor Analyses Including
Primary-Process Variables

Heath (1965)		Kahn (1965)	
Factor I (12.4% of variance)		*Factor I (24.3% of variance)*	
	Loadings*		Loadings*
Ror: % Formal	−.93	Ror: % Formal	−.92
% Level 1	−.87	% Ag 1 Content	−.74
% Content	−.71	% Lib 1 Content	−.65
Sum DD	− 52	Mean DD	−.67
Incongruence of self-image	−.73		
MMPI: Sc	−.63		
D	−.60		
Pd	−.58		
Hs	−.52		
Bernreuter: Nonsocial	−.56		
AVL: Political value	−.51		
Ror: Mean DDxDE	.74		
Mean DE	.68	Ror: Mean DE	.70
Content DD/Formal DD	.57	Form Level accuracy	.69
Clin. eval.: Organization	.64	Psychiatric eval.: Sane	.57
d%	.51		
PT: Adaptive improvement	.59		
Factor II (7.3% of variance)		*Factor II (14.5% of variance)*	
Grade average	.86	Education (years of)	.32
Maturity of self-image	.76		
Self-organization (judged)	.75		
Bernreuter: Dominance	.64		
CEEB: Verbal ability	.52	WAIS: Verbal IQ	.93
Terman Concept Mastery Test	.51	Full scale IQ	.97
TA-S: Score on threat items	.50	Performance IQ	.93
Rorschach: Number of Populars	.49		
% Level 2	.43	Rorschach: % Level 2	.39
Cognitive skill test	.44		
SVIB: Occupational level	.42		
Instability of self-image	−.59		
Bernreuter: Neuroticism	−.55		
MMPI: Si	−.48		

* 13 loadings of .40 to .49 are omitted. Loadings are approximately in order of descending size in the Heath study; when possible, a corresponding or comparable variable from the Kahn study has been placed on the same line. "TA-S" is a special thematic cognitive task devised by Heath; this score measures the ability to perform despite the "load" of threat in certain items. "PT" is his Phrase Association Test. For details about these and his self-image measures, see Heath (1965).

variables, plus ten other Rorschach measures (mostly Klopfer's scores), scores from his PT (Phrase Association Test); the SVIB; measures of congruence, stability, maturity, etc., of the self-image; MMPI scales; AVL values; the CEEB test; Terman's Concept Mastery test; the Bernreuter test; and a number of behavioral ratings and scores on specific cognitive tasks. His sample was 24 Haverford College students. Kahn (1965), on the other hand, factored a matrix of 17 Rorschach primary-process variables, plus four from the WAIS and 18 rated (or counted) measures from the clinical histories of 43 convicted murderers—aspects of their past adjustment, social class, nature of the crime, etc. Both solutions were orthogonal, and both were done by computer, but using different methods of rotation; neither knew of the other's work.

In both analyses, the first factor, which accounts for most of the variance, is most heavily loaded with primary-process variables, centering on % *Formal* with virtually the same negative loading. Level 1 and Content scores and DD also have high negative loadings, and DE a high positive loading. In Kahn's analysis, the only non-Rorschach variable to show up was the psychiatrist's judgment, on the basis of the history, of whether the prisoner was "sane" or "insane," which is paralleled in Heath's study by psychotic and other pathological scales from the MMPI. Perhaps an Eysenckian would identify this factor as "psychoticism"; Heath called it "Allocentrism-Autocentrism," while for Kahn it is "Primitive undefended primary process versus perceptual adequacy and good defense." In the study by Silverman *et al.* (1962) % Formal proved to be a prime indicator of psychosis, being in effect a measure of thought disorder.

The second factor in both cases is mainly a matter of the available measures of intellectual ability, with which is associated % Level 2, again with strikingly similar loadings! Heath calls it "Competence-Incompetence," Kahn "Intellectual Level." It would seem, then, that the ability to produce civilized or socially acceptable manifestations of the primary-process characterizes persons of superior cognitive competence. I am reminded of the psychoanalytic proposition that at its highest levels of effectiveness, secondary-process thinking still needs access to affect, to be used as a signal in judgment.

PERSONALITY CORRELATES OF MOTIVATIONAL MEASURES

I want now to turn to another set of tables of correlations, each of which presents measures of personality that are correlated .3 or better with a category from the Rorschach. The sample is the same 50 unemployed actors mentioned above; they were intensively studied during the years 1959–1961 at the Research Center for Mental Health, during which time they were used in a variety of experiments, took many tests of cognitive style and personality, including incidentally the WAIS, the IQ from which was not significantly related to any of the categories to be discussed here.

We assessed the personalities of our 50 Ss in two principal ways: first, we interviewed them, got them to write autobiographies, administered standard projective techniques like Rorschach and TAT, and collected on each man a dossier of these qualitative data plus the WAIS. Each member of the

Research Center's staff, about half of whom were advanced graduate students of clinical psychology, was assigned as "biographer" for one or two Ss. He studied the material in the folder, reached some tentative conclusions, and then called the man in for a final focused interview plus a Self-Interpretation of the TAT (Luborsky, 1953). After that, he recorded his judgments about the S in the form of ratings on a nine-point scale on each of 150 variables, which were culled from various sources (particularly from the variables used in personality assessment at the Harvard Psychological Clinic when I worked there as a graduate student). Subsequently, Dr. Harriet Barr of our staff had all of these variables intercorrelated and identified highly interrelated clusters on the one hand, and certain other items that had too little variance to be useful or had other psychometric disqualifications. The result of this statistical working over was a group of 74 usable, relatively independent, and apparently meaningful as well as face-valid measures of personality. I call your attention to the fact that the Rorschach was part of the dossier, but not the primary-process scoring; only a few of the judges were familiar with the scoring system, so the ratings have only a negligible degree of direct contamination. On the other hand, it should be kept in mind that the scoring system does reflect in part the processes of clinical analysis and interpretation that influence some of the ratings.

The second set of assessments are completely free of any such contamination: they are the objective test scores, which were not seen by the clinical raters. I am reporting correlations involving 74 scores taken from the following: Grygier's Dynamic Personality Inventory (1955), Guilford's Brick Uses (Guilford, Kettsur, & Christensen, 1954), Morris's Paths of Life (Morris & Jones, 1955), a few scales from Jenkins's How Well Do You Know Yourself? (1962), three tests of cognitive style, and Barron's (1953a) Ego-strength scale from the MMPI.

Since there were 148 items with which each Rorschach variable was correlated,[7] it is obvious that many correlations might have arisen by chance alone; and because of the uneven pattern of intercorrelations among the measures of personality, it is impossible to say that exactly 1.48 correlations of .36 or larger should turn up by chance for every variable since that is the .01 level for 48 degrees of freedom. As I view it, the question of the statistical significance of correlation coefficients is a rather academic one anyway, especially in the context of a fishing expedition such as this one obviously is. Nothing that I have to report to you should be taken with any great degree of confidence that it will turn up in another sample, except for the few points I can tell you about on which there is some replicated evidence. I am presenting these correlations as descriptive, not predictive statistics: they describe relationships that did obtain within one rather specialized and

---

[7]A heroic task which would have been impossible without the devoted and skilled labors of Philip Halboth, whom I wish to thank for his help with the computer.

unusual sample of young men. Some of them make such eminent good sense theoretically that they seem not to be determined by the parameters of this sample; others are intelligible primarily in terms of our actors' special characteristics. To anyone with any experience in this kind of personality research, however, it is an old story that very high and extremely "significant" correlations disappear or stand on their heads when one turns to another sample.

In the following tables, I have adopted the simplifying procedure of including only correlations of .30 or larger. By the conventional criterion, that puts most of them on the angelic side of the 5% level; more to the point, as I see it, is the fact that their absolute magnitude is large enough to begin to be interesting (see Cohen, 1965).

Let us warm up by glancing quickly at Table 11.4, which presents the correlates of the basic score yielded by the Rorschach, the number of responses, or R. A purely statistically minded hardnose might notice first of all that this table contains fewer than 7.5 correlations that are significant at the .05 level, and quite aside from the fact that I could have included a few .29s, the real point of the matter is that the two largest correlations are entirely consistent with clinical expectation: it is a well-established diagnostic rule that depression holds down responsiveness to the Rorschach, even (as here) within the normal range, and it is equally familiar from clinical experience that a wide range of interests tends to push R up. Clinical lore is not that supportive of the negative correlation with isolation, and I suspect that it is relatively specific to this sample. The main point I want to establish, however, is that we need to keep in mind only a few variables as strongly related to R, which I had gambled on because I have not expressed the rest of them as percentages of R as might have been prudent. For accidental and extraneous reasons, it would have been quite difficult.

Table 11.4.   Personality Correlates of Total Number of Rorschach
Responses (R)

Clinical ratings
−.46 Easily feels depressed, ashamed, inferior; turns hostility against himself
−.41 Has narrow interests
−.34 Uses isolation as defense
−.31 Experiences diffuse anxiety readily
−.31 Has diffuse and conflictful identity

Test scores
−.30 Importing (Paul, 1959) (p = .06)
−.30 Color-Word Interference (Stroop)

Note: N in this and all subsequent tables is 50 for correlations with clinical ratings; for test scores, it varies between 37 and 50. Hence, coefficients of identical size may have different significances.

Table 11.5.   Personality Correlates of Libidinal Level 1, Oral
Responses (L 1 O)

Clinical ratings
.39 Seeks and enjoys sensuous and/or sensual experience (n Sentience)
.35 Ego autonomy composite
−.34 Orderly and thrifty (n Order, n Retention)
−.33 Defensive and guarded
−.33 Suggestible and dependent on others to take initiative
−.33 Separation from or rejection by paternal figures an important
source of anxiety
−.32 Feels sexually inadequate
−.32 Has vivid imagery

Test scores
.37 Cholinergy (Jenkins)
.34 Cognitive flexibility (Brick Uses)
.33 Achievement motive (Scale Pa, DPI*)
.33 Creative, intellectual interests (Scale CI, DPI)
.32 Enjoyment of visual pleasures (Vistorexis, Jenkins)
.31 Interest in objects of phallic symbolic significance (Scale P, DPI)
.30 Initiative, self-reliance (Scale EI, DPI)
−.37 Passivity (Scale Wp, DPI)

---

*Dynamic Personality Inventory (Grygier, 1955).

With Table 11.5, we start to get into the meat of my presentation, if you'll forgive an oral metaphor (scored L 2 O, R-fig). Let me call to your attention a couple of themes here. First, these directly oral responses characterize men who enjoy sensory intake, and whose defensive and cognitive style seems open and flexible rather than compulsive and defensive. Rather surprisingly, they seem predominantly not to be infantile, passive oral characters but the opposite: active copers who take the initiative, feel adequate, and are effective. The best test correlate, Cholinergy, is defined by Jenkins (1962) as "a resilient tendency to feel energetic, happy, enthusiastic, secure, or optimistic." This is a pretty good match to the psychoanalytic conception of the "satisfied oral character."

Incidentally, the correlation with the Dynamic Personality Inventory's measure of creative interests is paralleled by an internal correlation of **.41** with the rated creativity of Rorschach responses, and by correlations of *.33* with two adaptive types of controls, successful reflection on the response process and successful use of contexts.[8]

Table 11.6, the correlates of the similar Level 2 Oral category, presents quite a congruent picture: again, we have ego autonomy and cholinergy, and openness to sensory pleasures (this time indicated by several of the Jenkins

*Throughout the text and tables, coefficients printed in *italics* are significantly different from zero at the .05 level (two-tailed); those in **bold face** are significant at the .01 level.

Table 11.6.   Personality Correlates of Libidinal, Level 2, Oral Responses (L 2 O)

Clinical ratings
.38 Ego autonomy composite
−.52 Self-punitive, disillusioned
−.40 Has a narrow range of interests (−.*32* with *R* held constant)
−.39 Has vivid imagery
−.38 Passively aggressive
−.37 Easily feels depressed, ashamed, inferior; turns hostility against himself (−.27 with *R* held constant)
−.*32* Feels unloved and unwanted
−.*31* Has diffuse and conflictful identity (−.24 with *R* held constant)

Test scores
.43 Cholinergy (Jenkins)
.*38* Enjoys nonmusical auditory sensations (Auditory orexis, Jenkins)
.*36* Has a strong desire for sexual stimulation (Sexorexis, Jenkins)
.*36* Expresses self in an uninhibited, natural, and enthusiastic manner (Emotional Spontaneity, Jenkins)
−.*37* Embedded figures, total time
−.*33* Colors alone, reading time (Stroop Color-Word)

scales) versus defensive narrowness. A new theme emerges, however, or a slight twist on the general effectance associated with L 1 O: instead of the test indications of creativity and achievement drive, we see indications of some rather specific cognitive competences. The more L 2 O responses, the shorter the time taken to disembed the figures in Witkin's version of the Gottschaldt test or to name colors in the noninterference series of the Stroop Color-Word test;[9] Guilford's measure of flexibility in shifting cognitive categories also yields a correlation of .*28* with L 2 O.

Happily, there does exist an independent body of confirming data in the work of von Holt and his collaborators (1960). In two successive samples of 27 and 23 college students, both male and female, my near-namesake was surprised to find that the sum of Level 2 Oral responses was positively related to solving the Hanfmann-Kasanin test ($p < .05$ in both samples, Mann-Whitney test). The hypothesis that occurs to me about these findings, aided by the data in Table 11.6, is that the receptive openness to experience connoted by L 2 O, particularly when the emotional stimulation of color is involved (as it is in both the Stroop and the Witkin EFT as well as the Hanfmann-Kasanin), enables the subject to keep looking analytically at complex visual stimuli without being shocked or disturbed by them until their many sensory attributes can be registered separately. (Jenkins' vistorexis scale was correlated with L 2 O to the extent of $r = .28$.) The tightly

[9]This is a partial replication of my finding that persons who did well on the Stroop (by a more complicated criterion than the ones used here) had significantly more L 1 O responses than those who performed badly (Holt, 1960c [Chapter 9]).

organized man, who does not have the kind of basic trust that Erikson (1950) describes as the desirable outcome of the oral phase, is in quite an unconscious way less able to drink in stimulation and therefore may be at a disadvantage in tasks requiring the conflict-free exercise of the receptive mode.

Through the kindness of a colleague, Dr. John S. Sullivan, I am able to cite some supporting data from an unpublished study of 44 volunteers for the Peace Corps who were trained at New York University a few years ago (Sullivan & Bernstein, 1963). They were given Rorschachs and a good many other tests, and my scoring system was applied to the Rorschach data, though with some modifications. Thus, the distinction between levels 1 and 2 was disregarded, and the sum of all oral responses for each S was divided by his total number of primary-process responses. This oral measure was significantly related to a number of others, most notably to the Social value (from the Allport-Vernon-Lindzey; $r = .42$) and to need Nurturance (as measured by Edwards' PPS; $r = .42$). The benign and kindly attitude toward others implied by these scales seems congruent with the general picture conveyed by Tables 11.5 and 11.6: It seems as if happy and satisfied men tend to generate images of open mouths, breasts, and sucking (L 1 O), or of food, drink, and associated objects and activities (L 2 O). But who else could look at an ink blot and find it running with milk and honey? Truly, for such a person, the world must be a good place.

I feel less willing to venture a hypothesis about why L 1 O should seem to be related to creativity and L 2 O to problem-solving, particularly because of indications from the internal correlations in the schizophrenic sample that the Level 2 response is associated with rated creativity of response and with measures of good control. There are several instances of contrasting or inverse patterns of relationship in the normal and schizophrenic samples, which deserve to be replicated and inquired into further.

Let us take a step up the psychosexual ladder with the aid of Table 11.7.

Table 11.7.   Personality Correlates of Libidinal, Level 1, Anal
Responses (L 1 A)

Clinical ratings	
.34	Regresses in the face of stress; sees self as immature and childlike
−.34	Intellectualization and intellectuality
−.33	Ego autonomy
−.30	Exhibitionistic, exclusive, feels superior
Test scores	
.52	Embedded figures, total time
.35	Unconventionality of outlook (Scale Ou, DPI)
.31	Interference score (Stroop Color-Word)
−.31	Creative, intellectual interests (Scale CI, DPI)

It does not look like much progress! But then, what can you expect of subjects who create an imagined world of feces and explicit anal anatomy? It appears from these correlations that they are somewhat decompensated intellectualizers who are far from being able to use their cognitive capacities either creatively or in problem-solving. Perhaps the tendency to project images of filthy messes, into which no one would like to look too deeply, seriously interferes with the ability to extract a figure from a rather messed-up design.

There is other evidence, from intratest correlations, that L 1 A indicates a somewhat more general malfunctioning of intellectual abilities: among the actors, the formal category Autistic Logic (Level 1) is correlated **.61** with L 1 A. This score is given for attempts to cast one's discussion of a response in a syllogistic form but with absurd or illogical results; thus, it is a kind of stab at an intellectual procedure which gets rather badly botched. My system contains another category, among the controls, that is even more directly related to intellectualizing: Cx I, or Intellectual Context, which is scored as either effective (plus) or ineffective (minus). In the sample of 81 VA schizophrenics, the correlation between L 1 A and Cx I− is (coincidentally, and very strikingly) **.81**! This is an exceedingly high correlation, enough to make one suspicious that it might be in some way an artifact of the scoring procedure itself; yet in the normal sample of 121, the corresponding coefficient was −.01!

With the oral scores, we found indications of what Abraham (1924) and Freud described as oral character traits; now, with the anal score, you may be wondering about the no-show of the familiar anal triad of negativism, orderliness, and thrift (Freud, 1908b). Remember, however that intellectualization is a prime defense of the obsessive-compulsive type, which is a more generalized way of describing the principal type of anal character-structure. Recall too that any such character-structure may take adaptive (compensated or healthy, if you will) and maladaptive (decompensated or pathological) forms. It is interesting that oral responses here were associated with adaptive forms of oral character formation, anal responses with maladaptive forms of the anal character. The difference, I believe, lies in the different degrees of social acceptability of the two types of imagery, plus the fact that reaction formation plays a larger role in the development of even the adaptive kind of compulsiveness than in oral character-formation. Therefore, only when an anal personality is poorly compensated and has not developed effectively operating opposites of messiness, or when it is seriously broken down as in a psychosis, do we encounter the emergence of such socially unacceptable responses as L 1 A's. Even then, it may take some degree of unconventionality for the nonpsychotic subject to mention it to the examiner.

There is relatively little to add about L 2 A, the supposedly more socialized form of anal imagery; its correlates are in Table 11.8. The strongest correlation suggests that queasy and easily disgusted persons may avoid

Table 11.8.   Personality Correlates of Libidinal, Level 2, Anal
Responses (L 2 A)

Clinical ratings
−.33 Goal striving in the face of frustration

Test scores
−.39 Tends to be disgusted or sickened by some foods (Food Aversiveness, Jenkins)
−.33 Colors alone, reading time (Stroop Color-Word)
−.32 Importing (Paul, 1959) (−.26 with R held constant)
−.31 Self-satisfied, socially conforming (Scale H, DPI)

even the indirect allusions to the rear end that make up this rather unsatisfactory category. The others are scanty and suggest no consistent pattern;
the same situation obtained in Sullivan's data. I am inclined to blame the
scoring criteria, which I may have let become too remote from anality in an
effort to keep this category from being so infrequently scored as to be
useless.

Table 11.9 takes us to the more attractive realm of sex, in which I make
no attempt to apply the psychoanalytic distinction between phallic and
genital since the visual subject-matter is essentially the same. L 1 S differs
very little from the usual content category, Sex, but I have not come across
published studies of its personality correlates. Perhaps that is because others,
too, have not found many of them, despite the fact that this is the most
frequently scored of the Level 1 Libidinal categories. Aside from the correlation with the Jenkins scale of sexual interest, which poses no interpretive
problems, Table 11.9 seems to contain mostly indications of the kinds of
defensive style that are relevant to telling the tester that you see sexual
organs or acts in his dirty pictures: in a sample of such free souls as actors,
where the average subject gives a sex response, anyone who does not is likely
to be smug, prim, or poorly controlled. It is interesting that in the total

Table 11.9.   Personality Correlates of Libidinal, Level 1, Sexual Responses
(L 1 S)

Clinical ratings
−.35 Uses reaction formation as defense
−.34 Has weak relationships with people; withdrawn
−.30 Fears losing control over his aggressions
−.30 Thinks in a ruminative, circumstantial, overdetailed fashion; vacillates

Test scores
.31 Has a strong desire for sexual stimulation (Sexorexis, Jenkins)
.49 Has unconventional outlook (Scale Ou, DPI)
−.38 Fascinated with height, space, and distance (Scale Ph, DPI)
−.34 Self-satisfied, socially conforming (Scale H, DPI)

normal sample of 121, which is dominated by male college students, the strongest nonobvious intra-Rorschach correlate of L 1 S was Cx I− ($R =$ .68). I am reminded of Anna Freud's (1936) observations about the growth of intellectualizing as a defensive struggle against sexual preoccupation in adolescents; when the preoccupation comes into the open, the defense is not working well.

The more socially acceptable version of sex is love and romance, which is the general theme of responses scored L 2 S (Table 11.10). The correlates of this score are puzzling on two counts: they suggest two unrelated clusters of pesonal attributes, neither of which has any obvious relation to sexuality. A hypothesis occurs to me, however, that makes some sense out of this table: the subjects are unemployed and mostly unmarried male actors in the age range when most men marry and settle into job and family, while these fellows are still struggling to get a foothold in a cruelly competitive, chancy profession. In such a plight, the actor with ego strength who is able to concentrate on the major task at hand, his work, will do well to shut out thoughts of love and marriage, and those who lack these achievement-oriented strengths will let longings of a relatively sublimated sexual kind into their conscious thoughts. At the same time, another subgroup in our sample seem to have excluded this kind of wishful fantasies because they feel unloved (and would find such thoughts threatening) or because they are too narcissistic to be oriented toward love. All of this is pretty speculative, because the base rate for L 2 S is low: the blots do not present many areas that lend themselves to such images as sweethearts kissing, wedding rings, or cupids.

The remaining three types of Libidinal Level 1 responses occur too seldom to be very meaningfully correlated with anything else (in the normal sample, their mean frequencies were all about one-tenth of a response). Since L 1 E-V and L 1 H were both significantly correlated with L 1 M, I combined the three and threw the resulting miscellany into the actors'

Table 11.10. Personality Correlates of Libidinal, Level 2, Sexual
Responses (L 2 S)

Clinical ratings	
−.40	Concentrates easily, not distractible
−.31	Positive attitudes toward work and responsibility (incl. n Ach)
−.40	Oversensitive to challenge and threat
−.31	Narcissistic, with fluid affect
−.30	Feels unloved and unwanted
Test scores	
.35	Importing (Paul, 1959)
−.33	Counteractively persistent (Scale EP, DPI)
−.30	Ego strength (Barron)

Table 11.11. Personality Correlates of Miscellaneous Libidinal
Level 1 Scores (Σ L 1 E-V, H, and M)

Clinical ratings
−.42 Uses reaction formation as defense
−.38 Fears losing control over his aggressions
−.35 Orderly and thrifty (n Order, n Retention)
−.33 Defensive and guarded

Test scores
.44 Cognitive flexibility (Brick Uses)
.35 Has unconventional outlook (Scale Ou, DPI)
.32 Consciously accepts sexual impulses (Scale S, DPI)
−.32 Gets upset by outstanding colors (Color Shock, Jenkins)
−.31 Conservative, rigid, sticks to routine (Scale Ac, DPI)

correlational matrix; Table 11.11 presents the outcome. The kinds of responses involved stress nudity; hermaphroditism or overtly homosexual responses; menstruation, childbirth, and urine. Pretty strong meat, and not for the easily shocked, conventional, compulsive person; so the correlations with clinical ratings and most of the correlations with test scores tell us. The sort of person, even in as bohemian and partly homosexual a group as actors, who comes right out with responses of these types not only has to be free of rigid, conventional proprieties, he is also likely to accept his own sexuality and to have considerable associative flexibility.

The only one of these three miscellaneous libidinal themes I shall consider further, because it is the only one that has any substantial frequency on Level 2, is the Exhibitionistic-Voyeuristic. My scoring scheme differs from most others in classifying responses that emphasize eyes and the acts of looking and peering as libidinal, on the strength of the classical psychosexual theory. Actually, even Freud wrote in a number of places (e.g., 1905d, 1910c) about nonsexual curiosity, and it is clear from the standpoint of modern ego-psychology that the primarily autonomous visual function can become drawn into the orbit of either libidinal or aggressive wishes. I should have realized that the extremely widespread superstition of the "evil eye" implies the weighting with hostility that such workers as Elizur (1949), Murstein (1956), and Holtzman *et al.* (1961) have incorporated into their scaling of hostility. At any rate, that is what turned out to be the fact in the actors; I correlated L 2 E-V with all the other primary-process scores, partialling out its substantial correlation with R (.52), and it ended up not significantly related to anything, but more highly correlated with aggressive than with libidinal scores. Though the coefficients are low, L 2 E-V is more closely related to Ag 2 P-S (.23) and to Ag 2 A-S (.27) than either is to any score except to one another.

If the meager batch of personological correlates in Table 11.12 say anything, they tend to agree: the related variables are measures of rather

Table 11.12. Personality Correlates of Libidinal, Level 2, Exhibitionistic-Voyeuristic Responses (L 2 E-V)

Clinical ratings
.38 Rebellious and defiant of authority (n Autonomy: Resistance)
−.33 Seeks substitute gratification in fantasy when frustrated
−.30 Uses undoing as a defense

Test scores
.31 Feels a need for freedom of movement and emotional independence (Scale OM, DPI)
.31 Likes adventure and active, pioneering exploration (Scale Pi, DPI)
−.36 Conservative, rigid, sticks to routine (Scale Ac, DPI)

---

sublimated derivatives of aggression—rebellion, rejection of dependence, impatience with authority and conservative conventions, and adventurous exploration (though there may be an implication of curiosity in that last DPI scale). There is a bit of slightly supportive evidence from Sullivan's Peace Corps trainees: his percent E-V score was most highly correlated with the Political Value (A-V-L; $r = .38$). One might expect the looking theme to be related to well-contained and controlled forms of aggression in this last sample, but it is particularly impressive that it showed so little libidinal tinge in the actors, who are involved in one of the most exhibitionistic of professions. But the phenomenon of stage fright ought to convince us that all those eyes out in the audience are a potential threat to an actor; the acceptance and recognition which the audience can also give are conveyed perhaps more to the actor's ear than to his own eye, but the Rorschach cannot tell us much about that.

Now that we have crossed the Great Divide of the dual instinct theory, let us consider next Table 11.13 and the Level 1 Aggression scores. Again, I grouped the varieties of Level 1 Aggression because of the rare occurrence of any of these gory, sadistic responses in a normal population—which is as it should be! These correlations suggest that the few Ss who did give Level 1 Aggression responses were among the least "normal" members of this theat-

Table 11.13. Personality Correlates of Level 1 Aggression Scores (Σ Ag 1 P-S, A-S, P-O, A-O, and R)

Clinical ratings
.42 Given to inferential thinking and primary-process intrusion
.34 Regresses in the face of stress; sees self as immature and childlike
.33 Seeks substitute gratification in fantasy when frustrated
−.34 Heterosexual versus homosexual

Test scores
.30 Values pragmatic adventurous action (Paths of Life, 6)
−.35 Values passive receptivity (Paths of Life, 9)

---

rical sample: those whose sexual orientation was primarily homosexual, and who showed signs of pathological regression in behavior and thought. Of course, the clinical rating of one item may have been much influenced by such primary-process manifestations in the Rorschach as Ag 1: "His thinking and speech generally show much evidence of the primary process," which was combined with the strongly correlated item "Highly given to inference; tries to figure out hidden meanings, reasoning in a biased and sometimes arbitrary way." The **.42** correlation may accordingly be discounted some-what, but not, I think, entirely. Note that the conscious values of these Ss stress the active versus the passive life, yet they are apparently not remarka-ble for their ability to act effectively, so that their bloody, violent fantasies may be substitutive gratifications occasioned by frustration.

Thanks to Dr. Marvin Kahn, who has made available to me some of his unpublished data, I can tell you about some of the correlates of extreme aggressive responses in a group of people all of whom have acted out in a way that would be scored Ag 1: murderers. In his sample, those who produced gory images—Level 1 Aggression—were more often psychotic (r = **.40**; the principal alternative being psychopathic personality), and tended to be young siblings (**.44**) in large families (**.48**) who, moreover, tended to have killed persons of close kin (r = .26). Perhaps the low man of the sibship is at the uncomfortable end of the pecking order and has the most competi-tors for whatever amount of parental love may be available; if there is not much, it is conceivable that such frustrations could foster murderous fanta-sies. It is instructive that not all murderers by a long shot react with Level 1 Aggressive responses to the Rorschach, only those with deeply injured personalities, people who probably harbor sadistic retaliatory fantasies for years before acting them out.

With responses scored Ag 2 P-S, we get at last to some decent frequen-cies; this category has the highest mean occurrence in all groups, the actors giving on the average almost five of these responses. Many kinds of potential aggressive threats occur in Rorschach responses: dangerous animals, threat-ening people, witches, devils and monsters, weapons, claws and teeth, volca-noes, etc. One might expect, therefore, that the next table (11.14) was going to

Table 11.14. Personality Correlates of Level 2, Potential Subject-
Aggression Responses (Ag 2 P-S)

Clinical ratings
−.33 Easily feels depressed, ashamed, inferior; turns hostility against himself
−.30 Orderly and thrifty (n Order, n Retention)

Test scores
.31 Ego strength (−.10 with R partialled out) (Barron)
.30 Self-reliant and takes initiative (Scale EI, DPI)
−.34 Obtains satisfaction from many kinds of odors (Olfactorexis, Jenkins)

---

be a fat one; but not so. There are not only not many correlations, but they are low and do not make a particularly intelligible picture.[10] Nevertheless, the actor who reported few of this kind of aggressive responses seems to have had difficulty in handling his own aggressive impulses, while being able to come out with plenty of them characterized the more self-reliant ones. Note, however, that the correlation with Barron's Ego Strength scale completely disappeared when R was partialled out.

My confidence in these results is not increased by comparing them with findings from the NYU Peace Corps trainees. Perhaps the closest thing to self-reliance in the variables that were appreciably correlated with the score, Sum of Ag P-S divided by total primary process, was the surgency scale from Cattell's 16 PF test—but this enthusiastic, lively versus glum, sober characteristic was correlated −.45. Similarly, the cyclothymia scale (warm, sociable versus aloof, stiff) was correlated −.38 and the Edwards PPS n Nurturance measure −.42 with potential subject aggression. In Sullivan's sample, there was a marked antithesis between this aggressive score and the libidinal ones, and a parallel tendency for Ss whose primary-process scores contained a large proportion of Ag P-S to lack warmth and vitality. Not surprisingly, they were given low ratings by their peers on leadership ($r = −.46$) and on predicted success in the mission (−.46). To be sure, this measure of aggression is not directly comparable with my uncorrected sum of Ag 2 P-S, and I cannot say that I can see a clear rationale for this particular ratio.

The story of what ought to be the next table, the personality correlates of Ag 2 A-S (active, subject-aggression, Level 2) is short and sad: it was unrelated to anything except the clinical rating "Plays the role of clown when with others" ($r = .32$). This is the more remarkable in view of the fact that it was correlated with a number of variables in the larger normal and schizophrenic samples; of all the primary-process categories, it was correlated most highly with human movement (.62), animal movement, (.37), and IQ (.22), and it was the only motivational variable to be significantly associated with youth in both of the large samples: the correlation with age is −.41 in the schizophrenics, −.33 in the normals. It is intelligible that the young man's type of response would be one in which fighting or destroying of some kind is actively going on, but within socially tolerable limits. Why, then, is this not a good predictor of active, vital struggling of some kind, among the actors?

Perhaps the trouble lies in the peculiarities of the sample; but if we look to the Peace Corps, we find cold comfort. The proportional measure of active, subject-aggression was correlated at the 1% level with only the following miscellaneous variables: Radical versus Conservative attitudes (16 PF; $r = −.48$), Theoretical value (A-V-L; −.42), and Computational interest (Kuder; −.42).

[10]It may be that the relationships with aggressive responses are predominantly curvilinear, as J. R. Smith and Coleman (1956) found them to be.

By now you will not be surprised to learn that the mirror image of this supposedly sadistic subject-aggression, namely object-aggression, is not better as a predictor of personality variables. Since there were decidedly fewer of either the potential or the active subtype than of any of my other aggressive scores, I combined Ag 2 P-O and Ag 2 A-O; examples of responses scored as Level 2 object-aggression are "a frightened face"; "people falling down stairs." This might at least seem a promising measure of anxiety; but my net brought up only the four highly miscellaneous minnows of Table 11.15.

In a follow-up to the assessment of the Peace Corps trainees, Sullivan and Bernstein (1963) report one striking and seemingly paradoxical finding: the biserial correlation between completion versus noncompletion of overseas assignment and percent Ag A-O was *plus* **.48**! The only other Rorschach variable to predict this criterion was a measure of the *in*effectiveness or inefficiency of controls and defenses for primary process. It happened, however, that the assignment to an African country came at a particularly unhappy time, when the people the Peace Corps volunteers were supposed to work with were involved in a border war. For this and for other reasons, there was very little the Americans could do that was constructive, while they were exposed to danger and considerable privation. Apparently the adaptive reaction under such circumstances was to pull out; judging by the ostensible meaning of the correlated Rorschach score, the ones who stayed expected, or were in some way positively oriented toward, being the objects of active aggression.[11]

Table 11.16 presents the last of these correlational results, the presumed motivational measure this time being Ag 2 R, results of aggression: broken objects, wounded animals, people with parts missing, and the like. About three and a half such responses may be expected in a normal record of 40 *R;* it is the second commonest aggressive score, the kind of thing traditionally interpreted by Rorschach workers as an indication of castration anxiety.

Table 11.15.   Personality Correlates of Level 2, Object-Aggression Responses
(Ag 2 P-O, Ag 2 A-O)

Clinical rating
−.30 Narcissistic, with fluid affect

Test scores
.32 Has strong drive for achievement (Scale Pa, DPI)
.31 Interested in children, needs to give affection (Scale C, DPI)
.31 Expresses self in an uninhibited, natural, and enthusiastic manner (Emotional Spontaneity, Jenkins)

[11]As Sullivan and Bernstein (1963) point out, this particular Peace Corps mission was anomalous in having the smallest number staying to the end; not a single one of the Peace Corps' own predictive variables was correlated with the criterion of completing the mission.

Table 11.16.   Personality Correlates of Level 2, Results of Aggression Responses
(Ag 2 R)

Clinical ratings
.30 Oversensitive to challenge and threat
.30 Concentrates easily, not distractible
.30 Uses projection and externalization as defenses
−.39 Separation from or rejection by maternal figures is an important source of anxiety
−.39 Has an adequate amount of reasonable self-esteem

Test score
−.32 Reserved and mistrustful, socially and ethnically prejudiced (Scale Ai, DPI)

Only the first of the correlated clinical ratings would appear to offer support to that assumption, plus perhaps the indication that these "injured" responses are given by people with weak self-esteem. I confess that I can make little sense of the rest of the correlations; and the few results from the Peace Corps trainees do not help much: it is unclear why Character or Superego Strength as measured by the 16 PF should be positively related (r = .43), though it makes some sense that castration anxiety should hold down sexual interest as measured by the Edwards PPS Heterosexual scale (−.49). Perhaps the 16 PF Superego scale actually measures guilt.

What are we to conclude about the measures of aggression that I have put forward? The results surely do not suggest that I hit upon a particularly happy way of cutting up the realm of hostility with my five-way division. In retrospect, it strikes me that I made entirely too simple an assumption that there was something sadistic about seeing potential or active aggressors. I forgot the basic lesson I had learned from Murray (1933) many years ago: that apperceptive projection may be either complementary or supplementary. That is, a snarling tiger may be seen in an ink blot by a person who fears and expects encountering hostility from others, or by someone who himself tends to be an active aggressor. Those who have divided the same realm up to make two scales, of anxiety and of hostility, may have had the better hunch.

Two leads about promising alternative ways to deal with the aggressive categories come from research by others who have been working with my scoring manual. In a series of interesting and significant studies which are unfortunately a little too complicated for me to summarize briefly enough here, Silverman (1963; Silverman *et al.*, 1962) has obtained good results by weighting the scores according to their DD values. Let me refresh your memory that the manual provides a rough scaling of the "shock value," outrageousness, or intrinsic demand that some kind of defense be instituted, for each type of scorable response. For example, an unelaborated image of "a wolf" gets a DD rating of 1, which is minimal; "a volcano," 2; "an erupting volcano" or "bloody headless bears," 3; "worms eating the eyes of a rabbit," 4;

"witches tearing a baby apart," 5. It would be relatively easy to add together the DD values instead of just counting aggressive responses, and if the experience of such workers as Murstein and Holtzman is any guide, it should provide a more useful measure.

The other idea is to take account of both drive and control categories simultaneously in statistical analyses, just as the clinician does.[12] In a striking study comparing the mothers of children who were schizophrenic, neurotic, and normal, Lavoie (1964) developed a successful way of doing this. *First,* for each response with scorable libidinal and/or aggressive manifestations, the separate DD values for all formal deviations of thinking in that response are added together, to provide an estimate of formal deviation for that response (which he calls *Fd*). *Second,* for each response with libidinal and/or aggressive manifestations, the manual's separate DD values for *all* manifestations of primary process in that response, either content or formal, are added up to provide an estimate (PP) of the total overt contribution of the primary process to that response. *Third,* this estimate (PP) is multiplied by the defense effectiveness score (DE) of the response, to provide an estimate of the level of adaptive regression *(Rego)* for that response. *Fourth,* the *mean* scores of formal deviations *(Fd)* occurring together with, let us say, aggressive manifestations, are obtained by adding together the *Fd* values of all aggressive responses and dividing the sum by the number of aggressive responses. Lavoie thus computed separate indexes for *Fd, PP, DE,* and *Rego* in (a) responses with primary-process manifestations of any kind, (b) responses containing at least one libidinal score, (c) responses containing at least one aggressive score, and (d) responses containing both an oral and an aggressive manifestation. He compared mothers of normal, neurotic, and schizophrenic children on each score, and then repeated all three kinds of comparisons (a, b, and c) with oral-aggressive responses taken out of the analyses.

By this method, he found many significant differences between mothers of schizophrenics and mothers of neurotics, the former having more formal deviations of thinking, especially of the level 1 type, and more poorly controlled primary-process scores of various kinds. He demonstrated, further, that there was a specific impairment in the mothers of schizophrenic children with regard to *oral aggression.* Their mean level of adaptive regression in oral-aggressive responses was not only lower than for mothers of the other groups, but all the differences with the mothers of neurotic children, with respect to primary process, defense effectiveness, and adaptive regression disappeared when oral-aggressive responses were taken out, although most differences concerning formal deviations of thinking remained significant.

---

[12][The work of Olweus (1969, 1973) strongly suggests that such an approach would be useful. He found that he could predict the overt aggressive behavior of boys from a measure of aggressive content in TAT stories only when combined with a measure of inhibitory control.]

Heath (1965) describes a similar method of considering drive and control simultaneously, making use of the rating of Defense Effectiveness for the latter purpose. He simply added up the DE scores for every response containing oral content, for example, which was treated as a measure of the adequacy with which orality was controlled. He then correlated this measure with an "anxiety threshold score" for items dealing with the theme of desertion (from his Phrase Association Test or PT), partialling out both the total number of Rorschach responses and the total score on the PT; the resulting coefficient was −.34, significant at the .10 level. The stimuli of the PT are five-word sentences, to which S is to respond with a brief phrase as quickly as possible; stimulus items suggest (among other themes) desertion of children by mother and father, aggressions toward the parents, and hetero-sexual relations; the responses are scored for various indicators of anxiety, like laughter, excessive length, fragmentation, etc. Using this same method, Heath also found correlations of −.33 between well-controlled aggressive responses in the Rorschachs of his Haverford students and poor control on aggressive PT items, and −.39 between well-controlled sexual responses to the Rorschach and poor control on sexual items of the PT; all p's less than .10 (two-tailed tests).

DISCUSSION

As I indicated earlier, I did not set out with the intent of turning the Rorschach into a test of specific motivational constructs, but rather with the hope of devising a way to pick up operational indicators of Freud's concept of the primary process. The cognitive theory epitomized by that concept assumes that there may be an intimate relation between motives and thought or perception, but also that cognitive functions may demonstrate considera-ble autonomy; hence, observable products of a person's cognitive activity may fall just about anywhere on the continuum between the logical poles of the primary and secondary processes, which are conceived of as ideal types. Although Freud's theory antedated the New Look of a couple of decades ago by almost half a century, it was a good deal more sophisticated in allowing for the actual variety of effects instead of the simple prediction that needs would distort perception.

It is this matter of the relative autonomy of cognition that stands in the way of nice, simple measuring devices based on projective techniques. As Klein (1956) puts it, if needs influence perception, how come we see the world so accurately most of the time? The answer may be found in the structures that develop, mediating veridical contact with reality and restrain-ing impulse; they are represented to some extent in my scoring by the controls and defenses. A good case can be made for the proposition that people differ a good deal more in the ways they cope with their wishes than in the basic strength of motives. By this token, the control and defense categories of the primary-process manual ought to be better predictors of independent personological measures than the content scores, and I believe that they are. At least, for a sample of 20 of the control scores, the mean number of correlations of .30 or greater with clinical assessment ratings was 5, while the corresponding mean for the motivational variables is 4. Since we have already had more than enough tables of correlation coefficients, I am going to leave the assertion at that, with a hint that I shall eventually publish the full results.

There is surely no support for a tension-reduction view of motivation in the data I have presented. According to that theory, a particular kind of wish would show up, other things being equal, in the Rorschach responses of people who had the wish in a strongly aroused but frustrated state. We found, instead, that such oral responses as images of food were given by men who were clinically evaluated as having been well-fed with love, not by those who had been deprived.[13]

Moreover, most of the time the personality correlates make best sense as indications of the types of people who are unable to keep certain kinds of preoccupation out of mind, or who have styles of inner control that allow affect-laden topics of conversation to be communicated to an examiner. In thinking about these results, I was reminded of some apt remarks made by Kagan (1964) in a recent discussion of personality assessment:

> The most significant change in thinking about human behavior is a gradual displacement of the traditional and overworked constructs of sexual, dependent, and aggressive motivation from a primary to a subordinate position, and the introduction of theoretical language describing cognitive standards and discrepancies from these standards. The loss in appeal of the concepts of hostile, sexual, or dependent motives arises from two sources. First, we acknowledge that these motives are typically linked to defensive responses that block behavioral expression of these wishes. As a result of this inhibition, it becomes difficult—and perhaps impossible—to assess motive intensity from the presence or absence of goal related behavior; for this behavior is not free from the contaminating effect of defensive tactics. Unfortunately, this statement is no less true if we substitute interpretation of projective stimuli for overt goal related behavior. . . . [Second,] *human beings develop standards about their behavior.* One of the major determinants of the occurrence of a class of responses is the person's cognitive evaluation of the degree of consonance between a response (it can be a thought) and the cognitive standard surrounding it [p. 151].

Can the Rorschach, then, be used to measure such standards and other cognitive controls that enter into motivation, if not the hypothetically under-

---

[13][I have deliberately used *men,* not *people,* because Rosen (1971) found that oral scores had quite different significances for male and for female college students.]

lying drives themselves? My answer would be a cautious and qualified yes.[14] I am encouraged enough by the convergence of similar findings from a variety of studies when more or less comparable data are available to feel affirmative; but not if one has in mind to transform the Rorschach into a specifically focused measuring instrument. Like other projective techniques, its great strength lies in its openness, the diversity of data it provides from different *S*s, and the broad range of possible inferences that can be drawn from it. The most I hope for from my research is to facilitate the process of clinical inference and to help clarify ways in which Rorschach data can be used to derive hypotheses about personality. But no research is going to make it into a first cousin of the Stanford-Binet as a measuring instrument; it will remain almost as diffuse as it is broad, and inferences based on it will necessarily be more probabilistic than is implied in the usual concept of measurement.

The apparatus of pseudoprecision in my method, I want to emphasize in closing, is simply a function of the exigencies of research. To test hypotheses, and even to facilitate the exploration of a large mass of assessments in relation to the Rorschach, it is necessary to treat qualitative scoring categories as if they were well-designed interval scales, which of course they are not. We *should* make as much use as we can of psychometric refinements in efforts to do as little violence to the nature of the data as possible, and to extract from the data as much of their clinical essence as may be. In the end, however, I do not expect formulas to emerge from all my fiddling with the computer, which will displace or surpass the trained clinical interpreter. Rather, I hope to come up with some ways of helping him understand better the nature of his data and some leads for the inferential, interpretive process.

---

[14]It is interesting that Klein (1961, p. 190) predicted that my attempt to measure primary process in the Rorschach would be significant mainly as a way of getting at cognitive style.

Other Methods

12

When David Rapaport taught me the clinical use of diagnostic psychological tests in 1946, the Szondi test (Szondi, 1947) was in routine use as part of the standard battery given virtually all patients at the Menninger Clinic. Unlike the others, it had virtually no semantic content, posed no adaptive challenge (thus requiring no perceptible ability), and was virtually unknown in this country outside of Topeka. Rapaport had learned it in Hungary and brought it with him as an empirically useful tool, which he hoped to learn to understand by using it.

A few years after my initial introduction to it, the Szondi test began to be generally available as a good deal of interest was stirred up by Deri's (1949) book. The following paper was published during this period, when the Szondi test was well-enough known to make a description seem superfluous. For a few years, papers on the test appeared in professional meetings and journals, but then it dropped out of sight. The research that was published was almost entirely negative, except for the present piece, and no satisfactory rationale was ever published. American psychologists were repelled by Szondi's (1952) own fanciful pseudobiological notions and the test seemed to violate common sense.

It consists of six sets of eight photographs of faces, on small cards. The examiner lays them out in a standard order, saying, "I am going to show you some faces. Look them over quickly and point to the one you like the best." After the subject does so, the examiner continues, "Which do you like best of the ones remaining?" Then he obtains two dislikes in the same way, in each instance removing the picture chosen, recording the identifying code on its back and beginning four piles in front of himself. They proceed in the same manner through all six sets, until there are four piles of selections. The examiner then spreads out the first of these, saying, "These are the ones you liked best. Take another look and show me what one you like best of all. . . . Which one do you like next best?" Similarly, he obtains judgments for the other extreme piles. The pattern of choices constitutes his data.

Each set contains one photograph of a person from the following groups: overt homosexuals (h), sadistic murderers (s), epileptics (e), hysterics (hy), paranoid (p) and catatonic (k) schizophrenics, depressives (d), and manics (m). Choices are classified as likes (+) or dislikes (−) in each of the preceding eight factors, which are grouped into four pairs referred to as vectors.

Another unusual feature of the test was the fact that it was supposed to be administered not once but repeatedly, preferably half a dozen times on different days. Any one momentary pattern of choices was said to be in large part a function of momentary states of the subject, so that only the temporal pattern was reliably characteristic and thus interpretable. Since to follow such a prescription was a nuisance, it was *widely ignored; most of the research allegedly intended to validate the Szondi made use of but a single administration. So in addition to the usual factors that plague test validation research (Holt, 1967g), ignoring this important aspect of Szondi's test doomed it to the appearance of invalidity while it was not being given a fair chance.*

The power of fashion should not be underestimated in psychology. The following paper attracted little interest from those who were eager to condemn the Szondi, and the test's few partisans were not research-minded enough to replicate and extend my findings; or perhaps they were deterred by the enormous labor of computing all the required correlations—an obstacle that has been brushed aside by the era of the computer. The paper has, of course, all the weaknesses of any piece of N = 1 research (see Vol. 2, Chap. 8). Fortunately, the decision to reprint the paper made me realize that I had neglected it for years, and now a student (Marie Lombardi) has replicated it with six subjects. We shall publish the results separately, but I can state here that they are positive, albeit in a complicated way. That is, for each subject there are at least three times as many strong and significant correlations between Szondi variables and questionnaire items as would be expected by chance, but the pattern is different in each case. Yet the existence of much more convergence in the lists of correlates than would be expected by chance, for most Szondi variables, indicates a small but meaningful common core of validity across at least seven subjects, of both sexes and from varying subcultures.

An Approach to the Validation of the Szondi Test through a Systematic Study of Unreliability

Research work with projective techniques is teaching us more sophisticated and basically valid conceptions of reliability. In the earlier days of psychological testing, we thought that a test was reliable if it (or its component parts, or equivalent forms) always gave us nearly the same scores. As soon as one starts dealing with more variable features of personality than total intelligence, using tools which are sensitive enough for the purpose, he discovers that it is unreasonable to require a test always to give the same results. Such a requirement would make sense only if we could properly conceive of personality as a static, fixed entity, instead of the dynamic (that is, moving and changing) process that it is. Would a pilot in the Rockies want a "reliable" altimeter that always gave the same reading? Certainly not. In such a case the instrument's validity would depend on its giving constantly changing values, as long as the plane was in motion. Of course, when the actual distance between plane and ground was constant, the reading should be also. A barometric altimeter, which varies with humidity as well as altitude, would then be less reliable than one which worked by radar.

A personality test that always gave the same results with the same subject would, like a watch that didn't run, have only a specious or *phenotypic reliability*. What we want instead is that a test should have *genotypic reliability:* that is, that there should be as constant as possible a relationship between any particular aspect of a test, such as a score, and its determinants in personality and situation. As it stands, the definition just given seems to imply the familiar constancy hypothesis of mechanistic psychology, which Köhler (1929) has so brilliantly shown to be as untenable as it is unfortunately widespread. It is just as fallacious in physics as in psychology, too: a physical phenomenon, such as the ascent of mercury in a barometer, does not have an invariant relationship with any one causal factor, such as atmospheric pressure. True, there is invariance in that a change in pressure (from a change in either altitude or weather) will produce a predictable rise in the column of mercury *under controlled conditions,* but the last specification means just that other events may likewise send the mercury up or down (such as temperature or surface tension).

Mercury barometers are not useless and to be discarded just because their scale readings are overdetermined. Fortunately, we know the principal sources of variance and can allow for them with tables which have been prepared for the purpose. In psychology, we do not discard the Rorschach test because an Experience Balance of 1:1 does not always have the same meaning, even though we have not gone far enough in quantification to provide tables of corrections. We use instead the inexact but workable clinical method in which we give meaningful consideration to the total pattern in order to illuminate the significance of any of the parts, and seek as much knowledge as possible of the subject's total situation at the time of testing so that allowance may be made for the influence of variable factors which the test is sensitive enough to reflect.

The study reported here proposes to make use of this very kind of sensitivity in order to test the validity of interpretative hypotheses that have been made about one projective technique, the Szondi test. The logic underlying the study is as follows: if there is a causal relation between the strength of a motive and choices of a certain type of picture, then investigation of their relationship may proceed by correlating choices with variations in the strength of the motive. Such variations may be obtained either by using a variety of subjects, who may be expected to have differing strengths of the motive, or by using a single subject at times when the motive's strength fluctuates. The former method is the one usually employed in validational studies, but I believe the method of the single subject has important advantages. One of the great difficulties in the way of statistical validation of projective techniques is the objection that one cannot take a single quantitative score out of its context and meaningfully correlate it with a criterion. Why not? Because in different patterns, for example, 4M may mean creative thinking, or introversion, or the presence of delusions, or Rorschach only knows what all. To a great extent, however, one gets around this difficulty by working with one subject at different times. Thereby many important psychological variables are controlled; all, in fact, that do not change appreciably during the period when the subject is studied. Thus the method of correlating single test measures with criteria is made a good deal more legitimate and more likely to yield results. There is less likelihood that existing relationships will be disguised or exaggerated by uncontrolled and unknown factors.

Of course, there does remain the possibility that a functional relationship found in one personality may be relatively specific to that one, and may not occur in others. It is still desirable to use as many subjects as possible for this reason. But the method of single subjects can get around this last objection even better than the usual cross-sectional study using many subjects. It is hard to know how to sample the total population of all possible kinds of personalities; most validational studies (except those done in connection with certain intelligence tests) don't even attempt to do so. Random sampling is out of the question, and one would hardly know how to stratify such a sample. The truth is that most of us don't seem to think of such considerations most of the time anyway, and consequently we have no way of knowing how far to generalize our results, or to what extent they are affected for better or for worse by the homogeneity or heterogeneity of our samples of personalities. We can at least avoid the last-named difficulty by taking subjects one at a time and getting as wide a variety of people as possible.[1]

Another principal stumbling block in the way of all validational studies remains: providing a satisfactory criterion. At this point, the traditional but somewhat malodorous expedient of validating one test against another with equally unknown validity becomes necessary. All that can be claimed for such efforts as these is that the meaningful consistency of results constitutes presumptive though not coercive evidence of validity.

What serves as a criterion in this study is a series of self-ratings. Perhaps the best way to clarify the point would be to describe the procedure. A single subject, a male college senior 24 years of age, was the subject; he was paid for his time. Starting in August 1948, he was tested every Thursday afternoon (except for a two-week period at APA convention time) for ten sessions; after a lay-off of about three months, there were two more sessions, again a week apart. On each occasion he was given the Szondi test, filled out a revision of the Horn Repeated Questionnaire, and took the Murray Mind Reading Test, a kind of abbreviated TAT; some diary materials were also obtained. These projective and autobiographic data will be further described, and their relationship to the Szondi test results reported, in a subsequent article.[2]

It should be stated that I got not only the questionnaire but the basic

---

[1]For a further discussion of methodological points treated in the preceding section see Holt (1950a). [That paper is too outdated to be included here; see instead Vol. 2, Chap. 8.]

[2][The subsequent article was never written, because the Mind Reading Test responses showed too little variability to permit any correlations to emerge and because the diary was too stereotyped and fragmentary to prove useful.]

technique of studying the covariation of "unreliable" test items as an approach to personality from Dr. Daniel Horn, who originated the latter idea, though interesting work with it has also been done by Cattell and Luborsky (1950). I collaborated with Dr. Horn on some early trials of the repeated questionnaire technique a number of years ago at the Harvard Psychological Clinic. His questionnaire was a condensation of some larger ones by Dr. H. A. Murray, and consisted of 100 items of the following sort: "1. I give my time and energy to those who ask for it." The unique feature of the instrument is its extended rating scale, deliberately designed for pheno-typic unreliability. It is a 12-point scale with no dead average; one is to rate the extent to which each statement is true of himself, as compared with his college associates as a group. The subject is instructed not to try to remember his previous ratings, but to rate himself each time as he feels at the moment. The hundred items contain in random order several statements bearing on each of 17 needs. To these I added 30 statements about other aspects of personality which, according to Rapaport's and my experience, seemed related to the eight Szondi factors.

The rationale of the repeated questionnaire assumes that variations in self-ratings of a need are related in some way to fluctuations in the intensity or readiness for gratification of the motive.[3] The exact nature of this relationship is obscure, though studies of the present kind may help us to develop some hypotheses about it. Even so, it seems reasonable to assume that if a measure obtained entirely independently, such as the number of choices in a Szondi column, is correlated highly with self-ratings on a questionnaire item, the two have a dynamic relationship. The simplest assumption is that both are effects of a common cause, namely the need that the item specifies.

RESULTS

In discussing the correlates of the Szondi variables, I should state first that some questionnaire items could not be correlated with anything simply because the subject gave himself nearly the same self-rating throughout, perhaps using only two adjacent points on the scale. Consequently, the absence of certain expected correlations cannot be taken as evidence that these expectations are based on false premises. For similar reasons, some of the theoretically possible Szondi measures that were tried varied too little in this particular case to show any relationship to anything else.

[3]Note that it is not necessary to assume the validity of self-ratings—only that they are *in some relatively constant way* related to the personality variables in question. This is a decided advantage of using a series of one subject's self-ratings as against single ratings by a large number of subjects, in which case it is necessary to assume that all subjects have some insight, and to about the same extent.

The use of correlational approach is novel in the Szondi technique; consequently there were no guide lines to assist in the choice of variables. All of the following were tried, therefore: the number of plus choices in any column, the number of minus choices, total choices (whether liked or disliked), and algebraic sum of plus and minus choices—four measures for each of the eight factors, making 32. At the time this experiment was designed, Deri's (1949) book was not available and the significance of the vectors was not clear to me; nevertheless eight additional measures were tried: the total of likes and of dislikes, separately, for each of the four vectors.[4]

One very general result that emerged from the giant matrix, when each Szondi variable was correlated with each item in the questionnaire, is that the correlational approach does seem to be a fruitful one. Large numbers of significant correlations appeared. Quite a few would be expected by chance alone, of course; since there was a great deal of dependence among the variables it is difficult to say how many, but it seems unlikely that so many large coefficients arose from random fluctuations. So many are there, in fact, only those that attain the 1% level of confidence (.70) are chosen for comment.

The relevant coefficients are to be found in Table 12.1. The following brief discussion is organized around an attempt to check the obtained findings against Deri's assumptions and interpretations as set forth in her book (1949), with which the reader is assumed to have some familiarity.

The correlates of h all may be easily reconciled with Deri's statements. It is an aspect of sexuality that is measured, she says (cf. #68), and specifically the tender, dependent (cf. #88) and passive type (cf. #60). What is puzzling is that the direction of the relationship runs in an opposite direction for the dependent, succorant item and the passive one (passivity being considered an opposite to counteractive effort). The correlate of negative choices in this column merely underlines the relationships to sexual (#26) needs implicated in the items correlated with the algebraic sum of h choices.

The other presumably sexual factor, s, should be expected to show an opposite direction in its correlations with sexual items, and so it does. Whereas the positive tendency in the h column (as measured by algebraic sum of h) was *positively* correlated with a diffuse sexuality item, the total likes of s pictures is negatively correlated with the same statement, #68. In this respect, it behaves somewhat like the dislikes of h, again as would be predicted from Deri's rationale.

[4][These "vectorial" variables were highly correlated with but few questionnaire items and seemed to add little. I therefore omitted them from Table 12.1, but neglected to explain their absence in the published paper. The original text went on to comment that total choices proved most useful. I have deleted the sentence, because in the replication study, cumulative figures across seven subjects show that number of dislikes was consistently most fruitful, followed by total choices.]

Table 12.1. Items from Self-Rated Questionnaire Correlated at 1% Level with
Selected Szondi Test Variables

Total h choices versus:

88. I tell my troubles to anyone who will listen (*n* Succorance) −.76

60. I try over and over again until I succeed at a difficult task (*n* Counteraction) −.70

Algebraic sum of h choices versus:

68. I seek sexual experience whenever possible (*n* Sex:Diffuse) +.79

Total dislikes of h versus:

26. I am inclined to select and fall in love with one girl (*n* Sex:Focal) −.76

Total s choices versus:

53. I rebel against dogmatic views and standards (*n* Autonomy:Resistance) +.74

13. I am shrewd in buying things cheap and selling them at a profit (*n* Acquisition) −.84

Total likes of s versus:

68. I seek sexual experience whenever possible (*n* Sex:Diffuse) −.89

Total e choices versus:

59. I prefer the company of men to the company of women (Latent *n* Homosexual) −.81

119. I have a strong sense of property and dislike to lose things through lending them (Anality; *n* Retention) −.73

87. I amuse myself with one girl after another (*n* Sex: Diffuse) −.72

Total likes of e versus:

87. I amuse myself with one girl after another (*n* Sex:Diffuse) +.71

Total dislikes of e versus:

119. I have a strong sense of property and dislike to lose things through lending them (Anality; *n* Retention) −.71

Total likes of hy versus:

23. I avoid dangerous situations and endeavors (*n* Harm avoidance) +.72

100. I enjoy doing something perfectly (*n* Achievement) +.70

4. I tend to boast of my claims to recognition (*n* Recognition:Exhibition) −.78

Total k choices versus:

9. I rely on the advice, consolation, or aid of an older person (*n* Succorance) −.74

Algebraic sum of k choices versus:

35. I sometimes have the desire to bully or hurt a weaker person (latent *n* Aggression:Sadism) −.70

Total likes of k versus:

88. I tell my troubles to anyone who will listen (*n* Succorance) +.75

Algebraic sum of p choices versus:

80. I like to commend or cheer a good performance (*n* Deference:Respect) +.82

53. I rebel against dogmatic views and standards (*n* Autonomy:Resistance) +.72

68. I seek sexual experience whenever possible (*n* Sex:Diffuse) −.72

Total d choices versus:

90. I stick at a task until I am satisfied with results (*n* Achievement) −.75

80. I like to commend or cheer a good performance (*n* Deference:Respect) −.73

Total likes of d versus:

1. I give my time and energy to those who ask for it (*n* Nurturance) +.71

Table 12.1 (*continued*)

Total m choices versus:

59.	I prefer the company of men to the company of women (latent *n* Homosexual)	+.84
110.	I love to eat (Orality; *n* Nutrience)	+.80
119.	I have a strong sense of property and dislike to lose things through lending them (Anality; *n* Retention)	+.79
124.	My idea of a good time is a stag party with plenty to drink (Orality; latent *n* Homosexual)	+.78
100.	I enjoy doing something perfectly (*n* Achievement)	−.86
58.	I sometimes indulge in self-pity (*n* Succorance:Intra-Nurturance)	−.84
125.	Sometimes I feel that I am not worth a darn (*n* Intra-Aggression:Ego-Ideal)	−.84
120.	I often think how I look and what impression I am making on others (*n* Recognition; Dependence on the opinion of others)	−.83
85.	I worry about the possibility of failure (*n* Infavoidance)	−.81
1.	I give my time and energy to those who ask for it (*n* Nurturance)	−.80
106.	I am systematic and methodical in my daily life (Compulsiveness; *n* Order)	−.78
74.	I like all sorts of people (*n* Affiliation:Diffuse)	−.76
73.	I am strongly attached to certain of my possessions (*n* Retention)	−.76
31.	I feel strong affection for some people (*n* Affiliation:Focal)	−.72

Algebraic sum of m choices versus:

4.	I tend to boast of my claims to recognition (*n* Recognition:Exhibition)	+.82
98.	I occasionally have daydreams in which I take the role of a powerful, omniscient leader (latent *n* Dominance:Omnipotence)	+.74
100.	I enjoy doing something perfectly (*n* Achievement)	−.73

Total likes of m versus:

4.	I tend to boast of my claims to recognition (*n* Recognition:Exhibition)	+.77
98.	I occasionally have daydreams in which I take the role of a powerful, omniscient leader (latent *n* Dominance:Omnipotence)	+.73
100.	I enjoy doing something perfectly (*n* Achievement)	−.81
2.	I am cooperative and obliging, responsive, and respectful to my superiors (*n* Deference)	−.70

Total dislikes of m versus:

90.	I stick at a task until I am satisfied with the results (*n* Achievement)	+.83
10.	I am more apt to give in than to continue a fight (*n* Abasement)	+.82

Note: The parenthetical indications of the variables to which the items pertain are of course not included in the Repeated Questionnaire.

Aggressively toned items should also be related to some of the *s* measures, however, and we look in vain for any correlate involving direct anger or its physical expressions. Knowing the subject, however, I do not find this surprising; he is a disarmingly friendly, even-tempered fellow who is much too well-mannered to get into brawls (the characteristic position of the *s* factor was minus). He does express hostility verbally at times, however; and it is in the verbal form of *n* Autonomy:Resistance (#53) that an aggressive item correlates with *s*. Item #13 is very puzzling; perhaps a hitherto unsuspected relationship between *s* and some kind of acquisitive need may obtain. Or it may be that the kind of shrewd business practice that is described represents a disguised, socially approved form of aggression for the subject. He dislikes the business world, though he prepared himself in college to enter it, and was at the time of the testing considering other less competitive kinds of employment, such as teaching.

Choices of epileptics, we are told, give a clue to controlling functions imposed on aggression, chiefly of a superego nature. What we see in the correlates of the e measures, however, is principally the sexual need, which the subject was keeping under satisfactory control (#87, #59). In an interview he blamed his lack of sexual satisfaction on his moralistic training. The superego function may well be involved, then, but not exclusively in its campaign against derivatives of aggression. The table shows us that it is principally the positive e choices that are entailed in this correlation. Is it then that the more pictures of epileptics he likes, the more he plays around with girls? Just the opposite state of affairs should, according to Deri, obtain, for the likes represent control, the dislikes a release of inhibition. Here we must remember that we are dealing with a man's *self-ratings*—the extent to which he feels a statement to be true of himself at the moment. It may well be that a high self-rating on even an item that refers to overt behavior, like #87, is really a measure of motive frustration much more than an accurate report of what the subject is currently doing. In general, this interpretation seems to help in understanding many of the correlations.

Item #119 was made up as a compulsive, anal characteristic aimed at d, but here it is tagging along with e, principally via dislikes. Perhaps its flavor of "proper" behavior and slightly moralistic tone may help us to fit it in under the concept of superego control. But we should not deceive ourselves with such facile *post hoc* reasoning. The explanation may fall plausibly upon some ears, but the relationship was not a predicted one, and it should be looked on as an indication that further research is needed.

For some obscure reason, the only measure of hy to yield correlations as high as .7 was the sum of likes. Its strongest relationship is with the very item that should theoretically be associated with positive hy choices: the exhibitionistic statement #4. The other correlations are both positive and may represent in the case of #100 "really doing something" instead of just boasting. The place of #4 in the cluster of items correlated with m (see below), strengthens this argument. Making a boastful show is for this subject a compensatory device in which he never actually engages to a noticeable extent, but which he may feel some urge toward when he is at a low ebb in his compulsive efforts. The n Harmavoidance item, #23, does not fit in with any of these trends; rather its covariation with an hy measure reminds us of the meaning of the hysterical column as a gauge of anxiety—something I should be inclined to stress more on the basis of my limited experience with the Szondi test than Deri does.

According to her, k measures (among other things) the narcissistic self-sufficient (thus, independence-seeking) trends in a person—especially the positive choices. And, indeed, plus k and the total of all k choices are correlated with dependent (n Succorance) items, #88 and #9. But the latent sadism item is a puzzler. Can it be that when the subject is feeling more independent, less bound by convention, that he is able to admit to himself more usually repressed aggressive urges? Hardly; for the more positive the k column, the *lower* his self-ratings on this item! I am unable to find any consistent explanation for the sign of this correlation.[5]

The psychological meaning of p, as set forth in *Introduction to the Szondi Test*, is vaguer (or, if one prefers, subtler) than that attributed to any other factor in the test. It might be paraphrased as some kind of expansive outreaching of libido toward objects. Such a concept may be linked to items #80 and #68; the only difficulty is that the correlation in one case is positive, negative in the other, while both items are on the surface positive statements of "outgoing libido." What to make of the n Autonomy:Resistance item (#53) in this context is difficult to know. It has little of the sound of the p factor as Deri presents it. It is of course possible to build up a rationalization of it, but it might be possible to do so for many other items; meanwhile, those that were tailor-made to tap the mild projective trends often shown by the subject failed to correlate significantly with anything in the Szondi test.

Anal compulsive trends (said to be indicated by the d column) are well-enough represented by item #90, though it is disappointing to find that self-ratings on so many other items presumably affected by the same kinds of needs or defenses (e.g., 100, 106, 73, 119) are much more closely related to m. (It might be added parenthetically that the perfectionistic statement, #100, does correlate at better than the .05 level with algebraic sum of d choices.)

Nurturance and Deference, the needs implied by #1 and #80, are not usually thought of as being the kind of anal trends that are associated with the d vector. The items refer to eminently socialized, noncompetitive types of behavior, in contrast to the need to manipulate and control objects that goes with d, Deri tells us. This very antithetical quality suggests that the key may be in the implied opposites of the statements. If I rate myself as low on noncompetitiveness, am I not thereby raising my competitiveness score, perhaps all the more because I am not aware of it? The trouble with this possibility is that it may account for the correlate of $d+$, but #80 and #90 are both negatively correlated with total d. It would be arguing that as the d column empties, the subject becomes more anal in one respect and less so in another! Some other explanation would be preferable. One abstraction that might encompass the correlates of d is conventional, somewhat moral "good citizenship." The good Rotarian is the man who works hard (#90), "boosts" his pals (#80), and lends a helping hand to good causes (#1). It would be interesting to see whether or not this same syndrome would appear in association with plus d in other cases.

[5][In retrospect, rationalizations come more easily: when the subject felt less self-esteem and self-sufficiency, he might have reactively felt like taking out his frustration on someone else.]

The most striking thing about Table 12.1 is the fact that the factor m had nearly as many correlates as all the other columns together. Every measure of m found similar significant correlates; they all will be discussed together, therefore. We find first of all the directly oral item #110: "I love to eat." There are some oral aspects to #124, also, but the main significance of this item seems to be its implications of unconscious homosexuality (see also item #59). This relationship is consistent with Deri's statement that the m and h factorial object-relationships are closely related. Then, there are several items which pertain to the ability to give love and emotional support to loved persons—items #31, 74, and 1. But why so many items: #100, 106, 73, 119, 90, referring to compulsive or retentive trends which one would have expected to be much more closely related to the "anal" factor, d?

The explanation may be found via a slight digression. I made a syndrome analysis by the Horn (1944) technique of the questionnaire items that are correlated significantly with Szondi variables. Eight relatively independent syndromes emerged. By far the largest comprised just the items listed under sum of m; the syndrome as a whole is correlated **.89** with total m choices. And in that syndrome, the central items are #125 and #120—which focus on what Robert W. White calls the *esteem-income:* from self, #125, also #58, and from others: #120, also #1, and perhaps #4. It is possible to interpret the whole m-related syndrome most parsimoniously, perhaps, in terms of this idea. The other items represent principally the ways in which this hard-working, conscientious fellow wins esteem from others and from himself: compulsive mechanisms (the "anal" items just menioned), the giving of affection and good fellowship in hope of receiving in turn (#1, 74, 31, 124, perhaps 59), being a "good guy" (#2, 10), and the intrapsychic consequences of so much concern over this problem: self-pity (#58), dejection (#125), self-consciousness (#120), anxiety (#85)—even some compensatory grandiose fantasies (#98). To put the matter in psychoanalytic terms, so much concern over one's income of esteem is characteristic of orally frustrated persons with an anxiety over the loss of love. Which brings us back to the basic rationale of the m factor as presented by Deri, though with a slightly different twist.

SUMMARY

In sum, the correlations obtained give a substantial measure of entirely independent support to Deri's statements about the meanings of the Szondi factors, though they also suggest a number of modifications and additions. Further, they tend to justify the methodological assumptions on which the study was based: that one can approach the psychological meaning of test scores (validity) through a study of their temporal variations and covariations (phenotypic unreliability).

13

Reversing the general chronological order, the next two chapters are among my earliest publications. Rereading them today, I find that they are worth rescuing from oblivion. The problems they address have not been overmuch studied, yet are important.

This paper on self-insight reports work I did as a graduate student, incidental to my dissertation research on self-evaluations, even though I did not get around to publishing it for a few years. It would of course have been impossible without the collaboration of at least a dozen of my teachers and fellow students, who provided the criterion judgments. It is a pleasure to recall the names of the Diagnostic Council members and to record my gratitude, even though not all of them are still alive: Henry A. Murray, Christiana D. Morgan, Juergen Ruesch, Silvan S. Tomkins, Daniel Horn, Robert W. White, Frederick Wyatt, Elliott Jacques, and Leopold Bellak. (I was the tenth member.)

The Accuracy of Self-Evaluations: Its Measurement and Some of Its Personological Correlates

One of the standard ways of studying personality is through the self-concept, or at least that aspect of it which the subject is willing to reveal in self-evaluations. Recently, the self-rated questionnaire has fallen into disrepute in some circles; it has been argued that most people are so self-deceptive, or so defensive about admitting many of the truths they know about themselves, that self-evaluation can be used only indirectly and cannot be taken at face value.

Such a statement cannot be called true or false. There appears to be a tremendous range of variation, from the completely self-deluded to the rare man with an accurate appraisal of himself. For clinical psychology, *variations* in the phenomenon of self-evaluation and its *interrelations* with other variables of personality are more interesting than an assessment of its general level for any group as a whole.

Insight will be used in this paper to mean "the degree to which self-evaluations are accurate." The insight that psychotherapists talk about, in contrast, should not be thought of as a mental state, an endowment, or attainment like one's level of intelligence, but as an emotional as well as intellectual *process*—a continuing journey defined by its direction rather than by an ultimate goal.[1] When the therapist says he wants his patient to become more insightful, he means that he wants to help the patient achieve an outlook that will permit him to continue, on his own, a process of self-understanding.

When Allport (1921) first proposed a method for measuring insight, he had no such conception in mind. Get a mathematical expression, he said, of the relation between self-judgments of personality characteristics and the judgments of objective scientists, who presumably come close to the truth. When Sears (1936) made his pioneering attempt to study relationships between self-evaluations and the judgments of others, he too spoke of insight but meant merely the accuracy of statements a person is willing to make about himself to a relative stranger in whom he has none of the trust and faith that a neurotic must have in his psychotherapist. It may be that the therapist's concept of dynamic-process-insight and the experimentalist's operationally defined product-insight are related. Perhaps the former is a necessary precondition for the latter. The task of the present communication, however, is limited to the study of an insight that is defined as the accuracy of experimentally obtained self-evaluations.

There are various levels of this kind of insight, dependent on the *aspects* of himself a person is called upon to assess, which might range from external facts like one's skin color to half-conscious motives. Different apparent accuracy would be brought about by variations in the *situation* in which self-judgments are called for—the nature of the experimenter, his relationship to the subject, the latter's understanding of the use to which the data were to be put, the public or private nature of the situation, etc. The *number* of judgments to be made must also have some effect on the resulting measure as long as perfect generality of insight is not assumed. These considerations make it necessary to specify in detail the procedure followed and to urge caution in generalizing the results of the present study.

THE MEASUREMENT OF INSIGHT

Procedure

The method used was basically that urged by Allport. A cooperative research project at the Harvard Psychological Clinic in 1941 and 1942 afforded an usually good chance to meet the requirement of good criterion

[1] My friend, Dr. Paul Bergman, suggested this formulation, for which I am grateful.

ratings against which to validate the self-ratings. During two years, 20 psychologists, psychiatrists, and other social scientists, led by Henry A. Murray, devised new techniques and re-explored old ones for the study of personality. The subjects (Ss) were ten more or less healthy college men, each of whom was seen by the experimenters (Es) for a minimum total of 40 hours; Ss were paid for their time. All Es learned a system of 148 personological concepts similar to those described in *Explorations in Personality* (Murray *et al.*, 1938), and worked in terms of these variables, the final ratings on which were taken as criteria in the present study. A six-point scale (0–5) was used for all variables, ratings being made in terms of the total population of Harvard undergraduates.[2] The Diagnostic Council of ten members split into two groups; each group reached an independent consensus for each S by pooling and discussing differences between the members' independent ratings; the overall reliability of ratings was about .80. In meetings of the reunited Council, differences between groups were ironed out, Ss were ranked for each variable, and final scores were given, without knowledge of the Ss' self-ratings.

Such consideration has seldom been given to the rating of a group of Ss on an array of needs, traits, facts of past history, abilities, defense mechanisms, etc. Another advantage was that this internally consistent set of variables had been used for a year or so by all of us and had been thoroughly assimilated (with a few exceptions, to be noted later).

The self-ratings were obtained during one of the Ss' initial visits to the Clinic, after they had been acquainted with the general nature of the experiments—to study normal personality—and had been assured of anonymity and the confidence in which all data would be kept. The Ss agreed to be as frank as possible. When ratings were obtained, the Ss went individually to a room where they were met by a pleasant, motherly woman who showed them the forms to be filled out, and then retired to the other side of the room ostensibly to read a book. From her reports, it was plain that the Ss generally forgot her unobtrusive presence. The ratings considered here were obtained from a blank called *Common Forms of Behavior*. It consisted of 36 items, each of which was the definition, mostly in behavioral terms, of one of the overt needs,[3] followed by a blank space for a rating of the degree to which the described behavior was true of oneself. Ss used the same 0–5 rating scale and the same reference population as did the Es.

Even with the assumption that our criterion ratings (called E-ratings hereafter) are highly valid, three types of questions are raised by the present approach to the measurement of insight.

---

[2]For further description of the scale, see Murray *et al.*, (1948, p. 32).

[3]For definitions of *overt needs*, see Murray *et al.* (1938, pp. 123–124, 252). In the self-rating form, the needs were not named; the definitions were substantially the same as those given in *Explorations*. An additional ten items, constituting definitions of such variables as Super-ego Integration and some miscellaneous needs not rated by the Diagnostic Council, were interspersed throughout the form.

1. *Which personality variables should be used?* Which kinds would give the best measure of the most important kind of insight? Such a question had probably never been asked in a study of this kind. That there may be different "insights" in the same personality, varying with the area that is evaluated, had been recognized.[4] But it is customary in the literature to speak always of insight whether overt behavioral tendencies, covert needs, abilities, or what not are being judged, as if it made no difference. The results here pertain only to overt needs; it would be interesting to compare insights of the various kinds mentioned, but unfortunately it was not feasible.

All but one of the 36 needs were included in the final measure of insight. The excluded one was the *n* (need for) Retention. The sum of the squared deviations between *S*- and *E*-ratings of this need was eight times as great as in the case of the variable showing the best agreement, *n* Rejection. Not only was this discrepancy measure far greater for *n* Retention than for any other, but the *S*s who were furthest from *E*-ratings of it were the ones who were most insightful by the criterion of the other 35 needs. Consequently it was discarded.

2. *What statistic is best for an insight measure?* To express mathematically the correspondence between two sets of numbers, the product-moment correlation coefficient is the first method that comes to mind, and it was the first that was used. The results were suspect, however. For example, it was easy to see that one *S*, Dupressy, came close to the mark most of the time and that he rarely went off more than one point. Another *S*, Nailson, on the other hand, had numerous discrepancies of two or three points. Yet *r* was .72 for Nailson, .19 for Dupressy, giving them ranks in the group of 1 and 9 respectively! How could this be?[5]

The product-moment formula is a function of the squared deviations between the paired scores, and the variances of the two distributions. This means that each of the two distributions of scores being correlated is corrected for its own degree of variability so they will be comparable, i.e., the *scales* used in the two sets of ratings are equated. Dupressy's scores (both *S*- and *E*-ratings) fell within a narrow range, which magnified little discrepancies; but Nailson's *E*-scores varied greatly, usually in the same direction as his own mark but much further, so that he came out well when the range of the *E*-scores was statistically reduced.

For many situations, this kind of equation of distribution is highly desirable; in the present case it was not. The *E*- and *S*-ratings *had already been equated for scale* since both were made in terms of the same 0–5 scale, 0 meaning very much below the average of Harvard undergraduates, 5 very much above. What was needed was a statistic which could reach a maximum value only when scores were identical.

[4]See Sears (1936).
[5]For the following explanation I am indebted to my friend, Dr. Daniel Horn. [See also the discussion of similar problems by Cronbach and Gleser, 1955.]

The intraclass correlation coefficient (r') meets this requirement but it still involves correcting for the variance in the scores to get a coefficient ranging from +1 to −1. Since the coefficient of insight did not need to have such a property in this case, a simple measure used, the sum of the squared deviations of S- from E-ratings (squared to eliminate signs and to weight more heavily big discrepancies). This measure (referred to hereafter as Insight—with a capital I to distinguish it from the general concept) was correlated .70 with Dr. Murray's ranking of Ss in order of their "insight into overt aspects of one's personality"—more highly than the other two. Finally, its personological correlates made more sense than those of the rank-orders based on r or r'.

These details are included as an example of the difficulties met when one uses a conventional statistic without considering the relevance of its underlying assumptions to the data at hand.

3. *How can the patterning of personality variables be considered?* The measure finally chosen unfortunately provides no solution for the problem of super-summativeness. Even if a subject marks every need correctly, he may conceivably have an erroneous notion of their interrelationships in his personality: which ones are more basic, which subsidiary; what themas they go to make up; what infantile complexes they are related to, etc. But the difficulties of quantifying this kind of insight resemble those of measuring "process-insight." Therefore, it should be repeated that the *Insight* considered here is intellectual, cross-sectional, and somewhat atomistic, consisting of the S's ability to assay objectively (or with the same biases as the Diagnostic Council) the overt motivational trends in his personality. We may better understand what kind of phenomenon this is if we look at the aspects of personality to which it is related.

PERSONOLOGICAL CORRELATES OF ACCURATE SELF-EVALUATION

Table 13.1 presents all of the rated variables of personality[6] with which Insight was appreciably correlated. It is reasonable to find that the most intelligent Ss knew themselves best. Of the five aspects of intelligence rated separately, only the initial pair of variables were correlated above .07 with Insight. They refer to creative facets of intellect; it would be interesting if further studies should bear out the implication that Insight may be a cause or a result of the ability to reorganize experience constructively.[7]

---

[6]Definitions similar to those used in the study for most of the variables may be found in Murray *et al.* (1938).

[7]In this connection, it is noteworthy that Mead's theory of the self (1934) posits an intimate connection between what he calls "self-consciousness" (taking the role of the other in relation to the self) and the ability to organize ideas and think constructively. My then wife, Dr. Louisa P. Holt (now Howe), brought this similarity to my attention.

Table 13.1.   Personological Correlates of Insight

Organizing Intelligence	**.77***
Originality of Thought	.49
Athletic Ability	*.75*
Athletic Achievement	*.67*
Endurance	.54
n Excitance:Adventure	.56
n Harmavoidance	−.50
Sentiment for Subjectivity and Passion	−.58
Exocathection	.52
n Change:Novelty	.46
Breadth of Interest	.62
n Dominance:Conduct	*.66*
Leadership (in Adolescence)	*.66*
Social Adjustment	.51
n Affiliation:Diffuse	.51
n Infavoidance	−.49
Social Ability	.48
Covert *n* Aggression	−.61
Fantasied *p* Dominance:Coercion	**−.78**
Projection	.50

*These are rank-order correlation coefficients. When $N = 10$, rho
  must be *.64* to be significantly different from zero at the 5% level,
  .77 for the 1% level.

The second group of correlates in Table 13.1 might represent some factor of *constitutional strength*. These athletic attributes probably just indicate the sturdier members of this rather nonathletic group of Ss, which contained no member of a college team. But the constitutional hypothesis may not be warranted, and the second and third groups of variables in Table 13.1 might be considered together as a larger syndrome of *active adventurous living in the world of reality*. Our typical insightful S is adventurous rather than timid; he turns away from the inner life to a diversity of interests in the real external world. This finding recalls G. H. Mead's theory that a person gains self-knowledge through learning more about others. Certainly when self-ratings are made in relation to the population of one's contemporaries and on observable forms of behavior, we should expect the introverted, timid, and narrow person to do poorly at it. He might, on the other hand, do very well if insight were being measured in terms of the covert themes he discerns in his soul-searching.

In light of these points, it should be expected that in our group of Ss, *dominance and social adjustment* are related to the present measure of Insight, as shown by the fourth group of correlates. Insight thus goes not only with enough strength in body and mind to control others, but also with a basically friendly attitude toward them, free of resentment or feelings of being pushed around.

In discussing these correlations, I have made statements imputing a causal relationship, where it seems the most natural explanation of the correlation. This is risky, because in any one of these correlations the causal relationship may go in one direction in one case and in the other in another case, with the most complex kind of interaction in a third. Furthermore, some of the results are most probably specific to this particular group of Harvard students, whose homogeneity may have allowed relationships to emerge that would not hold, would be obscured, or would be expressed differently in another group.

THE RELATION BETWEEN INSIGHT AND PROJECTION

The last correlate, Projection, is an unexpected one. So challenging a relationship cannot be brushed aside on the grounds of statistical unreliability. But isn't it a paradox? Doesn't projection involve a lack of accuracy in judgment that is antithetical to insight? In his experiment on the attribution of traits, Sears (1936) found that his least insightful Ss projected the most; his result has been widely accepted as proof that insight and projection are incompatible.

The Desirability of the Needs Rated. Closer examination shows, first, that Sears' rather crude measures, both of projection and of insight, were different from those used in the present study. His technique allowed him to state only that a subject was insightful or uninsightful, and projective or not. Secondly, all four variables he used were rated as undesirable by his subjects: stinginess (cf. *n* Retention), disorderliness (*n* Order), stubbornness (*n* Autonomy:Resistance), and bashfulness (*n* Infavoidance). By contrast, the variables used in my measure of Insight were well distributed between desirable, undesirable, and intermediate, according to the Ss' own ratings. When a measure of Insight based on the six *most* desirable variables is calculated (sum of the squared deviations), it is correlated +.54 with Projection, while a similar measure based on the six *least* desirable needs is correlated only +.04. Insight into the 23 intermediary variables is correlated +.36, so that there appears to be a linear relationship between the social acceptability of needs and the degree to which more projective persons self-rate them more accurately. This finding does not seem to be based on a greater *general* accuracy of self-rating on the most desirable needs (see below).

How then are we to understand it? When a tendency is thought shameful or if recognition of it in oneself arouses anxiety, the demand to rate the amount of it that one possesses is a threat to self-esteem, to which people will react according to the nature of their principal defense mechanisms. If projection is particularly characteristic of a person, he will tend to attribute the quality in question to others, by contrast to whom he will then seem to have little of it. His self-ratings, particularly if they are made in comparative terms, should therefore tend to be inaccurate. No such interference should enter in when desirable characteristics are being rated, because there is not as much of a threat to arouse the projective defenses.

These predictions are well borne out by data. The two Ss who were rated most projective *underestimated* in themselves those needs which they considered least acceptable socially and personally (as determined by a separate series of ratings using the Common Forms of Behavior blank): their respective average discrepancies were $-.7$ and $-.8$. Contrariwise, the two least projective Ss *overestimated* the needs which they considered least acceptable, their mean deviations being $+.8$ and $+1.4$. When the highly desirable needs are considered, both projective and nonprojective Ss overrated themselves by similar amounts: projective $+.5$, $+.9$; nonprojective $+.5$, $+1.2$.

Insight, Projection, and Intelligence. There still remains the main problem: why does the projective person do well in self-estimation when there is no problem of the social undesirability of what he rates? Perhaps because of the generalized sharpness, the observational acuity, and mental alertness that clinically are associated with projective tendencies. But these characteristics almost comprise a definition of certain aspects of intelligence. In diagnostic testing, a common working hypothesis is that projective trends may elevate a person's scores on certain subtests of the Wechsler-Bellevue Scale [or the WAIS] (Arithmetic, Similarities, Picture Completion). And indeed, Projection turns out to be correlated with Organizing Intelligence; rho is $+.48$. If Organizing Intelligence is then held constant by partial correlation,[8] the correlation between Insight and Projection drops to $+.23$. In this particular sample there is probably an unusually high mutual dependence of Projection and Intelligence, which may be a principal explanation of the correlation originally found between the experimental measure of Insight and the rated variable, Projection. Even when a correction is made for this overlap, however, the relationship remains a positive one. The principal interest of these findings is that they demonstrate that a positive association between Insight and Projection *can* exist in a certain type of population, and they point to the need for further research in which the measures of both traits should be systematically varied as well as carefully controlled.

VARIATIONS IN INSIGHT ACCORDING TO VARIABLES RATED

There were considerable differences between the variables in the ease with which the subjects as a group could give themselves accurate marks. The mean squared deviation between E-ratings and S-ratings for all 36 variables and all 10 Ss was 2.21. The five best-rated needs had a mean D^2 of

[8]I owe this fruitful suggestion to my friend, Dr. George S. Klein.

.9; they are, in order: n Rejection, n Dominance:Ideas, n Affiliation:Diffuse, n Dominance:Conduct, and n Excitance. The five worst-rated needs had a mean D^2 of 3.86; they are: n Seclusion, n Cognizance:Curiosity, n Change:Novelty, n Playmirth, and worst of all, n Retention. Dominant and affiliative needs, which are correlated in this group with Insight, were also among the easiest for the Ss to judge validly for themselves.

When the best- and worst-rated variables are compared, a number of sources of error emerge. Embarrassingly enough, most of them seem to be attributable to the Es rather than to the Ss.

Sources of Error: Definitions. In the case of several variables, errors in ratings seem to have been due to poorly worded definitions. The needs for Playmirth, Cognizance, and Change were in large part defined in terms of subjective feelings, moods, or attitudes rather than overt behavior, as they were supposed to be. It would seem more difficult to rate someone (yourself or another person, in relation to a given population) on the first of the following statements than on the second: "To enjoy good-natured jokes and jests" (n Playmirth); "To assemble, lead or organize a group" (n Dominance:Conduct). Other definitions suffered from including very diverse forms of behavior (n Change: "To seek new experiences . . . or to be somewhat changeable and inconsistent").

Influence of the Desirability of Needs. I asked the Ss to rate the desirability of each need, the extent to which it would be found in an "ideal man," on the same Common Forms of Behavior blank. It could be seen that they had a tendency to overrate those items they rated as admirable and to underrate by about an equal amount the less acceptable needs. It seemed worthwhile to investigate the possibility that relatively neutral forms of behavior might be more accurately rated. The needs were then divided into three groups: six most desirable or ideal forms of behavior, six least desirable, and the remaining 23 intermediary variables. The mean squared deviation between E- and S-ratings is 2.25 for most desirable, 2.10 for indifferent, and 2.15 for undesirable ones. There was thus only a negligible trend in the direction of the hypothesis. That strongly valent needs were no more deviantly rated than others by this group points to the special nature of the small population dealt with. All were college men, most of them considerably above average in scholarship, and some of them were chosen for study partly because they had interesting talents.

By contrast, consider the mean self-ratings of 99 men in the Army Specialized Training Program at Harvard who filled out the same Common Forms of Behavior blank.[9] The same scale was used so that if the group was fairly representative and the members marked themselves accurately, the mean rating for each need should be 2.5. The following needs deviated by

[9]The following data were kindly made available to me by Dr. Daniel Horn, who obtained the ratings from the Army Specialized Training Program.

more than a full point from the mean: *Underrated:* n Aggression:Physical, n Succorance, n Sex:Diffuse; *Overrated:* n Affiliation:Focal, n Sex:Focal, and n Blamavoidance. Here the influences of the social acceptability of the form of behavior and of wish are very clear. Few people can assess correctly their own direct expressions of aggression, sexuality, and dependence, while friendship, love, and moral behavior are goals which most people are only too eager to say they pursue.

Familiarity of Es with Variables Rated. To return to the original sets of data: three of the five needs on which agreement is poorest are among a group of five which were added at the end of the study. Thus, we did not have these variables specifically in mind when dealing with the Ss, and they were not put through the process of so many ratings, justifications, and discussions. Feeling that we knew the Ss very well, and that the forms of behavior in question had all actually been observed or inquired into, we made ratings on the needs for Acquisition, Physical Aggression, Cognizance:Curiosity, Playmirth, and Retention.[10] The last three were among the four needs into which the Ss had poorest insight, if our judgments were a criterion. It is likely that a person would know whether or not he was saving and thrifty and tended to hoard things, while the Es probably overlooked the fact that the definition was stated only in terms of physical objects and perhaps were influenced by clinically observable retentiveness of information and affection. The definition of n Playmirth almost invites one to rate his own sense of humor—a matter in which people are notoriously self-deceived. Allport (1937a, p. 224) found, for example, that 94% of a group of college students thought that their sense of humor was at least as good as average. If all the discrepancies were positive, such an explanation would be plausible, but actually four underrated and four overrated.

Observability of Relevant Behavior. Aside from the difficulty caused by the subjective elements in the definition of n Playmirth, it may be presumed that the Es had insufficient opportunity to observe the Ss in a relaxed, natural setting in which spontaneous, humorous playfulness might assert itself. This comment applies even more to the need for Seclusion, which is obviously difficult to observe. Contrariwise, turning to the variables well self-rated, the results are easiest to explain on the assumption that the self-ratings were generally valid, and that the Es were able to approximate them closely because the kinds of behavior rated were involved directly in the interaction between E and S in the Clinic. Situations were provided in which the Es could directly observe Ss arguing and attempting to influence behavior and ideas of others (n Dominance:Ideas and n Dominance:Behavior), as well as their generalized friendliness or aloofness (n Affiliation:Diffuse and n Rejection). It is more difficult to explain the good agreement on n Excitance. It was not well defined and not too easily observable, though it had the possible

[10] The need for Exposition, which was not self-rated, was also added.

slight advantage of being neither a very highly prized nor an undesirable form of behavior.

The conclusions suggested by these last findings are not particularly novel; they reaffirm what was already known about personality ratings. Definitions of variables must be clear and single-pointed. When ratings are being made on a scale that implies comparison of the subject (or self) with a group, the variable is best defined in terms of overtly observable behavior, so that a person can be expected to make comparisons without resorting to guess. (Of course, the nature of some variables inevitably makes this kind of definition inappropriate.) Finally, no matter how well a group of *E*s may feel they know their *S*s after exhaustive study, there are dangers in adding variables to be rated after the data have all been gathered and analyzed. Probably more valid results are obtained when all *E*s understand all variables clearly from the beginning and have them all in the back of their minds throughout their work with the *S*s.

14

This paper has a rather amusing history. It is a condensation of one chapter from the first draft of my doctoral dissertation (Holt, 1945, 1946a, 1947a). In that research, I had obtained numerous self-evaluations from subjects, including classical levels of aspiration, had intercorrelated them, and had interpreted clusters of interrelated variables as types of defense of self-esteem. I doubt that Ray Cattell, who was working in a nearby office in the Harvard Psychological Clinic, ever mentioned to me his later-published, three-dimensional Covariation Chart (Cattell, 1946) and the idea that the same data might be examined by either Q or R technique. Nevertheless, the thought occurred to me that it would be interesting to see how self-evaluations and defenses of self-esteem were structured in the same group of undergraduates, considered one at a time. I soon found that one such case study was all that I could manage, and it made up a chapter as long as many entire dissertations—in a manuscript that was already far too long.

I had begun work on level of aspiration as a thesis topic under Gordon Allport, had shifted to Murray as my sponsor when I began working at the Harvard Psychological Clinic, but now that I was writing it up, had to return to Allport since Murray had gone off to mysterious war work at the OSS. Allport generously agreed, but to my surprise asked me to take out the case study on the grounds that it was "too idiographic for this nomothetic dissertation!" Reluctantly, I did so, and a few months later made it into my contribution to Random Harpoonings, *an unpublished volume Bob White put together as a kind of Festschrift/parting gift for Murray.*

A few years afterward, after returning to clinical work in Topeka, I dusted it off, boiled it down to the present form, and presented it at the 1947 meeting of the Kansas Academy of Science.

An Inductive Method of Analyzing Defense of Self-Esteem

Clinical psychology today concerns itself to a large extent with defensive functions: the organism's conscious and unconscious efforts to ward off and nullify threats to all aspects of its psychological integrity, which are analogous to physiological mechanisms of defense against threats to numerous vital biochemical equilibria. Psychoanalysts were the first to describe psychological defense "mechanisms" from their intensive clinical observations. More slowly, psychologists who are in a better position to use experimental techniques have followed in their wake, seeking objective empirical demonstration of such strategies as repression and projection, and (what is more important) studying their concrete manifestations in a variety of situations.

There is a level of defensive functioning about which psychiatrists and psychologists are beginning to think and write, but it is still relatively unexplored.[1] Most of the classic psychoanalytic defenses have been conceived of as directed against anxiety, which in turn stems from fears of bodily mutilation, loss of love, or impotence in a catastrophic situation. Psychoanalysts, psychologists, and social workers have lately been paying attention to another important threat to human happiness: the loss of self-esteem (or self-respect). The role played by this factor in mental illness is a vexing problem in psychiatry, but the more seriously ego-psychology is considered, the larger self-esteem bulks, for it refers to the person's basic feeling of being able to live in peace with himself.

Because of methodological difficulties, problems of this sort have long been eschewed by psychologists who strive after scientific rigor. Reports of observations made incidentally to therapeutic contact with patients are unexcelled as stimulating leads but leave something to be desired as scientific data. The method of the case study has been suggested as ideal for work on problems of personal structure and dynamics, and, indeed, it is irreplaceable in the present state of psychological progress. It needs to be refined and sharpened considerably, however, if it is to be an advance over relatively uncontrolled observation. The work reported here is an effort toward the development of an inductive, at least theoretically repeatable method for the preparation of a topical case history of an aspect of psychodynamics. The aspect chosen here is the defense of self-esteem.

The writer of a case study usually faces impalement on one or the other horn of a critical dilemma: either he will be called down for having presented mere facts without conceptualization, or if he fits facts into a preconceived theoretical framework, he will suffer the critical wrath of those who espouse other general theories and say he has chosen facts to fit preexisting ideas of his own. I hoped to bypass this dilemma by developing a set of concepts and a way of ordering the data unique to the case, so that the facts might be arrayed and given implications of wider usefulness, by generalization, and still without recourse to concepts taken over ready-made from preexisting systems. An inductive method was needed, and the fact that the focus of interest was a relatively novel one called all the more for a fresh start without preconceptions.

The method is such a simple one that although I have not been able to

[1][This statement is obviously less true today than it was in 1947, when this paper was written.]

find a published description of it, it probably is not novel. Taking all of the materials available pertaining to one person, I read them through carefully looking for every situation, real or fancied, in which there was a threat of unpleasant consequences from the subject's point of view. All reactions to such situations were tentatively considered to have some degree of defensive significance, and each description of a defensive reaction was copied on a separate slip of paper. Such a broad definition obviously brought in more than reactions defensive of self-esteem, but it seemed better to do the cutting down and eliminating after this first gross selection.

At the time this study was done, I was one of more than a score of collaborating psychologists, psychiatrists, and social scientists intensively studying a small group of college students at the Harvard Psychological Clinic under the direction of Henry A. Murray. Each worker brought to bear on the subject an interviewing technique, psychological test, or experimental method that was her or his own specialty. Reports of each procedure and in most cases the protocols were available; these, the test data, and the subject's autobiography were the materials from which I gathered all indications of the subject's defensive behavior.

As a result of the first step, then, I collected 281 instances of one college student's defensive behavior. Already in the process of selection, it became apparent that there were definite groups into which the behaviors naturally fell, and I had arrived at a first hit-or-miss classification by the time the 281 slips had been gathered together. I then considered the first rough categories, which numbered about 100, with as few preconceptions as possible and with an effort to let the congruences in the data themselves determine what should be classified with what. The resulting combinations reduced the number of rubrics to 45. Elimination of those that were not clearly relevant to defense of self-esteem cut the number to 38.

You may ask if these 38 individual traits are supposed to be the "real" structure of the subject's esteem-defenses. Indeed, what is the proper level of generalization at which to stop? There are overlaps and similarities among the 38; they fall naturally into five main groups, which may be designated as more generalized defensive traits. Is this, then, the appropriate degree of abstraction to make of the original data? It is possible to go even further, and find a single cardinal trait or mode of defense, implicit in each of the five generalized mechanisms. The answer, of course, is that each of the levels of abstraction arrived at may have its own validity or usefulness for certain purposes, and that since all are conceptual, no level has any greater degree of reality than any other. At any level the utility of the concepts cannot be considered as established without cross-validational studies of the same or other persons.

When the groupings of defensive behaviors are examined, it may appear that the effort to do away with preconceptions was no more successful than might have been expected. No one, not the most antitheoretical of fact-grubbers can avoid some structuring of data in accordance with whatever principles of mental organization he already knows. Thus, it might be argued that the claim of inductive method is no more than pretense; that at best, I have succeeded only in imposing unconscious preconceptions on the data instead of conscious ones; that another worker, trained in very different ideas of psychodynamics, would come up with very different categories, using the same method. A good deal of this criticism I accept; yet I feel that there is so much force of meaningful cohesion in the materials themselves that anyone who honestly tried to feel these coherences would come out with substantially similar categories, though he might give them quite different names.[2]

The empirical focus of the study is a young man given the pseudonym of Grove. He is a personable, highly intelligent, listless fellow, who succeeded in graduating from Harvard *cum laude* with the aid of steady prodding by advisors. He was the older and weaker of two sons of an abusive, hated father and a weak, neurotic, and adored mother. His father openly preferred the more active younger brother, with whom Grove quarreled from the beginning. He was a shy, dreamy boy who withdrew from the others when they called him sissy; yet in adolescence he managed to develop reasonably good social relations. His high school work was outstanding, he was something of a leader in dramatics and writing, and he made a moderately good heterosexual adjustment. Coming to Harvard on a scholarship, he was lost in a huge impersonal world in which no one sought him out, and he gradually retired behind a shell of cool aloofness which hid his hurt. He went through college without any positive goals, living in the dread of being drafted into the war which appeared more and more imminent. The night of Pearl Harbor he had an anxiety attack, with the feeling that the earth was giving way beneath him; this and similar attacks brought him to the Clinic where he was studied intensively and received some therapeutic aid, which enabled him to enter the Navy on graduation. [After the war, he worked for a large corporation in New York City.]

In skeleton outline, here is the structure of his defenses of self-esteem at the time of the study. An example or so is supplied for each, which will illustrate the nature of the case materials used.

A. Passivity and Abasement

1. Planlessness " . . . he has never been certain of what he expected to gain from college or what he wanted to prepare for. . . . At the present

---

[2][At the time, it did not occur to me to get someone else to sort the basic observations and see to what extent he might reproduce my categories, and by the time I came to publish the paper, I no longer had the raw data. Nevertheless, it is worth emphasizing that the reliability of such clinical judgments can and should be tested.]

moment he is very confused as to his plans for the future, the value of his education, and his social relationships." (Autobiography)

2. *Procrastination* "I put off until the last two days; up all night before an exam. Papers are a terrific strain; I put them off and worry about it." (Interview)

3. *Immobilization* During Session I, Grove showed a greater than average amount of blocks, inhibitions, and general erratic behavior. (Emotional Conditioning Experiment; Haggard, 1943)

4. *Stereotyped Conformity* "He is a broken man.... He tries to find research in a pulp mill but by now he has become an automaton. He has no initiative and no spark, and his mind is warped." (TAT)

5. *Disillusioned Resignation* "She is completely disillusioned with what she thought there was in life other than what she had so she comes home and marries . . . and settles into a life style exactly like that her mother had . . . she resigns herself to it." (TAT)

6. *Compliant Giving In* [In his stories] *n* Rejection is high for the submissive character but he usually gives in at the end . . . he is the only subject whose characters acknowledge agreement. (Interpretation of Arguments Completion Test[3])

7. *Lowering of the Ego Ideal* "This fellow has been working in the lab trying to find a new form of gasoline that will revolutionize the market. [After 165 trials he finds it; an oil company buys it, but] the new gas is shelved, and the man realizes . . . that he will have to start all over again. He is disillusioned with science which has no more to offer him. He has given up the idea of benefiting man. He is a broken man..... " (TAT)

8. *Passive Resistance* "Am I going too slowly?" (Classification Test[4])

9. *Self-pity and Fantasies of Reliance on Older Persons* Subject: " . . . I think I've been busier feeling sorry for myself, I'm ashamed to say." Experimenter: "Why do you feel sorry for yourself?" Subject: "Well, that's always been one of my weak points—'well, look at poor me, I've always had such a hard life'— when of course I haven't." (Interview)

" . . . he finds another job, another good job because now everybody is willing to help him." (TAT)

10. *Reaction Formation: Rejection of Dependence* "I need some approval of others but I do not like to seek advice." (Interview)

[Hero hated father after being forced to kill his dog] . . . "father wanted to send him away to college but the boy wouldn't go, said no. He was quite nice about it. He said that he believed that he had taken as much as he could

[3]This passage is taken from an interpretation written by Christiana D. Morgan, who devised the test. It is described on pp. 61–62 of Murray and Morgan (1945) where there is also a good deal of discussion of Grove, his sentiments, and their origins (pp. 86–92; 167–169; 220–227; 277–279).

[4]An unpublished test of verbal conceptual thinking devised by Dr. Katherine McBride.

from his father and his father had supported him long enough and he would go out to find his own way." (TAT)

11. Being a "Good Boy" " . . . the fact that people no longer acclaimed him as especially smart hurt his pride. He was, however, a model pupil behaviorally." (Autobiography)

12. Objectivity About Himself; Self-criticism "This is an autobiography written in the third person. The writer felt this was the best way to obtain the objectivity necessary in a paper of this sort." (Autobiography)

13. Submission " . . . he found out that one of his best friends had stolen something from him, and so he went up to the friend and asked that the stolen article be returned [and the friend denied it] and this fellow said, 'well, all right then, we will forget it for the time being but if ever I miss anything again I'm going to see that you get what you deserve.'" (TAT)

B. Avoidance and Escape

1. Avoidance of Competition "He began to avoid the company of children who might draw him into any sort of physical contact . . ." (Autobiography)

"I had been sick for the first hour exam and out of town for the second—I didn't go to the final, and didn't get credit." (Interview)

2. Running Away from Rejection "Running away was very ineffective, I was out for sympathy. My mother brought this on; I thought she didn't want me around. I rode away on my bicycle, slept in the park." (Interview)

3. Refusal of Responsibility "The young man [was hypnotized, forced into a crime; he] was still completely unaware of everything that was happening and obeying everything the old man said . . . of course he didn't realize that he had done wrong because he was ready to come back. . . ." (TAT)

4. Shyness and Withdrawal " . . . at college, he refused to be gregarious and remained with the nucleus of friends he had met at the beginning of the year. His shyness around strangers increased and he would often go out of his way to avoid meeting new people." (Autobiography)

Experimenter: "How would you describe your usual reaction to failure?" Subject: "Oh, general depression and withdrawal for awhile momentarily." (Interview)

5. Reserve "The subject often desires to have others confide in him their secrets about personal and confidential matters, yet he is extremely cautious in confiding to others." (Autobiography, section written by roomate)

6. Escape into Fantasy "I began going to a lot of movies and tried to escape that way." (Interview)

"In a lecture, I can usually pay attention the first ten or fifteen minutes and then my mind wanders and I have to look on the next fellow's notes. . . ." (Interview)

7. Regressive Fantasy of the Return Home "In contrast to his desire for change and escape from home when he first came to college, he is now dissatisfied in a way and would almost prefer to be home."

"Even up to the present time the subject retains a childish desire to be with his mother whenever he is in trouble or has to make a decision." (Autobiography)

8. Forgetting . . . In Production 1, he "forgot" the bathroom and had to make it in an annex, and apologized: "The bathroom is pretty badly planned (laughs). There is no way of getting into it without going outside." (Dramatic Production Test[5])

C. Rejection and Aggression

1. Rejection of People: Overt, in Fantasy, and Generalized Rejective Sentiments "He acquired a cool manner resembling snobbishness which he applied in his contacts with the people about him." (Autobiography)

" . . . they have just had a violent quarrel and he's decided that he's going away and not coming back and that she can get a divorce from him if she wants. . . ." (TAT)

2. Negativism "He's against everything. He's always aiding small groups that are against the order of the day and against what everybody else is doing in general because he can never be satisfied with the world as it is. He always has a chip on his shoulder and a grudge to bear. . . ." (TAT)

3. Verbal Aggression: "Bickering" [The subject] has had a tendency to answer back . . .has sneered at his father. Developed quarreling as a technique of getting things. (Interview)

4. Fantasies of Retaliation " . . . the old man at the top is about ready to choke the man underneath." (TAT)

5. Resentment [Boy who is forced to take violin lessons finds that] "the sounds that came out just were not music to him; so little by little he began to hate music lessons . . . practicing just became a bore and a burden. . . . He began to hate his teacher. He began to dislike his mother for making him take lessons." (TAT)

D. Rationalization and Intellectualization

1. Verbal Denial Experimenter: "Would you say that your life is carried on efficiently, that you get things done?" Subject: "Yes—there's absolutely no plan about it. I get things done." (Interview)

---

[5]A quotation from a report on Grove's productions in this test, written by Dr. Elizabeth Nottingham. For description of the test, see Murray *et al.* (1938), pp. 552–582.

2. Extrapunitiveness: Blaming Others Experimenter: "Why did you give up the Dramatic Club?" Subject: "They took their art too seriously." (Interview)

3. Impunitiveness: Blaming Impersonal Factors [Yawns] "I was up all night, excuse me." (Sentiments Examination; Murray & Morgan, 1945, pp. 60–61)

4. Rationalization Experimenter: "Why did you turn and look at me when you got the shock?" Subject: "Well, you were the only one to look at." (Emotional Conditioning Experiment)

5. Intellectualization Asked if records were made; much interested, going to ask Dr. Murray for results of all tests if possible. . . . Again spoke of relief in knowing yourself, how it helped. (Conversation after an experiment)

6. Search for Information [After five minutes of drawing moonfaces] Experimenter: "Now would you draw just one more, please?" Subject: "I can't finish that? Is speed involved? I'm supposed to do this for so long?" (Frustration Experiment)

E. Fantasies of the Ego Ideal, Recognition, Achievement, and Counteraction

1. Ego Ideal of Achievement Through Kindliness "He was a great daydreamer and often though of himself as a Galahad riding off on a white horse or a kind doctor who helps all his patients. . . ." (TAT)

2. Fantasied Acclaim "He has a strong but unexpressed desire, carried over from younger years, to act on the stage or radio." (Autobiography)

3. Fantasies of Achievement [The hero] "gradually worked up until he owned . . . a corporation. . . so he was rather successful in spite of the fact that he didn't have his father's help." (TAT)

4. Fantasies of Restriving " . . . the farm isn't yielding anything any more, but still they keep on . . . their future is just nil . . . but they'll try again, year after year." (TAT)

5. Direct Compensation " . . . the fact that people no longer acclaimed him as especially smart hurt his pride. He was, however, a model pupil behaviorally. Gradually his work became better and he led his class by the fourth grade." (Autobiography)

6. Unadaptive Counteractive Effect After failure, he made more than twice as many movements of the test material, with poorer results. (Frustration Experiment)

In a report of this compass, it is unfortunately not possible to put much flesh on these bare bones, nor to give enough context to show convincingly the threat to self-esteem to which these defenses are (in part) reactive. If it seems paradoxical to consider some of these reactions defensive, I can only say that in general Grove chooses what seems to him a lesser evil to avoid a real hurt. Passivity and abasement set the style for all of the defenses. Avoidance and escape are like passivity in being refusals to meet the situation directly in its own terms. Counteraction is found principally in Grove's fantasy, which is itself the most passive kind of reaction, and prevalently serves as an escape from reality. His cognitive inner working-over of situations includes the more logical processes of rationalization, frequently in terms of an intellectualized framework of justification. To the extent that Grove's reaction to a threat is extrapunitive, it is either in fantasies of an aggressive sort, or in the most passive form of aggression: rejection.

All of his major defenses, then, are predicated on subjective restructuring of situations, rather than any overt or physical effort directed against danger to self-esteem. Thus we might tentatively say that at the highest level of integration, Grove's cardinal defensive trait is a passive retreat into an unreal world where matters are set aright.

About the limitations of the method: obviously, it can be no more comprehensive than the raw materials that are used. In the case of the subject studied here, the data cover only what was observed while Grove was in the Clinic and what he reported about himself in the autobiography and interview. It is true that projective tests and some dreams are included, but there are no free associations or similar materials. It would be interesting to apply the method to a transcription of some psychoanalytic interviews, though that was not possible in this case.

It may be in order to warn against one aspect of the method: its appearance of giving a quantitative measure of the importance or prominence of the various weapons in a person's defensive armory. The relative numbers of instances of different strategies can serve as only the roughest indication of their comparative importance in a person's life. For such quantities to take on meaning, it would be necessary to assume that the frequency with which a device was used for coping with threats was a valid indicator of its importance or was a matter of intrinsic interest. In addition, one would have to work with a comprehensive and representative sample of all areas of behavior—an almost impossible condition. The situation is also complicated by the fact that some defenses appear usually in fantasy though occasionally in overt action, and vice versa. (Grove had *many* hostile thoughts about his father, and only *once* struck him and knocked him down.) It might be fruitful in further applications of the method to treat real actions and those in fantasy or dream separately instead of lumping them, as was done here, and then compare the patterns obtained.

Though this kind of work is tedious and still contains much subjectivity, nevertheless it is reasonable to hope that patient application of some procedures such as have been described may be a fruitful way of harvesting from the riches of clinical case data new insights into the mechanisms of such human behavior as the defense of self-esteem.

References

Abraham, K. (1924). The influence of oral erotism on character formation. In *Selected papers.* New York: Basic Books, 1953.

Ackoff, R. L. *Redesigning the future.* New York: Wiley, 1974.

Allport, G. W. Personality and character. *Psychological Bulletin,* 1921, *18,* 441–455.

Allport, G. W. *Personality: A psychological interpretation.* New York: Holt, 1937. (a)

Allport, G. W. The personalistic psychology of William Stern. *Character and Personality,* 1937, *5,* 231–246. (b)

Allport, G. W. Motivation in personality: Reply to Mr. Bertocci. *Psychological Review,* 1940, *47,* 533–554.

Allport, G. W. The use of personal documents in psychological science. *Social Science Research Council Bulletin,* 1942, No. 49.

Allport, G. W. Personalistic psychology as science: A reply. *Psychological Review,* 1946, *53,* 132–135.

Allport, G. W. *Becoming: Basic considerations for a psychology of personality.* New Haven: Yale University Press, 1955.

Allport, G. W. The open system in personality theory. *Journal of Abnormal and Social Psychology,* 1960, *61,* 301–310. Reprinted in *Personality and social encounter.* Boston: Beacon Press, 1960.

Allport, G. W. *Pattern and growth in personality.* New York: Holt, Rinehart & Winston, 1961.

Allport, G. W. The general and the unique in psychological science. *Journal of Personality,* 1962, *30,* 405–422.

Allport, G. W. *Letters from Jenny.* New York: Harcourt, Brace & World, 1965.

Allport, G. W., & Odbert, H. S. Trait-names: A psycho-lexical study. *Psychological Monographs,* 1936, *47* (1, Whole No. 211).

Anderson, H. H., & Anderson, G. L. *An introduction to projective techniques and other devices for understanding the dynamics of human behavior.* Englewood Cliffs, N.J.: Prentice-Hall, 1951.

Aron, B. *A manual for analysis of the Thematic Apperception Test.* Berkeley, Calif.: Willis E. Berg, 1949.

Atkinson, J. W. Explorations using imaginative thought to assess the strength of human motives. In M. R. Jones (Ed.), *Nebraska symposium on motivation, 1954.* Lincoln: University of Nebraska Press, 1954.

Atkinson, J. W. (Ed.). *Motives in fantasy, action, and society: A method of assessment and study.* Princeton: Van Nostrand, 1958.

Baldwin, A. L. Personal structure analysis: A statistical method for investigating the single personality. *Journal of Abnormal and Social Psychology,* 1942, *37,* 163–183.

Balken, E. R., & Masserman, J. H. The language of phantasy: III. The language of the phantasies of patients with conversion hysteria, anxiety state, and obsessive-compulsive neuroses. *Journal of Psychology,* 1940, *10,* 75–86.

319

Barr, H. B., Langs, R. J., Holt, R. R., Goldberger, L., & Klein, G. S. *LSD: Personality and experience.* New York: Wiley, 1972.

Barron, F. An ego-strength scale which predicts response to psychotherapy. *Journal of Consulting Psychology,* 1953, *17,* 327–333. (a)

Beck, S. J. The science of personality: Nomothetic or idiographic? *Psychological Review,* 1953, *60,* 353–359.

Beier, E. G., Gorlow, L., & Stacey, C. L. The fantasy life of the mental defective. *American Journal of Mental Deficiency,* 1951, *55,* 582–589.

Bell, J. E. *Projective techniques: A dynamic approach to the study of the personality.* New York: Longmans, Green and Co., 1948.

Bell, J. E. The case of Gregor. *Journal of Projective Techniques.* 1949, *13,* 155–205; 433–468.

Bellak, L. *A guide to the interpretation of the Thematic Apperception Test.* New York: Psychological Corporation, 1947. (a)

Bellak, L. *Bellak TAT blank: For recording and analyzing Thematic Apperception Test stories.* New York: Psychological Corporation, 1947. (b)

Bellak, L. A study of limitations and "failures": Toward an ego psychology of projective techniques. *Journal of Projective Techniques,* 1954, *18,* 279–293. (a)

Bellak, L. *The Thematic Apperception Test and the Children's Apperception Test in clinical use.* New York: Grune & Stratton, 1954. (b)

Bellak, L. Freud and projective techniques. *Journal of Projective Techniques,* 1956, *20,* 5–13.

Bellak, L., & Bellak, S. S. *Children's Apperception Test.* New York: C.P.S. Co., P.O. Box 42, Gracie Station, 1949 (Set of ten cards and manual).

Bellak, L., & Jaques, E. On the problem of dynamic conceptualization in case studies. *Character and Personality,* 1942, *11,* 20–39.

Bertalanffy, L. von. Theoretical models in biology and psychology. *Journal of Personality,* 1951, *20,* 24–38.

Bertalanffy, L. von. *General system theory.* New York: Braziller, 1968.

Bijou, J. W., & Kenny, D. T. The ambiguity value of TAT cards. *Journal of Consulting Psychology,* 1951, *15,* 203–209.

Bleuler, E. (1912) Autistic thinking. In D. Rapaport (Ed.), *Organization and pathology of thought.* New York: Columbia University Press, 1951.

Block, J. A comparison of ipsative and normative ratings of personality. *Journal of Abnormal and Social Psychology,* 1957, *54,* 50–54.

Block, J. *The Q-sort method in personality assessment and psychiatric research: A monograph.* Springfield, Ill.: C C Thomas, 1961.

Boring, E. G. (1929) *A history of experimental psychology* (Rev. ed.). New York: Appleton-Century-Crofts, 1957.

Brunswik, E. Organismic achievement and environmental probability. *Psychological Review,* 1943, *50,* 255–272. Also in M. H. Marx (Ed.), *Psychological theory: Contemporary readings.* New York: Macmillan, 1951.

Buros, O. K. (Ed.). *The sixth mental measurements yearbook.* Highland Park, N.J.: Gryphon Press, 1965.

Buros, O. K. (Ed.). *Personality tests and reviews.* Highland Park, N.J.: Gryphon Press, 1970.

Buros, O. K. (Ed.). *The seventh mental measurements yearbook* (2 vols.) Highland Park, N.J.: Gryphon Press, 1972.

Cattell, R. B. *Description and measurement of personality.* Yonkers, N.Y.: World, 1946.

Cattell, R. B., & Luborsky, L. B. P-technique demonstrated as a new clinical method for determining personality and symptom structure. *Journal of Genetic Psychology,* 1950, *42,* 3–24.

Chein, I. *The science of behavior and the image of man.* New York: Basic Books, 1972.

Cohen, J. Factors underlying Wechsler-Bellevue performance of three neuropsychiatric groups. *Journal of Abnormal and Social Psychology,* 1952, *47,* 359–365.

Cohen, J. Some statistical issues in psychological research. In B. Wolman (Ed.), *Handbook of clinical psychology*. New York: McGraw-Hill, 1965.

Colby, K. M. *Energy and structure in psychoanalysis*. New York: Ronald, 1955.

Coleman, J. C. Changes in TAT responses as a function of age. *Journal of Genetic Psychology*, 1969, *114*, 171–178.

Coleman, W. The Thematic Apperception Test: I. Effects of recent experience; II. Some quantitative observations. *Journal of Clinical Psychology*, 1948, *3*, 257–264.

Combs, A. W. The use of personal experience in Thematic Apperception Test story plots. *Journal of Clinical Psychology*, 1946, *2*, 357–363.

Cournot, A. A. (1851) *An essay on the foundations of our knowledge* (M. H. Moore, translator). New York: Liberal Arts Press, 1956.

Cronbach, L. J. Statistical methods applied to Rorschach scores: A review. *Psychological Bulletin*, 1949, *46*, 393–429.

Cronbach, L. J., & Gleser, G. C. Processes affecting scores on "understanding of others" and "assumed similarity." *Psychological Bulletin*, 1955, *52*, 177–193.

Cronbach, L. J., & Meehl, P. E. Construct validity in psychological tests. In H. Feigl & M. Scriven (Eds.), *Minnesota studies in the philosophy of science* (Vol. 1). Minneapolis: University of Minnesota Press, 1956.

Dement, W., & Kleitman, N. The relation of eye movements during sleep to dream activity: An objective method for the study of dreaming. *Journal of Experimental Psychology*, 1957, *53*, 339. (b)

Deri, S. *Introduction to the Szondi test*. New York: Grune & Stratton, 1949.

Dymond, R. The relation of insight and empathy. *Journal of Consulting Psychology*, 1948, *12*, 228–233.

Dymond, R. Can clinicians predict individual behavior? *Journal of Personality*, 1953, *22*, 151–161.

Eagle, C. An investigation of individual consistencies in the manifestations of primary process. Unpublished doctoral dissertation, New York University, 1964.

Ehrenreich, G. A. Headache, necrophilia, and murder: A brief hypnotherapeutic investigation of a single case. Paper presented at the joint meeting of the Southwest Psychological Association and Kansas Psychological Association, Topeka, Kansas, 1959.

Elizur, A. Content analysis of the Rorschach with regard to anxiety and hostility. *Journal of Projective Techniques*, 1949, *13*, 247–284.

Erikson, E. H. Ego development and historical change. In *The Psychoanalytic Study of the Child* (Vol. 2). New York: International Universities Press, 1946.

Erikson, E. H. (1950) *Childhood and society* (2nd ed.). New York: Norton, 1963.

Erikson, E. H. *Identity, youth and crisis*. New York: Norton, 1968.

Eron, L. D. Frequencies of themes and identifications in the stories of schizophrenic patients and nonhospitalized college students. *Journal of Consulting Psychology*, 1948, *12*, 387–395.

Eron, L. D. A normative study of the Thematic Apperception Test. *Psychological Monographs*, 1950, *64* (9, Whole No. 315).

Eron, L. D. Responses of women to the Thematic Apperception Test. *Journal of Consulting Psychology*, 1953, *17*, 269–282.

Eysenck, H. J. The science of personality: Nomothetic! *Psychological Review*, 1954, *61*, 339–342.

Falk, J. L. Issues distinguishing nomothetic from idiographic approaches to personality theory. *Psychological Review*, 1956, *63*, 53–62.

Feffer, M., & Jahelka, M. Implications of the decentering concept for the structuring of projective content. *Journal of Consulting Psychology*, 1968, *32*, 434–441.

Fenichel, O. *The psychoanalytic theory of neurosis*. New York: Norton, 1945.

Ferenczi, S. (1913) Stages in the development of the sense of reality. *Sex in psychoanalysis*. New York: Basic Books, 1950.

Fleming, E. E. A descriptive analysis of responses in the Thematic Apperception Test. Unpublished master's thesis, University of Pittsburgh, 1946.

Frenkel-Brunswik, E. Dynamic and cognitive categorization of qualitative material: I. General problems and the Thematic Apperception Test. *Journal of Psychology*, 1948, *25*, 253–260.

Freud, A. (1936) *The ego and the mechanisms of defence*. New York: International Universities Press, 1946.

Freud, S. (1887–1902) *The origins of psychoanalysis*. New York: Basic Books, 1954.

Freud, S. (1899a)[1] Screen memories. *Standard edition* (Vol. 3). London: Hogarth, 1962.

Freud, S. (1900a) The interpretation of dreams. *Standard edition* (Vols. 4 & 5). London: Hogarth, 1953.

Freud, S. (1905) Jokes and their relation to the unconscious. *Standard edition* (Vol. 8). London: Hogarth, 1960.

Freud, S. (1905d) Three essays on the theory of sexuality. *Standard edition* (Vol. 7). London: Hogarth, 1953.

Freud, S. (1905e) Fragment of an analysis of a case of hysteria. *Standard edition* (Vol. 7). London: Hogarth, 1953.

Freud, S. (1906a) My views on the part played by sexuality in the aetiology of the neuroses. *Standard edition* (Vol. 7). London: Hogarth, 1953.

Freud, S. (1907a) Delusions and dreams in Jensen's "Gradiva." *Standard edition* (Vol. 9). London: Hogarth, 1959.

Freud, S. (1908a) Hysterical phantasies and their relation to bisexuality. *Standard edition* (Vol. 9). London: Hogarth, 1959.

Freud, S. (1908b) Character and anal erotism. *Standard edition* (Vol. 9). London: Hogarth, 1959.

Freud, S. (1908e) Creative writers and day-dreaming. *Standard edition* (Vol. 9). London: Hogarth, 1959.

Freud, S. (1910c) Leonardo da Vinci and a memory of his childhood. *Standard edition* (Vol. 11). London: Hogarth, 1957.

Freud, S. (1911b) Formulations regarding the two principles in mental functioning. *Standard edition* (Vol. 12). London: Hogarth, 1958.

Freud, S. (1919e) "A child is being beaten": A contribution to the study of the origin of sexual perversions. *Standard edition* (Vol. 17). London: Hogarth, 1955.

Freud, S. (1923b) The ego and the id. *Standard edition* (Vol. 19). London: Hogarth, 1961.

Freud, S. (1926d) Inhibitions, symptoms, and anxiety. *Standard edition* (Vol. 20). London: Hogarth, 1959.

Friedman, H. Perceptual regression in schizophrenia: An hypothesis suggested by the use of the Rorschach test. *Journal of Projective Techniques*, 1953, *17*, 171–185.

Friess, H. L. Wilhelm Dilthey. *Journal of Philosophy*, 1929, *26*, 5–25.

Fromm, Erika. The manifest and the latent content of two paintings by Hieronymus Bosch: A contribution to the study of creativity. *American Imago*, 1969, *26*, 145–166.

Gardner, R., Holzman, P. S., Klein, G. S., Linton, H. B., & Spence, D. P. Cognitive control: A study of individual consistencies in cognitive behavior. *Psychological Issues*, 1959, *1*(4).

Garfield, S. L., & Eron, L. D. Interpreting mood and activity in TAT stories. *Journal of Abnormal and Social Psychology*, 1948, *43*, 338–345.

Ghiselin, B. *The creative process*. Los Angeles: University of California Press, 1952.

Goldberger, L. Reactions to perceptual isolation and Rorschach manifestations of the primary process. *Journal of Projective Techniques*, 1961, *25*, 287–303.

Goldberger, L., & Holt, R. R. Experimental interference with reality contact (perceptual isolation): Method and group results. *Journal of Nervous and Mental Disease*, 1958, *127*, 99–112.

Goldfried, M. R., & Zax, M. The stimulus value of the TAT. *Journal of Projective Techniques and Personality Assessment*, 1965, *29*, 46–57.

---

[1]Dates of original publication, with letters distinguishing items from the same year, are taken from the definitive Freud bibliography in Vol. 24 of *The Standard Edition of the Complete Psychological Works of Sigmund Freud*. London: Hogarth, 1974.

Goldstein, M. J., Gould, E., Alkire, A., Rodnick, E. H., & Judd, L. L. Interpersonal themes in the Thematic Apperception Test stories of families of disturbed adolescents. *Journal of Nervous and Mental Disease.* 1970, *150*, 354–365.

Grygier, T. *The dynamic personality inventory.* Sutton, England: Banstead Hospital Management Committee, 1955.

Guilford, J. P. *The nature of human intelligence.* New York: McGraw-Hill, 1967.

Guilford, J. P., Kettsur, N. W., & Christensen, P. R. A factor-analytic study across the domains of reasoning, creativity, and evaluation. University of Southern California Psychology Lab. Report, 1954, No. 11.

Guilford, J. P., Frick, J. W., Christensen, P. R., & Merrifield, P. R. A factor-analytic study of flexibility in thinking. University of Southern California Psychology Lab. Report, 1957, No. 18.

Gurel, L., & Ullmann, L. P. Quantitative differences in response to TAT cards: The relationship between transcendence score and number of emotional words. *Journal of Projective Techniques,* 1958, *22,* 399–401.

Haggard, E. A. Some conditions determining adjustment during and readjustment following experimentally induced stress. In S. S. Tomkins (Ed.), *Contemporary psychopathology.* Cambridge: Harvard University Press, 1943.

Harrison, R. Studies in the use and validity of the Thematic Apperception Test with mentally disordered patients: II. A quantitative validity study. III. Validation by the method of "blind analysis." *Character and Personality,* 1940, *9,* 122–138.

Hartman, A. A. A basic TAT set. *Journal of Projective Techniques and Personality Assessment,* 1970, *34,* 391–396.

Hartmann, H. Comments on the psychoanalytic theory of the ego. *Psychoanalytic Study of the Child,* 1950, *5,* 74–96.

Hartmann, H. Ego psychology and the problem of adaptation. In D. Rapaport (Ed.), *Organization and pathology of thought.* New York: Columbia University Press, 1951.

Hartwell, S. W., Hutt, M. L., Andrew, G., & Walton, R. E. The Michigan Picture Test: Diagnostic and therapeutic possibilities of a new projective test for children. *American Journal of Orthopsychiatry,* 1951, *21,* 124–137.

Heath, D. H. *Explorations of maturity.* New York: Appleton-Century-Crofts, 1965.

Helson, H. Adaptation level theory. In S. Koch (Ed.), *Psychology: A study of a science* (Vol. 1). New York: McGraw-Hill, 1959.

Henry, W. E. The Thematic Apperception Technique in the study of culture-personality relations. *Genetic Psychology Monographs,* 1947, *35,* 3–135.

Henry, W. E. The Thematic Apperception Technique in the study of group and cultural problems. In H. H. Anderson & G. L. Anderson (Eds.), *Introduction to projective techniques.* New York: Prentice-Hall, 1951.

Henry, W. E. *The analysis of fantasy: The Thematic Apperception Technique in the study of personality.* New York: Wiley, 1956.

Henry, W. E., & Gardner, B. B. Personality evaluation in the selection of executive personnel. *Public Personnel Review,* 1949, *10,* 67–71.

Hitschmann, E. *Great men.* New York: International Universities Press, 1956.

Hoffman, P. J. The paramorphic representation of clinical judgment. *Psychological Bulletin,* 1960, *57,* 116–131.

Holt, R. R. Implications of some contemporary personality theories for Rorschach rationale. In B. Klopfer, M. D. Ainsworth, W. G. Klopfer, & R. R. Holt, *Developments in the Rorschach technique: Vol. 1. Technique and theory.* New York: World Book Co., 1954.

Holt, R. R. Gauging primary and secondary processes in Rorschach responses. *Journal of Projective Techniques,* 1956, *20,* 14–25. (b)

Holt, R. R. Formal aspects of the TAT—A neglected resource. *Journal of Projective Techniques,* 1958, *22,* 163–172. (b) Also in Bobbs-Merrill Reprint Series in the Social Sciences, P-481, 1966.

Holt, R. R. (with the collaboration and assistance of Joan Havel, Leo Goldberger, Anthony Philip, & Reeva Safrin). Manual for the scoring of primary process manifestations in Rorschach responses (7th ed.). New York: Research Center for Mental Health, New York University, 1959 (dittoed). (e)

Holt, R. R. Recent developments in psychoanalytic ego psychology and their implications for diagnostic testing. *Journal of Projective Techniques*, 1960, *24*, 254–266. (b)

Holt, R. R. Cognitive controls and primary processes. *Journal of Psychological Researches*, 1960, *4*, 105–112. (c)

Holt, R. R. Two influences on Freud's scientific thought: A fragment of intellectual biography. In R. W. White (Ed.), *The study of lives*. New York: Atherton Press, 1963. (a)

Holt, R. R. (with the collaboration and assistance of Joan Havel, Leo Goldberger, Anthony Philip, & Reeva Safrin). Manual for the scoring of primary process manifestations in Rorschach responses (9th ed.) New York: Research Center for Mental Health, New York University, 1963 (mimeographed). (c)

Holt, R. R. Imagery: The return of the ostracized. *American Psychologist*, 1964, *19*, 254–264. (b) Reprinted in E. P. Torrance & W. F. White (Eds.), *Issues and advances in educational psychology: A book of readings*. Itasca, Ill.: F. E. Peacock, 1969. Also abridged in B. L. Kintz & J. L. Bruning (Eds.), *Research in psychology: Readings for the introductory course*. Glenview, Ill.: Scott, Foresman, 1970.

Holt, R. R. A review of some of Freud's biological assumptions and their influence on his theories. In N. S. Greenfield & W. C. Lewis (Eds.), *Psychoanalysis and current biological thought*. Madison: University of Wisconsin Press, 1965. (a)

Holt, R. R. Ego autonomy re-evaluated. *International Journal of Psycho-Analysis*, 1965, *46*, 151–167. (c) Reprinted with critical evaluations by S. C. Miller, A. Namnum, B. B. Rubinstein, J. Sandler & W. G. Joffe, R. Schafer, H. Weiner, and the author's rejoinder [see 1967a], *International Journal of Psychiatry*, 1967, *3*, 481–536.

Holt, R. R. On freedom, autonomy, and the redirection of psychoanalytic theory: A rejoinder. *International Journal of Psychiatry*, 1967, *3*, 524–536 [see also 1965c, above]. (a)

Holt, R. R. (Ed.). Motives and thought: Psychoanalytic essays in memory of David Rapaport. *Psychological Issues*, 1967, *5*, 2/3 (Whole Nos. 18/19). (b)

Holt, R. R. The development of the primary process: A structural view. In R. R. Holt (Ed.), Motives and thought. *Psychological Issues*, 1967, *5*, 2/3 (Whole Nos. 18/19). (d)

Holt, R. R. Beyond vitalism and mechanism: Freud's concept of psychic energy. In J. H. Masserman (Ed.), *Science and psychoanalysis, Vol. 11: Concepts of ego*. New York: Grune & Stratton, 1967. And in B. Wolman (Ed.), *Historical roots of contemporary psychology*. New York: Harper & Row, 1968. (e)

Holt, R. R. Diagnostic testing: Present status and future prospects. *Journal of Nervous and Mental Disease*, 1967, *144*, 444–465. (g)

Holt, R. R. (with the collaboration and assistance of Joan Havel, Leo Goldberger, Anthony Philip, Reeva Safrin, & Carol Eagle). Manual for the scoring of primary process manifestations in Rorschach responses (10th ed.). New York: Research Center for Mental Health, New York University, 1969 (mimeographed). (d)

Holt, R. R. Artistic creativity and Rorschach measures of adaptive regression. In B. Klopfer, M. M. Meyer, & F. B. Brawer (Eds.), *Developments in the Rorschach technique, Vol. 3: Aspects of personality structure*. New York: Harcourt, Brace, Jovanovich, 1970. (c)

Holt, R. R. Freud's two images of man. *Western Psychologist Monograph Series No. 2*, 1971, 5–25. (a)

Holt, R. R. *Assessing personality*. New York: Harcourt, Brace, Jovanovich, 1971 (paperback reprint of 1969a, above). (c)

Holt, R. R. Freud's mechanistic and humanistic image of man. In R. R. Holt & E. Peterfreund (Eds.), *Psychoanalysis and Contemporary Science*, 1972, *1*, 3–24. (a)

Holt, R. R. The past and future of ego psychology. *Psychoanalytic Quarterly*, 1975, *44*(4), 550–576. (b)

Holt, R. R. Drive or wish? A reconsideration of the psychoanalytic theory of motivation. *Psychological Issues,* 1976, *9*(4, Whole No. 36). (a)

Holt, R. R. A method for assessing primary process manifestations and their control in Rorschach responses. In M. A. Rickers-Ovsiankina (Ed.), *Rorschach psychology,* rev. ed. New York: Krieger, 1977. (a)

Holt, R. R., & Havel, J. A method for assessing primary and secondary processes in the Rorschach. In M. A. Rickers-Ovsiankina (Ed.), *Rorschach psychology.* New York: Wiley, 1960.

Holt, R. R., & Luborsky, *Personality patterns of psychiatrists* (2 vols.) New York: Basic Books, 1958. (b)

Holton, G. *Thematic origins of scientific thought: Kepler to Einstein.* Cambridge: Harvard University Press, 1973.

Holtzman, W. H., Thorpe, J. S., Swartz, J. D., & Herron, E. W. *Inkblot perception and personality: Holtzman inkblot technique.* Austen: University of Texas Press, 1961.

Horn, D. A study of personality syndromes. *Character and Personality,* 1944, *12,* 257–274.

[Howe] Holt, L. P. Psychoanalysis and the social process: An examination of Freudian theory with reference to some of its sociological implications and counterparts. Unpublished doctoral dissertation, Harvard University, 1948.

Howe, L. P. Some sociological aspects of identification. *Psychoanalysis and the Social Sciences,* 1955, *4,* 61–79.

Hunt, R. G., & Smith, M. E. Cultural symbols and response to thematic materials. *Journal of Projective Techniques and Personality Assessment,* 1966, *30,* 587–590.

Jenkins, T. N. Measurement of the primary factors of the total personality. *Journal of Psychology,* 1962, *54,* 417–442.

Kagan, J. On measurement: Suggestions for the future. *Journal of Projective Techniques and Personality Assessment,* 1964, *28,* 151–155.

Kagan, J., & Lesser, G. *Contemporary issues in thematic apperceptive methods.* Springfield, Ill.: C C Thomas, 1961.

Kahn, M. W. A factor-analytic study of personality, intelligence, and history characteristics of murderers. In *Proceedings of the 73rd Annual Convention of the American Psychological Association, 1965.* Washington, D.C.: American Psychological Association, 1965.

Kaplan, A. *The conduct of inquiry: Methodology for behavioral science.* San Francisco: Chandler, 1964.

Kiefer, R. B. The Thematic Apperception Test pictures: A study of common stories as told by normal adult females. Unpublished master's thesis, University of Alberta, Edmonton, 1950.

Kilpatrick, F. P., & Cantril, H. Self-anchoring scale: A measure of the individual's unique reality world. *Journal of Individual Psychology,* 1960, *16,* 158–170.

Klein, G. S. The personal world through perception. In R. R. Blake & G. V. Ramsey (Eds.), *Perception: An approach to personality.* New York: Ronald, 1950.

Klein, G. S. Need and regulation. In M. R. Jones (Ed.), *Nebraska symposium on motivation, 1954.* Lincoln: University of Nebraska Press, 1954.

Klein, G. S. Perception, motives and personality: A clinical perspective. In J. L. McCary (Ed.), *Psychology of personality.* New York: Logos Press, 1956.

Klein, G. S. Cognitive control and motivation. In G. Lindzey (Ed.), *Assessment of human motives.* New York: Holt, Rinehart, Winston, 1958.

Klein, G. S. On inhibition, disinhibition, and "primary process" in thinking. In *Proceedings of the XIV International Congress of Applied Psychology: Vol. 4. Clinical psychology.* Copenhagen: Munksgaard, 1961.

Klein, G. S. *Perception, motives and personality.* New York: Knopf, 1970.

Klein, G. S., & Schlesinger, H. J. Where is the perceiver in perceptual theory? *Journal of Personality,* 1949, *18,* 32–47.

Klein, G. S., Spence, D. P., Holt, R. R., & Gourevitch, S. Cognition without awareness: Subliminal influences upon conscious thought. *Journal of Abnormal and Social Psychology,* 1958, *57,* 255–266.

Klinger, E. *Structure and functions of fantasy.* New York: Wiley-Interscience, 1971.

Klopfer, B., Ainsworth, M. D., Klopfer, W. J., & Holt, R. R. *Advances in the Rorschach technique* (Vol. 1). Yonkers-on-Hudson, N.Y.: World Book, 1954.

Kluckhohn, C., & Murray, H. A. Personality formation: The determinants. In C. Kluckhohn & H. A. Murray (Eds.), *Personality in nature, society, and culture.* New York: Knopf, 1953.

Klüver, H. Contemporary German psychology as a "cultural science." In G. Murphy (Ed.), *An historical introduction to modern psychology.* New York: Harcourt, Brace, 1929.

Koestler, A. *The ghost in the machine.* New York: Macmillan, 1967.

Köhler, W. (1929) *Gestalt psychology.* New York: Liveright, 1947.

Kris, E. On preconscious mental processes. *Psychoanalytic Quarterly,* 1950, *19,* 540–560.

Kris, E. *Psychoanalytic explorations in art.* New York: International Universities Press, 1952.

Landsberger, H. A. Final report on a research project in mediation. *Labor Law Journal,* 1956, *7,* 501–507.

Lapkin, B. The relation of primary process thinking to the recovery of subliminal material. *Journal of Nervous and Mental Disease,* 1962, *135,* 10–25.

Laszlo, E. *The systems view of the world.* New York: Braziller, 1972.

Lavoie, G. Les processus primaires et secondaires chez les méres d'enfants schizophrenes. Unpublished doctoral dissertation, Université de Montréal, 1964.

Leary, T. A theory and methodology for measuring fantasy and imaginative expression. *Journal of Personality,* 1956, *25,* 159–175.

Lindzey, G. *Projective techniques and cross-cultural research.* New York: Appleton-Century-Crofts, 1961.

Lohrenz, L. J., & Gardner, R. W. The Mayman form-level scoring method: Scorer reliability and correlates of form level. *Journal of Projective Techniques and Personality Assessment,* 1967, *31*(4), 39–43.

Luborsky, L. Self-interpretation of the TAT as a clinical technique. *Journal of Projective Techniques,* 1953, *17,* 217–223.

MacKinnon, D. W. Personality. *Annual Review of Psychology,* 1951, *2,* 113–136.

Markmann, R. Predictions of manifest personality trends by a thematic analysis of three pictures of the Thematic Apperception Test. Unpublished undergraduate honors thesis, Radcliffe College, 1943.

Masserman, J. H., & Balken, E. R. The clinical application of fantasy studies. *Journal of Psychology,* 1938, *6,* 81–88.

Mayman, M. Rorschach form level scoring manual. Topeka: Menninger Foundation, 1956 (Mimeographed).

Mayman, M. Form level scoring manual. Topeka: Menninger Foundation, 1960 (Mimeographed).

Mayman, M., & Kutner, B. Reliability in analyzing Thematic Apperception Test stories. *Journal of Abnormal and Social Psychology,* 1947, *42,* 365–368.

McClelland, D. C. *Personality.* New York: Dryden Press, 1951.

McClelland, D. C., Atkinson, J. W., Clark, R. A., & Lowell, E. L. *The achievement motive.* New York: Appleton-Century-Crofts, 1953.

McKellar, P. *Imagination and thinking: A psychological analysis.* New York: Basic Books, 1957.

McMahon, J. M. The relationship between "overinclusive" and primary process thought in a normal and a schizophrenic population. Unpublished doctoral dissertation, New York University, 1964.

Mead, G. H. *Mind, self and society.* Chicago: University of Chicago Press, 1934.

Meehl, P. E. *Psychodiagnosis: Selected papers.* Minneapolis: University of Minnesota Press, 1973.

Meehl, P. E., & Rosen, A. Antecedent probability and the efficiency of psychometric signs, patterns, or cutting scores. *Psychological Bulletin,* 1955, *52,* 194–216.

Michotte, A. (1946) *The perception of causality.* New York: Basic Books, 1963.

Miller, J. G. *Unconsciousness.* New York: Wiley, 1942.

Milner, M. *On not being able to paint.* New York: International Universities Press, 1957.

Morgan, C. D., & Murray, H. A. A method for investigating fantasies: The Thematic Apperception Test. *Archives of Neurology and Psychiatry,* 1935, *34,* 289–306.

Morris, C., & Jones, L. V. Value scales and dimensions. *Journal of Abnormal and Social Psychology,*
1955, *51,* 523–525.

Murphy, G. *Personality: A biosocial approach to origins and structure.* New York: Harper, 1947.

Murray, H. A. (1933) The effect of fear upon estimates of the maliciousness of other personalities. In S. S. Tomkins (Ed.), *Contemporary psychopathology.* Cambridge: Harvard University
Press, 1943.

Murray, H. A. *Thematic Apperception Test.* Cambridge: Harvard University Press, 1943 (set of 30
cards and manual).

Murray, H. A. Personal communication, 1959.

Murray, H. A., & Morgan, C. D. A clinical study of sentiments. *Genetic Psychology Monographs,*
1945, *32,* 3–311.

Murray, H. A. [*et al.*] *Explorations in personality.* New York: Oxford University Press, 1938.

[Murray, H. A. *et al.*] *Assessment of men.* New York: Rinehart, 1948.

Murstein, B. I. The projection of hostility on the Rorschach and as a result of ego-threat. *Journal
of Projective Techniques,* 1956, *20,* 418–428.

Murstein, B. I. Nonprojective determinants of perception on the TAT. *Journal of Consulting
Psychology,* 1958, *22,* 195–198.

Murstein, B. I. *Theory and research in projective techniques: Emphasizing the TAT.* New York: Wiley,
1963.

Murstein, B. I. Scaling of the TAT for Ach. *Journal of Consulting Psychology,* 1965, *29,* 286.

Murstein, B. I. Normative written TAT responses for a college sample. *Journal of Personality
Assessment,* 1972, *36,* 109–147.

Murstein, B. I., David, C., Fisher, D., & Furth, H. The scaling of the TAT for hostility by a
variety of scaling methods. *Journal of Consulting Psychology,* 1961, *25,* 497–504.

Newbigging, P. L. Influence of a stimulus variable on stories told to certain TAT pictures.
Canadian Journal of Psychology, 1955, *9,* 195–106.

Olweus, D. *Prediction of aggression on the basis of a projective test.* Stockholm: Skandinaviska
Testförlaget, 1969.

Olweus, D. Personality and aggression. In J. K. Cole & D. D. Jensen (Eds.), *Nebraska Symposium on
Motivation, 1972.* Lincoln: University of Nebraska Press, 1973.

Pappenheim, E., & Kris, E. The function of drawings and the meaning of the "creative spell" in a
schizophrenic artist. *Psychoanalytic Quarterly,* 1946, *15,* 6–31.

Parsons, T. (1937) *The structure of social action.* Glencoe, Ill.: Free Press, 1957.

Paul, I. H. Studies in remembering. *Psychological Issues,* 1959, *1* (Monograph No. 2).

Piaget, J. (1936) *The origins of intelligence in children* (M. Cook, trans.). New York: International
Universities Press, 1952.

Pine, F. Thematic drive content and creativity. *Journal of Personality,* 1959, *27,* 136–151.

Pine, F. A manual for rating drive content in the Thematic Appercaption Test. *Journal of
Projective Techniques,* 1960, *24,* 32–45.

Pine, F. Creativity and primary process: Sample variations. *Journal of Nervous and Mental Disease,*
1962, *134,* 506–511.

Pine, F., & Holt, R. R. Creativity and primary process: A study of adaptive regression. *Journal of
Abnormal and Social Psychology,* 1960, *61,* 370–379.

Polanyi, M. (1958) *Personal knowledge: Towards a post-critical philosophy* (Rev. ed.). New York:
Harper Torchbooks, 1964.

Popper, K. R. *The open society and its enemies.* Princeton: Princeton University Press, 1950.

Popper, K. R. *The poverty of historicism.* Boston: Beacon, 1957.

Rabkin, J. Psychoanalytic assessment of change in organization of thought as a function of
psychotherapy. Unpublished doctoral dissertation, New York University, 1966.

Rapaport, D. *Emotions and memory.* Baltimore: Williams & Wilkins, 1942.

Rapaport, D. Principles underlying nonprojective tests of personality. *Annals of the New York Academy of Science,* 1946, *46,* 643–652.

Rapaport, D. (Ed.). *Organization and pathology of thought.* New York: Columbia University Press, 1951. (a)

Rapaport, D. States of consciousness: A psychopathological and psychodynamic view. In H. A. Abramson (Ed.), *Problems of consciousness: Transactions of the Second Conference.* New York: Macy, 1951. (b)

Rapaport, D. Toward a theory of thinking. In D. Rapaport (Ed.), *Organization and pathology of thought.* New York: Columbia University Press, 1951. (c)

Rapaport, D. (1953) Some metapsychological considerations concerning activity and passivity. In M. M. Gill (Ed.) *The collected papers of David Rapaport.* New York: Basic Books, 1967.

Rapaport, D. Cognitive structures. In *Contemporary approaches to cognition: A symposium.* Cambridge: Harvard University Press, 1958.

Rapaport, D., & Gill, M. M. The points of view and assumptions of metapsychology. *International Journal of Psychoanalysis,* 1959, *40,* 153–162.

Rapaport, D., Gill, M. M., & Schafer, R. *Diagnostic psychological testing* (Vol. 2). Chicago: Chicago Yearbook Publ., 1946.

Rapaport, D., Gill, M. M., & Schafer, R. *Diagnostic psychological testing* (Rev. ed., R. R. Holt, Ed.). New York: International Universities Press, 1968.

Renaud, H. R. Group differences in fantasies: Head injuries, psychoneurotics, and brain diseases. *Journal of Psychology,* 1946, *21,* 327–346.

Roback, A. A. *The psychology of character.* New York: Harcourt, Brace, 1927.

Rock, M. H. Self-reflection and ego development. Unpublished doctoral dissertation, New York University, 1975.

Roe, A. Alcohol and creative work. *Quarterly Journal of Studies in Alcohol,* 1946, *6,* 415–467.

Roe, A. *The making of a scientist.* New York: Dodd, Mead, 1952.

Rosen, M. Trust, orality and openness to sensory experience: A study of some personality correlates of creativity. Unpublished doctoral dissertation, New York University, 1971.

Rosenzweig, S., & Fleming, E. E. Apperceptive norms for the Thematic Apperception Test: II. An empirical investigation. *Journal of Personality,* 1949, *17,* 483–503.

Rubinstein, B. B. Psychoanalytic theory and the mind-body problem. In N. S. Greenfield & W. C. Lewis (Eds.), *Psychoanalysis and current biological thought.* Madison: University of Wisconsin Press, 1965.

Rubinstein, B. B. Explanation and mere description: A metascientific examination of certain aspects of the psychoanalytic theory of motivation. In R. R. Holt (Ed.), *Motives and thought: Psychoanalytic essays in honor of David Rapaport.* New York: International Universities Press, 1967.

Sanford, F. H. Speech and personality: A comparative case study. *Character and Personality,* 1942, *10,* 169–198.

Sarbin, T. R. The logic of prediction in psychology. *Psychological Review,* 1944, *51,* 210–228.

Saretsky, T. The effect of chlorpromazine on primary process thought manifestations. Unpublished doctoral dissertation, New York University, 1961.

Sargent, H. D. An experimental application of projective principles to a paper and pencil personality test. *Psychological Monographs,* 1944, *57,* vi; 57.

Schafer, R. *The clinical application of psychological tests.* New York: International Universities Press, 1948.

Schafer, R. *Psychoanalytic interpretation in Rorschach testing.* New York: Grune & Stratton, 1954.

Schafer, R. How was this story told? *Journal of Projective Techniques,* 1958, *22,* 181–210. (a)

Schafer, R. Regression in the service of the ego: The relevance of a psychoanalytic concept for personality assessment. In G. Lindzey (Ed.), *Assessment of human motives.* New York: Holt, Rinehart & Winston, 1958. (b)

Schafer, R. Personal communication, 1959.

Schafer, R. *Projective testing and psychoanalysis: Selected papers.* New York: International Universities Press, 1967.

Schafer, R. *A new language for psychoanalysis.* New Haven: Yale University Press, 1976.

Sears, R. R. Experimental studies of projection: I. Attribution of traits. *Journal of Social Psychology,* 1936, *7,* 151–163.

Shneidman, E. S. Schizophrenia and the MAPS Test: A study of certain formal psycho-social aspects of fantasy production in schizophrenia as revealed by performance on the Make-A-Picture Story (MAPS) Test. *Genetic Psychology Monographs,* 1948, *38,* 145–223.

Shneidman, E. S. *Make-A-Picture Story ("MAPS") Test.* New York: The Psychological Corporation, 1949 (set of cards, figures, figure location charts).

Shneidman, E. S. (with W. Joel and K. B. Little). *Thematic test analysis.* New York: Grune & Stratton, 1951.

Shneidman, E. S. The case of Jay: Psychological test and anamnestic data. *Journal of Projective Techniques,* 1952, *16,* 297–345; 444–475.

Silberer, H. Report on a method of eliciting and observing certain symbolic hallucination phenomena. In D. Rapaport (Ed.), *Organization and pathology of thought.* New York: Columbia University Press, 1951.

Silverman, L. H. On the relationship between aggressive imagery and thought disturbance in Rorschach responses. *Journal of Projective Techniques and Personality Assessment,* 1963, *27,* 336–344.

Silverman, L. H., Lapkin, B., & Rosenbaum, I. S. Manifestations of primary-process thinking in schizophrenia. *Journal of Projective Techniques,* 1962, *26,* 117–127.

Singer, C. *A short history of scientific ideas.* London: Oxford University Press, 1959.

Singer, J. L. *Daydreaming: An introduction to the experimental study of inner experience.* New York: Random House, 1966.

Skaggs, E. B. Personalistic psychology as science. *Psychological Review,* 1945, *52,* 234–238.

Smith, G. J. W., Spence, D. P., & Klein, G. S. Subliminal effects of verbal stimuli. *Journal of Abnormal and Social Psychology,* 1959, *59,* 167–176.

Smith, J. R., & Coleman, J. C. The relationship between manifestations of hostility in projective tests and overt behavior. *Journal of Projective Techniques,* 1956, *20,* 326–334.

Smith, M. B. *Humanizing social psychology.* San Francisco: Jossey-Bass, 1974.

Smythies, J. R. The "base line" of schizophrenia: Part 1. The visual phenomena. *American Journal of Psychiatry,* 1953, *110,* 200–204.

Spranger, E. (1922) *Types of men* (P. J. W. Pigors, trans.). Halle: Niemy, 1928.

Stein, L. Historical optimism: Wilhelm Dilthey. *Philosophical Review,* 1924, *33,* 329–344.

Stein, M. I. *The Thematic Apperception Test: An introductory manual for its clinical use with adult males.* Cambridge, Mass.: Addison-Wesley Press, 1948.

Stephenson, W. *The study of behavior: Q-technique and its methodology.* Chicago: University of Chicago Press, 1953.

Stern, W. *General psychology from a personalistic standpoint* (H. D. Spoerl, trans.). New York: Macmillan, 1938.

Storment, C. T., & Finney, B. B. Projection and behavior: A Rorschach study of assaultive mental hospital patients. *Journal of Projective Techniques,* 1953, *17,* 349–360.

Stroop, J. R. Studies of interference in serial verbal reactions. *Journal of Experimental Psychology,* 1935, *18,* 643–661.

Sullivan, J. S., & Bernstein, I. Personality measures of Peace Corps volunteers to Somalia. Unpublished manuscript, New York University, 1963.

Symonds, P. M. *Adolescent fantasy.* New York: Columbia University Press, 1949.

Szondi, L. *Szondi Test.* Bern: Huber, 1947.

Szondi, L. *Experimental diagnostics of drives.* New York: Grune & Stratton, 1952.

Tapper, B. Dilthey's methodology of the *Geisteswissenschaften. Philosophical Review,* 1925, *34,* 333–349.

Tomkins, S. S. *The Thematic Apperception Test: The theory and technique of interpretation.* New York: Grune & Stratton, 1947.

Tomkins, S. S. The present status of the Thematic Apperception Test. *American Journal of Orthopsychiatry,* 1949, *19*(2), 358–362.

Tomkins, S. S. Discussion of Dr. Holt's paper. In J. Kagan & G. Lesser (Eds.), *Contemporary issues in thematic apperceptive methods.* Springfield, Ill.: C C Thomas, 1961.

Ullmann, L. P. Productivity and the clinical use of TAT cards. *Journal of Projective Techniques,* 1957, *21,* 399–403.

van Lennep, D. J. *Four-Picture Test.* The Hague: Martinus Nijhoff, 1948 (pictures, testblanks, and manual).

van Lennep, D. J. The Four-Picture Test. In H. H. Anderson and G. L. Anderson (Eds.), *Introduction to projective techniques.* New York: Prentice-Hall, 1951.

Varendonck, J. *The psychology of daydreams.* New York: Macmillan, 1921.

Veroff, J. Thematic apperception in a nationwide sample survey. In J. Kagan & G. S. Lesser (Eds.), *Contemporary issues in thematic apperceptive methods.* Springfield, Ill.: C C Thomas, 1961.

Voigt, W. H., & Dana, R. H. Inter- and intra-scorer Rorschach reliability. *Journal of Projective Techniques and Personality Assessment,* 1964, *28,* 92–95.

von Holt, Jr., H. W., Sengstake, C. B., Sonoda, B., & Draper, W. A. Orality, image fusions and concept-formation. *Journal of Projective Techniques,* 1960, *24,* 194–198.

Walker, R. G. A comparison of clinical manifestations of hostility with Rorschach and MAPS test performances. *Journal of Projective Techniques,* 1951, *15,* 444–460.

Weber, M. *The methodology of the social sciences* (E. A. Shils & H. A. Finch, trans. & ed.). Glencoe, Ill.: Free Press, 1949 (the material collected here was originally published from 1904 to 1917).

Weiss, P. The living system: Determinism stratified. *Studium Generale,* 1969, *22,* 361–400. Also in A. Koestler and J. Smithies (Eds.), *Beyond reductionism.* New York: Macmillan, 1969.

Weisskopf, E. A. A transcendence index as a proposed measure in the TAT. *Journal of Psychology,* 1950, *29,* 279–390.

White, R. W. Hypnotic test. In H. A. Murray *et al., Explorations in personality.* New York: Oxford, 1938.

White, R. W. Ego and reality in psychoanalytic theory. *Psychological Issues,* 1963, *3*(Whole No. 11).

Whitehead, A. N. (1925) *Science in the modern world* (Rev. ed.). New York: Mentor, 1952.

Wittenborn, J. R. Some Thematic Apperception Test norms and a note on the use of the test cards in the guidance of college students. *Journal of Clinical Psychology,* 1949, *5,* 157–161.

Wolff, P. H. Observations on newborn infants. *Psychosomatic Medicine,* 1959, *21,* 110–118.

Wyatt, F. The scoring and analysis of the Thematic Apperception Test. *Journal of Psychology,* 1947, *24,* 319–330.

Yankelovich, D., & Barrett, W. *Ego and instinct.* New York: Random House, 1970.

Zimet, C. N., & Fine, H. J. Primary and secondary process thinking in two types of schizophrenia. *Journal of Projective Techniques and Personality Assessment,* 1965, *29,* 93–99.

Name Index

331

Subject Index